Brain-Compatible Dance Education

by
Anne Green Gilbert

Photos by
Bronwen Anne Gilbert

Graphics by
Alecia Rossano

National Dance Association

Associate Editors & AAHPERD Staff: Virginia Wilmerding, Ph.D., University of New Mexico
Sandy Weeks, Ph.D., Texas A&M University – Commerce
Barbara Hernandez, Ph.D., (reviewer), Lamar University
Colleen Porter Hearn, NDA Program Administrator
Shelby Tombras, NDA Administrative Assistant
Lissa Sakata, NDA Assistant
Megan Stipicevic, NDA Administrative Assistant
Liza Young, (layout and design), AAHPERD
Sheila Ward, Ph.D., Norfolk State University

The National Dance Association (NDA) encourages authors to freely express their professional teaching practices and personal opinions through their writing. Therefore, materials and medical/technical terminology within this text represent the views of the author and do not necessarily reflect the position of NDA. The author's research, citations and reference structure herein may not completely follow AAHPERD publications guidelines. The author granted permission and provided all materials for publication. Copyright permission for any material that is not the original work of the author is the sole responsibility of the author and not the responsibility of NDA or AAHPERD.

Top cover photo by Patrick Bennett

An Association of the
American Alliance for Health, Physical Education, Recreation and Dance (AAHPERD)
1900 Association Dr., Reston, VA 20191

ISBN 0-88314-766-1

By providing a myriad of ideas and variations, Anne Green Gilbert encourages teachers to see all the possibilities of Brain-Compatible Dance Education for all ages and abilities.

IMPORTANCE OF DANCE EDUCATION

The National Dance Association recognizes the outstanding work that Anne Green Gilbert contributes to our field – especially in creative dance. We commend her for reaching out to the international community, teaching all ages the importance of the connection between a healthy lifestyle and the developing mind. Arts and health organizations across the globe urge us to dance in order to:

- Build self-confidence and achieve personal goals
- Improve core curriculum skills in math, science and language arts
- Develop muscle strength, flexibility and improve circulation
- Improve posture, balance and coordination
- Enhance self-expression and communication skills with creative decision-making
- Learn conflict-resolution skills and positive behavior through teamwork

All of these elements develop a highly creative quality of life. Although research on the effect of the arts on brain development is still in its "infancy," Anne leaps boldly forward to reveal her unique ideas on this subject through her extensive research and practical teaching applications.

National Dance Association Board of Directors

Learning is change. It is change in ourselves because it is change in the brain. Thus the art of teaching must be the art of changing the brain.

~ James E. Zull

This book is dedicated to the pioneers in creative dance education whose writings "changed my brain" and started me on the path to teaching, decades ago:

Ann Barlin
Joyce Boorman
Norma Canner
Geraldine Dimondstein
Gladys Andrews Fleming
Bonnie Gilliom
Margaret H'Doubler
Mary Joyce
Barbara Mettler
Ruth Murray
Virginia Tanner

ACKNOWLEDGEMENTS

My thanks and appreciation to:

All my students, young and old, who have inspired me for the past thirty-five years to be the best teacher that I can be. You are the reason that I keep dancing!

The Creative Dance Center teachers who have generously shared their creative ideas over the past twelve years: Ines Andrade, Deborah Birrane, Rachel Carnes, Sara Coiley, Christy Fisher, Terry Goetz, Krista Harris, Elizabeth Heard, Gail Heilbron, Anne Hundley, Ingrid Hurlen, Jesse Jaramillo, Helen Landalf, Dena Lee, Kate Lounsbury, Anna Mansbridge, Danielle Payton, Debbie Poulsen, Mary Reardon, Alina Rossano, Christine Roberts, Bridget Thompson and Mim Turnbull. It is an honor and pleasure to play and work with you.

My dance colleagues in the US and abroad from the National Dance Association, National Dance Education Organization, dance and the Child international and Dance Educators Association of Washington who have shared so much of themselves at conferences, through emails and in conversations. Thank you for your scholarship and friendship.

Martha Johnson for help with formatting, keeping the Creative Dance Center going and for putting up with my hair-pulling, complaining and general insanity in our little basement office. You are marvelous in so many ways!

Helen Landalf for editing the first draft of this manuscript and for giving me advice, counsel and much needed encouragement. I could not have written this book without them.

Colleen Hearn and the National Dance Association for editorial input and for publishing this book.

Eric Chappelle for your inspiring music that makes teaching dance such a pleasure. You are one talented composer!

Tom Bergersen for your heartfelt support and great accompaniment.

Alecia Rossano, Kaleidoscope graduate, for your wonderful graphics.

Katie Johnson for your interest in the BrainDance and your creative work with children and teachers. I value your friendship and support.

Kate Lounsbury for your help with the definition of dance concepts, your knowledge of Bartenieff Fundamentals and for taking care of my dogs when I teach away from home.

Ann Hutchinson Guest and Tina Curran for your friendship and generosity and for introducing me to motif notation and the Language of Dance®.

Betsey Wetzig for allowing me to share your fascinating theory on the Patterns of Coordination. You have given me some amazing tools.

Meg Robson Mahoney and Debbie Gilbert for advice on assessment. Your work with students and teachers in public education is exemplary.

Charlene Curtiss, Joanne Petroff and Debbie Gilbert of Light Motion Dance Company (and friends) for allowing Bronwen to photograph a rehearsal. You do important work.

Mary Lee Snorteland and Cheryl Marek for keeping my body and mind healthy during stressful times. You are great physical (and mental) therapists.

Kerri Lynn Nichols and Dionne Kamara for spreading the word about the BrainDance and the conceptual approach.

Patrick Bennett for your beautiful cover photo and other photography for Kaleidoscope.

Rachel Carnes for reading and advising.

Mila Parrish for advice on motif notation.

Monica Gutchow for supporting my work.

Marcia Lloyd for listening and offering advice.

Barbara Lacy for sharing ideas and encouraging me for so many years.

Tindley Whipple Gilbert for embracing our family and for believing in my work.

Huw and Griffith Gilbert, Kaleidoscope graduates, for your continuous encouragement, lively conversations and love for dance and me. You are amazing and talented sons.

Bronwen Gilbert, Kaleidoscope graduate, for your help with the Bibliography and for your dynamic dancing photographs that bring my words to life and show the joy that brain-compatible dance education brings to people of all ages. You are a beautiful and talented daughter.

David Gilbert for supporting my passion for dance for over thirty years, for reading the manuscript, offering suggestions and coping with my late night and long weekend writing sessions for over two years. You are my one true love.

FOREWORD

Brain-Compatible Dance Education is unique in its goals to integrate what is known about human growth and development and the maturation of the brain with the art of dance. Whereas sensory motor learning has always been an intrinsic part of the preparation of physical education teachers, strategies to graduate instructors of dance who support and can make use of current research in this field have been severely limited until now. *Brain-Compatible Dance Education* presents information on the anatomical make-up of this important organ and elucidates relevant and current theories of brain development. Most importantly, appreciation of the emergent mind of the developing human being is placed in tandem with what the physical and emotional act of dancing can do to support the learning process. Awareness of the value of sensory motor experiences in the plastic mind of a child is matched with pragmatic classroom guidelines and tips to support the teacher's educational intentions.

Brain-Compatible Dance Education offers practical applications for dance class derived and developed to support intellectual learning. Ten important principles of "BrainDance" are introduced. Concepts include the development of a meaningful curriculum, a meaningful environment, effective feedback and age appropriate curricular choices. Teachers of all dance forms will appreciate the strong philosophical and physiological basis for establishing dance as an integral part of the educational curriculum. Theories from known and respected motor learning specialists are in attendance with masters of dance education such as Laban and Bartenieff. A delineation of effective classroom strategies completes the preface of the book.

Brain-Compatible Dance Education is divided into lesson plan components, from the beginning warm-up of dance class to the final closure of cool down. The respective sensory motor goals are presented with simplicity and clarity. Movement behavior and sensory motor development concepts are supported and expanded upon by the thoughtful and integrated dance tutorials provided in the text, as well as a description of specific components of the National Dance Standards that are to be achieved. A thorough list of dance skills vocabulary is also provided at the beginning of each chapter.

All human beings first learn through movement. Movement must be an integral component of the learning process throughout the lifespan. *Brain-Compatible Dance Education* provides an intellectual rationale and offers practical suggestions for dance lessons from infants to adults. Dance as a form of communication is a common thread throughout all of the chapters. Dance as an art form is presented most powerfully in the chapters covering formal choreography and appreciation.

The reader of this book is encouraged to be a lifelong learner and show responsibility as a role model to his or her students. The teacher of dance is further encouraged to incorporate theories of multiple intelligences in dance class to reach all learners. This book will be an inspiration and reference in the development of class material for all levels of dance educators for years to come.

Virginia Wilmerding, Ph.D.
Department of Physical Performance and Development
University of New Mexico
Dance Science and Somatics Past Vice President,
National Dance Association
2005–2006 Board of Directors (President),
International Association for Dance Medicine and Science (IADMS)

PREFACE

In my book *Creative Dance for All Ages,* I wrote, "creative dance combines the mastery of movement with the artistry of expression." In other words, dance technique and composition skills – the craft of the art form – are integrated with creative and reflective experiences that develop the dancer's artistry. Teachers all over the world continue to ask me how to bring improvisation and choreography into dance technique classes of all styles and how to include skills and steps into a "creative" dance class. The only answer I ever think of is "Just do it!"

Now, *Brain-Compatible Dance Education*, as a companion to *Creative Dance for All Ages*, provides background materials and practical applications for dance teachers who wish to present a holistic approach in their classes. Since the first printing of *Creative Dance for All Ages* in 1992, great strides have been made in brain research as related to the understanding of how we learn and move. This research contains a wealth of information on the body-brain connection and the important role movement plays in developing the brain. *Brain-Compatible Dance Education* examines specific research and how it should be applied to effectively present dance lessons, engaging both teachers and students to think as well as to move.

While *Creative Dance for All Ages* focuses on fifteen dance concepts and many ways to embody each concept, *Brain-Compatible Dance Education* approaches the subject of teaching dance through an understanding of the lesson plan. After the introduction on brain-compatibility, the five core chapters focus on each of five lesson plan areas. Besides making connections between "how students learn best and how best to teach," each chapter contains new ways to explore dance concepts so to develop technical, compositional and reflective skills. The Appendices contain a wealth of information ranging from assessment to child development and lesson plans and resources for developing craft, artistry and more.

I hope you find this book helpful for planning lessons that meet the National Dance Standards and reflect best practices in dance education. *Brain-Compatible Dance Education* will make teaching and learning a joyful, meaningful experience for you and your students!

Anne Green Gilbert

Table of Contents

An Overview
Brain-Compatible Dance Education

In this chapter:

Elements of a Lesson Plan

Introduction

The Body-Brain Connection

- **Background**
- **Understanding the Brain**
- **Four Opportunities for Brain Development**

Ten Principles of Brain-Compatible Dance Education

Planning, Presenting and Evaluating Brain-Compatible Lessons

- **Lesson Plan Synopsis**
- **Planning the Lesson**
- **Presenting the Lesson**
- **Management Tips**
- **Special Issues**
- **Solving Space Problems**
- **Reflective Teaching**

In Summary

Brain-Compatible Dance Education

Elements of a Lesson Plan

NATIONAL STANDARDS for DANCE EDUCATION
National Standards for Dance Education, What Every Young American Should Know and Be Able to Do in Dance, Reston, VA: National Dance Association, 1994.

1. Identifying and demonstrating movement elements and skills in performing dance

2. Understanding choreographic principles, processes and structures

3. Understanding dance as a way to create and communicate meaning

4. Applying and demonstrating critical and creative thinking skills in dance

5. Demonstrating and understanding dance in various cultures and historical periods

6. Making connections between dance and healthful living

7. Making connections between dance and other disciplines

LESSON PLAN FORMAT

Warming Up

Exploring the Concept

Developing Skills

Creating

Cooling Down

DANCE CONCEPTS

Place, Size, Level, Direction, Pathway, Focus

Speed, Rhythm

Energy, Weight, Flow

Body Parts, Body Shapes, Relationships, Balance

Introduction

Ms. Jones begins dance class by leading her students through a series of exercises. She starts her favorite music, hands out scarves and instructs the students to pretend they are butterflies. As they run around the room, there is little creativity. In fact, some students swat each other with the scarves. Ms. Jones collects the scarves and asks the students to form lines at one end of the room. She then instructs them to gallop one by one like ponies across the floor. Ms. Jones notices that many students are talking and shoving; she thinks that reading a story might quiet them down. After reading the story, she tells them to "act out" what they have heard or seen. Several students react to the animal characters by making both appropriate and inappropriate noises while others just run around. Only a few seem to try their best to dance the story. After class, Ms. Jones wonders why her students never seem to improve.

Mr. Brown warmly greets each student by name and follows the weekly ritual that signals the beginning of the dance class. He leads his students through a movement sequence based on developmental patterns that prepares their bodies and brains for physical activity and learning. Mr. Brown introduces the lesson concept and together they explore it in a variety of ways. Contrasting music helps the students internalize the contrasting elements of the concept. After the structured exploration, he asks each dancer to reflect on which element of the concept is more challenging to explore. Next, Mr. Brown teaches a Russian folk dance that incorporates some of the skills they have practiced in previous classes. After the students practice the folk dance, Mr. Brown divides them into groups and asks each group to "re-choreograph," or create their own movement, for one of the dance sections. After they perform the new folk dances, they openly discuss their work. Class ends with deep breathing as Mr. Brown praises his students for their concentration and cooperation. Later, he reflects on the lesson and notes a few ideas for next week's class.

What is the difference between these two classes? Both Ms. Jones and Mr. Brown are professionals who have been teaching for many years. Both want more than anything for their students to grow as dancers and as responsible people. But Mr. Brown has an advantage – he understands how the brain works. He is able to plan and present lessons that coordinate two crucial elements, the students' bodies and minds. Mr. Brown is using a brain-compatible approach in his classes.

Brain-compatible dance education is based on current research about how we learn. This chapter outlines this research and conceptual principles that are used to plan and present the most effective dance class. The next chapter discusses another form of brain-compatibility, how to structure the teaching of developmental movement patterns (that help build the brain) into an effective mind-body warm-up called the BrainDance.

The Body-Brain Connection

Movement activates the neural wiring throughout the body, making the whole body the instrument of learning.[1]

Background

When I taught dance and physical education at the University of Washington in the early 1970s, I studied books by Newall Kephart, Bryan Cratty, Marianne Frostig and Jean Ayres. They wrote about stages of development, perceptual-motor skills, sensory integration and learning disorders. The connections they made between the brain and the body resonated with my experiences and thinking. In 1981, when I began teaching children in my private studio, I discovered that many of the exercises recommended by these authors were inherent in my methods. By exploring the concepts of Space, Time, Force, Body and Motion (adapted from Rudolf Laban's vocabulary), my students named body parts, practiced balance and developed eye-hand-foot coordination while exploring temporal, spatial, locomotor and nonlocomotor skills.

In the early 1980s, only a few of my students demonstrated learning and motor development problems. I used specific exercises from books mentioned above to guide them. I worked with the children for a few minutes before or after class and gave their parents exercises to use at home. In general, I saw gradual improvement.

By the 1990s, more and more students in my classes had not only motor or learning problems but also exhibited disturbing behavioral problems. These were caused by cultural changes that resulted in less movement in their lives. During the late 1960s and early 1970s, a generation of children spent hours sitting in front of televisions and in cars, rather than experiencing the joy of physical activity. In the 1980s, we saw the unfortunate results of children focusing on video games, viewing even more television and experiencing less unstructured play. The 1990s brought a plethora of computers and electronic games, families under stress, conflicting parenting advice, children spending more time being restrained in car seats, unnecessary baby equipment, children in long hours of day care without parental guidance, playgrounds disappearing, overly competitive sports for all ages and high-stakes testing in schools. No wonder children had so much trouble with learning and behavior!

Movement is the key to learning, but people today spend hours simply sitting. Even babies in utero experience less movement because mothers spend so much time in front of computers and televisions. The American Academy of Pediatrics recommends that children under the age of two should not watch television or work on computers; children over two should be limited to watching only educational material for no more than two hours a day on any kind of screen media.[2] When we watch television, we go into ocular lock, staring with no movement in our brains. In the critical years as their brains develop, children should move, dance, play and interact with peers rather than stare at screens.

Balance is the key to healthy living. Our sedentary life coupled with poor nutrition has caused an epidemic of obesity with an increase in serious learning and behaviorial problems. We have forgotten the importance of a balanced brain. Without a fully functioning lower and mid brain, the cortex must bare the burden of assuming more functions. Children are taught to read at an increasingly early age, which is inappropriate for healthy brain development. We over-schedule them with extra-curricular activities and competitive sports that leaves little time for free play and the development of motor skills, creativity and imagination. Children are pressured to learn and perform at levels that are not age-appropriate, with little opportunity to develop their social and emotional brains – the limbic system. Government and school districts put pressure on teachers to achieve high test scores, which leads to an even greater imbalance in the classroom and in society. Children become disengaged in their learning when rote education dictates and test scores are the priority.

Fortunately, the 1990s also provided an amazing amount of brain research based on advances in technology that allowed scientists to analyze images of the brain in action. Because I needed to understand my students' problems in order to guide them, I investigated a new generation of authors: Carla Hannaford, Eric Jensen, John Ratey, Patricia Wolfe, Shirley Randolph and Margot Heiniger. They presented ideas based on extensive research, which helped me refine my philosophy about brain-compatible dance education.

Understanding the Brain

The human brain is composed of two kinds of brain cells: glia and neurons. Glial cells are much more numerous than neurons and provide metabolic sustenance and a structural framework for the neurons. However, it is the neurons that perform the brain's work. The brain houses about 100 billion of these nerve cells. Each neuron has a cell body, one axon and many dendrites. The cell body contains the nucleus and oversees the cell's basic major metabolic functions. The axon, which may be a centimeter to a meter long, has two responsibilities: conduct information in the form of electrical stimulation and transport chemical substances. When an axon is insulated with a fatty substance called myelin, it conducts information faster because the myelin reduces interference from nearby reactions. Dendrites are branch-like wires that grow out of the cell body. Dendrites receive incoming information.

Neurons pass on information through synaptic connections: the end of the axon subdivides, sometimes forming many branches called axon terminals, then connects with the dendrites of another neuron. Information flows in one direction from the cell body, down the axon, to the synapse.

This information is carried inside a neuron by electrical impulses, but is transmitted across the synaptic gap from one neuron to another by chemicals called neurotransmitters.[3]

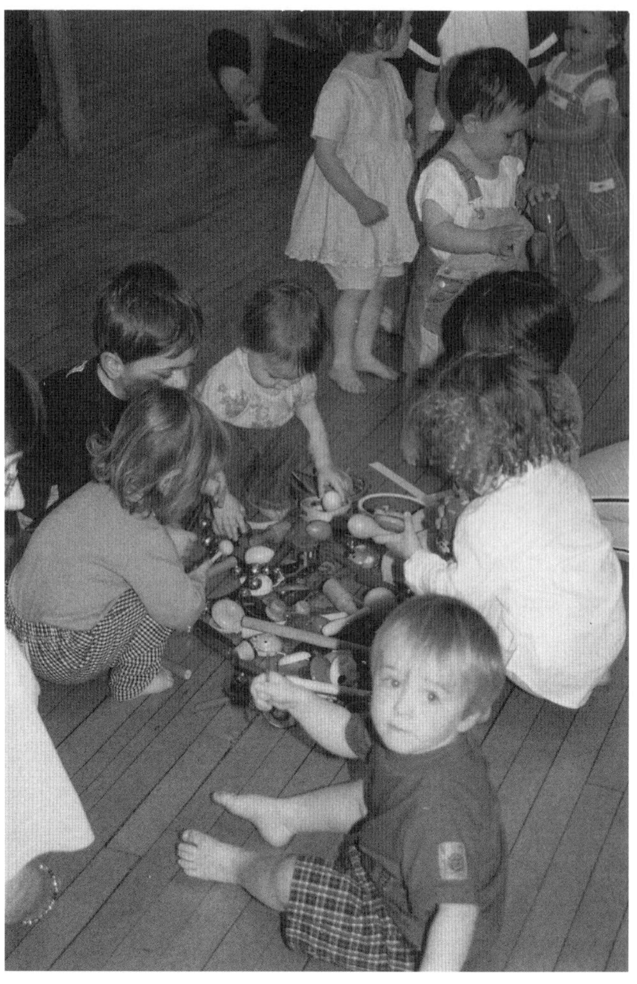

At three weeks of fetal development, the brain's billions of neurons begin developing through a process called neurogenesis. Within four months' gestation, these "building blocks" are for the most part fully formed. Neurons migrate to the areas of the brain where they are needed immediately after their formation. By the end of neurogenesis, most neurons take their final position so that all the major brain structures are in place.[4]

The most important part of brain development is synapse formation. While no new neurons are added after birth, many new synapses and dendrites grow at a rapid pace in the first few years of life. Synaptogenesis is a slower process than neurogenesis and migration. It begins at two months of gestation and continues through much of the first two years of life. Throughout this developmental phase, 1.8 million new synapses per second are produced.[5] To accommodate this huge synapse formation, neurons expand their dendrite surfaces by producing dendritic spines. As much as 83% of total dendritic growth occurs after birth.

How all the neurons and synapses correctly link together is one of the most intriguing puzzles of the brain. Neuroscientists are still trying to find all the answers to brain wiring, but it appears that there is a fine balance between "nature" and "nurture." Genes (nature) direct the growth of dendrites and axons to their approximate locations in the brain, but then environment (nurture) takes over, refining the rough circuits to customize the individual brain. For example, most children are born with the neurons to speak any language but, because of their environment, certain synapses are pruned and they only speak the words they hear daily. Babies' brains are "works in process" and sculpt themselves in response to the world around them.

All areas of the brain must work in an integrated way for the brain and body to fully function. A strong lower brain and mid brain, which develop primarily through sensory and motor activities in the first years of life, are vitally important for overall brain function. Without this coordination, basic processing that our lower brain handles automatically has to be conducted by our upper brain. This makes sensory processing more awkward and difficult.

The brain is programmed to develop in stages within a certain sequence. When that sequence is disrupted and stages are missed, the brain must compensate. As the brain develops, gaps cause problems in processing information, which can compromise cognitive function. By understanding the important work of each part of the brain, we realize the value of all parts working in harmony.

Lower Brain

The lower brain is the unconscious or automatic brain that regulates self-preservation to ensure survival. During its development between conception and fifteen months, an estimated 100 trillion nerve nets are created that link all of our senses with muscle movements. These nerve nets are encoded with the sensory-motor patterns upon which all of our learning will be based.[6]

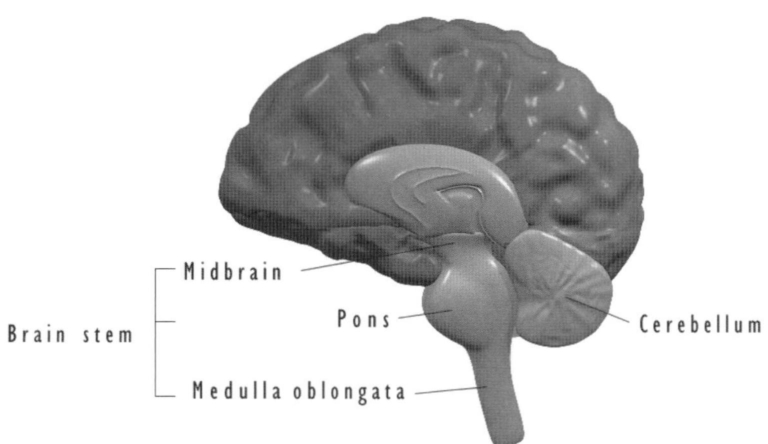

The lower brain houses the cerebellum and the brain stem, which includes the medulla oblongata, pons and midbrain. The brain stem, located at the top of the spinal cord, is the autopilot. All sensations must first go through the brain stem. The medulla oblongata, located in the brain stem, helps maintain and organize the brain stem. It controls circulation, respiration, breathing, heart rate and wake and sleep patterns.

The pons, located near the top of the brain stem above the medulla, controls the switchboard that carries messages from the spinal cord to the brain. The midbrain, located above the pons, serves as the nerve pathway of the cerebral hemispheres and contains visual and auditory reflex centers.

The cerebellum, located next to the brain stem and below the occipital area, is linked to coordination, balance, posture, muscle movements, cognition and emotions. It is critical to understand how much information the lower brain receives and processes.

> *The separation of physical, mental, emotional and spiritual faculties in our culture is a direct reflection of our by-passing the need to survive on an automatic physical level. This means on the one hand that automatic physical defense mechanisms on the low brain level are minimally stimulated to develop, while on the other hand, high brain mental consciousness is greatly emphasized.*
>
> *Less and less time is being spent on low brain development. For example, many of our infant rearing practices are emphasizing early and out of sequence eye-hand and bipedal activities (infant seats, baby bouncers, early walking) and less and less time is devoted to prone, supine and quadrupedal development which stimulates the lower brain. Infants are being placed in advanced postures before they have developed the means to move in and out of them on their own. Without fully developed automatic physical survival mechanisms, higher brain consciousness lacks a balanced grounding.*[7]

Mid-Brain

The mid-brain, sometimes called the limbic system, lies behind the frontal lobes, below the parietal lobes and above the brain stem. It combines conscious and unconscious thought and connects with the upper brain to allow emotional and cognitive processing. It also links with the lower brain to elicit physical signs of emotions. Think of it as the emotional and social brain. It houses many of the biochemical neurotransmitters that stimulate or inhibit activity in other parts of the brain.

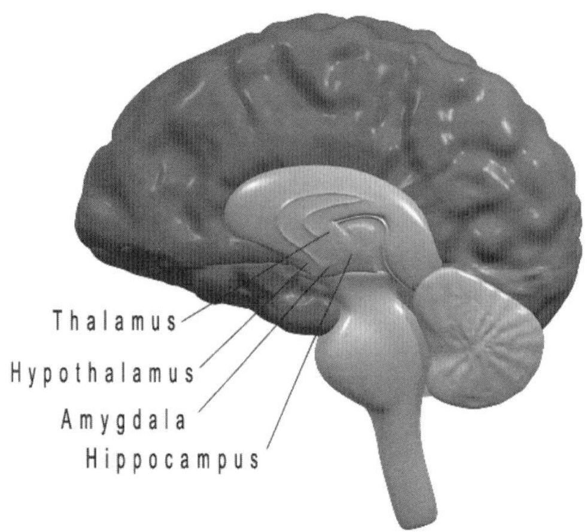

The mid-brain includes the thalamus, hypothalamus, amygdala and hippocampus. The thalamus serves as a receptionist for all incoming senses except smell. It also helps interpret temperature, pain, light and strong touch, and is related to emotion and memory.

The hypothalamus rules over the pituitary gland to act as a thermostat for appetite, thirst, digestion, hormone secretion and sleep patterns. It provides super-human strength or endurance in life-threatening situations. It is also involved in rage, pain, pleasure and aggressiveness.

Emotion is controlled by the amygdala, a critical processor for our senses. It contains twelve to fifteen distinct emotive regions; without it, we lose the capacity for imagination, nuances of emotion and key decision-making. It plays a role in emotionally laden memories, particularly those dealing with fear and threat. It helps us recognize facial expressions and body language and therefore helps us respond appropriately in social and emotional situations.[8] It is easy to understand why children with attachment disorders and rage issues are often diagnosed with problems in mid-brain functioning.

Memory is governed by the hippocampus. It uses sensory input, coming through the thalamus and emotions in the hypothalamus, to form short-term memory. Short-term memory, with nerve net activation in the hippocampus, can then enter permanent storage as long-term memory throughout the brain.[9]

The intricate wiring of the limbic system shows that in order to learn and remember something, there must be sensory input, a personal emotional connection and movement...emotions, and the release of neurotransmitters that they elicit, are intimately intertwined with cognitive function.[10]

Upper Brain

The upper brain, also known as the forebrain, includes the cerebrum, the largest part of the brain, which has two hemispheres (right and left). Each hemisphere has four lobes: the frontal, parietal, temporal and occipital. The two hemispheres are connected by white matter called the corpus callosum, a bundle of 200-300 million nerve fibers. The cerebrum has a crossover pattern so that each side of the body communicates with the opposite hemisphere.

The cerebral cortex, or neocortex, is the outermost layer of the cerebrum. It is one-quarter-inch thick, six layers deep and packed with brain cells or neurons – 85% of the total neurons in the brain. This part of the cerebrum is referred to as "grey matter" because the axons are not myelinated. Myelin is a white, fatty substance that insulates axons. The white matter of the cerebrum, made up of myelinated axons, quickly carries sensory information to the neocortex and then carries its motor commands to the body.[11]

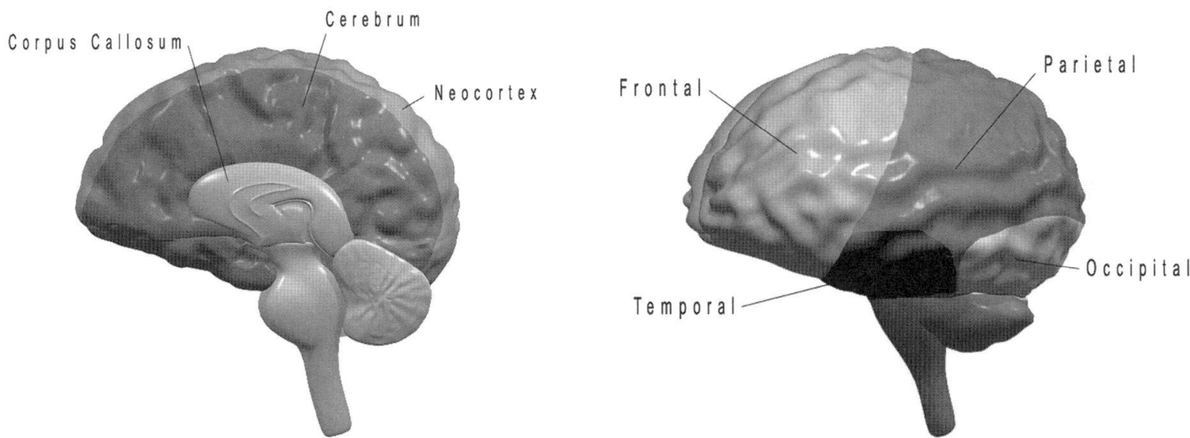

The frontal lobe controls voluntary movement, creativity, problem solving, verbal expression and planning. The parietal lobe handles proprioception (the body's understanding of its place in space), touch, pressure, pain, heat and cold. The occipital lobe processes vision by interpreting shape, color and movement. The temporal lobes are responsible for hearing, gravitational understanding (vestibular system), language and memory storage.[12]

Understanding the intricacies of the brain helps us realize the importance of integrating all parts of the brain. In order to learn, we must first have a sensory experience, then reflect and make connections. Finally, we must take action based on the experience. When we are aware that our first movements – even inside the womb – build our sensory-motor brain, we understand how important it is to move through all the developmental patterns. These patterns are discussed at length in the Warming Up chapter. A fully functioning body creates a fully functioning brain.

Four Opportunities for Brain Development

Conception to Birth: Cell Explosion

- Trillions of brain cells form and take their appropriate places in the brain.
- Chemicals ingested by the mother, severe stress, health problems and illnesses or lack of exercise may cause cell malformation in the fetus.

Birth to Age Three: Synaptic Connections

- Wires start to grow and connect. Brain mapping occurs through developmental movement patterns and sensory input.
- This is a critical learning period, as trillions of brain cells become available and "look for work."
- It is natural for brain cells that "don't find work" to die, but severe sensory deprivation may cause irreversible synaptic pruning (the elimination of synapses).
- An enriched environment with lots of "tummy time," a loving caregiver, behavioral boundaries and good nutrition encourages the development of a fully functioning human.

Ages Four to Twelve: Dendrite Expansion

- The brain glows with energy. Billions of brain cells are stimulated, dendrites branch out and synapses create countless neural connections.
- The brain learns fastest and most efficiently during these years. It grows and develops by learning to make sense of everything around it. Novelty, repetition and stimulation lay the foundation for later learning.
- An enriched environment with plenty of movement, multi-arts experiences, appropriate challenges, timely and positive feedback, good nutrition, caring adults and a focus on process rather than product, will continue the growth of a fully functioning human both in body and mind.

Ages 12 to Adult: Brain Plasticity

- This is a time to protect and stimulate the brain.
- The brain has plasticity. It is not a static system.
- Continued stimulation, especially staying active mentally and physically, will help the brain remap itself. One study shows that dancing three to four times a week significantly slows dementia.[13]
- Repeating the developmental movement patterns that wired the central nervous system in the first year of life fully integrates the brain and body.
- Good nutrition and safe behavior keeps the brain healthy.
- Lifelong learners and movers have fully functioning brains.

Ten Principles of Brain-Compatible Dance Education

Through understanding and using brain research, dance educators can plan brain-compatible dance classes. Understanding brain processes allows us to create the most beneficial learning environments for our students by employing the following basic principles:

1. Present Meaningful Curriculum

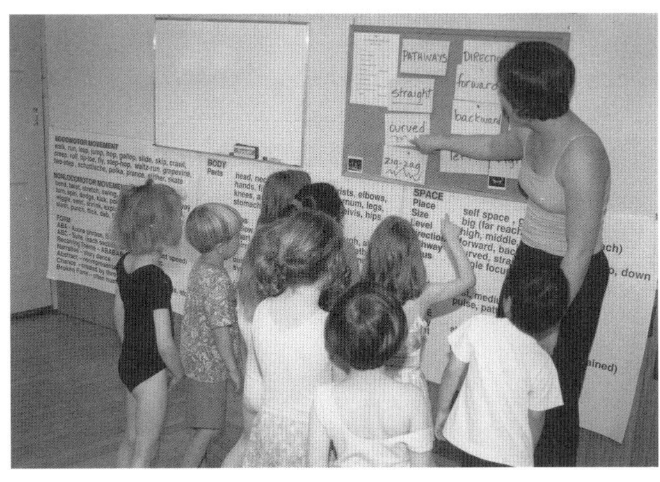

The brain is built for learning. It wants to make meaning out of experience. Conceptual content is more meaningful than random facts. Using a conceptual approach in dance class, rather than a rote, steps-only approach, creates a curriculum rich with novelty and meaning. This curriculum is based on fifteen dance concepts adapted from Rudolf Laban's movement vocabulary that relate to the other arts, interdisciplinary subjects and to many aspects of living. Using creative, critical thinking skills to fully explore relevant concepts stimulates the brain for powerful learning. When class content connects to a student's life, both the brain and body gain and retain knowledge.

2. Provide an Enriched Environment

A movement-enriched environment develops larger brain cells that have more dendrites; therefore they communicate better with one another. The enriched environment is achieved through a challenging multi-sensory curriculum involving problem solving, relevant projects, complex activities and critical thinking. An enriched environment also includes meaningful feedback.

3. Give Meaningful Feedback

The brain needs feedback to learn from experience. Students cannot learn, grow and develop without it. Meaningful feedback is positive, timely, frequent, learner-controlled and descriptive – not simply general. It must be multi-modal to reach all learning styles. For example, feedback might be expressed through positive words from a teacher or peer; from drawings, diagrams or photographs; from smiles and direct eye contact; from appropriate touch by self, teacher or peers as well as from manipulation of models and props. The intrinsic reward of achievement, as well as teacher and classmate appreciation, are far more meaningful than external prizes of treats and trophies.

4. Include Opportunities for Emotional Engagement

Emotions, thoughts and learning are linked. Experiences generate emotions, which generate thoughts and decisions, which generate both good and bad responses. Dance classes need to be positive and joyful as well as meaningful and challenging. Joyful movement causes the secretion of serotonin, a feel-good chemical that boosts self-esteem. When students are emotionally engaged, they not only want to return to class but also learn more and remember longer. Negative, stressful experiences are counterproductive in any learning environment. They may cause the secretion of the chemical cortisol, an excess of which can damage brain cells. Give students time to reflect on their feelings, thoughts and experiences.

5. Allow for Social Interaction

Social interaction encourages brain development. Students learn best through collaboration and peer coaching. Problem solving together evokes more ideas and choices. Additionally, working with others breaks down boundaries between genders, cultures and learning styles. Using a variety of groupings throughout the class – such as pairs, trios and small and large groups – creates a multi-dimensional, student centered learning environment. Collaboration is more brain-compatible than competition; solving problems together reduces stress and increases positive emotions.

6. Present Developmentally Appropriate Curriculum

Understanding developmental stages and providing appropriate curriculum make teaching easier and learning more attainable. (Developmental stages are discussed in Appendix A.) Many teachers unintentionally oversimplify or diminish the scope of the curriculum, especially with children. Young dancers are capable of learning more complex ideas than we think possible. Inappropriate classroom behavior is often the result of developmentally inappropriate curriculum. An appropriate curriculum must be genuinely challenging to get the brain's attention but achievable so students are not frustrated.

If there are class management problems, consider the students' level of development and experience. A wide range of ages or levels in one dance class can be problematic because the students' needs may be too varied to accommodate. Content that is too easy bores students and causes the brain to find something else of interest. Bored students may engage in inappropriate behavior just for some stimulation. Content that is too difficult frustrates students, causing the brain to shut down. Frustrated students stop participating altogether. Challenge students at the start, then modify activities if necessary.

7. Allow Students to Take Charge of Their Learning

Students who construct and re-create their own learning experience are more engaged; they retain information longer than students who are "fed" information. The best way to learn is to work out solutions or teach another person. Our brains have to understand material before we can explain this material to someone else. Allow students to take charge of their own learning through choices, peer coaching and problem solving. This will increase motivation, responsibility and emotional engagement. Approaches that alternate between directed teaching and student exploration/creation lead to greater student involvement and enhanced learning. Teachers need to step back from being in "complete" control and wholeheartedly accept the role of facilitator and mentor.

8. Provide both Novel and Repetitious Experiences

Synaptic connections in the brain are created through novelty. These new connections are then hard-wired through repetition. Too much novelty leads to confusion and frustration. Too much repetition leads to boredom. Find the balance between novelty and repetition for optimum learning.

The five-part lesson plan described in the Planning the Lesson section will help teachers create novel activities, as well as repetitious ones. To capture the students' attention, offer a variety of concepts, skills and music. Provide contrasts by alternating directed teaching with student choices. Group students in a variety of ways and use different teaching styles. The lesson plan sections, Exploring the Concept and Creating, offer many ideas for contrast and choice for novelty and excitement. Two other lesson plan sections, Warming Up and Developing Skills, provide ideas for including the repetition necessary for developing dance skills and technique. The lesson plan itself offers a repetitive structure that creates a sense of ritual, leading to lower levels of stress.

9. Offer a Curriculum that is Holistic and Sequential

Students learn better through studying whole ideas in context than through studying isolated parts. Alternate practicing skills with improvisation and dance making, rather than skills in one lesson and creating dances in another. Bringing dance history to life through concepts and movement, as well as by reading outside of class, is another example of learning through context.

Students also learn best when the curriculum is sequential rather than random. Focusing on one or two different dance concepts in each lesson is more beneficial than a hit-or-miss approach. Also, building on the knowledge and skills gained in previous lessons, rather than introducing only new material in each class, helps students learn more efficiently.

10. Provide Information about Proper Nutrition

Without good nutrition, water and oxygen, our brains and bodies cannot function properly. It is hard for students to learn when their bodies are filled with excess sugar, fueled by empty carbohydrates or are starving (as is the case with many dancers). It is important that students stay hydrated and have fresh oxygen when dancing. Educate them about the importance of a balanced diet. Provide a healthy environment, physically, emotionally and mentally, so the students' brains function fully.

Planning, Presenting and Evaluating Brain-Compatible Lessons

Lesson Plan Synopsis

1. Warming Up

- Introduce the lesson concept through a multi-sensory approach (hear, see, say and do).
- Perform the BrainDance.
- Include dance technique when appropriate.

2. Exploring the Concept

- Explore the lesson concept through structured improvisation(s) alone, in duets, trios and small groups and occasionally with props or musical instruments.
- Reflect on the exploration with peers.

3. Developing Skills

- Learn and practice dance skills and steps integrating the lesson concept.
- Learn and practice dance phrases, movement combinations and short dances.

4. Creating

- Generate new movement ideas based on the lesson concept through improvisation.
- Choreograph studies and dances incorporating choreographic devices, forms and principles.

5. Cooling Down

- Share and evaluate improvisation and choreography, review the lesson concept, stretch or reflect.

The Conceptual Lesson Plan

The thread that ties the whole lesson together is the concept chosen from the list on the Dance Concept Poster found in Chapter Two. It is easiest to start at the top of the list and progress downward: Week 1, Place; Week 2, Size; Week 3, Level; Week 4, Direction; Week 5, Pathway; Week 6, Focus; Week 7, Speed; Week 8, Rhythm and so forth. However, when teaching a short course (three to six weeks, for instance), include a few concepts from each main area of Space, Time, Force and Body.

An additional, thematic concept may draw on emotions, props, other subjects (such as math, science, art, music), literacy, social skills (such as partnering or conflict and resolution), dance history, dance in cultures or health. However, a theme should be secondary to the dance concept.

Five sections are addressed in each lesson. For a thirty-minute lesson, do one five-minute activity from each section. For a longer lesson, do two to three activities for Exploring the Concept and Developing Skills and then spend more time on Warming Up and/or Creating.

Below is an overview of each section of the lesson plan. Variations for technique classes and infant, toddler and preschool classes are found in the Appendices. Details about each lesson plan area are provided in the chapter focusing on that section.

1. **Warming Up** is a five to fifteen-minute teacher-directed activity that prepares the brain and body for the rest of the lesson. The BrainDance, described in Warming Up, is perfect for this! The warm-up might also include fifteen to twenty-five minutes (or more) of dance technique with a dance specialist. During the warm-up, introduce the concept for the day through a multi-sensory approach (hear, see, say and do). Dancers need to say and describe the words through movement while seeing the words visually displayed in order for the concept to be remembered and embodied.

2. Exploring the Concept is a five to fifteen-minute student-centered activity in which the concept is explored through a structured, problem-solving approach. Dancers can explore the concept in a number of ways, either individually or in pairs and trios. Encourage them to find new ways of moving to engage their critical thinking. Explore the concept in self space and general space, with isolated body parts, the whole body, alone and with others. Ask the dancers to reflect briefly on the movement experience as they share their thoughts through actions, voice, writing or drawing.

3. Developing Skills is a five to fifteen-minute teacher-directed activity in which locomotor and nonlocomotor skills are learned and practiced. This section can be extended to twenty-five minutes in longer classes that focus on technique. This section will need the most tweaking for different ages and skill levels. Skills are practiced while integrating the lesson concept. For example, turns should be practiced on different levels when the lesson concept is Level; skips may be practiced for several weeks by adding different Directions and then changes in Size, Level, Speed and Energy – according to the week's lesson. Combinations (dance phrases, routines or folk dances) emphasize the transitional flow between movements. Leaps, turns and partnering skills may also be included.

4. Creating is a five to thirty-minute student-centered and teacher-directed activity that includes improvisation or choreography. Dancers combine their knowledge of the concept with their developing movement skills to create original dances, either improvised or choreographed. This section provides an excellent opportunity for teachers to assess how well they have taught.

5. Cooling Down is a five to fifteen-minute activity that takes several forms. Begin by having students perform the improvisations or choreography created earlier. Discuss their observations: what concepts are seen, how movement problems are solved, etc. Alternatively, have dancers "visualize" as they review skills learned in class or do deep breathing and relaxation exercises. Very young dancers receive special praise, as well as rubber stamps on their hands and feet that relate to the lesson concept.

Lengths of Lessons

When classes are 60, 90 or 120 minutes, there is adequate time to present all five parts of the lesson plan. Adjust the length of each section depending on the goals of the class. When teaching dance technique, spend more time in Warming Up and Developing Skills than in Exploring the Concept, Creating and Cooling Down. When working on choreography, shorten the first three sections and spend more time in Creating and Cooling Down. Brain-compatible lessons need all five sections, even if they are brief.

Preschools and public schools often have only thirty minutes of class time. This is not a problem with toddlers through age five because we improvise rather than choreograph. This group also requires less work on technique or skill development. In a thirty-minute class, spend five minutes on each section because this age has a short attention span. Research indicates that people have attention spans of their age plus two minutes, so five minutes for each lesson section for a three-year-old is perfect! Adults, who reach their maturity at eighteen, have an attention span of about twenty-minutes.

Students in grades one through twelve need more than thirty minutes for a brain-compatible class. For the last ten years, I have been demanding at least forty-five minutes for this age group, although sixty minutes is optimal. If only thirty minutes is allowed for class, adjust the timing of the lesson plan. If classes meet for two thirty-minute periods weekly, divide the lesson by doing Warming Up, Exploring the Concept, Developing Skills and Cooling Down during the first class, and then, Warming Up, Creating and Cooling Down during the second.

The biggest problem when trying to include all parts of the lesson in a single class is that creating and sharing choreography takes time! Alternate improvisation with choreography or work on a choreographic project over several weeks.

To offer brain-compatible lessons, include all five sections of the lesson plan within either the week or the unit. Try different solutions, then ask students for their solutions and determine what works best for the situation. Time constraints make teaching frustrating. When possible, ask for more time and always use the allotted time in the most effective way.

Teaching Tip: *After teaching and practicing a short combination during the Developing Skills section, have half the class perform the combination for the other half. Ask the observers to reflect and comment on what they saw. Reverse the roles. End the class with a short improvisation for Creating. This is a simple way to practice audience and observation skills when there is limited time for longer choreographic study and reflection.*

Planning the Lesson

Planning lessons can seem daunting, but the structure just described will help. By keeping each part basic, the whole becomes complex. If each part is complicated, the lesson becomes overwhelming to teach and difficult for students to understand. The five-part plan creates a lesson that is both engaging and structured. Focusing on a new dance concept each week creates a curriculum that is layered and sequential. The five-part lesson plan provides a scaffold on which to build successful, brain-compatible lessons that are meaningful as well as appropriately challenging.

This plan alternates teacher-directed with student-centered activities, developing skills with improvisation. This alternation provides the repetition and novelty that helps all learners stay engaged. Students who prefer to learn skills, patterns and sequences feel more comfortable in the teacher-directed sections. Others prefer student-centered exploring, creating and improvising. When alternating skills and improvisation, all of the students are successful at some point in the lesson. When they are out of their comfort zone, they learn to take risks in a positive atmosphere and grow in a holistic way.

Teaching Tip: *Although I have taught for over thirty-five years, I still plan every lesson that I teach. I keep many notebooks full of lessons that I can refer back to for forgotten ideas and rework ideas that were not successful. With so many lessons each week spanning so many ages and levels, I could never remember what I taught the week before. Writing down my lesson plans has helped me evolve a sequential, brain-compatible curriculum.*

When I started teaching, I wrote everything I was going to say and do. I even hung a skeleton plan on the wall so I could readily see where I was going. Now my lesson details are quite brief, but, even after all these years, the map is very helpful. Students often attend classes at my dance studio for up to twelve years, so I want to make sure that the lessons grow with them.

When teaching short residencies in the public schools, keep a record of what works and what does not. Pull out successful lessons and with a few adjustments, create fresh, meaningful classes. With multiple grade levels, create one plan for the week that can be tweaked for different age groups. This makes planning and teaching much easier than creating five to ten different lessons!

Creating a lesson plan is like choreographing a dance. Each lesson should be balanced, harmonious, with a strong beginning, ending and a meaty middle. Alternate high-energy with lower-energy activities. To keep the students' attention, practice contrast and novelty through various spatial formations, a mix of music styles, meters and artists and the occasional addition of props. To be brain-compatible, the lesson also needs to include the three Rs:

- Relationships: include partner, trio and small group activities with peer discussion and coaching.
- Repetition (and Ritual): create rituals and offer movement experiences that are repetitive as well as novel.
- Reflection: give dancers the opportunity to reflect on their feelings, ideas and movement choices.

A lesson plan format with examples of lessons for all ages and spaces is located in the Appendices.

Presenting the Lesson

Planning a brain-compatible lesson is only part of the art of teaching. Presenting the lesson in a brain-compatible way is equally important.

Keep It SIMPLE!

This applies to directions, rules and planning classes. The brain functions better when fed smaller bits of information, like building blocks, that may be learned and built upon to create a more complex whole.

Choose appropriate objectives

What are the objectives of the lesson? What should the students know and be able to do? Select three to four specific objectives based on the *National Standards for Dance Education* and the list of Brain-Compatible Principles outlined earlier in this chapter.

Know the lesson plan

Go over the lesson plan before class, like a play script. Practice the directions and the transition between activities. If necessary, draw a skeleton plan on chart paper and post it for you and your students. When teaching, the body is flooded with adrenaline and the "rehearsal" and the chart will be appreciated.

Have music or accompaniment organized

Arrange compact disks in the order of use. Try to avoid using tapes because they can be difficult to cue between classes or when repeating an activity. Keep any musical instruments for accompaniment at hand and be familiar with the sound system or accompanist. For the traveling dance educator, it is best to have a portable sound system that can be clearly heard in all class spaces. Choose appropriate music with a variety of meters and styles. Music with clear contrasts is excellent for exploring contrasting elements. Present basic directions during the musical pauses. Developmentally appropriate music will help considerably with class management because the brain is very responsive to music.

Use the concept throughout the lesson

Instead of just stringing together a lot of "fun," unrelated activities, remember that the dance concept is the meaningful thread that runs through the whole lesson. The lesson's concept should be integrated into every section of the class.

Give directions clearly and simply

Do most of the explaining while the students move. They will pay more attention to you while engaged because they use more of their senses while moving than when standing, sitting or waiting to move. Explanations should be short and simple. Make sure your voice is heard over the music, otherwise give directions when the music pauses. Sometimes a portable microphone system is necessary when teaching in large spaces or to large groups.

Use your voice dramatically

Remember that novelty increases students' attention. Whisper when it is necessary for the students to listen to the you, as the teacher. Change vocal pitch, volume and tempo to encourage different types of movements, such as changes in level, speed and weight. Sing or chant directions, because the brain responds well to pulse and rhythm. Encourage students with a "cheerleading" voice. When changing activities, use a mysterious, magical voice that will grab student's attention. Tone expresses pleasure, humor, fear, anger, sarcasm, encouragement, acceptance, superficiality, despair, weariness, excitement and many other emotions and ideas that the brain tunes in. Use the voice well and use it wisely. Remember, also, "Silence is Golden." Besides speaking, try eye contact, sign language or let the music simply do the "talking."

Keep the flow going

Determining transitions ahead of time is an important part of presentation. A lesson will easily fall apart if the class repeatedly starts and stops. As soon as one part ends, tell young dancers what to do next: "I enjoyed watching your creative level changes. Now we are going to make puzzle shapes with a partner on different levels. Come and stand on the white line, please." As the students gather at the white line, set up the next piece of music and whatever prop or equipment is needed for the next part of class. Everyone is then ready to listen to directions and start dancing again. Students who are told what is coming next are less likely to act up between lesson sections. Fear and uncertainty are eliminated. While the dancers move, check the lesson plan to be prepared for the next transition.

With older dancers, keep the class flowing by giving directions and feedback to the whole group as they move. Rather than working with just one student, ask students to pair up and engage in peer coaching (under the teacher's direction) so that everyone is involved in learning. Stop for deeper reflection only once or twice in each lesson rather than after every activity.

Demonstrate

Demonstrate what the students should do, using the invaluable multi-sensory approach of "hear," "see," "say" and "do." Using student demonstrators captures the students' attention. After the volunteers give a brief demonstration under the teacher's guidance, repeat it as the other students direct them in what to do. Allowing the students to teach and repeat the directions is an effective way for them to understand and remember what is expected of them.

Give immediate feedback

Make corrections the moment there are problems. Immediate feedback is more brain-compatible than feedback at the end of class. Ask, "What is happening with this picture?" Demonstrate a movement or behavior incorrectly. Focus down on leaps, flail arms, lock knees, grab props, etc. Students make corrections, repeat the movement correctly and then tell how the new version is better. Encourage them to try moving correctly themselves, because when students are involved in the feedback process, body and brain learning is faster and lasts longer.

One method is to address the entire class rather than singling out specific students: "Remember to keep breathing," "I am proud of the way you are reaching your arms out into space," "Using focus will help you find your partner faster." All students respond to descriptive remarks. Another method is to pair up students to assess and help one another. We cannot improve as dancers without feedback. Creating a positive atmosphere means that we give feedback in a constructive and meaningful way.

Provide opportunities for all students to dance all the time

Students come to dance class to move. Make sure they are not spending too much time waiting in line or for directions. Bored students easily become misbehaving students. If there is an odd number of students during a partnering activity, create a trio or have the teacher dance with an individual. Because children have useful ideas ask them to include everyone, especially extra or special-needs students.

Students who misbehave usually need movement more than others, so find a way to dance with them and include them in the class. It is recommended that they not sit out. However, remember that a person cannot be forced to dance. Avoid power struggles. Allow a shy student more time to observe. Some public school students may not participate for religious reasons. If that student really wants to dance, talk with the parents about the educational values of the class.

Use a multi-sensory approach to reach all learning styles

It is the responsibility of the teacher to reach all students. Using a multi-sensory or multiple-entry-point approach to engage all learners will accomplish this. Include visual art activities such as drawing dance maps or sculpting shapes. Encourage students to write poems and stories about dance. Read about dance history and cultures. Let them create sound scores and dance to stories as they are being told. Provide hands-on activities such as molding shapes and manipulating props. Teach musical and numerical concepts such as moving to mixed meters and creating rhythmic patterns. Introduce aesthetic concepts, such as creating dances and talking about them. Include activities requiring logic, such as problem solving through improvisation and choreography. Develop social interaction by working in pairs and groups. Engage the emotions through the exploration of opposing dance elements and through self and peer reflection. If all students are engaged, the class will be much easier to manage.

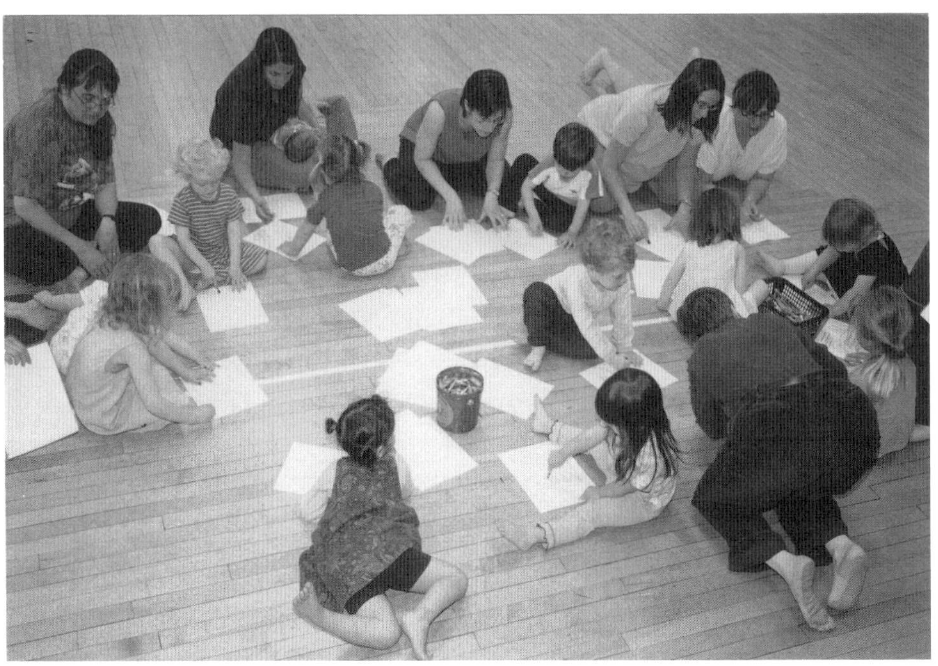

Provide time for reflection and peer- and self-assessment

Give students a few minutes during each class to reflect on their experiences, feelings and their development as dancers. Have them share these thoughts with a peer, a small group or the whole class. These moments develop self-expression, self-awareness and emotional growth. Reflection is valuable and thoroughly enjoyed by the students.

Management Tips

A conceptual, brain-compatible lesson plan helps considerably with class management. However, there are a few details that will make the lesson even more successful.

Use effective signals

Establish start and stop signals in the first few classes. The signal most often used for stopping and listening is a hand-clapping rhythm. Clap a basic pattern while the dancers echo it. Clap two to three patterns to get everyone's attention. Use this signal primarily for reflection and cooperative work that requires the dancers to talk to each other. Because clapping is heard over their voices, they quickly respond and turn their attention to the teacher. It also reinforces rhythmic patterns while reducing vocal strain.

Another way to signal dancers to stop is to pause or stop the music, say "Freeze!" and then give instruction. Capture the younger children's attention with a dramatic "Uh, oh!" followed by a direction or a new idea. Turn down the lights, hold up a hand or beat a drum or small gong. Saying "Shhhh" is usually ineffective.

For a starting signal, ask the dancers to take their positions, make a shape in their self space behind a partner by facing a partner in opposing lines at a certain count. Or say, "Begin dancing when you hear the music…here we go." Another attention-getting idea is, "Bill is looking at me. Raven is looking at me. Michiko is looking at me. Everyone is looking at me. Thank you! Please make a circle around the X by the time I count to five."

Try "Thank you for listening, we are ready to begin" or slowly count "5, 6, 7, 8." Dancers will quickly take their places and be ready to dance. Especially with young dancers, turn on the music to capture attention and give directions as they dance. Signals should encourage, not threaten.

Encourage appropriate movement

Begin each residency with a lesson on the Place concept. Lessons always go smoother when students are familiar with the terms self space and general space. Explore moving in self space – the space that belongs to them – by giving the students many ideas. Encourage them to change level, direction or speed, move different body parts, balance and use different energies and axial movements while in one place. Then have them move through general space. Remind them to explore different pathways and locomotor movements and to look for the empty space. By telling them to watch out for other people, they look for and bump into them! Asking them to look for the empty space solves this problem.

Alternate longer periods of dancing in self space with shorter periods in general space. Always suggest different ways to move, reminding dancers to look for the empty space. Reinforce appropriate movement with positive feedback. Help the inappropriate movers by holding their hands or dancing near them. If the class continues to have trouble with behavioral boundaries, use more self space activities rather than general space ones until they move in appropriate and safe ways.

Create Rituals

People love rituals that provide a sense of structure and security. For every age group, begin and end class the same way each week. By knowing what to expect, students feel safe and secure. They know that when dance class begins they will have a joyful, meaningful and positive experience. They look forward to the next class.

For parent/child classes, put a basket of small scarves on the floor for parents and children to gather around and play with before class. Class begins with a lively scarf dance relating to the day's concept. After that, move into the seated BrainDance with nursery rhymes (see the Warming Up chapter). These classes end with rubber stamps on hands and feet with lots of praise and encouragement.

Teaching Tip: *At the Creative Dance Center, preschool and primary dancers gather around me as we talk about their day and what they plan to do after class. For the first four classes we say each other's names to remember with whom we are dancing. It is BrainDance time when everyone has arrived. These classes end with stamps and praise.*

Modern Dance class for intermediate, middle school students and adults begins at the word board to discover the concept for the day. We embody it through the BrainDance. These classes end with a special circle where we review the lesson concept, do deep breathing exercises and applaud our accompanist and teacher.

In school residency class, begin with the introduction of the lesson concept and the BrainDance. End with quiet mirroring or relaxation exercises and positive feedback. In teacher training workshops, begin with brief introductions and an agenda or outline as a map for the time spent together. End with reflection and encouragement.

Starting classes with each student doing a solo movement that reflects something about him or her requires time and scares or embarrasses some students. It helps to get to know the students, but does it help the students? Create beginning and ending rituals that meet the needs of the students in order to give them a sense of security.

Use "I see" statements to indicate desired behavior and provide ideas

Use simple statements to cue desired behavior. For example, "I see dancers looking for the empty space" or "I see dancers moving safely through the space." "I see dancers listening to the music and changing their movements when the music changes" or "I see dancers moving on curved pathways." You may not immediately see these movements but as soon as you make the statement, the behavior will be seen. This gives dancers ideas without telling them what to do. Suggestions will motivate those who need ideas.

The brain does not comprehend the word "don't." When beginning with "don't," the brain will hear only the words that follow. "(Don't) bump into your neighbor... (Don't) run into the walls... (Don't) throw the instruments." This is actually commanding undesirable behavior! Practicing positive "I see" statements is much more beneficial.

Model appropriate behavior

Student behavior mirrors the teacher's feelings and behavior toward them. Be careful! One of the first things an infant recognizes is the mother's face. The normal brain then continues to respond to facial expressions throughout life. Greet each student with a hello and a smile. Be sure to learn all names and use them frequently (or use name tags). Respect and trust students. Be a guide rather than a boss or best friend. "Please" and "thank you" motivate appropriate behavior. For example, "Thank you, Santiago, for looking at me and listening. Thank you, Sue. Thank you, Kim. Thank you, Shanti. Now everyone is ready. Thank you!" Other effective statements are, "I am proud of Louis for waiting so patiently for his turn. I am proud of Chang. I am proud of Anna. I am proud of everybody!" These statements are as helpful with older students as with the younger ones.

To model participation in dance classes, move, move, move! Alternate dancing with the students and observing them. Move between students who talk or shove. Teach while standing between them or put a gentle hand on their shoulders for a second—model gentle touch with students. Many have never been touched gently and do not know how to be gentle themselves.

It takes a lot of patience to be a teacher. We are often expected to undo behavior learned at home. This takes time. Take care of yourself so that you can be a healthy model for your students.

Teach to the core, "ignore" negative behavior

Teach with a wide rather than a narrow focus. Give attention to students who follow directions and dance their best. They always outnumber the misbehaving or negative ones (with an appropriately planned and presented lesson). They form the core of the class. Reinforce the core through "I see" statements, smiles, eye contact and touch. If a student is having trouble moving safely, take hold of a hand and dance together. Be positive, help them! These children usually have problems with their sensory-motor system and need guidance. Dance near or with them while continuing to teach to the core. Please do not call attention to them; that can have a negative effect. They may need to sit down and take four deep breaths before rejoining class. Breathing and relaxation techniques help them self-regulate their behavior.

Severe, unsafe behavior may require removing a student for a short time. Discuss the problem with the parents or principal in order to work out a positive, cooperative plan. Doing the BrainDance at the beginning of every class will help considerably because it is an exercise that reorganizes the brain. Acknowledge all dancers who want to be in class who are trying to do their best! Eventually, the few who are off task will rejoin the other students when appropriately reinforced.

Establish a safe and nurturing environment

If students feel safe and cared for, they behave well and are comfortable exploring and sharing new ideas. The dance space should be inviting and colorful, well heated or cooled and ventilated. The floor should have a clean, appropriate surface and preferably be "sprung."

Even more important is how the emotional space feels. A democratic environment where the students' ideas are solicited and respected is more brain-compatible than an autocratic one. Be firm and nurturing at the same time. "Fun, firm and fair" is my motto. Children need a loving authority figure. When rules are clear, fair and abided by all, everyone feels safe. Providing reasonable boundaries is a positive way to teach respect for others. Many dancers were raised in tyrannical, autocratic dance studios and companies where they were yelled at, criticized and belittled. Let us not perpetuate this method of teaching! A nurturing, safe environment creates healthy people who enjoy dance throughout their lives.

Help non-participants

There are usually two types of non-participants, students who are shy or nervous about moving with a large group or students who demand attention through negative or manipulative behavior.

Let shy students enter class in their own time. For some, it takes minutes, for others it takes weeks. Suggesting ways to move by cueing with the dance concepts will help the shy or inhibited dancer. Some students are hesitant because they do not know what to expect. Outlining the lesson plan in the first class puts students at ease. Misbehavior often comes from fear of the unknown.

Give positive feedback to those students who are participating and ignore the manipulative student who refuses to dance. If the student is school-aged, remind the child that dance is a required subject, just like math or reading, and that everyone is expected to fully participate. Of course, you will be proud of his or her efforts. Remind tired teenagers that dancing gives them energy. Serotonin, a brain chemical that helps with self esteem, gets flowing with movement and makes them feel great. Another solution is to give a choice without anger in the voice: "Have fun dancing or please stand by the door until you are ready to join us." Make sure the choice is a viable one.

Children are not born misbehaving. Some have been inadvertently trained through parents' lack of establishing clear boundaries, while others have poorly functioning limbic systems (social and emotional brain). Inappropriate behavior always gets worse before it gets better. It seems easier to give in but, in the long run, it is better to persevere. The time it takes to correct behavior is always worth it.

Leave at home preconceived notions about who will and will not dance. Everyone – boys and girls, preschool, elementary, middle, high school, college students and adults – find joy in dancing when presented with brain-compatible lessons.

Special Issues

Clothing

Every dance studio has a dress code, from casual to formal. At the Creative Dance Center, most dancers participate with bare feet and choose their own dance clothes. Dance in school environments is another matter. When teaching short residencies in public schools, students should not remove their shoes unless they have possibly dangerous footwear (heels, floppy sandals or heavy boots). It takes up too much of the short time allotted. Dancing in socks might be okay, but could also be dangerous, depending on the floor surface. Clothes should be loose fitting but not too baggy. Girls should be encouraged to wear shorts under their skirts, or preferably pants on dance days.

Props

Be sure to have enough props, sports equipment or musical instruments for everyone. If this is not possible, then pair up dancers. One student in the pair dances with the prop while the other dances without; alternate roles several times. To prevent conflicts, provide just one color or type of prop or have plenty of props in three to four colors. One secret is to ignore the arguing students and compliment those who pick their props quickly to get ready to dance. "Susan is ready. Miguel is ready. Lan is ready. Ivor is ready. Here comes the music…thank you everyone, here we go!" Some students may still be deciding which color or instrument to take, but they soon join in when they see everyone having fun and receiving positive feedback for skillful dancing. If a student is very upset about not having a certain color, say, "Who is willing to offer a blue scarf to Simone? Thank you, Henry, I am really proud of you!"

Students with special needs

Integrate special-needs students into classes rather than create a separate curriculum for them. Start each quarter with lots of partnering work. Partners switch frequently at short intervals so everyone works together. This sets the tone for collaboration and understanding.

Because each special-needs child is unique, problems must be addressed as they arise. Help these students by encouraging them to explore new ways to challenge themselves. How can they move through the leaping course in a wheelchair? Perhaps they can wheel around the obstacles. If a skill is too difficult, help them discover ways to adapt and still keep the integrity of the movement. For example, Down syndrome students may step over the leaping cones until they learn to be "airborne."

As much as possible, treat everyone in class equally. The creative dance curriculum is very supportive because all students explore the dance concepts in their own ways. Problems are solved on the spot. Partner with one student to help with skills; allow another to do solo work if the group work becomes too stressful. Help students self-regulate their behavior when they get excited.

The conceptual approach is effective because the elements of the concepts are opposites. Special-needs students perform movements that may be unfamiliar, but are important for changing the way they move and think. For example, an overly aggressive student will do the familiar movements of "stamp" and "punch," but also the unfamiliar movements of "tiptoe" and "float." As the aggressive student works with these softer movements, the brain begins to change. New feelings of concern for others may emerge.

Tailor classes to meet the needs of the various groups of students with special needs. If necessary, break down movement patterns into shorter segments. Keep directions basic and pace the class. Work specifically with counterbalance and weight-sharing techniques with students in wheelchairs. With "learning disabled" and "behavior disordered" students, spend a lot of time on the BrainDance patterns described in the Warming Up chapter that integrate creeping and crawling throughout the dance class. Specific ideas for special-needs students are addressed in *Creative Dance for All Ages*. (Recommended resources are listed in the bibliographies in both of my books.)

Brain-compatible dance education offers many benefits to students of all abilities. Teachers are encouraged to be inclusive and explore ways to provide quality dance education for everyone.

Solving Space Problems

How the dance space is set up will help or hinder class management. Often inadequate thought is given to the teaching environment, nor may we have choices when determining the teaching space. Here are some helpful hints for dealing with less than optimal spaces. Remember that no matter how well a lesson is planned or presented, the space limitations can affect the lesson's outcome. Make the necessary adjustments and move on. Find a better space or convince supervisors that students deserve a space where they can truly learn to dance and create. Remember, complaining about the space will not change it. Be proactive and find solutions.

If the space is too small

- Present more self space than general space activities.
- Allow half the class to move while the other half observes, freezes in shapes or plays musical instruments. Alternate the roles of dancer and non-dancer quickly and frequently.
- Have opposing lines of dancers pass through each other when practicing skills or use figure eight formations.
- Use concentric circles instead of one big circle.
- Employ primarily scattered formations.

If the space is too large

- Set boundaries using traffic cones, floor tape or whatever is at hand. Hardware stores have tape that can be easily removed from the floor.
- Positively reinforce dancers who stay within the boundaries.
- Mark lines with floor tape at the ends of the room to identify the starting place for floor combinations and leaping courses. Tape an X in the middle of the room for gathering around and circle dances.
- Use a portable microphone and a good sound system that is heard throughout the space.

If the space contains too many distractions

- Cover all distractions (toys, playthings, musical instruments) with large sheets or cloths during dance class or place tape across areas where dancers should not enter.
- Post signs at doorways (lunchrooms and multi-purpose rooms) to alert people that "class is in session" and they may enter after it is over.
- Studio teachers should establish a policy of having parents in the dance room only during special visiting weeks.

If teaching in a classroom

- If traveling from classroom to classroom, give each teacher specific space set-up directions. Remember to compliment the teachers and students who have the space ready for the lesson. A rolling suitcase is effective for transporting all props and equipment.
- Sometimes it is easier not to move the furniture in a classroom. Often the space around desks and up and down aisles is greater than what is left when all the furniture is moved to one side. Also, the pathways are very interesting!

If the space is always dirty or the room and equipment are not set up

- Ask custodians for help. Give lots of positive reinforcement and provide an occasional gift, such as flowers or food. Occasionally invite them to watch class. Have the students give a special performance just for them.
- If necessary, buy a broom and ask responsible students to help prepare the space.
- Talk with the PTA and request parent volunteer help.
- Use scholarship students to help maintain the space in private studios.

Reflective Teaching

Reflecting about one's teaching practice is an important part of being a dance educator, as well as a learner. An effective teacher prepares a personal mission statement and writes lesson goals based on this statement. Lessons are planned and presented with the focus of meeting these goals. After the lessons are presented, reflect on how well the goals are met, compare teaching practices with personal mission statements and reframe problems for new action.

Evaluating One's Teaching: Basic questions to ask after the lesson

Did the students:

- See, hear, say and move the dance concept throughout the lesson?
- Display knowledge and understanding of the lesson concept?
- Execute the skills taught?
- Have the opportunity to use multiple thinking tools?
- Move safely?
- Construct their own learning for at least part of the class?
- Work together cooperatively?
- Reflect on their experiences, ideas and feelings?
- Respect one another?
- Take responsibility for their actions?
- Express enjoyment?

Writing a personal mission statement is an excellent way to become a reflective teacher. Jot down observations of master teachers to emulate, as well as teaching styles or theories to practice. Write down dreams and goals for both the teacher and the students. Reevaluate this statement often:

> *The goal in my first year of teaching was to survive! Now my mission is to create a positive learning environment in which all learners may succeed. May they grow and develop as critical thinkers, collaborative dancers and moral citizens of the world who understand and appreciate the art of dance.*

When encountering problems in class, return to the goals. "Are they too complex? Am I trying to accomplish too many things in a single lesson? Are they developmentally appropriate or are they too easy or too challenging? Am I overly critical of my students' accomplishments or of my own teaching? Have I left out an important element?" End by referring back to Principles of Brain-Compatible Dance Education.

When classes go well, ask why and make notes about successes. When classes are less successful, again ask why and seek solutions for the problems. Mistakes provide the path to growth. Blaming students is non-productive as is being overly self-critical. Remember the mantra: "Patience and Practice." Be patient with yourself and your personal mistakes; be willing to constantly learn and grow. Also, remember that practicing brain-compatible techniques will make you more proficient.

Review your mission statement frequently. Be honest about the reasons for teaching. "Am I teaching because I like to take control? Or am I teaching because I wish to be a guide? Am I teaching because I hope my students will fulfill a need? Or am I teaching because I want to fulfill the needs of students?" If making a difference in the lives of students is important, then attend professional conferences, share ideas with colleagues and read the books suggested in the bibliography on dance education, brain research and class management. Exemplary teachers are lifelong learners who constantly reflect on their beliefs and redefine their teaching techniques as they gain new knowledge.

Sharing this knowledge, as well as a love of dance with students will delight and satisfy a teacher throughout his or her teaching career. The students' joy will live long beyond that.

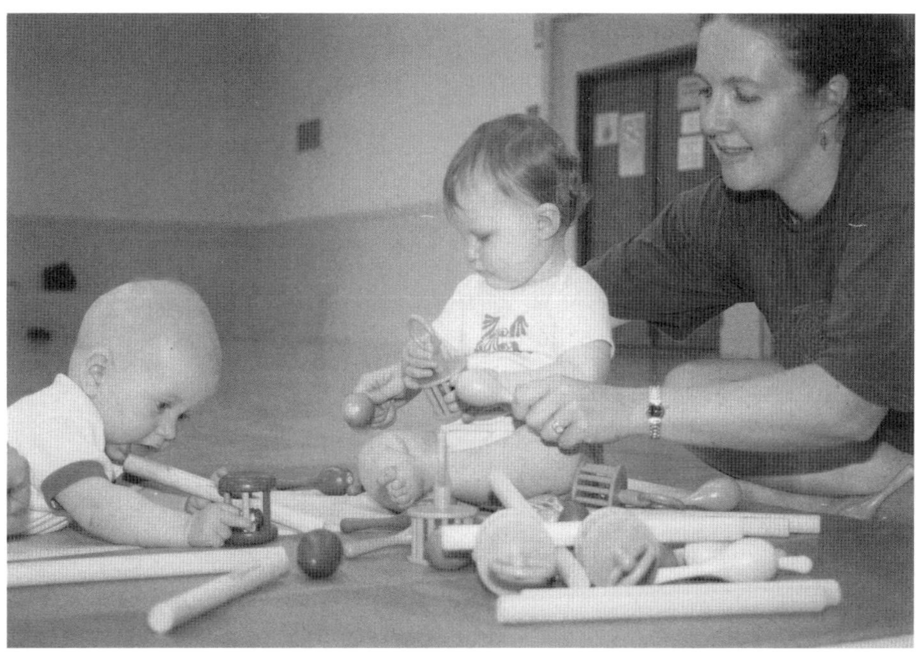

In Summary

Brain-compatible dance education concerns the best practices in teaching based on current research on how the brain learns:

- Sensory-motor activities build the brain. A fully functioning body reflects a fully functioning brain.
- The brain has plasticity. Sensory-motor activities form new neural pathways and synaptic connections throughout life.
- Students learn best in an enriched, multi-sensory environment where feedback is immediate and positive.
- Novelty encourages attention and repetition lowers stress. Novelty and repetition together aid learning and memory.
- The five-part lesson plan includes both teacher-directed and student-centered activities and provides opportunities for both technical and creative development. Therefore, it engages all learning styles.
- Concept-based lessons provide students with the tools to be critical thinkers and creative problem-solvers.
- Students model their behavior on the teacher's behavior. Positive thoughts, words and actions create positive results. Recognize the students who behave appropriately and minimize behavioral problems, unless safety is at risk.
- A safe and nurturing physical, mental and emotional environment decreases behavior problems and increases learning.
- A reflective teacher who is a lifelong learner guarantees students a brain-compatible dance experience.

Do not expect everything to always go perfect. ~ David, age 10

(Endnotes)

[1] Hannford, Carla. *Smart Moves: Why Learning is Not All in Your Head.* Arlington, VA: Great Ocean Publishers, 1995.

[2] *The Seattle Times*, 5 April 2004, p. A13.

[3] Jensen, Eric, *Teaching with the Brain in Mind* (Chapter 2). Alexandria, VA: ASCD, 1998.

[4] Eliot, Lise. *What's Going on in There? How the Brain and Mind Develop in the First Five Years of Life* (Chapter 2) New York, NY: Bantam, 2000.

[5] Ibid.

[6] Hannaford, op. cit. (Chapter 3).

[7] Interview with Bonnie Bainbridge Cohen, "Sensing, feeling and action." *Contact Quarterly reprint No. 1,* 1981, p. 6.

[8] Jensen, op. cit. (Chapter 8).

[9] Hannaford, op. cit. p. 54.

[10] Ibid. (Chapter 4).

[11] Ibid. (Chapter 5).

[12] Jensen, op. cit. (Chapter 2).

[13] *New England Journal of Medicine*, 348:2508-2516. June 19, 2003.

Chapter One
Lesson Plan Section 1: Warming Up

In this chapter:

BrainDance

1. **Breath** – Breathe deeply.

2. **Tactile** – Squeeze, tap, pat, scratch, brush all body parts.

3. **Core-Distal** – Reach out with toes, fingers, head, tail and curl back to your core.

4. **Head-Tail** – Move head and tail separately and together in all planes, wiggle spine.

5. **Upper-Lower** – Move all parts of upper half of body, then all parts of lower half of body.

6. **Body-Side** – Move all parts on right side of body, then all parts on left side, do horizontal eye tracking.

7. **Cross-Lateral** – Move across midline and connect upper and lower body quadrants, do vertical eye tracking.

8. **Vestibular** – Move off balance with swings, spins, tips and rolls on all levels and in all directions.

Some of these patterns are based on Bartenieff Fundamentals.

WARMING UP

Applicable National Dance Standards

The following standards from the *National Standards for Dance Education* will be achieved through the activities in this chapter:

- **Making connections between dance and healthful living**
- **Identifying and demonstrating movement elements and skills in performing dance**

Chapter Introduction

A brain-compatible dance class always begins with a rich, multi-layered warm-up that sets the tone for the entire class. The Warming Up section, primarily teacher-directed, prepares the brain and body for the day's lesson. The brain is prepared for thinking through a multi-sensory introduction of the lesson's dance concept. The dance concepts are listed and defined in the next chapter, Exploring the Concept. A multi-sensory approach – hear, see, say and do – is most brain compatible. Dancers of all ages remember and embody the dance concepts when they see, hear and say the words while describing them through movement. For example, when the lesson's concept is Level, the dancers read and speak the words "high level" as they move body parts on a high level. Then they read and say "middle level," while moving the whole body on a middle level. Finally they read and say "low level" while moving the body on a low level. The teacher further engages the students by asking questions about the concept, such as, "Where on the body do you think low level space ends and middle level space begins?"

Clearly display all dance vocabulary on the wall, in pocket charts, on overheads or by Power Point. This allows everyone easy reference to the conceptual vocabulary throughout the lesson. Also, write the lesson's concept on the board or pin the specific word cards in a "Word Corner."

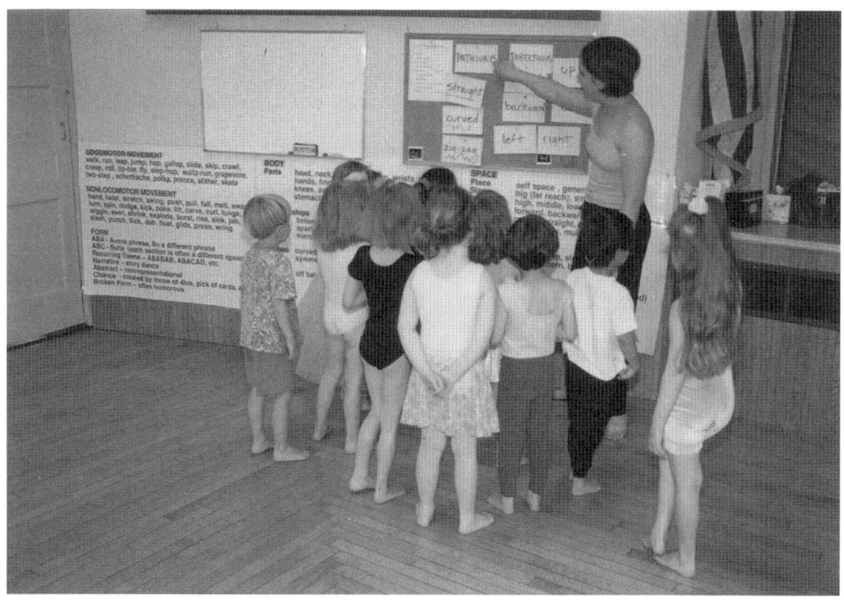

The lesson's concept may be introduced before, during or after the warm up exercises. The exercises may take five to eight minutes in a thirty-minute class, fifteen to twenty minutes in a sixty-minute class or thirty to forty-five minutes in a ninety-minute dance technique class. The most effective warm up exercise to prepare students for active moving and focused thinking is a series of movements called the "BrainDance."

What is the BrainDance?

Background

The BrainDance is an exercise I developed in 2000, based on the fundamental movement patterns that babies discover in their first year. These movement patterns wire the central nervous system by laying the foundation for appropriate behavior and attention, eye convergence necessary for reading, sensory-motor development and more. Before developing the BrainDance, I used a variety of ways for quickly warming up students in a thirty-minute class. I tried other methods for preparing the body for the rigorous dance technique in longer classes or before performances. None of these methods were satisfactory; the students did not become focused or very warmed up. I was also becoming frustrated with my school residencies; it was harder to teach in the public schools – the students seemed more difficult and less focused than ever before. More students who came to my private studio also had learning and behavior problems.

The seeds for the BrainDance began in the 1970s when my interest in the body-brain connection was sparked by Newall Kephart's work. During the 1980s, Krista Harris, a Certified Laban Movement Analyst, introduced me to the Bartenieff Fundamentals. I greatly enjoyed and felt better after moving through the fundamental patterns. The Bartenieff Fundamentals are, like many somatic practices, based on the developmental movement patterns that babies progress through in building the central nervous system and brain. I integrated the Fundamentals into my studio classes for children eight and older and was thrilled by the technical and expressive strides they made!

At the same time, I reconnected with colleague Bette Lamont, who was working with Florence Scott in Neurodevelopmental Movement Therapy. Her ideas for helping children with learning and behavior problems were fascinating; I agreed with the theory that crawling, creeping and other basic movements helped integrate our brains and bodies. Everything connected.

Although Bartenieff Fundamentals and neurodevelopmental patterns would be helpful in my school residencies, I was not given the time or space in classrooms for students to lie down on the floor and learn the patterns fully. So, I created a short sequence of standing exercises that quickly moved students through eight movement patterns in developmental order. It seemed like a "quick fix" for a big problem. The results were amazing and I named the standing sequence BrainDance.

After incorporating the BrainDance into my classes, I saw a profound difference in my students and myself. Because the BrainDance is based on the primary developmental movement patterns that wire our central nervous system, the brain is reorganized each time we move through them. The BrainDance is sequential and holistic. It effectively integrates the mind and body. The BrainDance also aligns the body by making us aware of all our connective parts – how they move separately and together. The BrainDance helps students become focused, energized and ready to learn. I, as the teacher, am relaxed and ready to teach.

I have received a great deal of positive feedback from people around the world who have used the BrainDance in many different situations and with many different ages. Teachers describe positive changes in students' behavior and improvement in test scores. It is not the whole answer to the many problems we face today as educators, but offers positive outcomes and provides a great warm up!

Developmental Movement Patterns: Origins of the BrainDance

A baby first communicates through movement. Brain development is stimulated by crawling, creeping, rolling, turning, walking, skipping, reaching, swinging and much more. The brain's plan for development involves specific and intensive motor activity that makes full use of the baby's complicated nervous system. This system must go through a series of developmental stages before the brain can operate at its full potential. The baby learns to "program" motor and perceptual responses. Nerve and brain cells learn to connect through whole body movement and sensory stimulation.

This process, called neurological organization, describes the evolution of the central nervous system from conception to eight years of age. Throughout the first year, infants engage in tasks that lead to walking and talking. By twelve months old, the brain has learned 50% of everything it will ever know![1]

While the baby is in the womb, neurogenesis (the birth of brain cells) takes place. Cells move to areas of the brain where they are needed. With babies' first breath, oxygen fills the brain, beginning the growth of dendrites and axons – the brain's "wires." Sensory integration and bonding develops as the baby begins tactile communication with the mother through touch and breastfeeding. Touch, movement, vision and hearing are equally important to the baby's developing brain.

The brain continues to develop as it creates synaptic connections through fundamental movement patterns. What appears to be random squiggling in the torso, arms and legs is called Core-Distal movement. Core-Distal movement is a baby's way of reaching out to discover the world.

Core-Distal movement soon turns into a more organized pattern called Head-Tail movement. By two months of age, an infant, if given exercise time on the tummy, begins to stretch the head to see the world. This develops important neck and shoulder strength for sitting and writing, as well as alignment of the cervical and lumbar spine.

By two-and-a-half to seven months of age, most babies begin to organize the Upper-Lower pattern by pressing (grounding) the lower body half (legs and pelvis) into the floor, so the upper half (arms, head and torso) can move and vice versa. The right and left sides of the body are also articulated through Body-Side movement and grounding. Physical grounding leads to emotional grounding. The articulation of body halves through mobility and stability also allows the baby to travel toward or away from a noise or object. Early belly crawling evolves into more mobile crawling that helps develop the horizontal eye tracking skill necessary for learning to read.

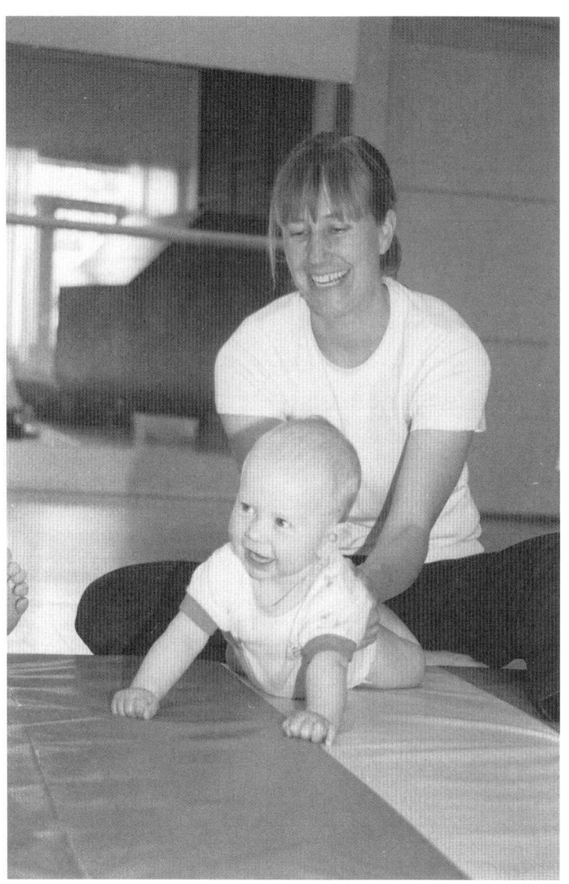

The baby develops a sensory and motor world that lays the foundation for the next stage of creeping. Sometime between seven months and a year, the baby puts distance between the body and the floor by pushing up onto hands and knees. The curvy little baby legs align with hip sockets and feet in preparation for standing. The baby creeps on hands and knees in a Cross-Lateral pattern that will soon result in cross-lateral walking. Creeping on hands and knees triggers vertical eye tracking. The convergence of vertical and horizontal eye tracking is essential for reading and writing.

Creeping also triggers the Vestibular System as balance is required to stay upright on hands and knees. The Vestibular System plays a critical role in all learning. The senses that we rely on for the rest of our lives depend on a properly functioning Vestibular System. This system analyzes movements through the whole body. It helps us know where we are in space by coordinating vision with movement. It also aids balance, locomotion, coordination and keeps us alert and responsive. This system, that begins developing in the womb, continues to develop during the first fifteen months of life through rolling, rocking, swaying and cross-lateral movements. Along with observable changes during the period of creeping, countless other neurological tasks are stimulated and organized through movement, such as detailed perception and focusing, body temperature regulation, waking and sleeping cycles, the suppression of newborn reflexes and the emergence of a more mature human being.

Humans are genetically programmed to develop through specific fundamental neural motor patterns, but our environment determines how successfully this happens. Babies who are not given ample opportunity to roll, crawl, creep, rock, turn, stretch, clasp, focus and babble may develop gaps in sensory motor functioning that later appear as developmental disabilities. These gaps result in focusing and filtering problems, reading problems, sensory integration problems or poor social skills.

How do babies miss these instinctive activities? For convenience, love and safety, we keep babies off the floor too much of their first year. An infant spending too much time in a car seat, jumper, walker, being held or lying on his or her back on a blanket, cannot move through the critical developmental patterns during the first twelve months.

The fear of Sudden Infant Death Syndrome has caused a widespread campaign to force babies to sleep and play on their backs. But babies should not spend most of their waking time on their backs. They should play on their stomachs! Mothers were once told to keep babies on their tummies to avoid choking. Now that the trend is reversed, we observe gaps in the normal growth and development of children who spend too much time on their backs.

Today, babies spend an average of six hundred hours a year riding in car seats and more hours sitting in the same plastic car seats at home, in stores and while waiting for siblings. I call this syndrome "baby-in-a-bucket." While car seats are important in saving lives in the event of a car accident, they hinder normal growth and development when used as a multi-purpose container.

Babies need to spend time on their tummies to develop fundamental movement patterns to wire the brain and lay the foundation for reading, writing, socializing and other healthy behavior. When prevented from moving through these patterns, learning and behavior problems may develop. The good news is that moving through these patterns at any age may correct flaws in the perceptual processing and integrate the body with the brain to enhance learning.

The BrainDance is an effective warm-up exercise that incorporates these patterns, reorganizes our brains, connects and aligns all parts of the body, delivers blood and oxygen to the brain, stimulates the Vestibular System, helps us to center and focus and brings clarity to all our movements.

Basic BrainDance for Ages Six through Adult

When first introducing students to the BrainDance, explain the rationale behind the patterns. Keep the explanation simple and brief for young students by saying, "I am going to teach you a series of movements that we all did when we were babies. Doing these movements every day will keep our brains and bodies strong and healthy." Then, move through the patterns, naming each while briefly explaining its function. After the BrainDance, ask the dancers how they feel. Their positive comments will validate the experience!

Older students should be given a more detailed description of how the brain works. Teach the BrainDance concepts in greater detail over several weeks or lessons. It is important to help the dancers connect brain function with learning and healthy living.

Following is a general description of each BrainDance pattern. A list of benefits is included for each pattern with explanations for BrainDance variations. The Basic BrainDance is a good model for building complex exercises. There are many movements other than the ones that follow that may be performed within each pattern. The only rule for the BrainDance to be effective is to include all the patterns and perform them in the order listed, beginning with Breath and ending with Vestibular. The Basic BrainDance with variations may be viewed in my videos/DVDs, *BrainDance* and *Teaching Creative Dance*.

1. Breath: Take four to six deep breaths through the nose and out the mouth, filling the belly, diaphragm and lungs. While breathing, center the body by pressing both feet on the floor (weight evenly distributed) and align all body parts: knees over feet, pelvis neutral (rather than tipped forward, backward or to one side), shoulders over pelvis (scapulae reaching toward tailbone), back of the neck long and jaw relaxed rather than stretching forward.

2. Tactile: Strongly squeeze all body parts and body surfaces with the hands, as though massaging the muscles. Tap all body parts and surfaces lightly and brush all body surfaces smoothly. Try other touches such as scratching, patting and slapping. Try touching the outside and inside of arms and hands, face, neck, front of torso, down both legs and feet and then up the back of legs, buttocks, back, shoulders and head (face, ears, scalp, etc).

3. Core-Distal: Reach from the center out, through and beyond the fingers, toes, head and tail (distal ends). Curl the distal ends back to the torso (core). Try whole body movements that grow and shrink, stretch and curl. Reach into different planes, directions and levels.

4. Head-Tail: First move just the head and just the tail (pelvis) in different directions with changes in size and energy. Play with movement that brings the head and tail together and apart while curving the spine forward and backward and side-to-side. This looks like the yoga exercise "cat-cow," but it is done standing. Try circling the head and tail. Keeping the knees bent helps to release the tail. End with a spine wiggle to accentuate the spine's flexibility.

5. Upper-Lower: Ground the lower half of the body by pressing the feet on the floor, bending the knees slightly. Stomp first to activate the legs and feet. Keeping the lower body grounded, swing the arms in different directions, stretch and dance the upper body (arms, head and torso) in different ways. Dance technique teachers might explore port de bras in their particular dance style.

Next, ground the upper body by reaching the arms into space with energy, as though hugging the earth. Try other arm positions, such as placing hands on the hips or touching little fingers to the shoulders with elbows reaching out and slightly forward. While keeping the upper body grounded, march in place, do knee bends in parallel and turnout, jumps, leg brushes, grapevine steps and other lower body actions. Dance technique teachers might explore pliés and relevés or other lower body steps in their particular dance style.

6. Body-Side: Ground the left side of the body by pressing the left foot on the floor and extend the left arm into space like the letter "K." Try other grounding positions such as one hand on one hip or the arm reaching down to the ground. The grounded side should be stable or still but energized to support the mobile side of the body. Keeping the left side grounded, dance the right side of the body in many different ways. Swing, bend, twist and stretch in different directions, with changes in energy. Be sure to include "half" of the head, pelvis and torso in these movements along with the leg and arm. Then ground the right side and dance the left side. Dance technique teachers might explore tendus, battements and other body-side movements in their particular dance style.

Next, simulate belly crawling, like a lizard up a wall. Crawl with arms and legs open to the side, with one side reaching up and the other side stretching down. Perform another body-side movement with elbows slightly bent, like a "W." Bring the whole left half of the body (arm, leg, pelvis and torso) over to meet the right half then open up the left half. Bring the right half over to meet the left half, like opening and closing a book or clam.

To develop horizontal eye tracking, repeat the "book" movement several times by following the opening hand with the eyes as it moves right to left or left to right. For more horizontal eye tracking practice, touch one finger of the right hand to the nose and look at the left hand while stretching it to the left side. Touch a finger of the left hand to the nose and look at the right hand while stretching it to the right. Repeat this several times. A third eye-tracking exercise is to follow one thumb with the eyes, without moving the head, while moving the thumb from left to right. The thumb should be at eye level about ten inches from the nose.

7. Cross-Lateral: Simulate creeping on hands and knees by doing a standing crawl with legs and arms parallel in front of the body. This looks like climbing a ladder. To practice vertical eye tracking, let the eyes travel up and down while "crawling." Look at one hand (or ceiling and floor) as it reaches high and then low. Another way to practice vertical eye tracking is to look at one thumb without moving the head as it moves up and down, about ten inches from the front of the body.

After practicing vertical eye tracking, do a cross-lateral "boogie" dance. Find as many ways possible to move cross-laterally, such as touching right knee to left elbow, right hand to left knee, left hand to right foot (crossing both behind and in front), swinging both arms sideways across the midline, spiraling and skipping in place with arms swinging. Dance technique teachers might include specific cross-lateral movements based on the particular dance style they are teaching.

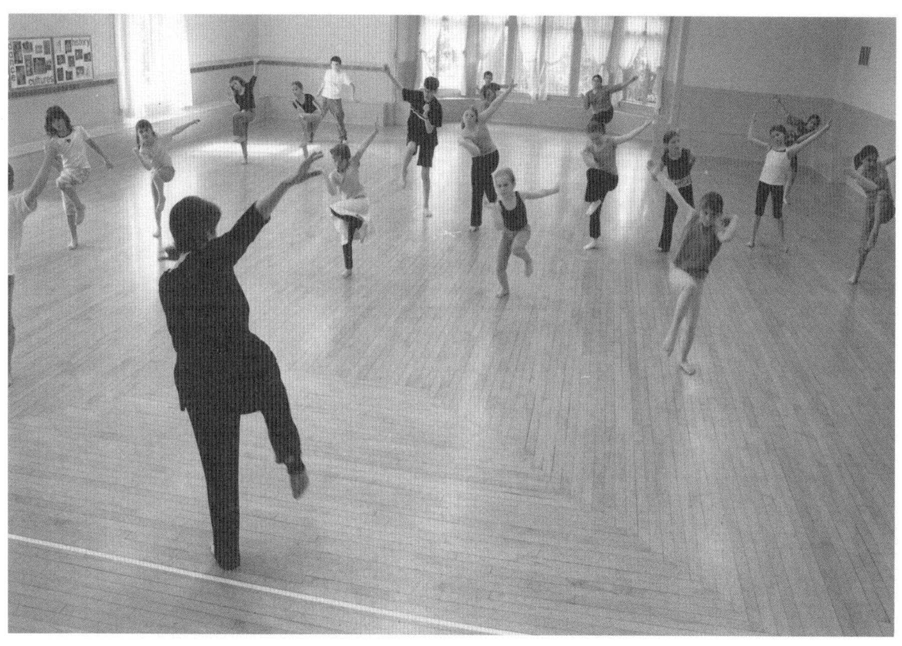

8. Vestibular: Spin in one direction for fifteen seconds or until dizzy (maybe only five to ten seconds), breathe and rest for fifteen seconds, then spin for fifteen more seconds in the other direction. Do not "spot" when turning; it is important to get dizzy to stimulate the balance system. Take three to four deep breaths to center oneself after spinning.

For more vestibular stimulation, try tipping in different directions, swinging the whole body forward and back and side-to-side, rolling on the floor and spinning on a low level on bottom, stomach and back.

Once students are familiar with the eight patterns of the BrainDance as a warm-up activity, refer to these patterns throughout the dance class. They will help students realize their maximum cognitive, physical, emotional and social potential.

Specific benefits of each pattern follow on the next page. Also, refer to Peggy Hackney's *Making Connections: Total Body Integration through Bartenieff Fundamentals*.

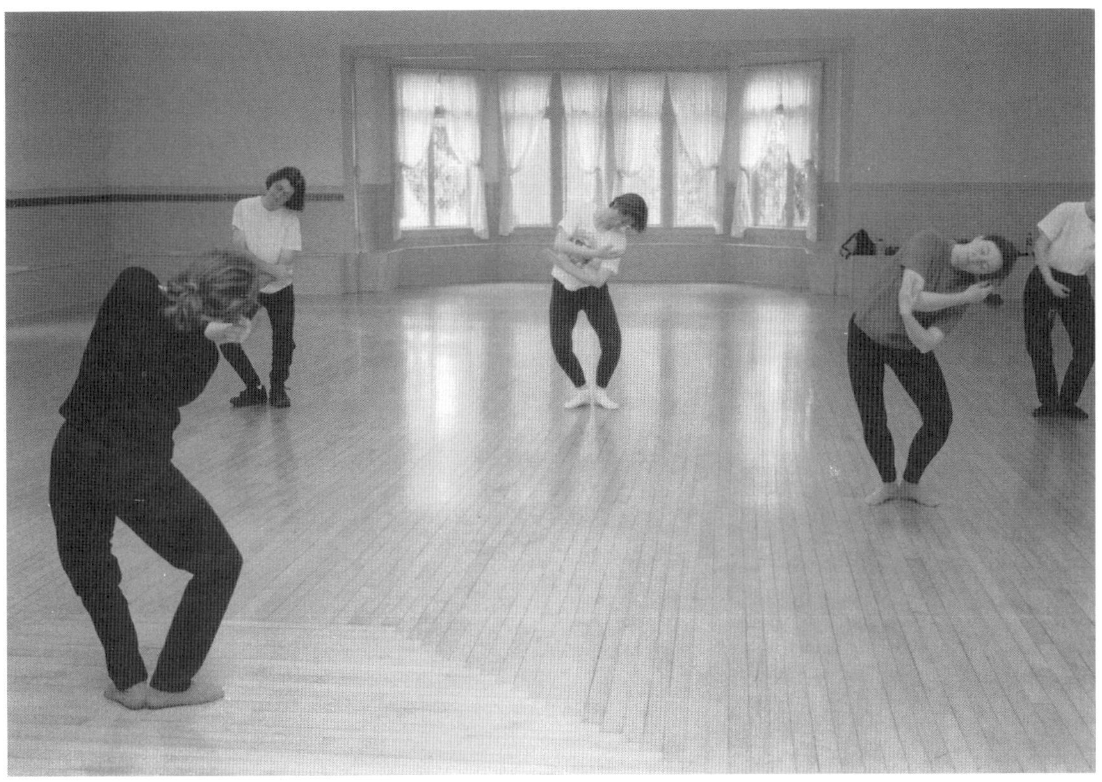

Benefits of Each Pattern

Some patterns are based on the Bartenieff Fundamentals

1. Breath: Deep breathing is essential for a fully functioning brain and body. The brain consumes one-fifth of the body's oxygen. All movements and rhythms are based on breath.

2. Tactile: A variety of touch leads to bonding, sensory integration, proprioception (knowing where the body is in space) and appropriate behavior.

3. Core-Distal: Reaching out with distal ends (fingers, toes, head and tail) connects us to the world beyond ourselves (interpersonal intelligence) and creates full body extension. Curling back to the core (pelvis and trunk) returns us to our own self (intrapersonal intelligence) and creates an awareness of core support for correct alignment and a sense of aliveness.

4. Head-Tail: Being aware of the interactive relationship between the head and tail (pelvis) leads to a full use of both ends of our spine for propelling us through space with ease, both on and off balance. Release of the head and tail creates an open path for our central nervous system to fully function. This pattern also strengthens back, neck and shoulder muscles used in sitting, writing and focusing on book, screen or blackboard.

5. Upper-Lower: Grounding the lower half, by yielding the weight of the body into the earth, allows the upper half to reach into space and relate with people. Grounding the upper half allows the lower to shift weight and travel through space toward someone or away from danger. Grounding and articulating body halves encourages emotional stability. We learn to reach for goals and set boundaries.

6. Body-Side: Grounding the right side allows the left side to be fully expressive and vice versa. Right or left dominance is felt; left and right brain hemispheres are strengthened. Body-side movements develop horizontal eye tracking necessary for reading.

7. Cross Lateral: Connecting body parts from opposite quadrants creates complex, three-dimensional movements such as spirals. Crossing the midline of the body connects both sides of the brain through the corpus collosum, which is essential for developing higher thinking skills. Cross-lateral movements develop vertical eye tracking necessary for reading.

8. Vestibular: Moving off balance develops the balance or Vestibular System. Stimulating the Vestibular System strengthens eye tracking, hearing, proprioception, balance and coordination.

Teaching Tip: BrainDance for Broad Assessment

When teaching the BrainDance, there may be students who have trouble performing one or two patterns smoothly. These individuals appear to move in a less integrated way than many of their peers. This lack of integration may indicate one or more gaps in the wiring of the central nervous system that may cause problems in behavior, social skills, attention or reading. These individuals may show improvement in these areas over time by doing more work in all the patterns on a daily basis. Instead of focusing on students who are having difficulties, present the BrainDance to the whole class, giving constructive feedback to the entire group.

Students having problems with specific patterns need to strengthen earlier patterns before the problem patterns can be improved. Students benefit most when presented with variations of the whole BrainDance at the beginning of every class and then work on specific patterns at different times during the class. An individual with severe problems might work with a movement therapist who is familiar with sensory integration, neurodevelopmental patterning or vision therapy.

Variations of the Basic BrainDance for Ages Six through Adult

Many of these variations can be viewed on my video/DVD, *BrainDance* (2003), listed in the Bibliography.

Whatever variation of the BrainDance is explored, always move through the patterns in order, from Breath through Vestibular. The Vestibular System actually starts developing in the womb and continues through fifteen months. Spinning and swinging make a good ending to the BrainDance, so place the Vestibular pattern there. Practice specific patterns separately in other parts of the lesson, with all eight patterns being performed in order as a warm-up exercise.

Remember that each pattern lays the foundation for the next one. Remind students to keep thinking about and using the early patterns as they move through the later patterns.

In crowded classrooms, lead the students through standing variations of the BrainDance. In gyms or dance studios where there is open space, have the students perform the BrainDance in a combination of levels, such as lying, sitting and standing.

Integrating Dance Concepts

After teachers and students are comfortable doing the basic BrainDance, integrate the lesson's dance concept into the BrainDance. Integrating the concepts is more challenging, which causes the brain to make new synaptic connections. It is also a great way to embody the concept from the very beginning of class.

Integrating the concepts also helps the students discover greater movement possibilities within each pattern. They might choose to recreate the movements when improvising or choreographing later in the lesson. This conceptual exploration of the BrainDance patterns will also deepen their understanding of body mechanics as they develop dance skills and technique.

Integrating a concept into the BrainDance is easy. Just explore the patterns relating to the lesson's concept. If the concept is Balance (on balance and off balance), have the students take balanced breaths for centering, then play with inhaling on balance and letting the exhale move them off balance and vice versa. In the Core-Distal pattern, have them stretch and curl on balance and then let the distal stretch pull them off balance with the movement back to core, bringing them back into balance.

In the Upper-Lower pattern, the students will discover how important it is to ground one half of the body (be on balance) to support the movements of the other half. Strongly ground the lower body while trying many unusual movements with the upper half in all the planes. Then do not ground the lower half in order to see if it is possible to do the same upper body movements with as much expression. Continue this exploration in the Body-Side and Cross-Lateral patterns. Can the whole body be out of balance or off balance and still move with safety and expression or does some part of the body need to be on balance? This is a good foundation for an exploration of counterbalance later in the lesson.

For the Vestibular pattern, explore different variations of spinning with eyes closed, changing speed or on different levels. Discuss which variations cause the students to feel more off balance. Explore ways to spin without feeling dizzy or off balance, such as spotting. Explore off- and on-balance turns.

Integrating the concepts into the BrainDance provides students with meaningful information about how they move and think. Ask students for ideas on integrating the lesson's concept. Not only will they be more involved in the lessons, the teacher will also develop a greater pool of ideas to draw from next time that concept is taught.

Integrating Dance Technique

Integrating the BrainDance into any style of dance technique class and vice versa makes the whole experience even more brain-compatible. The first four patterns of the BrainDance are the basis for moving with good technique. We often tell our students to breathe, but during the BrainDance they actually practice breathing. The tactile pattern will make partnering and contact work easier, because the students first explore all kinds of touch on their own bodies. The Core-Distal pattern helps students move with core strength for full extension of the arms and legs. The Head-Tail pattern awakens the two ends of the spine that propel us through space. Work in this pattern will help dancers move through space in a connected, relaxed way.

In the last four patterns, integrate the specific technical exercises. Particular arm movements for a dance style (port de bras) can be fully practiced in the Upper Body pattern. Pliés and other leg movements are practiced with the lower body. Tendus, brushes and similar one-legged movements are practiced with the corresponding arm movements in the Body-Side pattern. More complicated Contra-Lateral movements are practiced in the Cross-Lateral pattern. Turns, springs, falls, rolls and full body swings are practiced in the Vestibular pattern. Students change profoundly when the BrainDance is incorporated into technique class and technique into the BrainDance.

Spending more time in each pattern while working on technical skills generates important brain to body connections. The students' technique will become more expressive and articulate after doing the BrainDance. They will also develop an excellent movement vocabulary to use for feedback. For example, "That movement actually uses the Head-Tail pattern more than the Core-Distal pattern. Try focusing on moving with a Head-Tail initiation and see if it helps you do that movement easier and with more expression." Students also learn to use the patterns for self-assessment and to give peers articulate feedback.

Mirroring and Shadowing

Once the students are familiar with the BrainDance, have them create their own mirror or shadow movements by working in pairs, trios or quartets. Call out the patterns if necessary. Change leadership with each pattern or repeat each pattern with a new leader. Play with relationship by asking partners to stand near and far from each other.

Traveling

Perform all the patterns traveling through general space or alternate self and general space, leading to many new ways of dancing and discoveries such as the difference between a Body-Side and a Cross-Lateral walk.

Music and Rhymes

The brain is very responsive to music, so dancers are more inspired to do the BrainDance when accompanied by music or rhythmic patterns such as rhymes. Rhymes to accompany each BrainDance pattern for ages zero to five are listed on the following pages. For older students, Eric Chappelle, the Music Director for the Creative Dance Center, has composed exceptional music for conceptual dance classes and the BrainDance. *Music for Creative Dance, Volume II,* #21 is useful for doing the BrainDance quickly, as the whole piece is just over five minutes long. Change patterns on each pause in the music. *Music for Creative Dance, Volume III,* #17-19 is fun to use because it changes meters and ends with a lively reel for the last three patterns. *Music for Creative Dance, Volume I,* #15 has a soft, rhythmic quality that provides a steady, continuous beat in counts of six. Repeat the song several times for a longer BrainDance. *Music for Creative Dance, Volume II,* #13-19 comprises seven brief pieces that have world themes. Start with the breath pattern in silence, then begin the music, changing patterns on each new musical section. Experiment with lively music to energize students, slower music to calm them. *BrainDance Music* is an entire compact disk with a variety of spoken and instrumental pieces to accompany the BrainDance for all ages. Although nursery rhymes and songs are most often used with very young children, these can be fun for older students as well! Explore and experiment.

Lying or Sitting on the Floor

Create a BrainDance sequence that is performed lying and/or sitting on the floor. Move through patterns while lying on the stomach, back, sides, on hands and knees and sitting. If familiar with the Bartenieff Fundamentals, yoga positions, Pilates exercises, etc. incorporate them into the BrainDance. Also incorporate a floor barre into the BrainDance, which is most successful when done on a smooth, non-carpeted surface. Another variation is to perform the first four patterns sitting and the last four standing.

In a Chair

Do the BrainDance while sitting in a stable, non-folding chair. This variation is appropriate for students over age five. Students will discover new ways of moving through the patterns that they were unable to do while standing. School-aged students are very creative while dancing in their chairs. The chair BrainDance is particularly useful for older adults and students with special-needs. Be careful when teaching the eighth pattern (Vestibular) to older adults. Many older adults have balance problems. They should gently sway or tip the body side to side and forward and backward or swing the head gently side to side and around in easy circles. Have them hold onto the arms or seat of the chair. Older individuals might take turns holding the teacher's hands while doing this pattern.

With Props

Props add a new dimension to the basic BrainDance. Dancers hold two small scarves of different colors, one in each hand. The scarves provide a visual and tactile aid to distinguish the different patterns. Foam sticks are also used for tactile stimulation; when held or manipulated with different body parts, students can feel and visualize the various patterns. Stretchy bands and body socks, made from spandex, are other fun props. The push and pull of the stretchy material helps dancers become aware of body parts, halves and quadrants. Working in pairs with the stretchy bands adds another layer of interest and challenge.

With Emotions

Performing each pattern with different emotions, or doing several patterns with the same emotion, adds variety and often humor to the BrainDance!

Basic BrainDance with Rhymes for Toddlers through Age Five

Rhymes provide an excellent accompaniment for the BrainDance. Young children enjoy responding to rhymes and songs while developing rhythm and language through the repetition of words spoken and sung in a pulse or pattern. It is not necessary to "teach" these rhyming exercises. By performing these exercises with flow and a dramatic voice, the young students will naturally follow along! When teaching classes where adults are present, briefly explain the benefits of each pattern as it is performed. The Basic BrainDance with rhymes can be viewed in my video/DVD, *BrainDance*.

The local library may offer resources of nursery rhymes and other children's songs with even more ideas. After becoming familiar with the exercises described here, feel free to create movements within the context of each pattern. Children up to two years old will need help from a parent or caregiver to move through some of the BrainDance patterns. Very young dancers should sit between the legs of the parent while the parent moves the child through the patterns.

Repeating the rhymes, week after week, is beneficial for helping young dancers learn rhymes and exercises. Repetition also increases their sense of security. Vary the movements by incorporating the lesson's concept. Perform some of the movements "stronger" and "lighter" when exploring Weight, "quicker" and "slower" when exploring Speed or "bigger" and "smaller" when exploring Size.

The following is a BrainDance sequence that works well in a forty-five to sixty minute class. It takes fifteen minutes to go through the rhymes.

1. Breath: "Bubble Gum"

Students sit in a small circle and wiggle fingers and toes while chanting the rhyme below.

"Bubble gum, bubble gum in a dish,
How many blows do my dancers wish?"

One student names a number. Everyone blows (like blowing out a birthday candle) that same number of times, moving backward to form a bigger circle. "Pop" the bubble with a clap of the hands and move in again while exhaling. Repeat the rhyme two or three times.

2. Tactile: "Hickory, Dickory Dock"

Parents and their young children do tactile movements together. Older dancers touch their body parts as the song directs.

"Hickory Dickory Dock. The mouse ***squeezed*** *up the clock.*	Use hands to squeeze up legs, along torso, to top of head.
The clock struck one.	Clap once.
The mouse ***squeezed*** *down. Hickory Dickory Dock.*	Reverse direction of squeezing.
"Hickory Dickory Dock. The mouse ***tapped*** *up the clock.*	Use hands to tap up legs, along torso, to top of head.
The clock struck two, the mouse said, 'Whooo.'	Clap two times.
Hickory Dickory Dock.	Reverse direction of tapping.
"Hickory Dickory Dock. The mouse ***patted*** *up the clock.*	Use hands to pat up legs, along torso, to top of head.
The clock struck three, the mouse said, 'Whee!'	Clap three times.
Hickory Dickory Dock.	Reverse direction of patting.
"Hickory Dickory Dock. The mouse ***brushed*** *up the clock.*	Use hands to brush up legs, along torso, to top of head.
The clock struck four, the mouse said, 'No more!'	Clap four times.
Hickory Dickory Dock."	Reverse direction of brushing.

3. Core-Distal: "Twinkle, Twinkle Little Star."

"Twinkle, twinkle little star How I wonder what you are. Up above the world so high Like a diamond in the sky. Twinkle, twinkle little star How I wonder what you are."	Reach out (grow big) and curl in (shrink small) during alternate lines of the rhyme or reach out slowly while reciting each line, then quickly get small while saying the last word of each line (star, are, high, sky).

4. Head-Tail: "Bounce Like a Ball"

Sit with knees bent and soles of the feet together or legs crossed. Make a circle with the arms as if hugging a ball. Parents can hold their young children's hands and stretch them forward so the children curl over.

For more tactile stimulation, make foot and leg "sandwiches" by spreading imaginary peanut butter and jelly on the bottoms of the feet or tops of the legs. Tap in raisins, slap on bananas and brush on honey before stretching the head toward the tail or floor.

"Bounce, bounce, bounce like a ball,
Bounce, bounce,

Curl torso over feet or legs and bounce gently.

Stretch big and tall.

Stretch the arms, the back and the top of the head straight up toward ceiling.

Put your hands in your lap

Bring the arms down.

And look at the wall.
Reach for your toes, curl up very small
And...fall!

Reach head backward and look up at the ceiling. Curl into a ball and roll backward onto the back. Parents can scoop up young children and roll back with them in their laps.

Now sit up tall."

Sit up and repeat the rhyme with legs extended in front of the body.

5. Upper-Lower: "I Stretch My Hands"

"I shake (stretch, punch, poke float, etc.)
my hands up high,
I shake my hands down low.
I shake my hands above my head,
I shake them below.
I shake them to the left,
I shake them to the right,
I shake them all around,
And shake with all my might!"

Sit on the floor and follow the words of the song. Repeat the song, moving the legs and substituting the word "feet" for "hands."

Ages three through five can also do "Pussy Cat." Do the yoga exercise "cat-cow" while chanting this verse:

"Pussy cat, pussy cat, arching your back.
Pussycat, pussycat, furry and black.

Arch and release back several times while kneeling on hands and knees.

"Pussy cat, pussy cat, wag tail and head.
Pussy cat, pussy cat, curl into bed."

Wag or wiggle head and bottom from side to side while kneeling on hands and knees and then curl down into a ball.

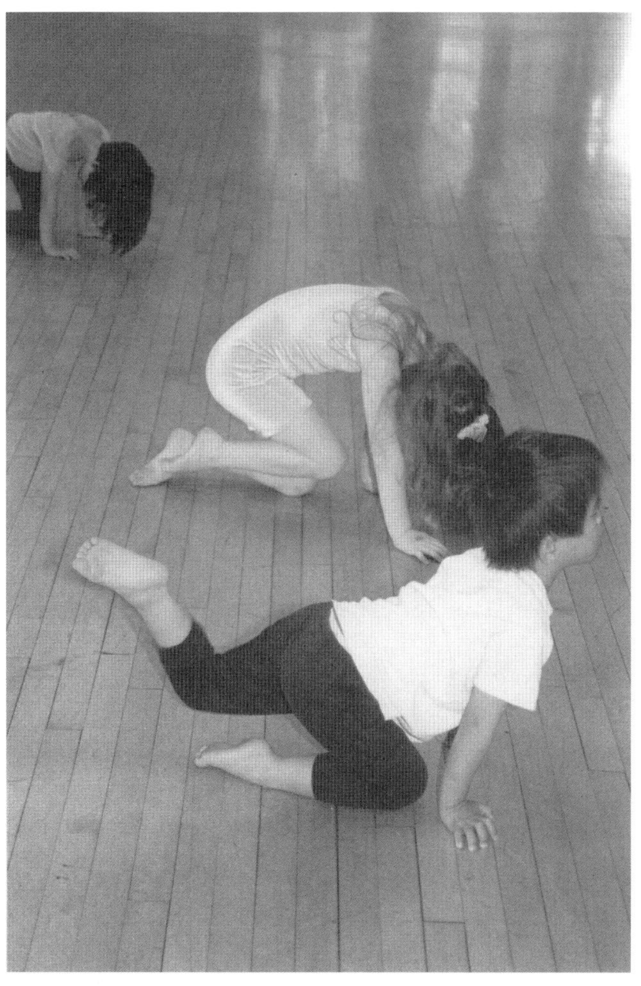

6. Body-Side: "One, Two, Buckle My Shoe"

Lie down on the left side of the body (very young dancers supported by parents). Lift and lower the right leg and arm on each verse (with the help of parents, if necessary). After singing the song once, roll to the other side and repeat the rhyme while moving the left arm and leg up and down.

This pattern can also be done sitting. Just lift and lower the left arm and leg, then the right arm and leg or move each body side in some fashion.

"One, two, buckle my shoe.	Lift and lower right arm and leg.
Three, four, shut the door.	Lift and lower right arm and leg.
Five, six, pick up sticks.	Lift and lower right arm and leg.
Seven, eight, lay them straight.	Lift and lower right arm and leg.
Nine, ten, let's do it again!"	Roll to the other side of the body and repeat, by moving the left arm and leg.

On the second side, end by sitting up while saying, *"Nine, ten, a big fat hen!"*

Here is a seated variation for four to five year-olds. For horizontal eye tracking, encourage students to look back and forth from the left hand to the right hand when the hand opens to the side.

"One, two, buckle my shoe.	Open the left arm and leg to the left side, close right arm and leg to the left side.
Three, four, shut the door.	Open the right arm and leg to the right side, close the left arm and leg to the right side.
Five, six, pick up sticks.	Open the left arm and leg to the left side, close right arm and leg to the left side.
Seven, eight, lay them straight.	Open the right arm and leg to the right side, close the left arm and leg to the right side.
Nine, ten, a big fat hen."	Spin on bottom.

7. Cross-Lateral: "Miss Mary Mack."

"Miss Mary Mack, Mack, Mack *All dressed in black, black, black*	Crisscross legs.
With silver buttons, buttons, buttons *Up and down her back, back, back.*	Crisscross arms.
She asked her mother, mother, mother *For fifty cents, cents, cents*	Crisscross arms and legs. Continue crisscrossing arms or legs with dancers under age three.
To see the elephant, elephant, elephant *Jump over the fence, fence, fence.*	Alternate reaching each arm across the midline of the body.
He jumped so high, high, high *He touched the sky, sky, sky* *And never came back, back, back*	For vertical eye tracking, alternate reaching right and left hands up and down with gaze following the hand.
'Til the fourth of July, ly, ly."	Drum hands on the floor for grounding.

8. Vestibular: "Humpty Dumpty"

"Humpty Dumpty sat on a wall, Humpty Dumpty had a great fall.	Tip side to side, then fall backward on the word "fall."
All the king's horses, and all the king's men couldn't put Humpty together again.	Spin toddlers on their backs. Older dancers can spin themselves.
"Humpty Dumpty sat on a wall, Humpty Dumpty had a great fall.	Rock backward and forward, then fall on the stomach on the word "fall."
All the king's horses, and all the king's men couldn't put Humpty together again."	Spin on stomach using hands to push oneself around.

The dancers are now in a position for belly crawling!

Crawling, Creeping and Walking Patterns:

End the sequence of seated BrainDance rhymes with a series of crawling, creeping and walking patterns that mirror the stages of infants' motor development. These patterns benefit dancers of all ages, including the parents in parent and child classes.

Belly crawling:

"I'm a scaly little lizard
And I'm crawling along.
I'm a scaly little lizard
And I sing my tongue song."

Crawl forward on the belly, alternating pushing with the left foot while pulling with the right hand and pushing with the right foot, pulling with the left hand. Try to look back and forth at the hand nearest the mouth for horizontal eye tracking. Then wiggle the tongue. Repeat the song while crawling backward.

Hand/knee creeping:

"I'm a furry little puppy
And I'm creeping along.
I'm a furry little puppy
And I sing my tongue song."

Creep forward on hands and knees, then pant. Look up and down for vertical eye tracking. Repeat the song while creeping backward.

Hand/foot walking:

"I'm a great big bear
And I'm walking along.
I'm a great big bear
And I sing my tongue song."

Walk forward on the hands and feet with the head down and tail up. Make a soft growling sound. Repeat the song while walking backward.

Upright walking:

"I'm a great big person
And I'm walking along.
I'm a great big person
And I sing my tongue song."

Walk forward on two feet and then sing, "Tralala." Repeat the song while walking backward. Older dancers might skip forward and backward.

Standing Exercises for More Practice on the Last Four Patterns

Now that the dancers are standing, conclude the rhyming BrainDance with four exercises that emphasize the last four BrainDance patterns. These standing exercises help dancers learn to work against gravity. They develop the vestibular system while laying the foundation for dance technique that will be introduced as the dancers get older.

Upper-Lower: "The Itsy Bitsy Spider"

"The itsy bitsy spider *Went up the waterspout.*	March in self space.
Down came the rain *And washed the spider out.*	Use hands to "wash" body from head to toe twice.
Out came the sun *And dried up all the rain.*	Open arms. Older dancers also turn around.
And the itsy bitsy spider *Went up the spout again."*	March in self space.

Body-Side: "London Bridge"

"London Bridge is falling down,
Falling down, falling down.
London Bridge is falling down,

Hold hands with a parent or partner, tip side to side from one leg to the other to the rhythm of the phrase.

My fair dancers."

Slide sideways to the right or left.

"Build it up with wood and clay,
Wood and clay, wood and clay.
Build it up with wood and clay,

Tip side to side.

My fair dancers."

Slide sideways in the other direction.

Cross-Lateral: "Baa, Baa Black Sheep"

"Baa, baa black sheep have you any wool?	Swing one leg and the opposite arm forward, then backward in a cross-lateral pattern.
Yes sir, yes sir, three bags full.	Jump or hop up and down, crisscross arms when developmentally appropriate.
One for the master, one for the dame.	Take two to four big steps or skips forward with swinging arms.
One for the little one who lives down the lane.	Tiptoe forward while stretching alternate arms above head.
Baa, baa black sheep have you any wool?	Run backward.
Yes sir, yes sir, three bags full."	Jump or hop up and down, crisscrossing arms when developmentally appropriate.

Repeat the song twice, swinging the other leg and opposite arm the second time through the rhyme.

Vestibular: "Twist in the Washing Machine"

"Twist and twist in the washing machine. *Twist and twist 'til you're all clean.*	Twist from side to side.
Twist and twist in the washing machine. *Twist and twist now you're all clean!"*	Spin around several times.

For more spinning, sing, "Spin and spin in the washing machine," and spin throughout the whole song! Stop and breathe on, "You're all clean!" Then spin the other way and sing, "Spin and spin in the drying machine." Stop and breathe with, "You're dry and clean!"

Variations of the BrainDance with Rhymes

In small spaces or thirty-minute classes, do the first four seated rhymes listed that practice the first four patterns: Breath, Tactile, Core-Distal, Head-Tail. Do the last four standing rhymes for the last four patterns: Upper-Lower, Body-Side, Cross-Lateral, Vestibular. Performing these eight exercises takes six to seven minutes. Moving through all eight patterns will benefit the students. If teaching in a space with a non-carpeted floor, include belly crawling sometime during the lesson. Belly crawling is a pattern many children need to repeat if there is a lack of tummy time or because they live in carpeted homes. (It is very difficult to belly crawl on a carpet.)

Five-Minute Variations of the BrainDance with Songs

Below are two quick BrainDances, performed to familiar children's songs while sitting. If the songs are unfamiliar, just make up a tune. Children four to five years old can do these as standing BrainDances.

"This is the Way"

1. Breath:

"This is the way we breathe in and out,
Breathe in and out, breathe in and out;
This is the way we breathe in and out
To make our brains work well!"

Recite the rhyme and then take a moment to breathe deeply.

2. Tactile:

"This is the way we tap our arms,
Slap our legs, brush our chest;
This is the way we pat our whole body,
To make us feel awake!"

Recite the rhyme while tapping, slapping, brushing and patting the whole body.

3. Core Distal:

"This is the way we stretch really big,
Curl really small, stretch really big;
This is the way we curl and stretch,
To reach out to the world!"

Stretch and curl the whole body several times.

4. Head-Tail:

"This is the way move head and tail,
Move head and tail, move head and tail;
This is the way move head and tail,
And now we wiggle our spine!"

Wiggle head and bottom in different directions, then undulate the spine.

5. Upper-Lower:

"This is the way we shake our arms high,
Shake our arms low, shake our arms wide;
This is the way we dance with our arms,
We move our upper body!

"This is the way we kick our legs high,
Kick our legs low, kick our legs side;
This is the way we dance with our legs,
We move our lower body!"

Shake the arms, then kick the legs. Substitute other arm and leg movements such as punch, twist, stamp or jump.

6. Body-Side:

"This is the way we move our right side,
Move our right side, move our right side;
This is the way we move our right side,
We move one side at a time!

"This is the way we move our left side,
Move our left side, move our left side;
This is the way we move our left side,
We move the other side!"

Move the right arm and leg and then the left arm and leg, bending and stretching, shaking, twisting, etc.

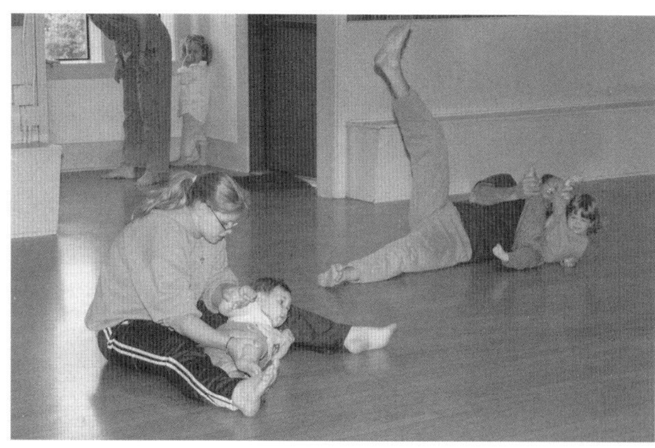

6a. Horizontal Eye Tracking:

"This is the way we look side to side,
Look side to side, look side to side;
This is the way we look side to side,
So we can learn to read!"

Follow one hand with the eyes as the hand moves left to right, right to left.

6b. Vertical Eye Tracking:

"Now our eyes go up and down,
Up and down, up and down;
Now our eyes go up and down,
We're doing our eye tracking!"

Follow one hand with the eyes as the hand moves up and down.

7. Cross-Lateral:

"This is the way we cross arms and legs,
Cross arms and legs, cross arms and legs;
This is the way we cross arms and legs,
We're crossing our whole body!"

Crisscross arms and legs, alternating top arm and leg each time.

8. Vestibular:

"This is the way we spin around,
Spin around, spin around;
This is the way we spin around,
And now we all fall down!"

Spin around, then fall down.

"The Wheels on the Bus"

1. Breath:

"The wheels on the bus get filled with air
Filled with air, filled with air;
The wheels on the bus get filled with air,
So take a big deep breath!"

Take deep breaths.

2. Tactile:

"The wipers on the bus go tap, tap, tap,
Pat, pat, pat, scratch, scratch, scratch;
The wipers on the bus go slap, slap, slap
All over you!"

Do the described actions to body parts.

3. Core-Distal:

"The doors on the bus open and close,
Open and close, open and close;
The doors on the bus open and close,
So you can come on board!"

Stretch and curl the whole body.

4. Head tail:

"The windows on the bus go up and down,
Up and down, up and down;
The windows on the bus go up and down,
So you can look outside!"

Curl the head forward and stretch the head backward or do the yoga exercise "cat-cow."

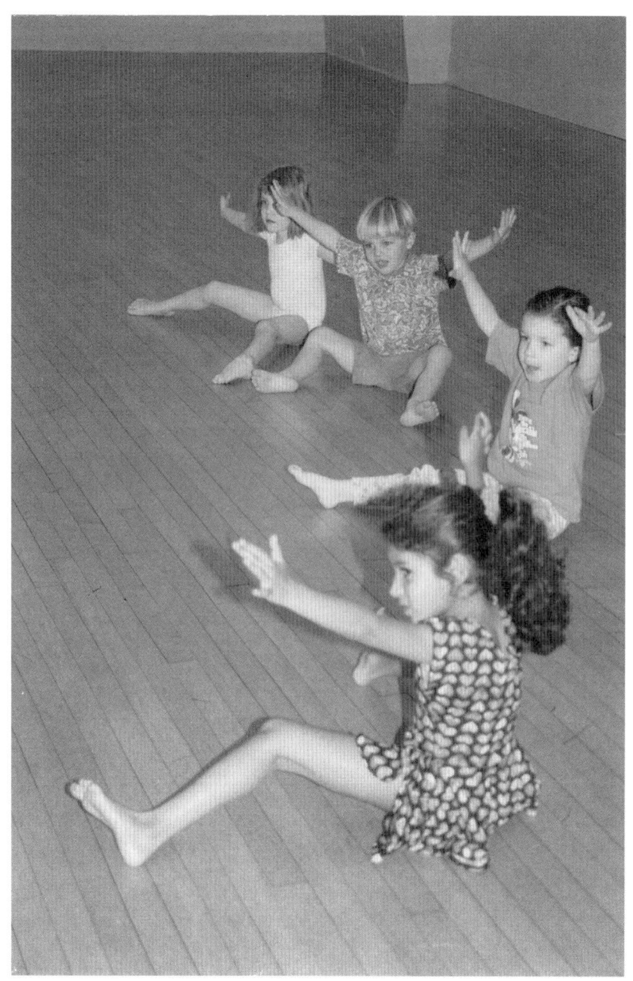

5. Upper-Lower:

"The people on the bus wave hello,
Wave hello, wave hello,
The people on the bus wave hello,
They say howdy do!"

Move with the upper body.

"Our feet on the bus go bumpity bump,
Bumpity bump, bumpity bump;
Our feet on the bus go bumpity bump,
All around the bus!"

Stamp.

6. Body Side / Horizontal Eye Tracking*:*

"The kids on the bus
They look out the windows,
Look out the windows,
Look out the windows;
The kids on the bus
They look out the windows,
They look side to side."

Open the left arm and leg to the left while looking left, then close to center. Open the right side while looking right and then close to center. Repeat left and right body-side opening with eye tracking until the verse ends.

7. Cross-Lateral/Vertical Eye Tracking:

"The people on the bus they pull the cord,
Pull the cord, pull the cord;
The people on the bus they pull the cord,
And say, 'Let me off!'

Look up and down for vertical eye tracking, while pulling an imaginary cord by alternating left and right arm stretches.

"The driver on the bus he turns the corner,
Turns the corner, turns the corner;
The driver on the bus he turns the corner and we all tip over!"

Twist arms to the left as if steering the bus, while crossing left leg over right leg. Reverse the action.

8. Vestibular:

"The wheels on the bus go round and round
Round and round, round and round;
The wheels on the bus go round and round
All over town!"

Spin around.

BrainDance for Infants

Infants naturally move through their own BrainDance in their first year of life if given enough tummy time with bare feet on a non-carpeted surface. However, a parent with an infant or a teacher in infant and parent dance classes may explore some of the BrainDance exercises with rhymes as described earlier in this chapter.

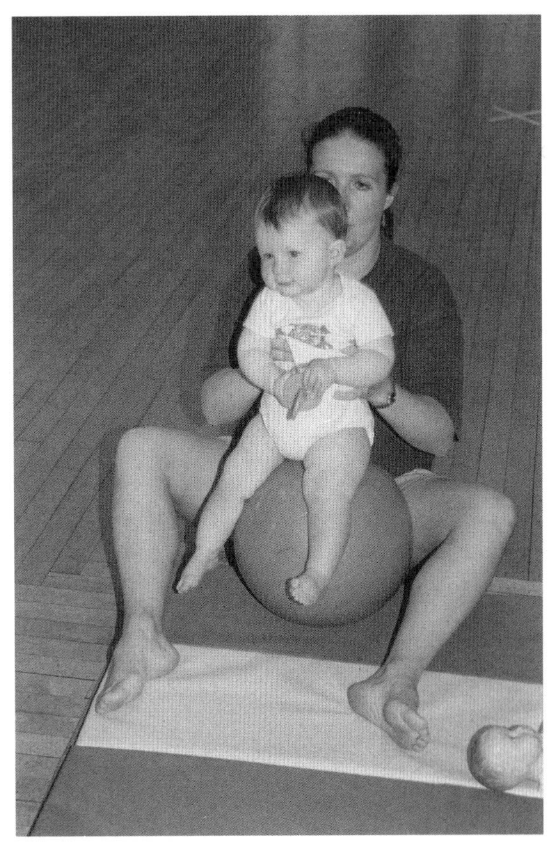

Perform some of the exercises gently with the baby lying on his or her tummy, back and side. Explore other movements within each pattern and play or sing favorite rhymes such as "Row, Row, Row Your Boat" and "Hey Diddle, Diddle."

Small therapy balls (twelve to fifteen inches) are fun to work with at this age. Most babies at four to five months can sit with their hips on the ball when held by adults. Hold the baby securely while rolling the ball slightly in different directions. By tipping the baby forward, backward and side-to-side, the Vestibular System is stimulated.

Lay the baby's tummy on the ball and hold the baby securely at the waist. Roll the ball forward so that the baby arches the back and head, strengthening the Head-Tail pattern. While in this position, place a favorite toy or rattle in front of the ball. Encourage the baby to practice the upper body reach and grasp pattern by allowing the baby to reach down for the toy as the parent rolls the baby and the ball forward.

When the baby has the toy, roll the baby and ball back to a neutral balance position.

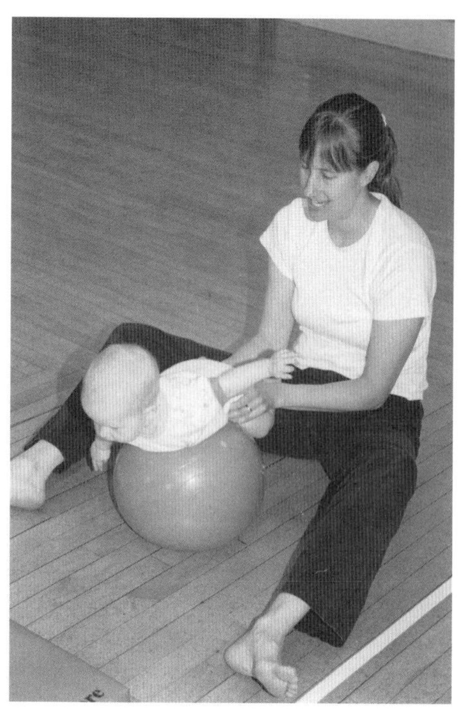

Parents should be encouraged to lie on their own tummies in front of their babies to model the early patterns, then model crawling and creeping as the babies progress to the later patterns. However, it is important to allow infants to progress at their own rate. Although it is beneficial for an infant to progress through the patterns in specific order, each baby will spend a different amount of time in each pattern. It is inappropriate to "teach" the patterns to an infant, unless the infant has serious developmental delays. Nor should a parent "push" an infant through the patterns to encourage early walking. An adage says, "The later one walks, the smarter one is." Learning to walk between twelve and fifteen months is natural.

Teaching parent and infant classes is especially rewarding. Educating adults about the importance of movement while helping their babies develop into happy, healthy, toddlers is a joyful experience!

In Summary

The BrainDance, with its many variations, is an excellent warm-up for all ages, spaces and lengths of lessons. This series of exercises is used for:

- **Neurological re-patterning**: re-mapping the brain to develop better behavior, attention, memory, eye-tracking, proprioception, motor skills and sensory integration.
- **Body connectivity and alignment**: becoming aware of the visceral and muscular systems that support the body, leading to the correct use of body structures that helps dancers be injury-free and move with ease.
- **Broad assessment**: becoming aware of students who need more individual help with development patterns or require specific movement therapy.

Now that a brain-compatible warm-up has been developed, you are ready to plan the next section of the lesson called Exploring the Concept.

We start every class with BrainDance and I teach more in the remaining 24-25 minutes than I ever have in 30. ~ Randy, Music Specialist

The BrainDance makes me feel awake. I feel ready to learn. My brain feels alive. My body feels good. ~ Students in Pocatello, Idaho

(Endnote)

[1] Lamont, Bette. "Learning and Movement." *Pathways*. Spring, (1996): p. 4-5.

Chapter Two
Lesson Plan Section 2: Exploring the Concept

In this chapter:

DANCE CONCEPTS

SPACE

Place	self space, general space
Size	big (far reach), medium (mid-reach), small (near reach)
Level	high, middle, low
Direction	forward, backward, right, left, up, down
Pathway	curved, straight, zigzag
Focus	single focus, multi-focus

TIME

Speed	fast, medium, slow
Rhythm	pulse, pattern, grouping, breath

FORCE

Energy	sharp, smooth, shaky, swingy
Weight	strong, light, active, passive
Flow	free, bound

BODY

Parts	head, neck, shoulders, arm, wrists, elbows, hands, fingers, hips, pelvis, trunk, spine, stomach, sternum, ribs, legs, knees, feet, toes, heels, ankles, etc.
Relationships	over, under, around, through, above, below, between, beside, near, far, in, out, together, apart, connected, etc.
Shapes	straight, curved, angular, twisted, symmetrical, asymmetrical
Balance	off balance, on balance

EXPLORING THE CONCEPT

Applicable National Dance Standards
The following standards from the *National Standards for Dance Education* will be achieved through the activities in this chapter:

- **Identifying and demonstrating movement elements and skills in performing dance**
- **Applying and demonstrating critical and creative thinking skills in dance**
- **Making connections between dance and other disciplines**
- **Understanding dance as a way to create and communicate meaning**

Chapter Introduction

After dancers have warmed up, they are ready to explore the lesson's concept. In this section of class the concept is explored through a problem-solving approach that, depending on the length of the lesson, lasts five to fifteen minutes. Movement explorations are structured so that dancers are encouraged to find new ways of working with the concept, thus increasing their cognitive and motor skills.

A teacher directed/student choice format is very effective: dancers alternate following specific directions with movements of their own choice. In this way, they learn new ways of exploring the concept from the teacher and then manipulate their movements using their own creative ideas. This is a brain-compatible approach to engage all learners, because the dancers are self directing their learning.

Focus on exploring the lesson's concept in self and general space by using isolated body parts, the whole body, working alone and with others. It is also essential for students to explore the concept through the other dance concepts, so they learn other ways of moving. For example, when

exploring Level, cue the dancers to move on different levels while varying the speed, energy, pathway, direction, focus, shape and flow of their movements. By using just the Level vocabulary during the lesson, the dancers may move on different levels only in their particular movement signature. They may not think of other ways to vary or augment their movements. Because the dance concept language is so basic, it is not necessary to introduce all the concepts before using them. Exploring the lesson concept in relation to the other dance concepts provides students with a greater depth of exploration of a particular lesson, which then leads to holistic learning and better understanding.

When introducing any exploration, keep directions simple and clear while demonstrating the activity with student demonstrators. Next, have the dancers find partners, groups or personal space to begin the exploration. Play music, giving further directions as the dancers move. Music pauses are helpful, because one can cue during the breaks. Music containing contrasting qualities provides helpful cueing for dancers by signaling changes in energy, levels, speeds, etc.

It is natural for young or inexperienced older dancers to copy the teacher's movements. This is one way to learn. Even with experienced dancers, encourage students to copy each other's movements during exploration and improvisation, so to experiment with new ways of dancing. Copying increases kinesthetic vocabulary. To help dancers choose their own movements, alternate dancing with the class and stepping aside to observe. Continue to offer movement ideas for support. As the weeks progress, fewer cues will be given (if teaching conceptually). The dancers imitate less as their knowledge and confidence grow with every class.

The activities in this part of the lesson need little adjusting for different ages and levels of experience. All students enjoy exploring the concept if the directions are clear and the explorations are engaging. Favorite dance games may be developed or made more challenging by adding concepts, varying accompaniment and props, combining two or more activities or modifying groupings. This section of the lesson plan is excellent for partner or small group work. Collaboration creates a friendly, cooperative atmosphere, develops social skills and makes learning more fun and brain-compatible.

Finding appropriate accompaniment to motivate students is critical to a lesson's success. Sometimes teachers can use their voices, body percussion (i.e. clapping, stomping, snapping) or musical instruments (such as drums and rhythm sticks) to accompany the students' explorations. Other times, recorded music can be used or a teacher may have the luxury of music played by an accompanist. Providing a variety of sounds and rhythms within each class is important. By using only one style of music (classical, new age, jazz), students may not be motivated to explore new movements and styles. If only a hand drum is used throughout the entire lesson, they will not experience harmony and melody. Even if a percussionist plays in class, try to include recorded music during the Exploring the Concept part of class. (My accompanist enjoys playing along with the compact disc.) Appropriate, motivating music makes the class more brain-compatible! Refer to the Appendices for dance class music suggestions.

It is beneficial to follow an exploration with a moment of "reflection" to help dancers make important body-mind connections. This exercise gives students an opportunity to analyze a preference for being a leader or a follower, to notice what movements they may choose naturally, to assess how they create alone or in concert with others and reflect on what movements they find challenging. If students make these basic choices through their experiences in dance class, they will be able to make more complex decisions in life. Reflection early in the lesson begins the critical thinking process and lays the foundation for deeper reflection later in the lesson. Ask dancers to share their feelings through an action, a word or a phrase. Sometimes, they will share these feelings with a peer, other times with several peers or the whole class. Remind them that their choices are based only on the previous exploration and that their feelings may change from day to day. Below are examples of reflective questions that a teacher might ask students after an exploration:

1. "Think about this question for a moment and then demonstrate the answer with your body position. If you enjoyed moving more to the fast music, sit down. If you enjoyed moving more to the slow music, stand up. Please make a clear choice and tell yourself why you made that choice."
2. "Was it easier for you to dance with strong or light weight? If you chose strong, form a low, strong shape. If you chose light, form a high, light shape. How do you move through your day? Do you move more often strongly or lightly? Why is it beneficial to move in unfamiliar ways? Share your thoughts with a peer."

3. "When you moved with small movements to the loud music, did you feel differently than when you moved with small movements to the soft music? If you felt differently, sit. If the music did not change your feelings, stand. What about dancing with big movements to the soft music? Which combination felt most natural to you?"

4. "Which part of the exploration was most challenging for you? Turn to the person near you and share your thoughts."

5. "Stand if you preferred being the leader. Sit if you preferred being the follower. Think of one or two words to express why and speak them loudly when I call your name."

6. "Turn to someone near you and share one new thing you learned about yourself during the exploration."

Explanation of Dance Concepts

I adapted the fifteen dance concepts for use in my classes from Rudolf Laban's movement vocabulary. Rudolf Laban (1879-1958) was a teacher and theorist who formulated principles of movement that laid the groundwork for modern dance education. His work in Germany and England also led him to create a system of dance notation called Labanotation, from which motif notation is derived. (See Appendices for an explanation of motif notation.)

Many dance educators around the world use Laban's vocabulary in their classes. However, the exact words and sometimes meanings differ from educator to educator. When I started teaching young dancers, I simplified Laban's principles into fifteen concepts containing contrasting elements for use with preschoolers. Young dancers understand and explore basic antonyms such as high and low, fast and slow, curved and straight, etc. When teaching intermediate or advanced students, explore the concepts in greater depth, with more complex vocabulary. Feel free to adapt the dance concepts defined here to specific lessons and students. What is key to brain-compatibility is using any dance language that is conceptual rather than only step- or skill-based.

SPACE Concepts

1. Place

Self space is the space a person occupies and is known as a kinesphere (movement sphere). The term **self space** is synonymous with **personal space** and often designates the place in which dancers move with nonlocomotor (axial) movements. Ask dancers to find their "perfect spot." This is a self space spot with plenty of room around it, so the dancer can move safely and freely.

General space is shared by dancers as they travel with locomotor movements through space. Encourage dancers to look for the **empty space** so they move safely. Remind them that as they travel through general space, they take their kinespheres or self spaces with them. Wherever they stop, they are in their self space.

2. Size (Range)

Small size may also be considered as "near reach." Dancers form small shapes and movements when they bring body parts close to their centers. Verbs that encourage dancers to change size and to do smaller movements are shrink, contract, narrow.

Medium size (mid-reach) is the most common natural range of motion. Spend more time exploring small and big size. However, when moving from small to big or big to small, one automatically moves through medium size.

Big size may be considered as "far reach." Dancers form big shapes and movements when they reach far from their centers. Verbs that encourage dancers to change size and do bigger movements are grow, expand, widen.

3. Level

Low level space is the space (or area) from the floor to the tops of the legs. Novice dancers often confuse small size and low level as the same concept. Verbs that encourage moving to a low level are sink, melt, fall.

Middle level space is the space (or area) from the tops of the legs to the armpits. Dancing in the middle level creates interesting and challenging movements. Verbs that encourage moving in middle-level are bend, crouch, lunge.

High level space is the space (or area) from the armpits to infinity. Novice dancers often confuse big size and high level as the same idea. Verbs that encourage moving to a high level are rise, elevate, ascend.

4. Direction

Forward is when the intention is frontal and the front of the body leads.

Backward is when the intention is back or behind and the back of the body leads.

Sideways is when the intention is side. The right side of the body leads or reaches to the right. The left side of the body leads or reaches to the left. The left arm and/or leg may reach across the body to the right side, giving an even stronger impression of "right side" and vice versa.

Upward is when the intention or focus of the body is up. This is not to be confused with moving at a high level. A dancer can move at a low level with several body parts reaching up to give the impression of "upward."

Downward is when the intention or focus of the body is down. This is not to be confused with moving at a low level. A dancer can move at a high level with body parts and focus reaching down, giving the impression of "downward."

Diagonal combines three directions. For example, the arm may reach up, side and back pulling one in a (backward) diagonal direction.

Planes – Each of the three planes consists of two primary and two secondary directions. The **sagittal** or "wheel" plane involves forward and backward movement with some up and down. The **vertical** or "door" plane involves up and down with some side movement. The **horizontal** or "table" plane involves right and left side with some forward and backward movement. It may be instructive and challenging to first explore each two-dimensional plane separately. Explore moving through two or three planes to create complex and compelling three-dimensional movement.

5. Pathway

Straight pathway follows a straight line. It is most natural for the body to be vertical as it moves along a straight pathway.

Curved pathway follows a curved, circular or meandering line. To curve the spine to the left or right side is most natural when moving in a curved pathway circling left or right. One can also move in a curved pathway in a forward and backward direction.

Zigzag pathway follows short, straight lines that move from side to side or forward and backward. Moving along a zigzag pathway, it is most natural to quickly shift weight and focus.

Diagonal is not a pathway because one can move in a diagonal line from corner to corner in any pathway. Pathways may be created on the floor with steps and in the air with arm and torso movements. Novice dancers often confuse the concepts of Pathway and Shape; when working with these dancers, focus on floor pathways.

6. Focus

Single (direct) focus is viewing one person or object, or having a single or direct intention with the body or a body part.

Multi (indirect) focus is viewing several people or objects. Focus and movement may be scattered.

Other elements that should be explored are **Internal** and **External** focus. **Internal** focus suggests looking within, being reflective. The gaze may be lowered, eyes may be closed or dancers may have a glazed or daydreaming look. **External** focus suggests dancers are aware of their surroundings with an attentive gaze. After dancers perform, discuss the audience's focus. How does the performers' focus affect the audience's focus?

TIME Concepts

7. Speed

Medium is a comfortable walking speed.

Slow is slower than medium speed and appears to have the intention of taking all the time in the world.

Fast is faster than medium speed and has an urgent intention.

Because novice dancers sometimes have trouble distinguishing between slow, medium and fast, it is helpful to explore very slow and fast speeds. Another consideration is **Duration**, the length of time (short, medium or long) of a movement. A dancer might perform one sustained movement through an eight-count phrase or eight quick movements during the same eight-count phrase. Duration may also be explored during lessons on Energy.

8. Rhythm

Pulse is a constant, even beat like the heart beat and is sometimes called the "underlying beat." Pulses may be different speeds, but are always in a measured, even rhythm.

Grouping puts pulses into groups to create different meters. Music is composed of different groups of twos and threes (duple and triple meter). The accent or stress that occurs on the first beat of the group or measure helps determine the meter.

Pattern is a series of pulses of varying speeds that create an uneven rhythm.

Breath is the rhythm of the lungs and is non-metered.

FORCE Concepts

Many educators have differing opinions about the concepts in this category. These complex concepts are related to Speed and Rhythm, as well as to each other. Clarify them in a basic way for young children. Experienced dancers may discuss the relationships between concepts to deepen their understanding.

9. Energy (Dynamics, Qualities)

Smooth (sustained) energy is continuous, with a sense of lingering. Some verbs that generate smooth movements are float, glide, press, pull, meander, skate, stretch, carve and melt.

Sharp (percussive) energy starts and stops quickly, with a sense of urgency. Verbs generating sharp movements include slash, punch, dab, flick, jump, prance, kick, poke and dodge.

Swingy (pendular) energy drops into gravity heavily and quickly and then suspends into lightness, taking more time on the ascent than on the descent. Some verbs that generate swingy movements are swing, sway, rock, tip, twist, roll, waltz and undulate.

Shaky (vibratory) energy is exhibited through small, quick, back-and-forth movements. Verbs generating shaky movements include shiver, bounce, wiggle, quiver, tremble, pulsate, vibrate and jiggle.

10. Weight

Strong weight requires the use of muscular force against resistance (gravity). Images that suggest strong movement include pushing walls away, giants stomping, shadow boxing and dancing on Jupiter.

Light weight requires little muscle force with little or no resistance. Images that suggest light movement include floating feathers and balloons, a breeze, flicking flies away and dancing on the moon.

Other elements to explore include **Passive** weight (heavy or limp, giving into gravity), **Active** weight (enlivened, moving against gravity in an energetic way) and **Shared** weight. "Sharing weight" means giving a person one's weight (or taking someone's weight), which is the essence of contact improvisation. These three elements deal with body perceptions; exploring them with teenagers and adults is valuable. **Lifts** may also be explored during lessons on Weight.

Some educators use the terms "tight" and "loose" to refer to Weight. They are adjectives relating to muscle tension rather than elements of the concept of Weight. Muscles are more tense or tight when dancing with strong weight, sharp energy, bound flow and fast speed**.** Muscles are less tense or loose when doing the opposite. This vocabulary helps dancers understand movement mechanics.

11. Flow

Free flow is fluid movement that is not easily stopped. Think of the body as a container with movement pouring freely in and out of it. Free flow movement is uncontrolled and off balance. Images that are helpful for exploring free flow include a rushing river or a leaf blowing in the wind.

Bound flow is careful and restrained movement that can be easily stopped. Here, the flow of movement is contained within the body. Bound flow movement is controlled and on balance. Images that encourage bound flow include wind-up toys or water slowly freezing.

Stillness is an important element to include in a variety of lessons. It is easily introduced in a lesson on Flow. A still dancer is completely bound, but expresses a continuous flow of energy. Stillness is exciting because it has an active, rather than passive, sense of weight. It creates a sense of anticipation. A **Pause** is shorter in duration than stillness. It is like a comma or a breath. **After flow** is a movement that occurs after dancers become still. A small reach into space, like an afterthought, may be used for dramatic effect.

Other ideas that can be explored are **Successive** and **Simultaneous flow**. Successive flow travels from one adjacent body part to another, like the movements of a snake. Many Indian, African, Asian and South Pacific cultures use successive flow in their dances. Simultaneous flow occurs when body parts move at the same time. Simultaneous flow happens in the joints (bending, straightening) and is often seen in the dances of Western cultures.

BODY Concepts

12. Body Parts

Novice dancers usually think about moving arms and legs, but forget about the many body parts that can be moved separately, such as the neck, spine, hands, feet, fingers, toes, hips, stomach, elbows, knees, shoulders and even the tongue. Sections of the body can also be explored, including upper and lower body halves, right and left body sides and upper and lower quadrants. Consider internal organs such as the heart, lungs and stomach. Dancers become articulate, integrated performers by exploring body parts in isolation and in tandem.

13. Body Shapes

Straight shapes are composed of two- or three-dimensional straight lines and are formed on any level, in any direction or size.

Curved shapes are composed of two- or three-dimensional curved lines or circles, spheres, cones, semi-circles, etc. They are formed on any level, in any direction or size.

Angular shapes are composed of two- or three-dimensional bent lines with acute, obtuse or right angles, such as squares, triangles, rectangles, pyramids, etc. They are formed on any level, in any direction or size.

Twisted shapes are composed of rotated, curved lines or spirals, figure eights, etc. They are formed on any level, in any direction or size and are three-dimensional.

Novice dancers enjoy forming shapes in self space. Experienced dancers may travel through space, consciously evolving their movements while transitioning from one shape to another.

Other ideas to explore include **Symmetrical** and **Asymmetrical** shapes. Novice dancers should explore symmetry and asymmetry individually, while experienced dancers may work in pairs, trios and quartets.

Students often ask, "What is the difference between shape and stillness?" A shape is a discreet form (shaped with intention) held still or moved through as a transition between movements. Stillness is an absence of motion without intentional form but expressing a sense of outpouring energy. It is an enlivened freeze

14. Relationship

Dancers move in relationship to other people, the environment, objects and their own body parts. Relationship words are prepositions that tell where one is and include over, under, around, through, in, out, on, off, in front, behind, beside, between, above, below, etc. This is a favorite concept because people enjoy interacting with others and playing with props. It is an important concept for students with underdeveloped proprioceptive or social skills because exploring Relationship helps develop these skills.

15. Balance

On-balance is the state of stability, no matter how many body parts support a person. To stay balanced in unusual shapes use **counterbalance.** Think of six separate strings pulling equally from the body's center in each direction while being suspended in space. Focus on one spot, ground the mind and body, breathe and maintain core support. Ask young dancers to touch their stomachs and "be quiet inside." This helps them engage the core, breathe slowly and balance.

Off-balance is falling out of balance. This happens when one of the imaginary strings pulls more than the other strings and causes the body to tip or fall, giving into gravity. Moving off-balance requires risk-taking and is exciting to do and observe. Encourage novice dancers to "fall in a ball" when they practice falling to the floor. They spiral down and roll on the buttocks and upper back to avoid bumping knees and elbows on the floor.

Exploring the BrainDance helps develop the vestibular system that is used when moving both on- and off-balance.

It is fun to **counterbalance** with other dancers by pulling or pressing against each other, maintaining an equal fulcrum of support with a shared balance in self space or while traveling.

> ***Teaching Tip:*** *Each concept is unique, but does not exist in a vacuum. The concepts are related and interdependent. When dancers move, they use a variety of dance concepts. However, it is useful to focus on one concept during each lesson for the first time through all fifteen. The dancers then give their full attention to the concept in order to explore it in depth. Remember, even though one concept is the focus of a lesson, it is always explored in relation to other concepts, which helps reinforce the interrelatedness of all the concepts. After students explore all fifteen concepts, occasionally have them focus on two concepts for similarities and subtle differences.*

Motif Notation

Please refer to the article on motif notation in the Appendices for a thorough description and selected symbols.

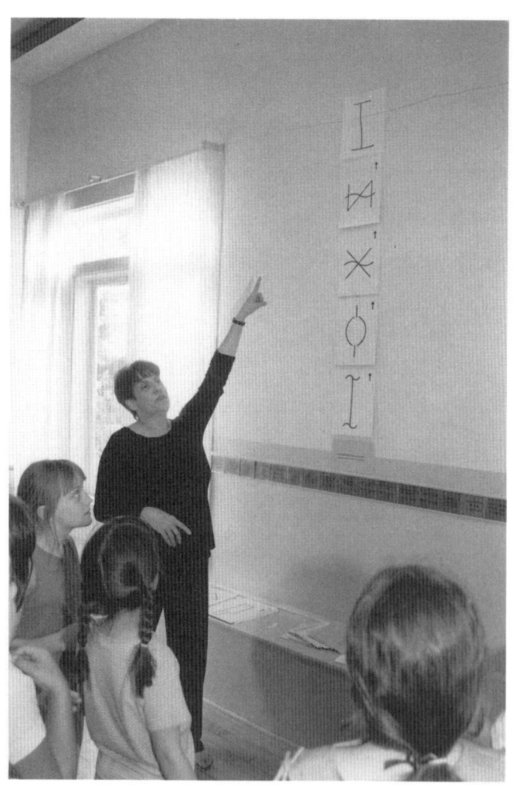

Motif notation is a symbol system that is a visualization of the conceptual vocabulary. Incorporating motif notation creates a multi-sensory lesson that is brain-compatible. Dance vocabulary is made visual through symbols that can be read, spoken and written.

Introduce motif symbols with dance concepts at the word board. Dancers learn the symbol for the concept and then do the appropriate movement while looking at the symbol and the word. Motif notation is a pictorial language that people of all cultures and reading levels can understand.

Once the dancers learn several symbols in the Exploring the Concept section of the lesson, they use these symbols to construct and notate movement combinations in the Developing Skills section. They expand these combinations, using motif notation to choreograph and notate their dances in the Creating section of class. For the basic elements of motif notation, see the Movement Alphabet as identified by Ann Hutchinson Guest in the Appendices.

Exploring the Concept: Structures for Dancers Working as Individuals

For a brain-compatible lesson, find the balance between individual and collaborative explorations. Start the Exploring the Concept section with an individual improvisation, followed by a partner or trio exploration. If there is not enough time for two short explorations, present one that combines individual improvisation with partner work.

Teaching Tip: Cueing *is an invaluable teaching strategy. When working with dancers new to the conceptual approach, offer a lot of support through cues and suggestions. While the dancers move, call out suggestions using the key phrases "try" and "I see." Students who need help with exploring the concept will welcome this support. Dancers with their own ideas will not be distracted.*

For example, when exploring the concept of Pathway, offer the following cues:

- *"Try moving on a curved pathway at a low level...backwards...quickly...with strong weight... with smooth movements."*
- *"I see dancers moving on a straight pathway at a high level...sideways...in straight shapes...with single focus...skipping...punching."*
- *"If you need a new idea, copy someone else's movement and then make it your own."*
- *"Look at the movement chart for more ways to move on different pathways."*
- *"Listen for the change in the music and then vary your pathway movement by changing speeds or energy."*
- *"Every time I call out the word 'change,' move in a new way."*

Exploring Contrasts

Because the elements of the dance concepts are antonyms (high and low, sharp and smooth, strong and light, straight and curved, on and off balance, single and multi-focus, etc.), one basic way to Explore the Concept is by alternating the vocabulary. For example, when exploring Size, encourage students to find ways of moving with small movements; then move with big movements. Next, have students explore different ways of dancing small and big by changing size while moving in different directions. Dancers continue alternating small and big movements four to five times while you suggest other ways to explore the concept through changes in speed, pathway, energy, etc.

Alternating contrasting elements in short intervals is more brain-compatible than exploring each of the contrasting words once for a longer period of time. This repetitive process helps dancers discover and practice novel ways of moving by exploring the lesson's concept through other concepts. Another way to create contrasts is by the "directed and free" approach. Direct dancers to explore the concept, then allow them to freely explore without suggestions or cues. *Creative Dance for All Ages* contains many ideas for exploring the concept through contrasts.

Contrasting Music

One of the easiest ways to motivate movement contrasts is to play music with **contrasts**. Eric Chappelle composed *Music for Creative Dance, Volumes I–V* (compact disc collection) specifically for exploring the dance concepts. Dancers of all ages respond to the beautifully crafted instrumental pieces that are motivating and supportive. His music makes teaching and class management easy. Each disc includes a booklet that I wrote, with four or five suggestions for applying each piece of music.

Below are ways to explore concepts through contrasting music. Although specific music is suggested for each activity, other music or accompaniment may be applied. However, the suggested music makes the basic activity unique. Conversely, the music suggested can be used to explore all concepts. Props, musical instruments or body percussion may be added to augment the exploration. Remember to ask a reflective question after the exploration.

Self and General Space

Dancers alternate moving in **self space** and **general space**. Introduce nonlocomotor movements for self space and locomotor movements for general space or show random word cards and let the dancers read them. Read the words for preschoolers. It is helpful for young students to have a visual object such as a spot or hoop to mark their self space. They dance through general space with the spot or hoop, then put it down and perform nonlocomotor movements on the spot or in the hoop.

Suggested Music: *Music for Creative Dance, Volume II,* #21

Big and Small

When the music is soft, have students dance with **small movements**. When the music is loud, have them dance with **big movements**. Then have them dance with big movements when the music is soft and small movements when the music is loud. Include age-appropriate images such as balloons expanding and contracting, elves and giants dancing, plants growing and withering. Remember to encourage use of other concepts to avoid mimetic movements.

Suggested Music: *Music for Creative Dance, Volume I,* #14

High and Low

Dancers explore ways of moving on a high level. When the music changes, they will hear a descending scale in the suggested music. At that point, have them sink to explore low level movements. When the music changes again (descending scale is repeated), they rise to explore new ways of dancing on a high level. Encourage dancers to find various ways of moving on different levels by changing direction, size, energy and pathway. For the rising and sinking section, suggest images such as smoke rising, water dripping, ascending and descending on escalators or elevators, rockets blasting off or leaves falling.

Suggested Music: *Music for Creative Dance, Volume II,* #7

Forward and Backward

For younger dancers, call out a new direction to move each time the music changes. The dancers could imagine that an invisible puppeteer is pulling their strings in six different directions. When the dancers have explored each direction once, let them choose their own directions for the remaining music. With older dancers, call out two opposing directions (forward and backward or right and left) each time the music changes and have them move from one direction to the other. The image of body parts having an argument about which direction to move helps motivate this exploration. Encourage experienced dancers to move in different planes.

Suggested Music: *Music for Creative Dance, Volume I,* #13

Curved and Straight

When the music is slow, the dancers move in curved pathways. When the music is at medium speed, they move in straight pathways. When the music is fast, dancers move in zigzag pathways. Also move in straight pathways to slow music, zigzag pathways to medium music, curved pathways to fast music, etc. Encourage dancers to add arm movements to accentuate each pathway. They might imagine their feet and hands are painting the space with different colored paths and lines.

Suggested Music: *Music for Creative Dance, Volume IV,* #1

Single Focus and Multi-Focus

Students alternate forming shapes in self space by using single focus (viewing different objects in the room), or through general space with multi-focus (looking at all the dancers). Say specific objects for the students to focus on for the single focus section. Encourage them to focus and move on different levels in different directions during both the single and multi-focus sections. For an additional challenge, add a third section when they close their eyes and dance in self space.

Suggested Music: *Music for Creative Dance, Volume III,* #15

Fast and Slow

Dancers move with different degrees of slowness (slow, slower, slowest), alternated by different degrees of quickness (fast, faster, fastest). Dancers might move one body part that the teacher names and then increase speed as they add more body parts. They slow down as they "subtract" body parts of their own choosing.

Suggested Music: *Music for Creative Dance, Volume I,* #9

Meter and Non-Meter

Dancers alternate moving their own way to the non-metered music with moving to the pulse of the metered music. Encourage students to move with long and short breaths on the non-metered music and then use a variety of body parts, levels and directions to highlight the accents on the metered music.

Suggested Music: *Music for Creative Dance, Volume II,* #1

Sharp and Smooth

When the music has a smooth quality, dancers explore smooth, sustained movements. When the music changes quality, dancers move with sharp, percussive energy. Encourage dancers to explore different ways of moving smoothly by changing size, level, direction or pathway each time the music repeats the smooth quality. With young children, use the image of a spacecraft floating different ways through space. In between floating through space, land first on a kicking planet, then a poking planet and finally a jumping planet. Dancing with pieces of plastic or fabric during this activity stimulates tactile and auditory senses.

Suggested Music: *Music for Creative Dance, Volume IV,* #6

Strong and Light

Dancers alternate light and strong movements by complimenting the music, as well as moving "against" it. Call out different verbs each time the music changes such as, glide, punch, float, slash, flick, press, dab and wring. Older dancers explore active and passive weight.

Suggested Music: *Music for Creative Dance, Volume I,* #1

Free and Bound

Dancers begin in bound shapes and then loosen up until they flow freely though space. At a signal or the change in the music, they "bind their flow" until they are completely frozen. The change between free and bound flow should be gradual, rather than sudden. Include age appropriate images such as ice and water, machines and people, sparks and smoke, contained and flowing lava, tree branches in winter and in summer. To avoid mimetic movements, encourage the use of many dance concepts or ask the dancers for images.

Suggested Music: *Music for Creative Dance, Volume I,* #4

Whole Body and Body Parts

Dancers alternate dancing with one body part and with the whole body. Let them choose the body part and how to move it or call out different body parts and specific movements, such as arms floating lightly and legs stamping strongly. The students can freely choose movements when dancing with the whole body.

Suggested Music: *Music for Creative Dance, Volume III, #4* or *Volume II* #3

Symmetrical and Asymmetrical Shapes

Dancers move through general space while imagining that the space is molding them into asymmetrical shapes. When the music changes, the teacher calls out, one at a time, two or three specific symmetrical shapes such as "big curved symmetrical," "straight symmetrical," "twisted high symmetrical." The dancers form the shapes in self space. Encourage them to observe each other's creative, symmetrical shapes.

Suggested Music: *Music for Creative Dance, Volume III*, #8

Under and Over

The teacher names places or the dancers imagine fanciful surroundings like forests, amusement parks or playgrounds. They move in these surroundings by darting between, jumping over, crawling under, climbing through, and dancing around imagined objects or people.

Suggested Music: *Music for Creative Dance, Volume II,* #20 or *Volume III,* #13

On-Balance and Off-Balance

Dancers alternate stable (balanced movement) with tipping (off-balance movement). Between the changes, they may form a still or counterbalance shape for a certain number of counts or as the music directs. A boat in a storm rocking and rolling side-to-side and back and forth motivates off balance movements. The students dance on balance when the sea is calm and then form counterbalance shapes when the anchor is down.

Suggested Music: *Music for Creative Dance, Volume I,* #11 or *Volume II,* #9

> ***Teaching Tip**: When exploring contrasts (i.e., high and low), think of contrasting ways to structure the activities and alternate between them.*
>
> *"Copy my movements/dance your own way."*
> *"Copy my movements, make your own shapes/copy my shapes, do your own movements."*
> *"Dance in self space/dance in general space."*
> *"Dance by yourself/dance with a partner."*
> *"Dance with the prop (or instrument)/put the prop down and dance without it."*
> *"Dance the way the music makes you feel/dance the opposite way (or against the music)."*
> *"Dance you own way/copy someone else's movements."*
> *"Dance with your whole body/dance with a body part(s)."*

Music with Pauses

Music with pauses is helpful in guiding dance explorations and improvisations. During each pause and with everyone's attention, call out a simple direction, dance step or dance concept . This music is also excellent for "directed and free" explorations. The pause signals the dancers to alternate the teacher's movement suggestions with their ideas. The *Music for Creative Dance, Volumes I-V* collection contains several pause selections. Particularly useful is the "Potpourri" at the end of each volume. Manually pause a piece of music to provide longer pauses for more complex directions, positive reinforcement, changing partners or to practice "being still." Below are explorations using music with pauses.

Body Halves

Dancers alternate dancing upper body halves in self space and lower body halves through general space. If pauses signal when to change halves, remind the dancers which half they will be moving next. Say "right half...left half...upper right and lower left...one quarter of your body...three quarters of your body." This activity is useful to teach fractions. Give appropriate directions and goals for each age and level of experience.

Suggested Music: *Music for Creative Dance, Volume IV,* #4

Leading Parts

At each pause, say a body part. When the music plays, dancers use that part to lead them through space while integrating varying directions, pathways, levels, energies or balances, based on the lesson's concept.

Suggested Music: *Music for Creative Dance, Volume III,* #2

Listen and Move

Dancers listen to the music and then dance the way it makes them feel. At the pause they become still, ready to listen to the dynamic change in the music. Describe what is seen to reinforce the dancers' choices. For example, "I see twisted low level movements...I see strong jumps...I see dancers moving like leaves in the wind."

Suggested Music: *Music for Creative Dance, Volume IV,* #18

Directed and Free

Dancers alternate copying the teacher's pulse and moving to their own tempo. Music pauses signal the change from teacher-directed to personal choice. For variation, the directed pulse may be through body percussion or rhythm instruments, with the free choice section being body movements alone. Dancers echo the teacher's rhythm patterns in the directed section and create their own patterns during free choice.

Suggested Music: *Music for Creative Dance, Volume III,* #9

Act and React

At a pause in the music, say, "Shake the space." When the music plays, the dancers will shake body parts on different levels. At the next pause, say, "Let the space shake you!" This time, the dancers "react" as though the space is shaking them! Call out "action" or "reaction" phrases at each pause with many verbs including squeeze, press, tickle, slash, twist, chop, paint, pull and flick. Compare the body parts used and feelings generated based on how the dancers act or react to the space.

Suggested Music: *Music for Creative Dance, Volume II,* #3

Freeze and Move

Dancers alternate holding a shape in self space and moving that shape through general space. They freeze in a shape in self space for eight counts of music; after a pause, they dance that shape through space for eight counts. At the next pause, they form a new shape and hold for eight counts, then they dance away in that shape. This can be tricky because the dancers alternate "freezing" and "moving" during the music. The pause signals only the change from holding a shape to dancing a shape. During the pause, the shapes are determined by the teacher (curved, high, strong, big, letter "A," numeral three, etc.) or by the dancers' choice. A basic variation is to dance the shape through space to the music and then "freeze" at the pause.

Suggested Music: *Music for Creative Dance, Volume II, #5*

Opposite Lands

Another way to explore contrasts is through the dance game, **Opposite Lands**. Divide the room in half by marking a line with cones, spots or tape. Dancers move with a certain type of movement on one side of the room. When the music changes, they cross to the other side of the room and dance the opposite way. They continue to travel back and forth between the two lands, moving as the teacher and music direct. Dancers find this quite delightful!

In a classroom, use an open area for the land where movements are faster, stronger or bigger. The area in and around the desks is the opposite land where movements are slower, lighter or smaller.

On the following pages are some specific explorations of Opposite Lands. Bring variety to familiar activities by adding props or musical instruments.

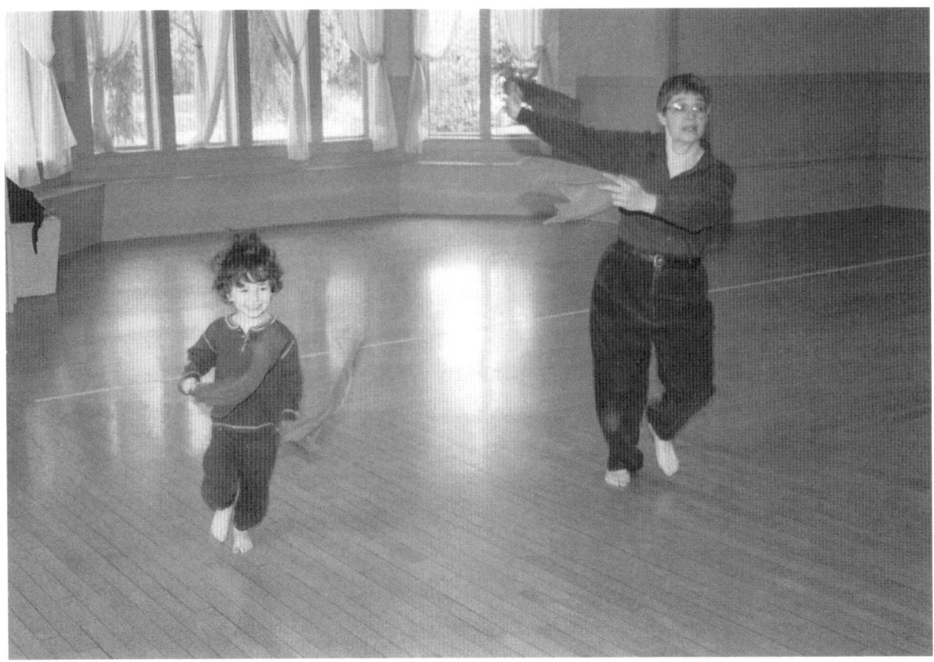

Baby and Giant Lands is a favorite of preschoolers.

In one land, students pretend to be moms and dads playing musical instruments softly and dancing quietly as they put their imaginary babies to sleep. On the loud music, they run to the opposite land to become giants, who are having a wild party in the woods and play loudly and dance strongly. Of course, the giants wake the babies when the music becomes quiet again; the students run back to the other side to soothe the babies and put them back to sleep. This exercise is repeated over and over until the music stops! This exploration is effective with or without instruments.

Suggested Music: *Music for Creative Dance, Volume I,* #14

Water and Ice Lands

Dancers use free-flowing, watery movements in **Water Land**. In **Ice Land**, they pretend to slowly freeze, moving with more and more bound flow, until frozen in shapes. In Ice Land, the dancers connect in pairs to represent small icebergs or in a large group for a glacier, before melting and flowing back to Water Land.

Suggested Music: *Music for Creative Dance, Volume I,* #4

Shrinking and Growing Lands

In **Big Land**, dancers use large movements, reaching far from center. Then they shrink, dancing with small movements in **Small Land**. Young dancers enjoy having imaginary shrinking and growing powder "sprinkled" on them as they change lands.

Suggested Music: *Music for Creative Dance, Volume IV,* #6

Variations

- Older dancers enjoy working with the concept of molecules. In one land, they are steam, dancing far from each other with big movements. Next, they are water, dancing a little closer to each other with medium movements. In the third land, they are ice, dancing close to each other with small movements. Then the dancers melt back to Water Land, expanding their movements as they return to Steam Land with large movements. Designate three spaces for this dance or have the dancers move back and forth between two spaces, reminding them which form they are describing through movement.
- Each time the dancers return to a land (the opposite side of the room), they imagine the walls have closed in and the space has shrunk. The dancers' movements and the space between dancers become smaller each time they change "lands" until they are dancing close together with tiny movements. The last land might change back to Big Land!

  Suggested Music: *Music for Creative Dance, Volume II,* #14-18

Pulse and Pattern Lands

In one land of Simple Machines or Robots, dancers move their whole body or body parts to an even, measured pulse as directed by the teacher. In the opposite land where more complex machines or robots dwell, dancers move to their own rhythm patterns created by body movements, claps, stamps, snaps, sounds and silence.

Suggested Music: *Music for Creative Dance, Volume III,* #2

Sea and Shore Lands

Dancers imagine one land is the ocean and they dance on a boat in stormy seas, tipping and falling off balance. Then they land on shore, where they dance with stable, balanced movements.

Suggested Music: *Music for Creative Dance, Volume III,* #4

Hide and Seek Lands

Dancers seek a special object in one land. Suggest that they look high and low in different directions along different pathways. As they change lands, they find their special object and dance while looking at it with single focus. The object can be something or someone in the room or one of their body parts.

Suggested Music: *Music for Creative Dance, Volume I,* #1

Flock and Fly Lands

Dancers move in one land, like a flock of birds. They walk along, pecking and hunting for worms or insects, then scatter to the other land where they fly in different ways with free flow.

Suggested Music: *Music for Creative Dance, Volume IV,* #6 or *Volume III,* #8

Happy and Sad Lands

Each land represents a different emotion. Use two opposing emotions or use a new emotion each time the dancers switch lands. Call out the emotion to travel to the new land. Have the dancers react to the music by changing emotions and lands at a music cue.

Suggested Music: *Music for Creative Dance, Volume II,* #20 or *Volume III,* #13

Props

Props are helpful in exploring contrasting movements. They are both a visual and tactile extension of the concept. Students see and feel their scarves move high and low, lightly and strongly, quickly and slowly, forward and backward, over and under, freely and rigidly. Props engage a variety of senses to make familiar activities novel, increasing student attention and making the lesson brain-compatible.

Props that are most versatile for exploring a variety of concepts include small scarves, big scarves, pieces of plastic (thin plastic tablecloths cut into 20" squares), stretchy bands (a loop of spandex material 12" wide and 6' around), spandex streamers and foam sticks (pipe insulation or swimming floats cut into 12" long pieces). Other props include therapy balls and cones of different sizes, spots cut from thin yoga mats, large pieces of cloth (sheets, cotton tablecloths, silk), musical instruments, ribbon rings, body sox, hula-hoops and folding gym mats. Below are some specific ways for using props to explore contrasts.

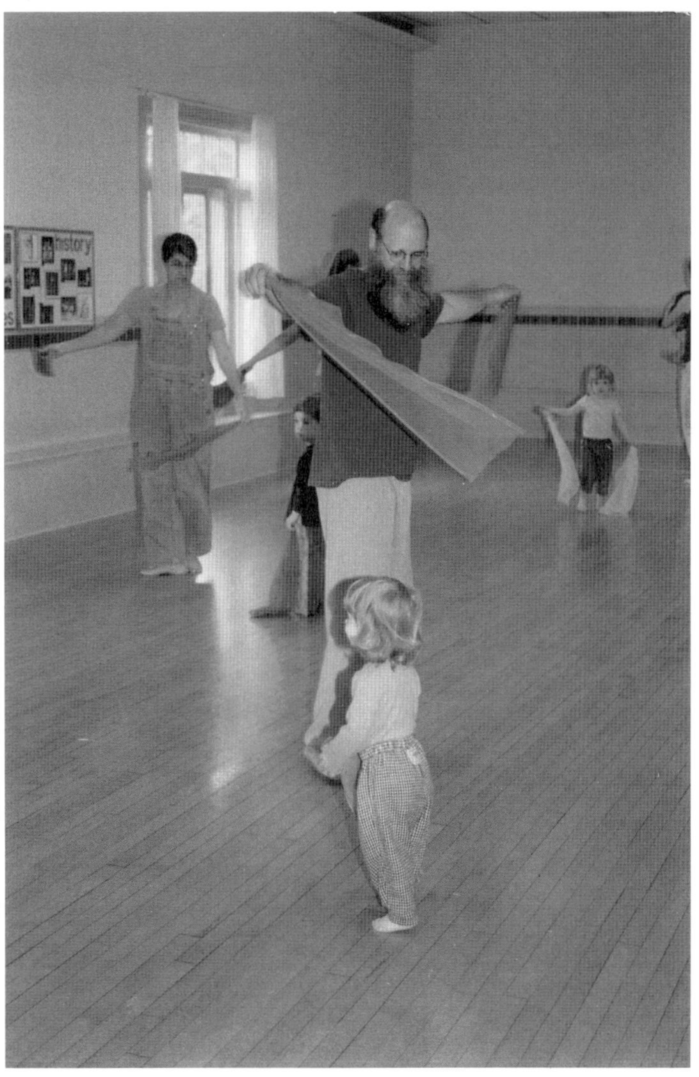

Scarves

- Dancers explore the words under, over, around, through, beside and between with a scarf. When the music pauses, they follow the teacher's directions. For example, "Form a shape under the scarf…over the scarf…and around the scarf." "Put the scarf around you." "Put the scarf between body parts." "Balance the scarf on a body part." "Shake the scarf in back of you." "Toss the scarf above your head."
- Dancers move their bodies and scarves freely, then bind the scarves to move bodies and scarves with bound flow.

Spots cut from thin yoga mats

- Dancers use spots as steering wheels and drive through general space as the teacher says locomotor movements. Put the spot down and practice nonlocomotor movements on the spot.
- Dancers leap over spots in general space, then stop on the spot and form shapes in self space.
- Dancers move with different movements in different pathways from spot to spot "connecting the dots."

Foam sticks (pipe insulation or swimming floats cut into 10"-12" pieces)

- Each dancer holds a stick as if holding a balloon and dances lightly through the space; then moving strongly, drums the floor with the stick or taps one's body parts. They may roll the stick on the floor by poking it lightly with their toes and then stomp strongly on the stick. Dancers may also roll their whole bodies back and forth on the sticks as if making cookie dough.
- Holding two sticks with a partner, dancers push and pull each other forward and backward. They may slide, swing and tip sideways right and left; move up and down as in an elevator; turn up and over together ("dishrag"). Foam sticks can also connect partners in folk dances.
- In groups of three to five, dancers use foam sticks to create snowflakes by connecting the sticks in interesting patterns. They then melt and dance away like wind and rain.

Hoops

- Dancers move through general space while holding the hoops. They dance in, out, over and around the hoops in self space.
- Dancers balance the hoops on body parts and form balancing shapes inside, outside and over the hoops.
- Scatter four to five hoops in the space. Dancers move around the hoops. On a signal, they form a shape with one body part inside a hoop, connecting with other dancers who gather at the same hoop.
- Each dancer stands in a hoop and plays a musical instrument. The first pause in the music signals them to leave the instrument in the hoop and begin dancing through general space without it. The next pause signals them to find a new hoop and play the instrument inside that hoop. Continue to alternate playing instruments in hoops and dancing away without them.

Stretchy Bands

- Dancers form geometric shapes with stretchy bands, then freely dance with the stretchy bands.
- Dancers dance alone with stretchy bands through the space, then connect with other students and move together.
- Adult and child couples love to play "horsy" with the child inside the stretchy band and pulling against it as the adult holds the imaginary reins.
- Pairs: one dancer forms a big shape with the stretchy band and the other dancer moves through the empty space created by the stretchy band. The dancer with the stretchy band releases it and the other dancer picks it up to form a new shape.

Streamers

- Dancers draw different pathways on the floor with the streamers, then draw them in the air as they dance. Dancers might also place the streamers on the floor in straight, curved and zigzag lines and perform locomotor movements beside the streamers, tracing the pathways.
- Dancers form acute, obtuse or right angles with the streamers and their bodies. They then draw geometric figures in space or dance freely with the streamers. They also form geometric shapes with other dancers and streamers.
- Balance the streamer on different body parts and then dance freely with the streamer.

Cloths or Sheets

- Dancers take turns forming shapes under the sheet, emphasizing different body parts, levels, sizes and directions, all depending on the lesson concept. Classmates watch and guess the elements of the concept or try to copy the mystery shape.
- Adults pull very young dancers on the sheets in different directions and pathways with varying energy. With the help of the teacher or another adult, they swing the child in the sheet as if in a hammock.
- Cloths with specific designs such as fish, leaves, animals and butterflies may be used creatively with preschool children. Direct young dancers to place body parts on designated colors, shapes and objects. They may dance under, on or over the cloth when held by fellow students.

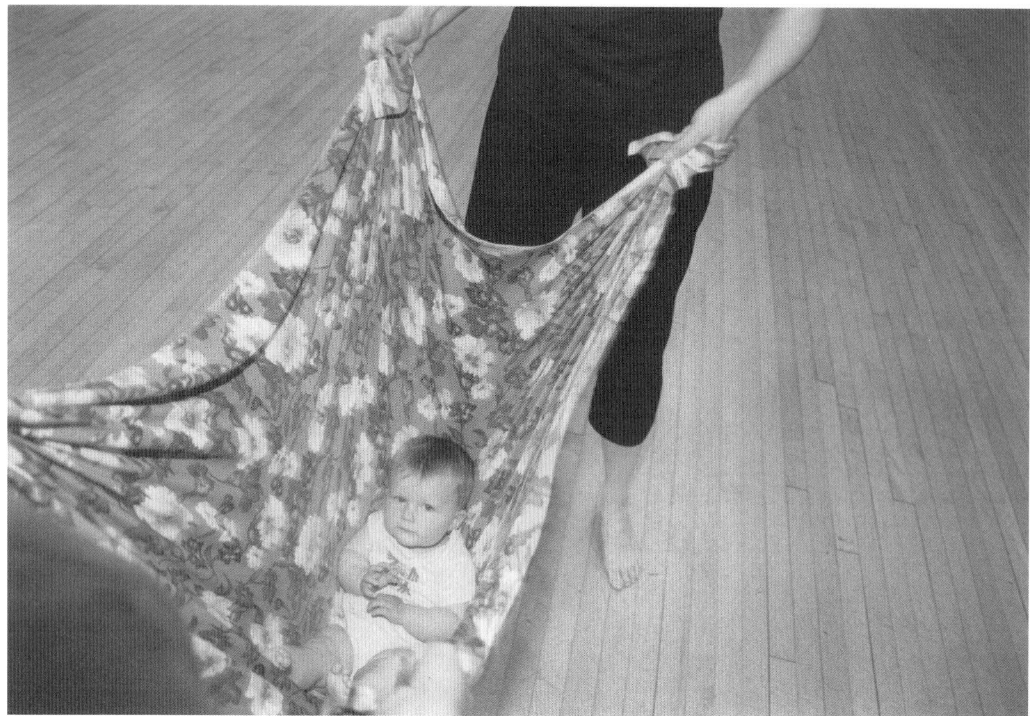

Plastic (squares cut from thin plastic tablecloths)

- Dancers move their bodies and the plastic with different energy (sharp, smooth, shaky, swingy).
- Dancers move the plastic with upper body parts (floating, punching, swinging, stretching) and then with lower ones (kicking, sliding on, poking, balancing on).
- Dancers squeeze the plastic into little balls and hide it in their hands or behind their backs while dancing with little movements. They open the plastic and dance with bigger movements.
- Pairs: one dancer moves the plastic in different ways as the other dancer imitates the plastic with body movements and shapes. They reverse roles.

***Teaching Tip**: When using props during Exploring the Concept, think of ways to use these props besides just holding them.*

- *Move the prop with feet for eye-foot coordination.*
- *Toss and catch the prop for eye-hand coordination.*
- *Tap, brush and press the prop on body parts for tactile stimulation.*
- *Jump over or step on and off the prop for vestibular development.*
- *Form shapes and move on, under, around or inside the prop to develop spatial awareness.*
- *Connect to a partner with the prop and dance together for social development.*

Exploring Concepts in Pairs, Trios and Small Groups

Dancing together is beneficial for people of all ages. We all have a movement signature, a way of moving that is particular to each of us. When we move with others or copy another dancer's movements, we expand our movement vocabulary as a form of kinesthetic brainstorming. The more movements we know and try, the more problems we solve. Through improvisation we become more creative and confident!

When we explore ideas together we practice leadership and followship skills. Alternating leader and follower roles dispells dancers' inhibitions and gives them opportunities to practice both skills. Knowing when to lead and follow, understanding the capabilities of both roles, is a beneficial life skill. Human beings seek relationships and learn about themselves and others through connections with many people. Students enjoy working together to develop social skills through this interchange.

The easiest way for students to form partnerships or trios is to say, "By the time I count to five, stand elbow to elbow (knee to knee, foot to foot, etc.), with another dancer (or two dancers). Raise your hand if you do not have a partner and find someone else's raised hand to connect with." A student "left over" can work in a trio or partner with the teacher. For quartets, have students get into pairs and then have each pair connect body parts with another pair by a given count.

The most important part of working with partners, especially at the beginning of the term, is to change them often, even several times within one activity. Ask pairs to form a few shapes together and then dance to another partner. Do this for three to four minutes, until everyone has worked together. Ask dancers to move together for eight counts, take eight counts to find a new partner, move with the new partner, find a third partner, etc. After a few weeks of finding and changing partners, barriers break down and everyone cooperates. Positive feedback always helps.

Favorite group explorations for dancers of all ages are presented in the following pages. Some activities may be familiar to readers of *Creative Dance for All Ages* and others are new. They can be used to explore any dance concept. Focus on a particular concept throughout the exploration, cueing dancers to use other concepts for movement variety.

Chopsticks

A chopstick is a unique and exciting prop. I have used them successfully with hundreds of students ages five through adult, in public schools and private studios, without an injury or problem. Dancers love the challenging, delicate quality of the chopstick.

Basic Chopsticks with Leaders

"Connect elbows with a partner by the time I count to five. Decide who will be Leader #1 and who will be Leader #2. Leader #1, pick up one chopstick and return to your partner. Balance the chopstick between your and your partner's flat palms. When the music begins, move through the general space with Leader #1 leading and the chopstick balanced between your palms. Move on different levels, in different directions and pathways, changing speed and energy. If the chopstick falls, just pick it up and balance it between your palms again. When I give the signal (or the music changes), Leader #1 takes the chopstick and forms shapes in self space. Leader #2 copies the shapes. When I give another signal (or the music changes), Leader #2 leads the movement through general space and then forms shapes for Leader #1 to copy. Continue changing leadership until the music ends."

Suggested Music: *Music for Creative Dance, Volume 1,* #1

Reflection: "Close your eyes and think about which part of this exploration you enjoyed. If you enjoyed being the leader, sit down. If you enjoyed being the follower, stand up. You cannot make a middle level shape. Decide, just for this moment, which you liked best." If time allows, ask students for one word to describe their choices.

Chopstick Variations

Chopsticks without Leaders

Pairs move with the chopstick balanced between palms. Both dancers share leadership and move cooperatively. At the signal or when the music changes, they put the chopstick down and each person dances in one's own way around or near the chopstick. Continue dancing together with the chopstick (occasionally changing the hand used to balance the chopstick) and apart without the chopstick, until the music ends.

Suggested Music: *Music for Creative Dance, Volume III,* #15 or *Volume 1,* #1

Chopsticks and Prepositions

Partners balance a chopstick between the palms and dance together through the space. At the signal or when the music changes, Leader #1 forms a shape as the teacher calls out a preposition (over, under, around, through, behind, in front, above, below, beside, between, on, off, in, out, etc.). Leader #2 forms a shape relating to Leader #1 that shows the designated preposition. Leader #1 forms a new shape and the teacher calls out another preposition. While following the teacher or music, alternate leaders, traveling with the chopstick and creating prepositional shapes.

Suggested Music: *Music for Creative Dance, Volume III,* #15 or #8 or *Volume 1,* #1

Chopsticks and Trios

Three dancers balance three chopsticks between three palms to form a triangle. Advanced dancers may balance the chopstick between shoulders, feet, hips. Dancers move together without traveling, changing levels, etc. At the signal or when the music changes, each of the three holds one chopstick. Leaders #2 and #3 shadow (copy) Leader #1's movements through general space. Alternate the two sections. Dance in one spot with chopsticks and then follow each leader through general space.

Suggested Music: *Music for Creative Dance, Volume 1,* #16

Reflection: "Turn to your partners and tell them which part you thought was more challenging, moving together in self space or shadowing through general space and why. Which part was more enjoyable, being the leader or a follower?"

Chopsticks, Body Parts and Shapes

Partners balance a chopstick between their palms. Moving with the chopstick between them, they form different shapes. They think of being "shape shifters" as they dance. When the teacher signals a change, Leader #1 holds the chopstick alone and makes a shape while Leader #2 connects one body part to Leader #1. Leader #1 forms a second shape and Leader #2 connects two body parts to Leader #1. Leader #1 forms a third shape and Leader #2 connects three body parts to Leader #1. Alternate leadership until the music ends.

Suggested Music: *Music for Creative Dance, Volume 1,* #15 or *Volume II,* #9 (Move through space on the reel music and connect body parts on the "shhh" sounds.)

Reflection: "Turn to your partner and say which part of the exploration you thought was more challenging, shape shifting with the chopstick between you or connecting body parts in shapes? Why did you make that choice? Show each other one new shape that you made during the dance."

Shadows and Mirrors

In **shadowing**, a dancer stands front to back with a partner and the person in back copies the movements of the person in front, as in "follow the leader." In **mirroring**, two dancers face one another and imitate the other's movements. Shadowing and mirroring may be done in small and large groups.

When working with novice dancers, do more shadowing than mirroring. Standing face to face and thinking of new movements or copying unfamiliar movements can be inhibiting. Shadowing is less stressful because the leader cannot see the follower. Also, locomotor movements are usually easier for novice dancers. Shadowing is most effective in general space. Experienced dancers possess an expanded movement vocabulary and feel less inhibited with mirroring. An easy way to practice mirroring is to combine it with shadowing, so that dancers develop mirroring skills while recuperating through shadowing.

Basic Partner Shadow

"By the time I count to six, connect knees with a partner. Decide who will be the first leader. Leader #1 stands in front of Leader #2. Now, Leader #1 dances through general space while Leader #2 shadows (copies) the movements. When the music pauses, stop and turn around so that Leader #2 is in front. Each time the music pauses, change leadership." The teacher may direct the movement by calling out concepts or basic movements during the pauses.

Suggested Music: *Music for Creative Dance, Volume I,* #16

Variations

- **Shadow** while holding props or playing instruments.
- **Connect** body parts with a partner during a pause in the music.
- **Form** letters, numbers, abstract forms or relationships (over/under/around/through) during a music pause before switching leaders.

Integrate the lesson's concept:

- **Place:** the dancers alternate shadowing in general space and self space.
- **Body Parts:** the leader focuses on moving certain body parts for the partner to copy. When the music pauses, partners connect body parts to form a shape.
- **Level:** each leader moves on a different level, then partners form a shape together on the opposite level during the pause.
- **Weight:** leaders move with strong and light weight, forming weight-sharing shapes together before changing leadership.

Shadow Variations

Triangle and Diamond Shadow

Triangle and **diamond** formations are well suited for older or experienced dancers who enjoy the challenge of maintaining their formation while moving through space. Trios form triangles with a leader in front and two followers side by side (with space between them) behind the leader. Quartets form a diamond, with all four dancers facing the same direction. The leader is in front of the other dancers and cannot see them. When the leader turns to face another dancer in the formation, the leadership changes. If everyone is shadowing the leader, they all follow the leader to face a new leader! Explore the many variations listed under "Basic Partner Shadow."

Suggested Music: *Music for Creative Dance, Volume II,* #13-19 or *Volume IV,* #8

Emotion Shadow

This variation may be done in pairs, trios or quartets. The leader listens to the music and moves the way the music makes him or her feel (happy, proud, scared, confused, etc.). The follower(s) copy or shadow that movement. When the music changes, the leader faces another dancer who, as the new leader, decides on appropriate movements that match the mood of the music. Continue until the music ends.

Suggested Music: *Music for Creative Dance, Volume II,* #20 or *III,* #13

Reflection: "Tell everyone in your group what you felt while you were moving. Did everyone in the group experience similar feelings? Did the leaders move in ways that you anticipated or did some movements surprise you?"

Line Shadow

Dancers form short lines of three to five dancers; three works best with younger dancers. They shadow the leader's movements in and through space. When the music pauses, the leader runs to the end of the line and the next person becomes the leader. Encourage the dancers to copy the person directly in front of them instead of following the first person in line. Try this activity with any of the variations listed under "Basic Partner Shadow."

Suggested Music: *Music for Creative Dance, Volume I,* #16*; Volume II,* #21*; Volume III,* #20 or *Volume IV,* #18

Reflection: "What was most challenging about following in a line? What was most challenging about leading a line? Share your thoughts with your group."

Blind Shadow

Dancers choose a partner and decide who is Leader #1 and who is Leader #2. Leader #2 will stand behind and to one side of Leader #1 with the left hand on the leader's right shoulder or the right hand on the left shoulder. Leader #2, with closed eyes, keeps the other arm close to the side of his or her body. Leader #1 moves carefully, leading the "blind" partner in and through space. Encourage the leader to move the upper body, including torso and shoulders, in unusual ways: adding bends, jumps, starts and stops, curvy movements, changes in speed and direction. Leaders should not move at low levels because this is dangerous for the follower. Change leaders when the music changes or when there is a signal.

Suggested Music: *Music for Creative Dance Volume, IV* #10, #12 or #17

Reflection: "When you were the follower, what did you feel – nervous, relaxed, excited, confused? Share feelings with each other. Are your feelings the same as your partner's? Why do you think this is so?"

Variation

- The leader takes the follower on a "journey." When the music stops the follower and leader share their versions of the journey with each other. Before this activity begins, each dancer may write a short story or draw a map of the journey to inspire movement.
  Suggested Music: *Music for Creative Dance Volume, II #20 or Volume III* #13

Basic Partner Mirror

The teacher may direct the movement by suggesting concepts or basic movements during the pauses. "Connect elbows with a partner by the time I count to five. Decide who will be the first leader. Leader #1, stand face to face with Leader #2 about two feet apart. Now, Leader #1, dance in self space while Leader #2 mirrors (copies) your movements. When the music pauses, change leadership. Leaders, if you want to travel through general space, remember you must always face your partner as if you are looking in a mirror."

Suggested Music: *Music for Creative Dance, Volume I,* #16

Mirror Variations

Mirror and Shadow

Dancers find partners (or trios) and choose who will lead first for shadowing. When the music pauses, changes quality or a signal is given, partners face each other. Leader #1 continues to lead, with Leader #2 mirroring Leader #1's movements in self space. Change leaders for shadowing and mirroring. Continue to change leaders until the music stops. Direct dancers to explore the lesson's dance concept while shadowing and mirroring.

Suggested Music: *Music for Creative Dance Volume, III,* #4 or #11

Reflection: "Which part was easier for you to lead – shadowing or mirroring? Which part was easier for you to follow? Why do you think this is so? Share your thoughts with your partner."

Variation

- Pairs shadow each other to the pulse of the music. On cue, they face each other and take turns doing a rhythmic pattern (i.e., jump, jump, clap, clap, clap) in four counts, echoing their partner's pattern. Leader #1 should do four patterns with Leader #2 echoing before returning to shadowing (32 counts). Shadowing provides recuperation from the more complex rhythm section.

Group Mirror and Dance Away

All dancers face one leader (the teacher or a selected student) and mirror the leader's movements in self space. When the music changes, all dance their own way through general space. Alternate self space mirroring with general space improvisation. Remember to focus on the lesson's concept. For example, when it is Size, the leader will demonstrate many ways of growing and shrinking. When the dancers do their own dance, they too will explore Size.

Suggested Music: *Music for Creative Dance, Volume I,* #9 or *Volume IV,* #6

Reflection: "If you enjoyed copying the leader's shapes, sit down. If you enjoyed dancing your own way, stand up. Turn to a person near you and tell her or him why you made this choice." (Each student can tell the whole group if time permits.)

> ***Teaching Tip**: When mirroring with very young dancers, I keep the movements simple and name each movement as I do it. "I am making a big shape... now I am shrinking into a tiny shape... now I am stretching into a strong, big shape... I am squooshing into a narrow shape. Now show me your own big and small dancing shape in general space."*
>
> *Sometimes, I surprise them by saying, "I am making a big, big shape. Oh! I popped into a little shape and you all followed me! Great watching! Who can look like me in this tall narrow shape? Oh! I burst into a wide shape! I can't fool you!"*
>
> *With experienced or older dancers, I make my movements more complicated without frustrating them. I try to move many body parts and bring in other concepts. When they dance away, I may offer suggestions or challenges such as, "Have you tried changing Size while traveling in different pathways? Have you moved with big movements on a low level and small movements on a high level?"*

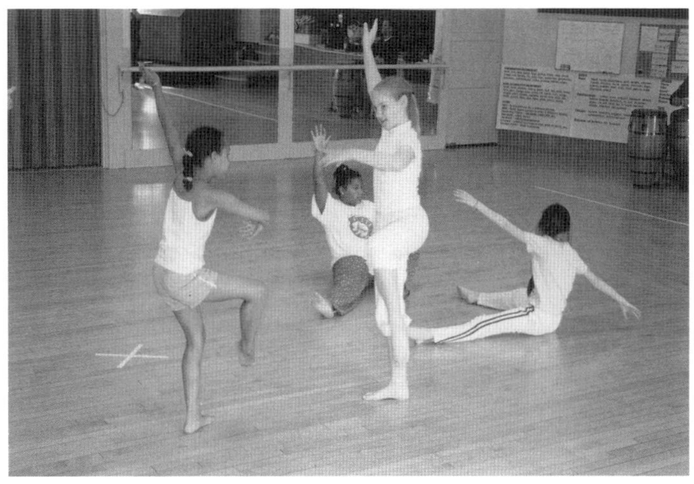

Partner Mirror and Dance Away

Dancers mirror each other in pairs while taking turns being the leader. When the music changes or at a signal, partners dance through general space away from and then back to their partner. This free dancing is a nice recuperation from mirroring in self space. Offer suggestions to novice leaders during mirroring to discourage inhibitions. For example, "Try changing levels...try moving slowly or quickly...try moving legs instead of arms...can you make your movements smoother or sharper?"

Suggested Music: *Music for Creative Dance, Volume II,* # 21

Reflection: "Tell each other which role was more challenging and why – being the leader or being the follower."

Connected Mirror

By the count of five, dancers connect all ten fingertips with a partner's fingertips. Partners decide who will lead first. As the leader moves in and through space, the pair remain connected through their fingertips. Change leaders when the music changes or at a signal. After a few repetitions, change partners or change the body part connections. Experienced dancers may explore connecting elbows, knees, backs or hips.

Suggested Music: *Music for Creative Dance Volume, IV,* #18

Space Between Mirrors

Partners face each other with arms outstretched and palms together. They then pull their palms away so they are about ten inches apart. Leader #1 moves through space, changing directions, levels and speed, while Leader #2 tries to keep ten inches between the palms at all times. This is challenging and fun! Dancers may move faster than in the connected mirror. Change leadership and partners several times. As a variation, dancers may mirror with space between other body parts.

Suggested Music: *Music for Creative Dance Volume, III,* #6

Etch-Sketch (Based on Etch-A-Sketch®, Ohio Art Company)

This mirror variation is based on a popular toy. The Etch-A-Sketch® is a screen with two knobs that are turned to make designs. One knob controls vertical lines, the other controls horizontal lines.

Pairs stand face to face and are scattered around the room. Leader #1 moves backward, right, forward, left – constantly changing directions. As the partner mirrors the leader's changes in direction, the follower appears to be drawing designs in space. The leader must be aware of all dancers in the space by carefully moving the follower through the space in front, behind and around others who are doing the same thing! When the music changes or on cue, the follower becomes the leader. Change leadership and partners several times. It is fun and challenging to direct the movement away from one another and back together before changing leaders.

For novice dancers, the focus is on directions and moving safely. Encourage experienced dancers to create unique movements while directing their partners through the space!

Suggested Music: *Music for Creative Dance, Volume IV,* #7

Reflection: "What made this improvisation challenging? What made it fun? Share your ideas with your partner."

Blind Mirror

Partners press palms together (do not interlock fingers). With closed eyes, Leader #2 follows Leader #1 as they move carefully in self space. When the music changes, partners switch roles.

Suggested Music: *Music for Creative Dance, Volume III,* # 7

Reflection: "Which did you find more relaxing – being the leader or the follower – and why?"

Variations

- Partners blind mirror sitting down.
- Leader alternates moving "blind" partner in self space and general space.
- Blind mirror with feet pressed together instead of palms.
- Partners alternate blind mirroring and dancing away from each other.

Zombie and Magician Mirror

Pairs stand face to face and are scattered around the room. Leader #1, the "magician," has a prop. Thin, plastic tablecloth material (twenty-inch square pieces), scarves or streamers, work well in this lesson. The magician moves the prop in many different ways, relating to the lesson's concept. The "zombie" mimics the prop's movement. The zombie only reacts to the movements of the prop. Change leaders several times. Encourage self and general space, as well as isolated and whole body part movements.

Suggested Music: *Music for Creative Dance, Volume I,* #9 or #16

Reflection: "Tell your partner which role you enjoyed more and why – zombie or magician? Did the zombie always move the way you thought it would?"

Variation

- Instead of a magician, the leader is a "musician" who holds a rhythm instrument (bells, sticks, shaker). The musician plays different tempi, rhythmic patterns and meters. The leader might also play the instrument loudly and softly or at different levels and in different directions. The "zombie" follows the instrument's movements and sounds! Allow experienced pairs to work on their own, but help younger dancers by giving directions, "Play quickly…play slowly…play up high…try down low…play side to side…play sharply…play smoothly."

> ***Teaching Tip***: *"Zombie and Magician Mirror" is an excellent lead-up to regular mirroring because followers are so focused on the prop that they are not embarrassed or inhibited by dancing face to face with a partner. Remember to give the leaders ideas if they are repeating the same movements over and over. For example, "Try changing levels… move with different speeds and types of energy… travel through space… try making just the head move by moving just the top of the prop… make just the legs move… try making just the zombie's torso move…"*

Connected Shapes

Students enjoy connecting with one another in different group shapes. These activities develop collaborative skills, balance and spatial, logical-mathematical and bodily-kinesthetic intelligences.

Shape Fences

Students connect with each other one at a time in a line of shapes, like a fence. The lesson's concept directs the type of shapes the dancers form, including shapes on levels, in different directions, connecting different body parts, in different pathways, etc.

Basic Fence

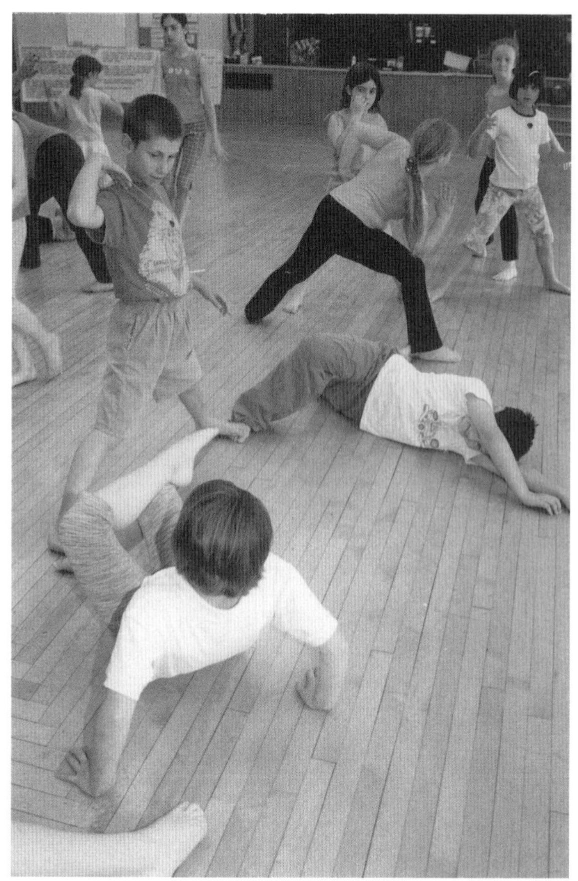

With a large group, divide the class into two or more separate fences. "Everyone, come to the end of the room. One dancer will start the fence by forming a shape. When your name is called, dance along the path of the fence line, observe the creative shapes that are in place and then connect to the last person in the fence. When all dancers are connected, the first dancer in line will break away from the fence, dance along the fence and reconnect at the end of the line of shapes. Hold your shape in the fence until the person next to you breaks away from the fence. Then dance down the fence again and make a new shape at the end of the line."

Suggested Music: *Music for Creative Dance, Volume I,* #3

Reflection: "Did you notice a shape that you had never seen before as you traveled along the fence? If so, try to form that shape. Think about what muscles you used to hold your shape in the fence. Grade yourself from 1 to 3, with 1 being the best, on how well you stayed still and connected in the fence (this assessment is optional). Share your answers with a person near you."

Fence Variations

Multiplication Fences

Explore sets of numbers by creating patterns in twos, threes or fours. For example, in sets of threes, every third dancer connects in a high shape (the other two in low shapes) and all the dancers yell out the numbers three! six! nine!, etc. as the high shapes connect. With sets of four, the fourth dancer makes the high shape (or big, strong, twisted or tipping shape).

Comparative Fences

Teach comparatives through fences that show patterns of big, bigger, biggest shapes; tall, taller, tallest shapes; or strong, stronger, strongest shapes.

Pathway Fences

After making a straight fence with straight shapes, dancers "build" one in a curved pathway with curved shapes or form a zigzag fence with zigzag shapes in a zigzag pathway. These fences are challenging and require teamwork, problem-solving skills and spatial intelligence. Remind dancers to closely follow the fence line (pathway) as they dance to the end of the fence.

Suggested Music: *Music for Creative Dance, Volume III,* #16

Stretchy Band Geometric Fences

Dancers make shapes in the fence using stretchy bands to form triangles, squares, diamonds, figure eights, etc. Dancers moving along the fence dance in, out, around and through the stretchy band shapes before making geometric shapes connecting to the last shape in the fence. Dancers enjoy finding ways to carry or hold the stretchy band as they travel along and through the fence.

Suggested Music: *Music for Creative Dance, Volume IV,* #13

Preposition Fences

This exercise is similar to the exploration above, but is performed without stretchy bands. Dancers relate to the fence as they travel along it by moving under and over, around and through, beside and between and in and out along shapes in the fence. Have dancers say the prepositions as they perform the corresponding actions.

Machines

In this improvisation, dancers randomly connect to each other, rather than in a line or fence. Dancers may connect anywhere in the shape, changing levels, relationships, etc.

Basic Body Part Machine

"When I call your name, connect one body part to a dancer in the machine. Form your shape on a level opposite to the person you connect with so the whole machine has an interesting shape. After everyone is connected, I will switch the machine on and each dancer in the machine will move one body part in a repetitive movement. Once you have a movement, make a sound to accompany it." The machine might start and stop several times on a signal. After moving, the machine may break apart and the dancers dance away to reassemble it in the same or different place in the room.

Suggested Music: *Music for Creative Dance, Volume I,* #3

Reflection: "Which body part did you move in the machine? Move it now. Is it the same or different from most of the other dancers? Share your sound and movement with a person near you and tell each other whether you feel the sound matches the movement or is different."

Machine Variations

Basic Machines

Each dancer thinks of a simple machine or tool (pulley, screw, wheel, inclined plane, lever or wedge) and creates an axial (self space) movement to describe it. By connecting one at a time to others, the group creates a complex machine! With a large group, it is fun to have half the dancers create the complex machine while the other half walks around it, noticing all the different simple machines. Dancers can add sounds to the machines. Viewers might name the complex machine (toy-making machine, doughnut machine, house cleaning machine). Change groups several times.

Suggested Music: *Music for Creative Dance, Volume I,* #5

Preposition Machines

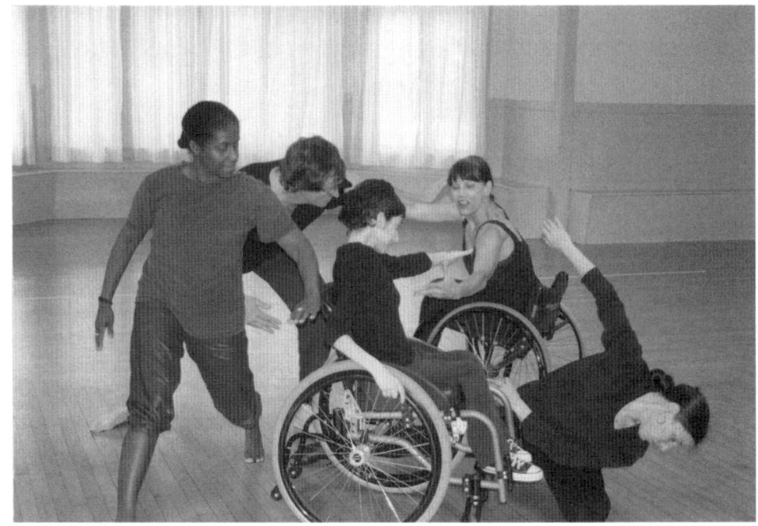

Ask dancers to create an "Over" machine. Each dancer connects to another dancer in a shape that describes "Over." Try an "Around" machine…a "Beside" machine…an "Under and Over" machine…an "Around and Through" machine. Discuss the many relationships and other prepositions that occur by chance when describing just one or two prepositions. How can the dancers be clear about which preposition they are trying to show?

Suggested Music: *Music for Creative Dance, Volume II,* #2

Tempo Machines

Dancers connect to one another and move a body part at a speed different from that of the other person. Dancers "outside" the machine accompany the tempo of a dancer in the machine with body, voice or instrument. With young dancers or parent and child classes, the whole machine could start slowly and then speed up until it breaks apart or slows down to stillness.

Suggested Music: *Music for Creative Dance, Volume I,* #3

Concept Machines

Use this exploration to focus on any of the fifteen dance concepts (Level, Speed, Energy, etc.), subject area concepts (math, science, language arts, etc.) or social themes (conflict, resolution, collaboration, etc.). Dancers focus on the lesson concept when making the machine while changing levels, directions, energy, weight, focus, shapes, etc. For subject areas, dancers form letters or numbers and connect in alphabetical or numerical order. They create landforms or solar systems. For social themes, shapes describe feelings that connect to opposite feelings or one machine describes "conflict" and another "resolution."

Emotion Machines

Dancers connect to one another while expressing a particular emotion though movement. Each machine expresses one emotion (anger), opposing emotions (happiness and sadness) or mixed emotions (anger, fear, sorrow, excitement, boredom).

Connected Counts

This exploration is based on " Fifteen Counts" by dance educator and author Mary Joyce.

This is a favorite because the students enjoy the collaboration required. Teachers appreciate that only half the students are moving through the space at a time, which aids class management.

Basic Connected Counts with Movement Skills

"Find a partner. One of you will dance in self space for a certain number of counts while the other travels through general space. The general space dancer will travel away from and back to the partner and end in a connected shape by the time I finish counting. Change roles. Sixteen counts floating..." (Count from one to sixteen.) "Did you make it back in time and are you in a connected shape? Now change roles. Twelve counts galloping...remember that the self space dancer has to gallop in place while the general space dancer gallops away and back by twelve counts. Fifteen counts twisting...eight counts jumping...ten counts turning." Continue to call out numbers and movement skills. The complexity of the movement skills depends on the dancer's experience.

Suggested Music: It is easier to count without music. Use a drum, rhythm sticks or body percussion for accompaniment. When counting, vary the pitch, volume and tempo to engage the dancers.

Reflection: "Discuss with a partner which movements felt more natural in self space and which felt more natural in general space. Why?"

Connected Counts Variations

Connected Counts with Dance Concepts

Call out different counts to explore one concept such as Level. For example, "Fifteen counts low level…twelve counts high level…nine counts middle level…eighteen counts moving high and low…ten counts moving from a high level to a low level (a challenge for the general space dancers)…sixteen counts moving from a low to a high level…eight counts moving low and smoothly…twelve counts moving high and sharply…thirteen counts turning on a middle level." Remind the dancers to end each phrase with a connecting shape that describes the concept. By using other concepts to explore one concept, the teacher and students can go on indefinitely! Repeat the command twice so each dancer has the opportunity to explore the idea in both self and general space.

Connected Counts with Math

Apply math to tell dancers how many counts they will use. For example, "5 + 10 moving backward." (Count from one to fifteen.) "Did you make it back in time and are you in a connected shape? Now change roles. 9 + 9 moving curvy…18 – 6 moving strongly…3 x 4 skipping…2 + 4 + 6 moving lightly." To make the exercise more instructive, let the dancers' connected shape answer the math problem. For example, when solving the equation "5 + 10 moving backwards," they would make the numeral 15 with body shapes. The self space person always represents the numeral in the one's place and the general space person might represent the numeral in the ten's place or they might form the numeral together if it is less than ten.

Students remember the equations better if they form the entire problem with body shapes while saying them aloud. For example, for the equation 5 + 10 = 15, they form a 5 with the body and say "five," form a plus sign, form a 10, form an equal sign and form the numeral 15, saying each number and sign while forming it with their bodies.

Connected Counts with Syllables

Self space dancers place the same number of body parts on the floor as the number of syllables in the word (i.e., for the word "watermelon," they place four body parts on the floor). Dancers in general space do the same number of actions away from their partner (i.e., four jumps). Dancers then repeat the words with their movements as the general space dancers do their actions returning to their partners. Both dancers say each syllable as they do their movements. On the next word, they reverse roles.

Variation

- **Spelling:** Focus on spelling the words instead of counting its syllables. For example: if the word is "house," the self space dancer spells "house" with whole body letters and voice. The general space dancer spells "house" through space, writing the letters on the floor or in the air with a body part as each letter is spoken. They repeat the actions as the general space dancer moves back to the partner. They say the word as they form a connected shape, illustrating the word's meaning. They reverse roles on the next word.

Back-to-Back

This exploration provides an easy way for dancers to connect with a partner or trio. It also develops appropriate touch and bonding. The command "back-to-back" signals dancers to stand with backs connected to another dancer.

Basic Back-to-Back

"When I say 'back-to-back,' quickly stand with your back touching another dancer's back. Now form a shape together reaching forward. You do not have to keep backs connected. Now dance away, moving in a forward direction. When I say, 'back-to-back,' connect backs with a new partner." (Younger dancers may return to the same partner each time). "Form a shape together reaching backward. Dance away, moving in a backward direction. Look behind you to move safely." The lesson's concept directs what kind of connected shapes the pairs make. The dancers then use the same concept to improvise through general space. This example is geared toward the Direction concept. The structure works well for mixing up groups and finding new partners quickly and simply.

Suggested Music: *Music for Creative Dance, Volume I,* #16

Reflection: "Share with your last partner your favorite part and why – connecting backs and making shapes together or exploring the concept through general space."

Back-to-Back Variations

Back-to-Back Pulse

Dancers stand back-to-back, following the teacher's pulse as they bounce together and clap their hands, slap thighs, etc. Then they dance away, moving to their own rhythm. Continue alternating back-to-back pulses with free, rhythmic solo dancing. It is fun and tactile to bounce backs and bottoms together in a steady pulse!

Suggested Music: *Music for Creative Dance, Volume III,* #2

Back-to-Back Movements

Dancers stand back-to-back as they do directed nonlocomotor movements such as floating, bending, twisting and stretching. They try to stay connected as they move. Then they dance away with a locomotor movement that the teacher names or with one of their own choosing.

Suggested Music: *Music for Creative Dance, Volume II,* #21

Back-to-Back Concepts

Each time the dancers connect back-to-back, name a different concept. For example, "Explore Size by one of you forming a big shape and the other a small shape…reverse roles…now dance away growing and shrinking. Back-to-back with a new partner. Form a connected shape on opposite Levels…now dance away, rising and sinking. Back-to-back with a new partner. Form a counterbalanced shape together. Now dance away off balance, tipping and falling."

Suggested Music: *Music for Creative Dance, Volume I,* #15

Shape Museums

This concept is based on an idea by dance educator Barbara Lacy.

Shape Museum is a dance game involving statues and dancers who constantly change roles. Shape Museum is a popular exploration for several reasons:

- Dancers love to form shapes.
- Dancers enjoy relating to others for short periods of time.
- Dancers enjoy being creative.
- Dancers enjoy alternating between moving and being still.
- Dancers enjoy the challenge of copying and learning from other people.
- Only half the dancers move at one time, which is helpful for small spaces and class management.

Basic Shape Museum

"Connect elbows with a partner by the count of five. Decide who will be a statue inside the museum and who will start outside the museum." (This is a simple way to divide the group in half.) "When the music begins, dancers outside the museum enter the museum and choose any statue by standing in front of it. Copy its shape exactly. After you have copied a statue, it comes to life and dances away to copy another statue. Hold your own shape until someone copies you, then dance away to copy another statue." With younger dancers, Shape Museums may be done in pairs. They remain partners for the entire exploration while alternating the roles of statue and dancer.

Suggested Music: *Music for Creative Dance, Volume I,* #6

Shape Museum Variations

Puzzle Shape Museum

When the music begins, dancers enter the museum and choose a statue. They form a shape fitting into the negative or empty space of the statue, just like a puzzle piece fits another. Puzzle shapes relate without touching. When the dancer forming the second puzzle piece is still, the original statue moves carefully away to form a puzzle shape with a different statue. When the statue moves away, the dancer will be left with a new shape with lots of empty space in it! The new statue holds that shape until another dancer comes to fit into the shape like a puzzle piece. This is an excellent activity for developing spatial intelligence and for discovering many new shapes. It develops the ability to find empty or negative space, an important concept for athletes and dancers.

Suggested Music: *Music for Creative Dance, Volume IV,* #3

Reflection: "If you formed a shape that you had never made before, sit down." (Most of the dancers should sit down.) "Turn to a person near you and tell him or her which you enjoyed doing more and why – dancing around and making the puzzle shape with the statue or being the statue and waiting to see how another dancer would relate to your shape?"

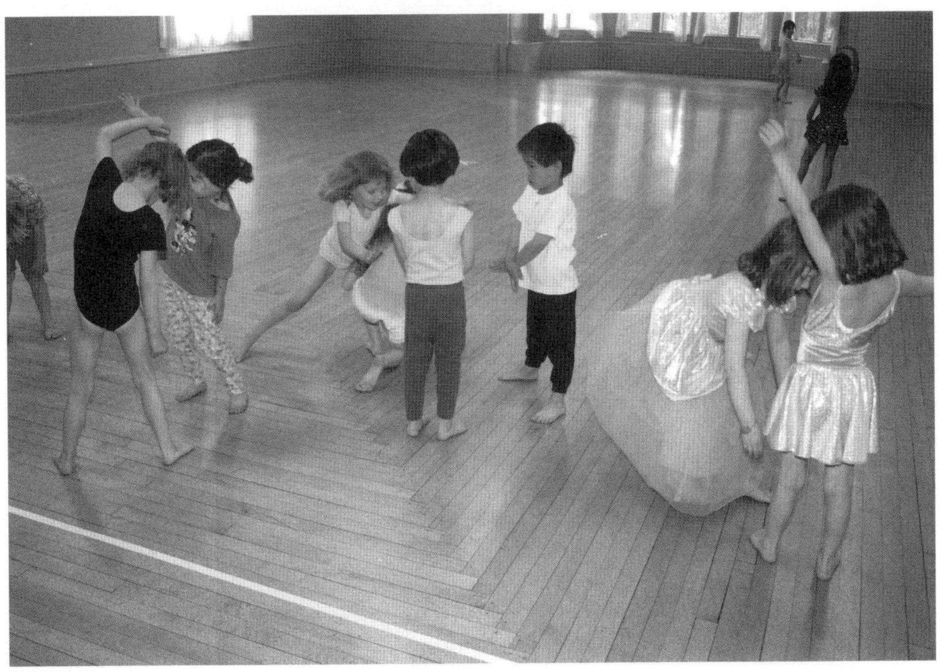

Variations

- This is a favorite activity for dancers ages three through five when done in **pairs**. After a quick demonstration of **puzzle** shapes with a partner, have dancers pair up and make puzzle shapes together, fitting into each other. At the signal, both dancers dance away. They return to each other on your cue and form a new puzzle together. Continue by encouraging dancers to make puzzles on different levels and to dance away using a variety of dance concepts.
- A dancer goes to a statue, says a **preposition** and creates a shape demonstrating that relationship. For example, a dancer says "around" and makes a shape, putting the arms around a leg of a statue. Instead of having dancers think of their own prepositions, call out prepositions and have the dancers all do the same preposition at the same time. This is a good way to see if the students understand prepositions. Fun prepositions include: over, under, around, through, in, out, above, below, on, off, in front and behind.
- Add **stretchy bands:** dancers (without stretchy bands) climb through the negative space made by the statue's stretchy band shape. The statue drops the stretchy band and dances away while the dancer picks up the stretchy band and makes a new statue with the band.

Robotic Shape Museum

This activity requires a prop made from pipe insulation or foam sticks used for swimming (available from many department stores). Cut foam into foot-long pieces. Each dancer outside the museum holds a stick in each hand. Each dances to a statue using the sticks as robotic arms, manipulating the statue into a new shape. The dancer with the sticks copies the new shape just created. The statue takes the sticks and dances away to find a new statue and changes it with the robotic stick arms. This continues until the music ends. This fun activity is a unique experience that molds a person into a new shape with sticks instead of hands. Encourage the robots to reshape legs, heads, hands and spines, as well as arms.

Suggested Music: *Music for Creative Dance, Volume 1V,* #2 or #11

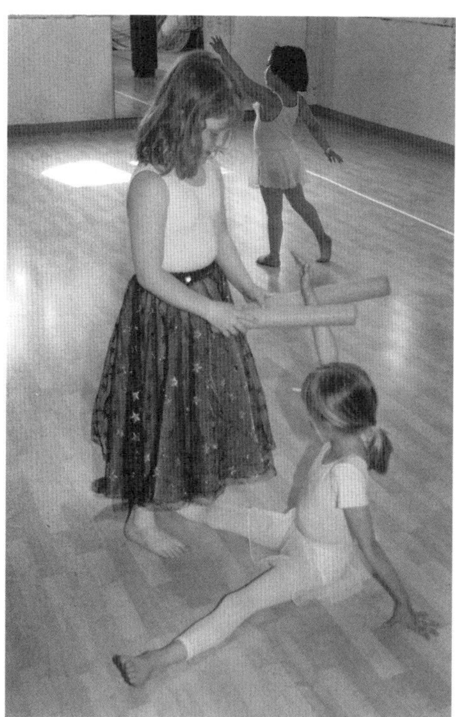

Reflection: "Find a partner and tell each other how you felt during this activity. How was this different from activities where you use your hands to reshape another dancer? Which part did you enjoy more and why – molding the shape or being molded into a new shape? Which part was more challenging?"

Variations

- In this variation, the statue has the robotic arms and the dancer uses them to mold a new statue. The statues hold a stick in each hand. A dancer dances to a statue, takes hold of the ends of the sticks being held by the statue and molds the statue into a new shape. When the new statue is complete, the statue releases the sticks. The dancer, continuing to hold the sticks, copies the newly created statue. This continues until the music ends.
- The dancer molds the statue into a shape with the sticks pointing in a certain direction (forward, backward, right, left, up, down). After the dancer has copied the statue, the statue comes to life and dances away in the direction the sticks are pointing. This is an excellent activity for the concept of Direction.

Aerobic Shape Museum

Statues inside the museum repeat movements in self space, such as twisting, stretching, bending, swinging and jumping in place. Encourage the statues to move on different levels with different rhythms and speeds, recreating movements from the BrainDance. When the music begins, dancers outside the museum enter and copy a statue's movements. After the dancer copies the statue's movements and the statue has become the dancer and danced away, the new statue changes the self space movements.

Suggested Music: *Music for Creative Dance, Volume II*, #2

Symmetry Shape Museum

The statues form symmetrical shapes inside the museum. When the music begins, dancers outside the museum enter and dance to a symmetrical statue. Carefully, using appropriate touch, dancers move one body part of the statue to create an asymmetrical shape. Dancers copy the asymmetrical statue and the statue dances away. The asymmetrical statue waits for a dancer to change it back to a symmetrical statue. Dancers must use their spatial intelligence to look at the statues carefully! If the statue is symmetrical, it must be changed to an asymmetrical shape. If the statue is asymmetrical, it must be made symmetrical. Remind the statues to hold their shapes until someone changes and copies them. They are then free to dance away.

Suggested Music: *Music for Creative Dance, Volume 1V,* #10

Reflection: "Form a symmetrical shape if you find that type more challenging to create. Make an asymmetrical shape if you find that type more challenging. Which was more challenging to recognize? Form that one."

Variation

- Dancers move two body parts, then three or four body parts, to create asymmetrical and symmetrical statues. Encourage experienced dancers to gently bend or twist necks, spines and hips, as well as arms and legs. This will make it more challenging to decide whether a shape is symmetrical or asymmetrical.

Muscle and Joint Shape Museum

Statues stand inside the museum in a neutral position (not in a shape). When the music begins, dancers outside the museum enter and dance through general space around, between, in front of and behind the statues. While dancing, they gently brush the statues' arms, legs, backs or shoulders. As the statues are touched, they move with big, smooth movements, twisting, stretching and swinging larger muscle groups. The statues look like trees blowing in the wind. At the signal, dancers lightly touch joints such as elbows, knees, shoulders, wrists, ankles or backs of necks. As the statues are touched this time, they move those joints. Dancers enjoy watching the statues magically change shape with quick bending or straightening motions. They now look like puppets or robots. Change roles: dancers become statues and statues become dancers.

This is a useful variation for introducing bones and muscles, sharp and smooth Energy or free and bound Flow. Props may be added. Use the foam sticks from Robotic Shape Museum to touch joints and roll smoothly over muscles or scarves to brush muscles and dab at joints.

Suggested Music: *Music for Creative Dance, Volume I,* #1

Reflection: "If you enjoyed moving your joints more, sit down. If you enjoyed moving muscles more, stand up. Turn to a person near you and explain why you chose your answer."

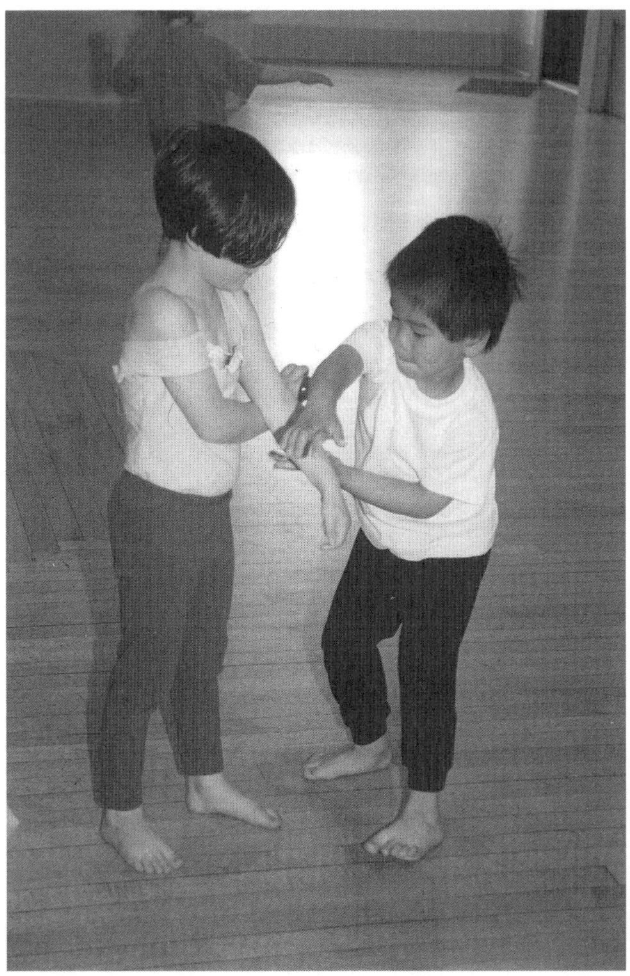

Sculptor and Clay Shape Museum

Statues stand or sit inside the museum in a neutral position (not in a particular shape). When the music begins, dancers outside the museum enter and find a statue to mold. They choose three body parts to move gently to create a new statue. Dancers copy the new statue they just created. The statue is now free to dance away.

Suggested Music: *Music for Creative Dance, Volume I,* #8

Reflection: "If you enjoyed sculpting more, sit down. If you enjoyed being sculpted, stand up. Think of one or two words (i.e., creative, challenging, being touched) that describe why you made your decision. Say the words out loud when I call your name."

Variations

- Dancers touch (instead of manipulate) three of the statue's body parts and the statue chooses how to change shape. The dancer copies the shape the statue created and the statue dances away.
- Sculptor and Clay may be done in pairs. The sculptors might be directed to shape the clay into designated shapes, such as those that describe emotions, letters, numerals, verbs, nouns, adverbs, adjectives, etc. or into shapes of their own choosing. Sculptors should always copy the statue they made, which is the signal for the statues to come to life, dance away and then return to mold their partner into a new shape.

- **Erosion Pairs:** Dancers take turns being the mountain (clay), the wind and rain (sculptor). One dancer forms a mountain. The other dancer dances once around the mountain with lots of flow, as the wind and rain erode the mountain. The dancer stops in front of the mountain and moves one body part to make the mountain smaller and lower (erosion). The sculptor copies the new mountain; the statue then comes to life and flows once around the new mountain. Dancers continue to alternate between being the mountain and the wind and rain that erode the mountain until both dancers are small "rocks" on the ground. They stand up and repeat the erosion together, mirroring each other as they recreate the shapes they made moving from big, high mountains to small, low rocks. This activity is fun for exploring free and bound Flow, Size, Level, Relationships and Focus. When exploring Focus, the mountain might have eyes closed.
- **Action and Reaction Pairs:** One dancer stands in self space with eyes closed. The other dancer gently touches a body part while the dancer with eyes closed moves this body part toward the touch. After five to ten touches on the body, the partners change roles. The second time, the dancer with eyes closed moves the body part away from the touch. Reflect on the difference in feeling between moving away and toward the touch.

Emotion Shape Museum

This exploration is based on an idea by dance educator and author Helen Landalf.

Statues inside the museum make small, round, low shapes scattered through the space like seeds. Dancers outside the museum enter and "water" a statue by gently stroking the back of the statue three times. The "seed" grows slowly into a full-body shape that describes an emotion, imagining that the feeling starts growing in the toes and fills the whole body until standing in a clear shape. The dancer who watered the seed then copies the emotion statue and the statue dances away. The new one shrinks to a seed and waits to be watered, and the cycle begins again.

Suggested Music: *Music for Creative Dance Volume I,* #15

Reflection: "Who tried on a new emotion or one that you seldom feel? What was that emotion? Form a shape that represents it. How did it feel to copy someone else's emotion? Share your feelings with a friend. Was the emotion clear? How did it feel to let go of your emotion and dance away? What was your favorite part of this exploration?"

Variation

- Young dancers do this in pairs. The teacher directs the action by commanding, "Water the seed three times: one, two, three. Now Seed, grow into an angry shape. Dancers, copy the shape. Seeds dance away. Shapes melt into a seed. Dancers, go water your seed three times." After directing the action through four rounds of watering and growing into specified emotions, allow the dancers to do the activity on their own.

> ***Teaching Tip:*** *It is helpful to demonstrate the Emotion Shape Museum with two or three dancers while giving directions. Before beginning this improvisation, brainstorm many emotions with the students or create a chart of emotions to which the students can refer.*

Illusion Shape Museum

This exploration is based on an idea by dance educator Dee Winterton.

Pairs of dancers inside the museum create "illusion" statues: one of the dancers is a "pedestal" and the other a statue resting on the pedestal. The statue creates the illusion of being dependent on the pedestal by leaning or balancing on the pedestal in a creative shape. The individual dancers outside the museum enter and go to a pedestal/statue pair. When the dancer touches the pedestal gently, the pedestal melts away and leaves the statue balanced in space! Then the pedestal dances away. Meanwhile, the statue changes into a pedestal and the dancer becomes the new statue. The systematic cycle is pedestal becomes dancer when touched; statue becomes pedestal after balancing; and dancer becomes statue balancing on the new pedestal.

Suggested Music: *Music for Creative Dance, Volume II,* #10

Reflection: "Find a friend and share your feelings. Which part of the activity did you find more challenging and why – being the pedestal or the statue? Do you think you created more realistic illusions as the improvisation went on? What did you do to improve?"

> ***Teaching Tip:*** *A demonstration is worth a thousand words! Keep reviewing directions as the dancers explore. Encourage experienced dancers to create more realistic illusions by making more challenging shapes. There is some weight sharing in the improvisation, but statues are ultimately responsible for their own weight – thus the illusion.*
>
> *A basic way to divide the dancers is to ask them to form trios by connecting elbows in nine counts. Ask one dancer from each trio to go to the other end of the room to be outside the museum. The two remaining dancers form a pedestal and a statue inside the museum.*

Variations

- As a lead-up to the exploration described above, younger dancers may work in pairs. One dancer is the pedestal and one is the statue. After a few seconds of holding the shapes, the pedestal dances away and the statue tries to balance without the pedestal. The dancer returns to the statue, roles are then exchanged.
- Pairs form illusion statues in the museum. Other pairs enter the museum, dancing together while lightly connected by fingertips of one hand. A dancing pair copies an illusion pair, which allows the illusion pair to come to life and dance away while lightly connected to each other. After copying an illusion pair, the dancers may form a new illusion statue.

Creating Additional Explorations

Create more explorations by tweaking familiar explorations, using the following ideas:

Add/Subtract/Exchange Props

- **Add** a prop to an exploration such as Shape Museum. Dancers dance with a streamer and then drape it on the statue before copying the statue. The statue comes to life and dances off with the streamer. Statues form shapes with stretchy bands. The dancer copies the shape without a stretchy band. Then the statue dances away and leaves the stretchy band behind for the new statue to use for a new shape.

- **Subtract** a prop from an exploration in which it is frequently used, such as scarves to explore Flow. Encourage the dancers to use only their bodies and provide images and conceptual cues to encourage movement without the prop.
- **Exchange** one prop for another. If stretchy bands are frequently used when exploring a particular concept, next time try dancing with the plastic. Dancers will find new ways of exploring the concept by using different props.

Combine Two Concepts

Exploring two concepts at the same time helps teachers and students discover similarities and differences between the two, especially for new activities.

- **Size and Level:** A pair of dancers forms shapes on opposite levels while stretching a stretchy band into a big shape. Another pair, dancing close together with small movements while changing levels, moves through the empty space created by the stretchy band. The dancers holding the band let it pop into a small shape and dance away changing levels. Then the "small" dancers pick it up and stretch it into a big shape.
- **Balance and Speed:** Dancers move slowly in self space while balancing on one body part. Then they dance quickly through space until stopping on cue to hold a balanced shape. After exploring this activity for a few minutes, dancers try moving quickly while balanced on one body part in self space and then move through space slowly, stopping on cue to hold a balanced shape. This may also be done with a partner by having the dancers mirror each other in the self space section and dancing away in the general space section. Discuss whether it was easier to balance after moving quickly or slowly.

Mix and Match Music

- Use the music generally played for Levels to explore Size, Flow or Focus to discover new ideas.
- Try an instrumental piece instead of a song and vice versa.
- Vary the music tempo. Sometimes do Shape Museums to slow music and other times to faster music. Mirror to slow music and then shadow to faster music.

Combine Two Explorations

The second time you explore a concept (or when working with experienced dancers), combine two favorite explorations such as:

- **"Opposite Lands"** and **"Sculptor and Clay:"** One land could be "Puppet Land" in which pairs take turns changing each other's shapes by touching (or moving) three body parts. The opposite land is "Human Land" where the dancers move all their body parts freely.
- **"Fences"** and **"Shadowing:"** Pairs shadow each other as they travel along the fence of shapes. The leader connects to the last person in the fence and the shadow has to copy that shape before connecting to the partner. When they break away to reconnect, the follower becomes the leader.

Change the Spatial Design

- Try familiar "Opposite Land" explorations using the whole space rather than alternating halves.
- Try familiar explorations usually done in scattered space in an "Opposite Land" format.
- Try "Machine" explorations in "Fence" formations and vice versa.
- Shadow when you usually Mirror and Mirror when you usually Shadow.

Form New Relationships

- Do familiar individual activities in pairs.
- Do pair activities in trios or quartets.
- Vary group activities by dividing the group in half. Alternate by having half of the students dance while the other half remains still.
- Combine individual explorations with partner activities. For example, have the dancers dance in general space, focusing on one element of a concept (light weight) and then form shapes with other dancers in self space, focusing on the opposite (strong weight). Or dance as individuals during the first section of the music and then shadow a partner during the second one.

In Summary

Exploring the fifteen dance concepts through a directed and free approach engages all learners:

- Integrating supplemental concepts such as social skills, math and language arts increases learning.
- Supportive, appropriate music is essential for motivating students and generating new ideas.
- Props add visual and tactile elements to the explorations.
- Exploring concepts by oneself develops creativity and confidence.
- Exploring concepts in pairs and small groups develops collaborative skills (interpersonal intelligence) that increases an individual's movement vocabulary (bodily-kinesthetic intelligence).
- Reflection following an exploration develops self-awareness (intrapersonal intelligence) and encourages body-brain connections.

After the fun and excitement of Exploring the Concept, students are ready to gain a deeper understanding of the concept by using it to practice skills and movement combinations in the Developing Skills section of the lesson.

No matter how many times you do an exploration, it never has to get old. ~ Aurora, age 11
Dance isn't just about steps, it's about imagination. ~ Emily, age 9

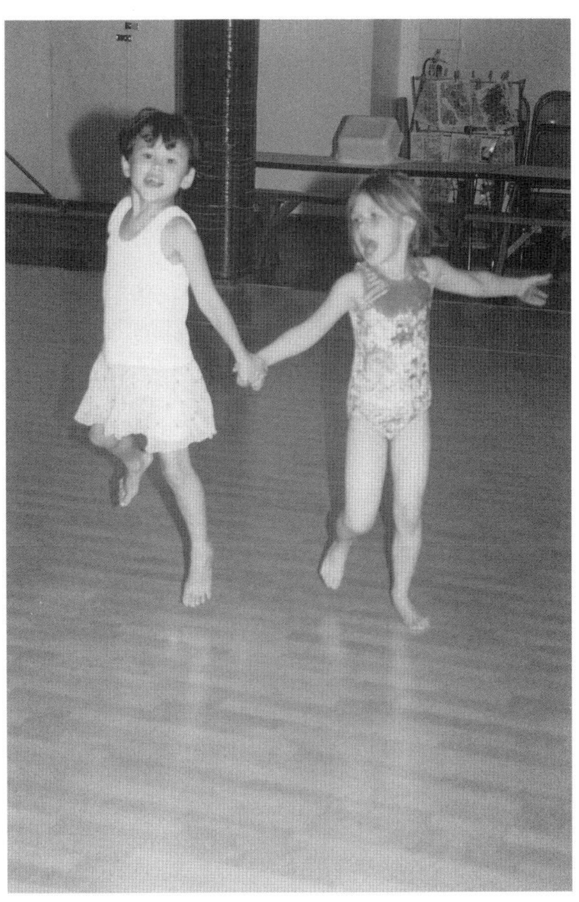

Notes

Chapter Three

Lesson Plan Section 3: Developing Skills

In this chapter:

MOVEMENT SKILLS

A Sampling

Locomotor Movements

Roll
Fly
Walk
Creep
Crawl
Run
Skip
Slide
Polka
March
Stomp
Gallop
Prance
Jump
Hop
Step-hop
Grapevine
Waltz Run
Schottische
Tiptoe
Leap

Nonlocomotor Movements

Bend
Fall
Swing
Twist
Push
Bounce
Press
Turn
Balance
Wiggle
Lunge
Stretch
Throw
Wring
Dab
Spin
Sway
Slash
Clap
Tip
Curl
Lift
Flick
Poke
Freeze
Shake
Pull
Dodge
Fall
Burst
Carve
Glide
Float
Punch
Melt
Rock

DEVELOPING SKILLS

Applicable Dance Standards

The following standards from the *National Standards for Dance Education* will be achieved through the activities in this chapter:

- **Identifying and demonstrating movement elements and skills in performing dance**
- **Demonstrating and understanding dances in various cultures and historical periods**

Chapter Introduction

Once dancers have explored the lesson's concept, they are ready to develop movement skills integrating the concept. Learning and practicing skills develop and fine-tune the dancer's body. Improvisation and problem solving develop the dancer's mind. Integrating these two concepts of brain and body into a dance class creates a whole dancer.

In the Developing Skills section of the dance class, practicing basic locomotor (traveling) and nonlocomotor (axial) skills requires ten to twenty minutes. In classes over one hour, the time is extended to twenty to thirty minutes to include more dance technique.

Combinations of movements (phrases, routines, patterns and folk dances) will also be learned during the Developing Skills section. Practicing movement combinations helps dancers develop transitional flow. Transitional flow is the "glue" between movements that turns separate actions into a phrase or dance. Dancers also practice the important skills of phrasing, sequencing and memory. Leaps and turns, so valuable for vestibular development, may be introduced as discrete skills or included in movement combinations. This section is excellent for practicing partnering skills.

The Developing Skills section is similar to the Warming Up section and is more teacher-directed than Exploring the Concept. There is less problem solving and less novelty. This part involves repetition for hard-wiring specific skills that build the dancer's instrument – the body.

However, remember that novelty sparks the attention needed to learn and remember skills. Integrating the dance concept into the lesson will accomplish this goal. For example, practice skipping in different Directions one week, with changes in Size the next and on different Levels the following week.

Integrating a dance concept into the teaching of skills encourages dancers to perform in different styles with varying emotions. Dancers of all ages gain a higher level of proficiency when they practice skills through many different concepts. The conceptual approach is extremely helpful for developing the skills of very young dancers who are not as enamored of practicing steps as are older dancers. The integration of a new concept each week makes practicing basic skills more enjoyable and brain-compatible for everyone.

This section of the lesson plan needs the most adjustment for age and level of experience. The dance teacher needs to be aware of the physical and cognitive development of the students to present the skills that are most appropriate at each level. Suggestions for age appropriate material appear in this text, but ultimately every teacher will discover what works with each group. Student behavior and progress will be the best guide. Are they challenged? Are they frustrated? Are they injury-free? Is their technique improving?

In *Creative Dance for All Ages*, two chapters are devoted to Locomotor and Nonlocomotor Movement. Many skills are explained in the context of both development and dance concepts. Rather than repeat that information, a Dance Skills chart listing movements for students to practice is provided below.

Dance Skills

This chart suggests possible movements and skills. Teachers may add others that they enjoy.

With ages two through five, introduce and practice the following skills:					
Locomotor (Traveling) Skills					
crawl/slither	creep	roll	walk	march	stomp
run	fly	tiptoe	leap	jump	hop
gallop	slide	skip (age four +)			
Nonlocomotor (Axial) Skills					
bend	twist	stretch	swing	melt	fall
shake	turn	push	pull	clap	float
flick	sway	rock	tip	balance	wiggle
poke	punch	freeze	bounce	kick	stillness

With ages six through eight, continue practicing the previous skills and add the following steps:
Locomotor (Traveling) Skills prance step-hop hinge-slide skate waddle shuffle grapevine (age 8+) waltz run (triplet) schottische (three steps and a hop) pas de cheval ("step of the horse" – a pawing action with one foot) pas de chat ("step of the cat" – a soft spring from one foot to the other with bent knees) chaineé turns (continuous turns that travel through space, creating a "chain-like" path) **Nonlocomotor (Axial) Skills** lunge dab slash glide burst spin rise sink grow shrink dodge whirl twitch jab explode shiver contract curl carve sway spiral

With ages nine through adult, continue practicing the previous skills and add the following steps:
polka mazurka leap turn barrel turn chest roll side fall front fall split fall back fall pirouette sissonne (take off from two feet and land on one foot) assemblé (take off from one foot and land on two feet)

Formations for Practicing Skills and Movement Combinations

Practice separate skills and movement combinations in many formations to introduce novelty into this repetitive part of class. Moving in different formations helps dancers develop spatial awareness while encouraging the use of different floor patterns in the dancers' choreography.

A quick way to organize dancers into formations is to use counts. For example, "By the time I count to sixteen, form four lines with four people in each line. Look at the lines as they form and see where you are needed." All students move right away instead of waiting for the you as the teacher to count them off. Other examples include, "We need five groups with four or five people in each group. Where are you needed?" "Form one big circle around the X in ten counts by connecting elbows with people on either side of you."

Scattered formations and lines work well with young children. As students develop in age and experience, begin to add circles, opposing lines and other variations as described on the following pages.

Dancers practice skills and combinations:

Scattered through the space (as individuals, partners, trios or quartets).

 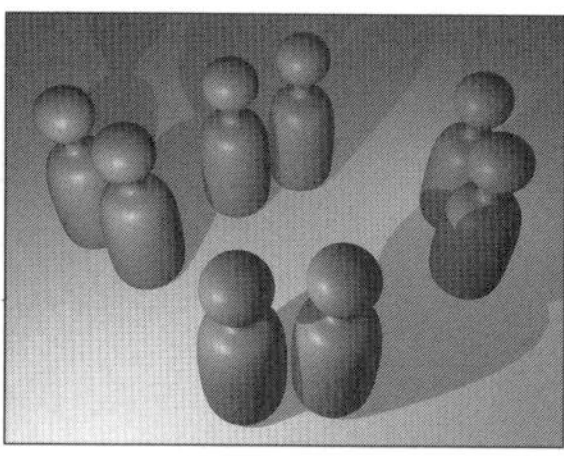 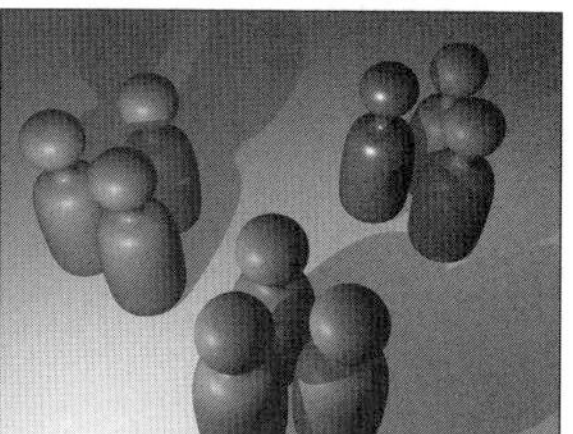

In horizontal lines (shoulder to shoulder) moving from one side of the room to the other.

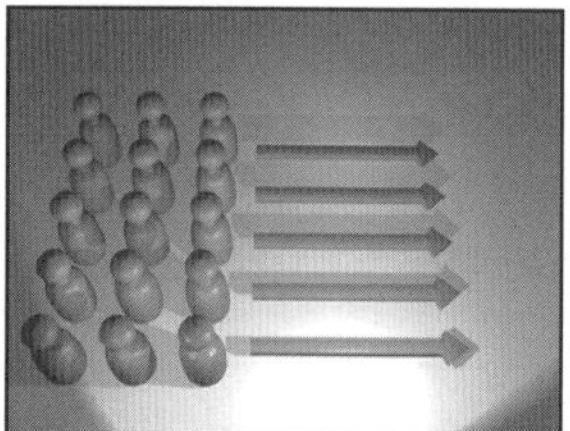

In opposing lines, moving toward and away from each other.

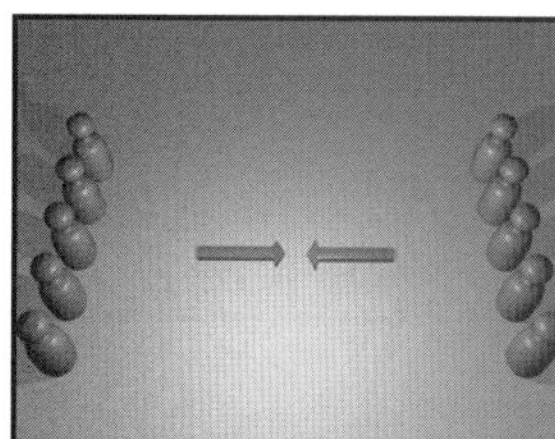 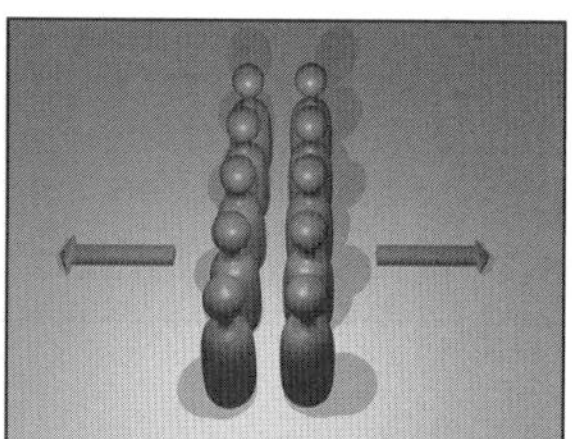

In opposing lines, moving toward and then passing through each other.

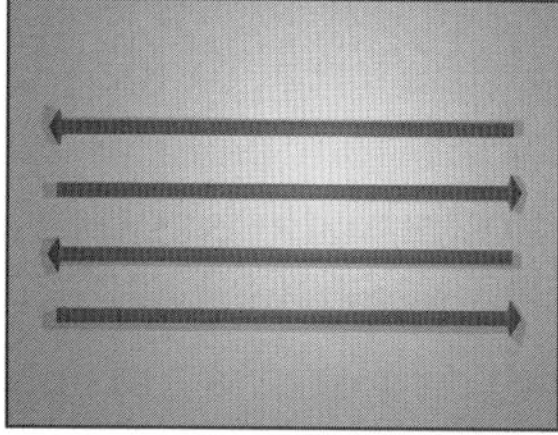

In follow-the-leader lines of three to five dancers, moving straight across the room or weaving through space.

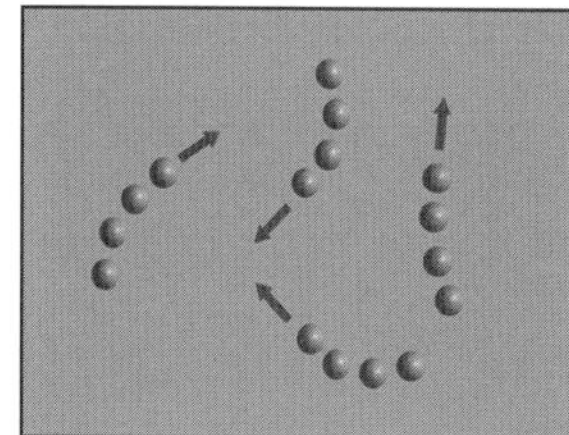

Moving from one corner to the opposite corner.

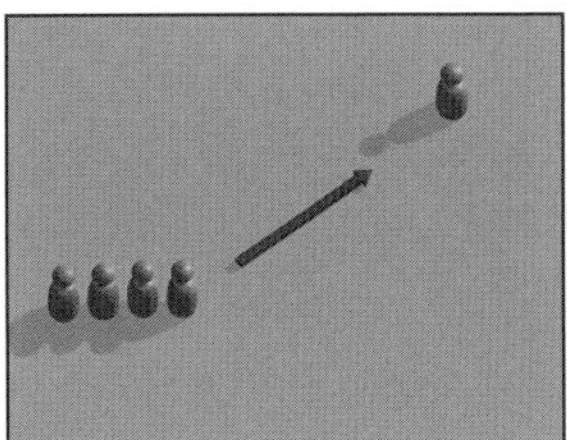

In a horseshoe formation, starting apart and coming together, starting together, going apart or in a single horseshoe (not shown).

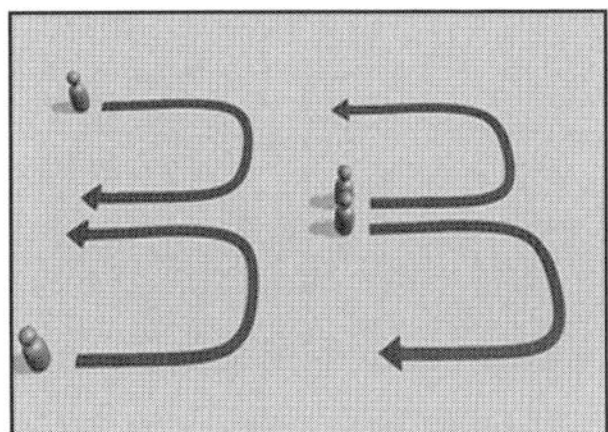

Moving in a figure eight pattern, connecting all corners of the space.

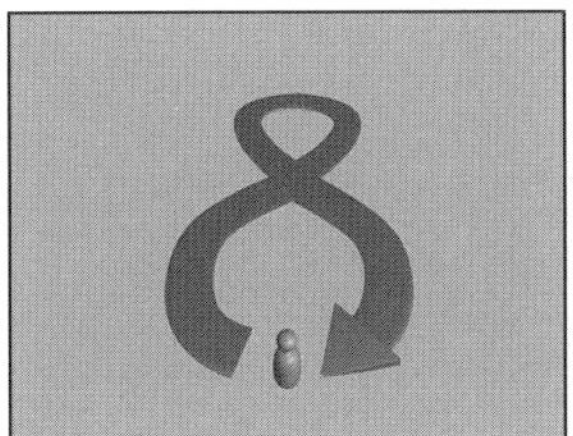

In an oval, rectangular or square formation around the edges of the room.

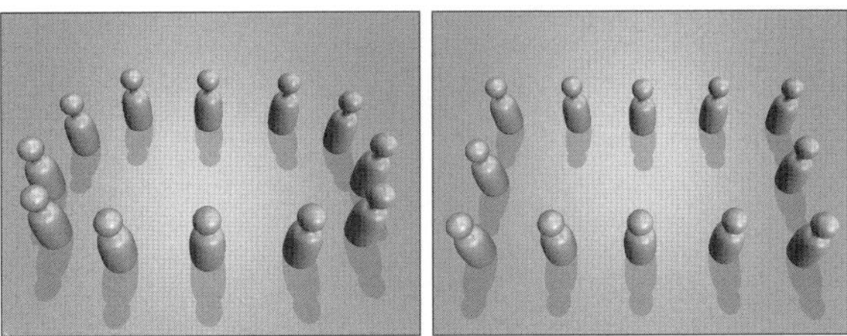

In a single circle, holding hands or not holding hands.

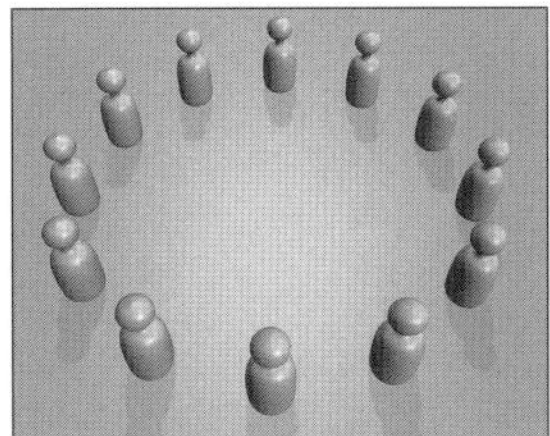

In concentric circles.

In small circles of four to eight people.

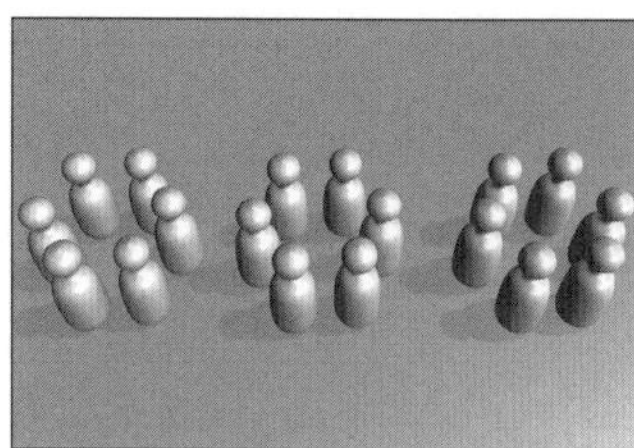

In triangles, with a leader in front and two followers behind and side by side (rotate to change leaders).

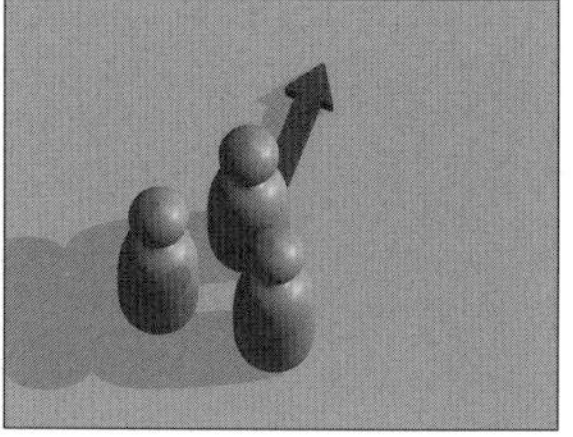

In diamonds.

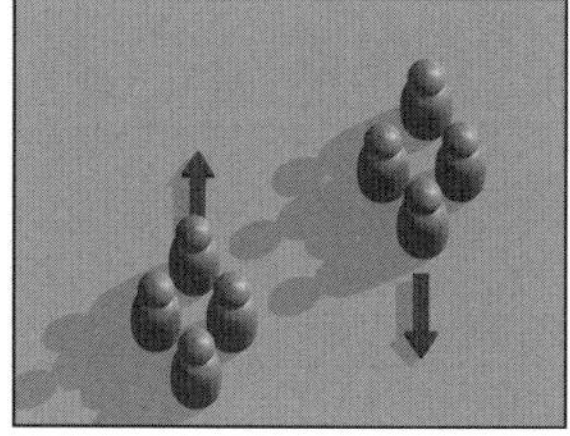

One group practices the skill or combination in half the space while another group watches. Alternate dancing and observing without changing places.

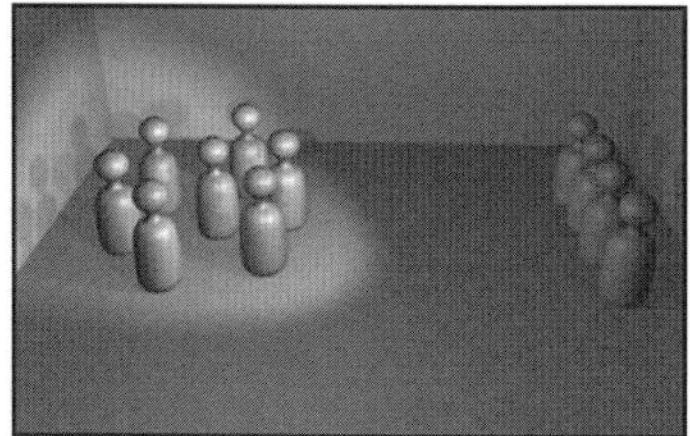

Basic Skill Development

Developing single skills through repetition can feel like drilling mathematics. Going over and over the same skill until a student is proficient before moving on to the next is not brain-compatible. The brain continues to process information when a person is asleep. Introduce a skill or combination one day, then practice it on subsequent days to help the brain remember. This process locks in the skill or combination more successfully than trying to perfect it in one class or rehearsal. Varying ways of practicing skills creates the challenge and novelty needed to get the brain's attention for learning.

Practice basic skills

- through the dance concepts.
- in many different formations.
- with a partner.
- to different accompaniment – music, drum beats, counts, body percussion or words.
- with a prop.
- within the context of a simple combination of familiar skills.

Skills to Include in Every Class: Leaps and Turns

Leaping and turning – favorite parts of a dance class for all ages – develop the Vestibular System, so include these basic skills in all of your classes. *Creative Dance for All Ages* contains many suggestions for leaping and turning exercises through dance concepts.

Young dancers from ages two through seven need objects to leap over, such as small cones, milk or egg cartons, spots cut from yoga mats, shoes or any other object that is safe to leap over. Set up leaping courses for these ages in the various pathways found in the Formations chart. Turns can be easily included within the leaping course.

Older dancers may practice complex leaping patterns without objects. Combining different numbers of leaps with runs challenges these dancers. Practicing leaps with turns and twists increases the challenge, as does adding shapes with special arm movements. Combining leaps with other forms of springing off the ground adds more variety and challenges.

Have all ages practice leaps and turns through the lesson's dance concept, using the following ideas to inspire their creativity. When using objects to leap over, set them up in ways that encourage and support the dance concept. For example, when practicing leaps on different Levels, stack several cartons on top of each other or use cones of varying heights.

- **Place**: Combine leaps and turns through general space with turns and jumps in self space.
- **Size**: Practice narrow leaps and turns, wide leaps and turns.
- **Level**: Practice low, middle and high leaps and turns.
- **Direction**: Older dancers practice side leaps and leaps that change directions in the air, while younger dancers practice forward leaps with arms in different directions.
- **Pathway**: Leap in straight, curved and zigzag pathways to practice body mechanics involving changes in focus, weight shifts and upper body shapes.
- **Focus**: Practice looking out (instead of down), while leaping; practice "spotting" while turning.
- **Speed**: Alternate quick, small leaps and turns with slower, bigger leaps and turns.
- **Rhythm**: For older dancers, create rhythmic patterns by combining leaps, runs and turns: leap, leap, run, run, run, leap, turn, turn (for older dancers). Put four cones fairly close together and one cone farther apart to create a pattern for younger dancers.
- **Energy**: Alternate soaring leaps with bursting leaps, practice leaps and turns with smooth, sharp and shaky arm movements.
- **Weight**: Combine light leaps and strong turns with strong leaps and light turns.
- **Flow**: Alternate continuous leaps and turns with leaps and turns followed by stillness or held shapes.
- **Body Parts**: Practice leaps and turns that are initiated by different body parts or are performed with a special body part focus.
- **Body Shapes:** Practice leaps and turns with straight, curved and angular arms, legs and torsos. Younger dancers enjoy making letters like "T," "O" and "Y" with their arms as they leap.

- **Relationships**: Practice leaps over people and objects, leaps and turns with partners and in small groups and leaps and turns that move away from partners and back together.
- **Balance**: Practice leaping and turning with a vertical spine, as well as leaps and turns that seem to go off balance and are more horizontal, such as barrel turns. Younger dancers may practice balancing after turning or alternate leaping with balanced shapes.

Obstacle Courses for Toddlers through Seven Year Olds

Young dancers develop their brains through sensory-motor activities. Obstacle courses encourage this development while practicing the basic skills of walking, running, jumping, hopping, crawling and creeping. Use whatever objects are at hand to create challenging obstacle courses. Encourage parents to create obstacle courses at home, it is much more beneficial to move along an obstacle course than to watch television!

For ages walking through four, set up a variety of objects in an oval, figure eight or horseshoe. For ages five through seven, spend more time practicing leaping, but include one or two special objects, such as a bench and tunnel, for novelty and attention. Have dancers move through the course several times in one direction, then several times in the opposite direction, receiving positive feedback as their skill level increases.

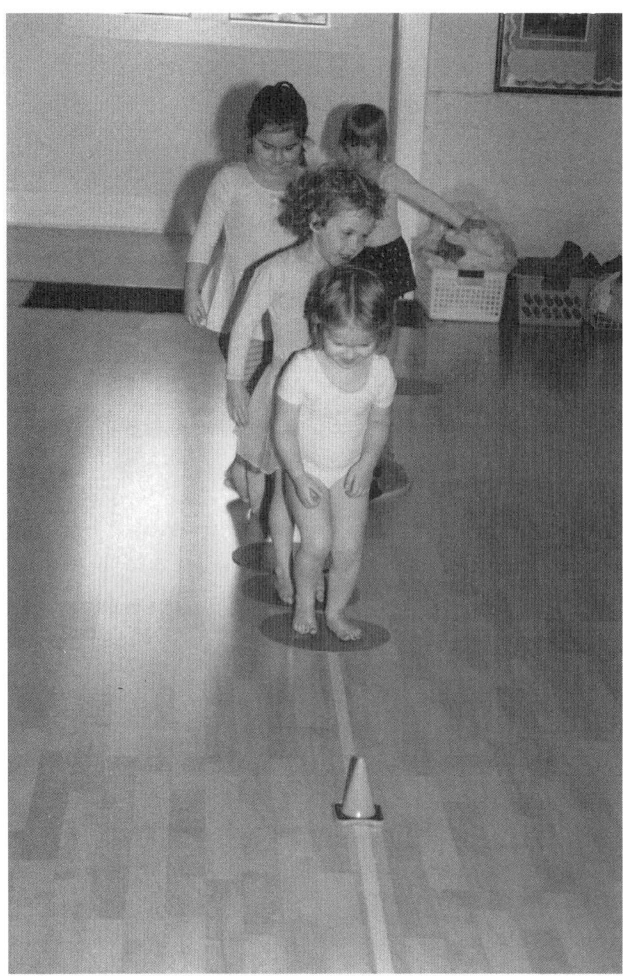

Objects that can be included in obstacle courses

- Small and medium-sized traffic cones (or milk cartons) to leap over.
- Large traffic cones to dance around or to move between as in a slalom course.
- Picnic benches to walk across and jump off.
- Spots (about twelve inches in diameter cut from thin yoga mats) placed in various pathways for dancers to tiptoe, walk, run or jump on.
- Piano benches to crawl onto and off.
- Small, stable stools to step on and jump off.
- Folding gym mats used for rolling or made into a triangular tunnel for crawling through.
- Sturdy portable ballet barres for hanging to develop arm strength.
- Thick, spongy mats for jumping.
- Objects to crawl under and over, such as a stretchy band strung between two large cones.
- Therapy balls, corralled by hula-hoops, for bouncing and rolling on.
- Hula-hoops for jumping in, circling around or crawling through.
- Very large scarves for hiding under.
- Big buckets (placed on their sides) for sitting in and rolling back and forth for vestibular development.

Combining Movements

Besides practicing basic skills, dancers need to perform movements in combinations or patterns. Learning and practicing movement phrases of varying lengths develops sequencing, memory and flow which leads to the ability to learn and perform complete dances.

Combinations Using Rhymes and Songs for Ages Two through Seven

The use of rhymes and rhythm while practicing locomotor and nonlocomotor skills stimulates language development and beat competency. Encourage young dancers to sing along with you.

1. To the tune of "Frère Jacques"

Focusing on **Place**
"Now we're walking; now we're walking; hop, hop, hop; hop, hop, hop.
Running, running, running; running, running, running; now we stop; now we stop!
Now we're sliding, now we're sliding; jump, jump, jump; jump, jump, jump.
Running, running, running; running, running, running; bump, bump, bump; bump, bump, bump.
Now we're turning, now we're turning; creep, creep, creep; creep, creep, creep.
Running, running, running; running, running, running; now we sleep; now we sleep."

Focusing on **Direction**
"Marching backward; marching backward; hop, hop, hop; hop, hop, hop.
Running, running forward; running, running forward; now we stop; now we stop!
Sliding sideways, sliding sideways; jump, jump, jump; jump, jump, jump.
Running, running backward; running, running backward; bump, bump, bump; bump, bump, bump.
Turning around, turning around; creep, creep, creep; creep, creep, creep.
Running, running sideways; running, running sideways; now we sleep; now we sleep."

Focusing on **Weight**
"Tiptoe lightly; tiptoe lightly; hop, hop, hop; hop, hop, hop.
Stomping, stomping strongly; stomping, stomping strongly; now we stop; now we stop!
Floating lightly, floating lightly; jump, jump, jump; jump, jump, jump.
Stomping, stomping strongly; stomping, stomping strongly; bump, bump, bump; bump, bump, bump.
Flicking lightly, flicking lightly; creep, creep, creep; creep, creep, creep.
Stomping, stomping strongly; stomping, stomping strongly; now we sleep; now we sleep."

Focusing on **Pathways**
"Walking straight path, walking straight path; hop, hop, hop; hop, hop, hop.
Running, running curvy; running, running curvy; now we stop; now we stop!
Sliding straight path, sliding straight path; jump, jump, jump; jump, jump, jump.
Running, running curvy; running, running curvy; bump, bump, bump; bump, bump, bump.
Turn in self space, turn in self space; creep, creep, creep; creep, creep, creep.
Running, running curvy; running, running curvy; now we sleep; now we sleep."

Create combinations of this pattern using other concepts such as Size, Energy and Speed.

2. To the tune of "Row, Row, Row Your Boat"

Substitute other locomotor and nonlocomotor skills for *italicized* words. Substitute other dance concepts for the words in **bold**.

"*Skip, skip, skip* your feet, *skip* them on the ground.
Swing, swing, swing your arms, *turn* yourself around.

"*Stomp, stomp, stomp* your feet **strongly** on the ground.
Flicking, flicking, flicking, flicking, **lightly** turn around.

"*Kick, kick, kick* your feet **sharply** down the street.
Floating, floating, floating **smoothly,** make a shape that's neat!

"*Run, run, run* your feet **quickly** down the street.
Stretching, stretching, stretching **slowly** in a shape that's neat!"

3. Use the song "This is the Way…" to explore many movements and concepts. Create different verses using one concept, changing body parts and movements.

Weight
"This is the way we stamp our feet, stamp our feet, stamp our feet.
This is the way we stamp our feet so very, very strongly!
This is the way we float our arms, float our arms, float our arms.
This is the way we float our arms so very, very lightly.
This is the way punch our knees, punch our knees, punch our knees.
This is the way punch our knees so very, very strongly!
This is the way we dab our finger, dab our finger, dab our finger.
This is the way we dab our finger so very, very lightly!"

Speed
"This is the way we kick our feet, kick our feet, kick our feet.
This is the way we kick our feet so very, very quickly!
This is the way we twist our arms, twist our arms, twist our arms.
This is the way we twist our arms so very, very slowly.
This is the way we shake our whole body, shake our whole body, shake our whole body.
This is the way we shake our whole body so very, very quickly!"

Level
"This is the way we stretch our arms, stretch our arms, stretch our arms.
This is the way we stretch our arms way up high.
This is the way we crawl on the floor, crawl on the floor, crawl on the floor.
This is the way we crawl on the floor way down low."

4. Perform these movements to the tune of "Skip to My Lou." This version focuses on **Direction**. Substitute other steps and dance concepts depending on the needs of the students.

"Skip, skip, skip to the front; skip, skip, skip to the front; skip, skip, skip to the front;
Skip to the front, my dancers.
"Dance in the general space, how do you do? Dance in the general space, how do you do?
Dance in the general space, how do you do? Make a shape, my dancers.
"Jump, jump, jump to the back; jump, jump, jump to the back; jump, jump, jump to the back;
Jump to the back, my dancers.
"Dance in your self space, how do you do? Dance in your self space, how do you do?
Dance in your self space, how do you do? Make a shape, my dancers.
"Slide, slide, slide to the left; slide, slide, slide to the left; slide, slide, slide to the left;
Slide to the left, my dancers.
"Dance in the general space, how do you do? Dance in the general space, how do you do?
Dance in the general space, how do you do? Make a shape, my dancers.
"Slide, slide, slide to the right; slide, slide, slide to the right; slide, slide, slide to the right;
Slide to the right, my dancers.
"Dance in your self space, how do you do? Dance in your self space, how do you do?
Dance in your self space, how do you do? Make a shape, my dancers.
"Stretch, stretch, stretch way up; stretch, stretch, stretch way up; stretch, stretch, stretch way up; Stretch way up, my dancers.
"Dance in the general space, how do you do? Dance in the general space, how do you do?
Dance in the general space, how do you do? Make a shape, my dancers.
"Bend, bend, bend way down; bend, bend, bend way down; bend, bend, bend way down,
Bend way down, my dancers.
"Dance in your self space, how do you do? Dance in your self space, how do you do?
Dance in your self space, how do you do? Make a shape, my dancers."

5. Sing "Old MacDonald" and name many body parts and actions.

"Old MacDonald had some feet, e, i, e, i, o.
And with those feet he liked to jump, e, i, e, i, o.
With a jump, jump here and a jump, jump there,
Here a jump, there a jump, everywhere a jump, jump.
Old MacDonald had some feet, e, i, e, i, o.

"Old MacDonald had some arms, e, i, e, i, o.
And with those arms he liked to poke, e, i, e, i, o.
With a poke, poke here and a poke, poke there;
Here a poke, there a poke, everywhere a poke, poke.
Old MacDonald had some arms, e, i, e, i, o.

"Old MacDonald had some legs, e, i, e, i, o.
And with those legs he liked to kick, e, i, e, i, o.
With a kick, kick here and a kick, kick there;
Here a kick, there a kick, everywhere a kick, kick.
Old MacDonald had some legs, e i, e i, o.

"Old MacDonald had a head, e, i, e, i, o.
And with his head he liked to nod, e, i, e, i, o.
With a nod, nod here and a nod, nod there;
Here a nod, there a nod, everywhere a nod, nod.
Old MacDonald had a head, e, i, e, i, o."

6. Perform these movements to the tune "Clap Your Hands." Focus on one concept and call out different actions. Change the speed, pitch and rhythm of the voice to accommodate the actions.

Speed
"Shake, shake, shake your hands, shake your hands so quickly.
Stretch, stretch, stretch your legs, stretch your legs so slowly.
Kick, kick, kick your feet, kick your feet so quickly.
Press, press, press your hands, press your hands so slowly."

Weight
"Stamp, stamp, stamp your feet, stamp your feet so strongly.
Tap, tap, tap your toes, tap your toes so lightly.
Punch, punch, punch your fists, punch your fists so strongly.
Float, float, float your arms, float your arms so lightly."

Level
"Jump, jump, jump your legs, jump your legs up high.
Slap, slap, slap the floor, slap the floor down low.
Poke, poke, poke your fingers, poke your fingers high.
Slide, slide, slide your feet, slide your feet down low."

7. Practice movements and rhyming words at the same time. The last two words in each line are emphasized. Allow these words more time to create a rhythm pattern. Allow one count for each of the first four words, two counts for each of the final two words, or a rhythm that works with the words. It is the rhythm that is important, not the counts. Ask the dancers for creative ways to dramatize the rhyming words. Use a dramatic voice and encourage the dancers to speak with you.

Words that end in "op"
"Gallop, gallop, gallop, gallop, mop! mop!
Turn, turn, turn, turn, pop! pop!
Slide, slide, slide, slide, flop! flop!
Jump, jump, jump, jump, stop! stop!"

Words that end in "ip"
"Hop, hop, hop, hop, tip! tip!
Creep, creep, creep, creep, flip, flip!
Float, float, float, float, slip! slip!
Punch, punch, punch, punch, drip! drip!"

Words that end in "ing"
"Skip, skip, skip, skip, spring! spring!
Roll, roll, roll, roll, fling, fling!
Leap, leap, leap, leap, ring! ring!
Poke, poke, poke, poke, sing! sing!"

8. Create basic chants for different body parts. Vary the rhythm. For young children, choose one four-line chant and repeat it several times. For older children, add a new four-line chant each week for three to four weeks to create a longer combination. Encourage the dancers to chant along with you. An underlying drumbeat, recorded or live, is fun for added accompaniment.

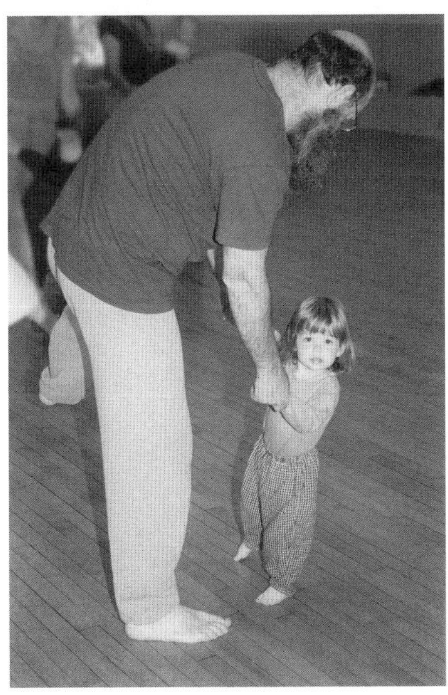

"Legs, legs, legs, legs	Kick legs four times.
Hands, hands, hands, hands	Chop with hands four times.
Knees, knees, knees, knees	March four steps.
Elbows, elbows."	Circle elbows slowly two times.
"Feet, feet, feet, feet	Jump four times.
Hips move slowly	Circle hips once slowly.
Toes, toes, toes, toes	Tiptoe four times.
Shake your head so very quickly."	Shake head quickly eight times.
"Hips, hips, hips, hips	Wiggle hips side to side four times.
Shoulders, shoulders	Lift shoulders up once and press down once.
Foot, foot, foot, foot	Hop four times on one foot or twice on the right foot and twice on the left foot.
Ten toes balance."	Balance in a shape for four counts.
"Legs, legs, legs, legs	Slide or gallop four times.
Backbone, backbone	Twist right and left.
Hands, hands, hands, hands	Clap hands four times.
Run your feet so very quickly."	Run eight little steps.

9. Try these rhymes and create new ones. Repeat four to five times; vary by adding Direction, Pathway, Speed or Energy or by dancing with and without a partner. I learned the first listed rhyme from colleague Carolyn Rosenfeld.

"Gallop and gallop and gallop and go, gallop and gallop and gallop and whoa! (forward)
Gallop and gallop and gallop and go, gallop and gallop and gallop and whoa! (backward)
Gallop and gallop and gallop and go, gallop and gallop and gallop and whoa! (zigzag path)
Gallop and gallop and gallop and go, gallop and gallop and gallop and whoa!" (to a partner)

Repeat these additional rhymes several times as described in the example above:

"Slide and slide and slide and flop; slide and slide and slide and stop!"
"Jump and jump and jump and tip; jump and jump and jump and drip!" (melting action)
"Turn and turn and turn and jump; turn and turn and fall in a lump!"
"Hop and hop and hop, get small; hop and hop and hop, get tall!"

Movement Combinations for Ages Three through Seven

An effective way to create basic movement combinations for young children, without using rhymes, is to choose three or four skills to perform in sequence.

Three Skills On and Off a Spot

Each dancer places a spot (perhaps a circle cut from a yoga mat) in his or her self space. Choose three skills to practice and include a shape in the combinations. If not using music, create a little song by saying the actions in a rhythm: "Jump, jump, jump on the spot; slide away, slide away; make a shape and hold it; now fly back to your spot." Find music with strong phrasing and call out the first action of each set: "jump…slide…shape…fly…." Remember to use music with varying meters: 2/4, 4/4, 3/4 and 6/8. Included are just a few ideas to get started. Patterns can be repeated several times, adding arm movements or changing Level, Direction or Pathway for variation. Remember to integrate the lesson's dance concept into the movement combination as in example #1. The lesson's concept will help decide what new skills to practice or how to practice familiar skills.

1. Kick on the spot (strongly).
Sneak away from the spot (lightly).
Make a strong shape looking at the spot.
Fly back to the spot (lightly).

2. Float on the spot.
Slide away from the spot.
March backward to the spot.
Balance in a shape on the spot.

3. Jump on and off the spot.
Turn away from the spot.
Make a low shape.
Crawl back to the spot.

4. Make a shape over the spot.
Roll away from the spot.
Stretch up high.
Tiptoe back to the spot.

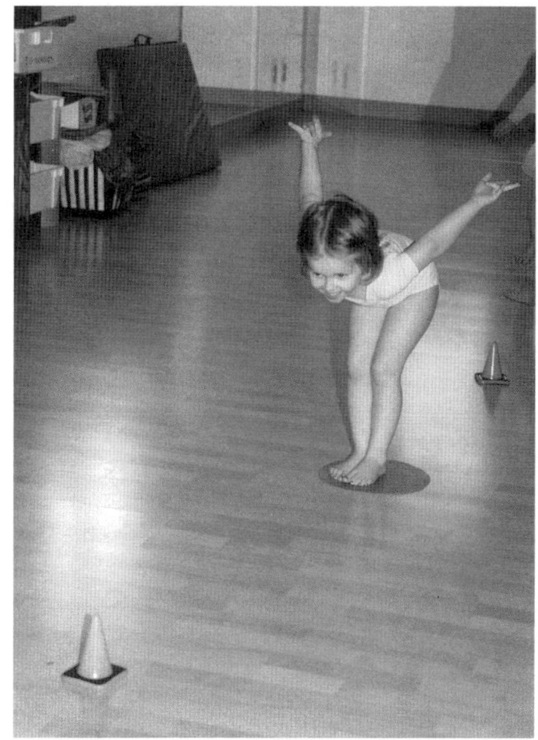

Eight Counts

Individually or together, the teacher and dancers choose two locomotor and nonlocomotor skills and place them in order. The teacher and/or dancers may choose the skills individually or together. Perform each movement for eight counts (or sixteen, six, twelve – whatever seems right for the music). Ask the students which skill they want to start with and which skill they want to finish with. This ensures a strong beginning and ending. Ask them which skill should be second and which third. Thinking about the lesson's concept helps determine the skills chosen. For example, if the concept is Level, dancers may include tiptoe and crawl. If the focus is Energy, they may choose float, press, swing and shake. Below are examples of concept-driven combinations.

Direction: Slide, turn, run, stretch backward.
Size: Tiptoe, stretch, leap, poke.
Pathway: Curvy run, swing, zigzag jump, march.
Speed: Creep, float, gallop, wiggle.
Weight: Press, tiptoe, stamp, flick.
Flow: Fly, freeze, swirl, walk.
Body Parts: March (knees), twist (spine), tiptoe (toes), nod (head).
Body Shapes: Kick (straight), twist (curved), march (angular), form two shapes.
Balance: Tip, spin, hop, shake.

Start with four skills in a combination, then vary the combination by integrating the weekly dance concept. For example:

Week #1: Level: Crawl, stretch, tiptoe, twist.
Week #2: Size: Big crawls like a tiger, stretch into a huge shape, tiptoe baby steps, small twists.
Week #3: Pathway: Crawl in a straight pathway, stretch, tiptoe in a circle, twist.
Week #4: Speed: Crawl slowly, stretch slowly, tiptoe quickly, twist medium speed.

After four lessons, we are ready to practice some new skills!

Skill Stories for Ages Three through Seven

Introducing skills through stories helps young children learn in an enjoyable way. The main focus for dance stories should be on the skills, not the characters or plot. Young dancers do not really care if the story makes sense, but rather that it is fun, exciting and has a nice rhythm and flow. These stories serve only as examples. It may be easier for you to make up your own stories than to memorize the ones here. Another excellent resource is *Movement Stories for Children Ages 3-6* by Helen Landalf and Pamela Gerke.

To create your own stories, choose the skills to be practiced. Think of what type of story with what characters might work to practice the skills. Write a basic outline and post a list of skills with the outline on the board or chart paper. As the story and the dance evolve, ideas for embellishing the outline will spontaneously occur. Remember again that the story does not have to make complete sense!

Always integrate the week's concepts into the story. A story may be used for almost any concept. By varying the adverbs that modify the skills, the weekly concept is easily integrated. For example, the characters might move strongly, quickly or sharply and then lightly, slowly or smoothly. Level is easily introduced into any story. Pathways might be accentuated. Free and Bound Flow might be the focus. Body parts such as legs, head, hips, arms and feet are easily highlighted. Stories are always used to practice skills in relation to the lesson's concept!

Animal Stories

These stories often focus on skills such as galloping, running, crawling, jumping, leaping, kicking, turning, flying and being still. Add partnering and ballet steps such as pas de chat, pas de cheval, chassé, chaineé turns and boureés. Emphasized words are in bold.

"Once there was a pony who lived all alone in a small field surrounded by a big fence. (Start in a **shape**.) The pony was lonely and **pawed (pas de cheval)** the ground every morning. Then the pony would **trot (prance)** around the small field, looking for other horses. Every so often the pony

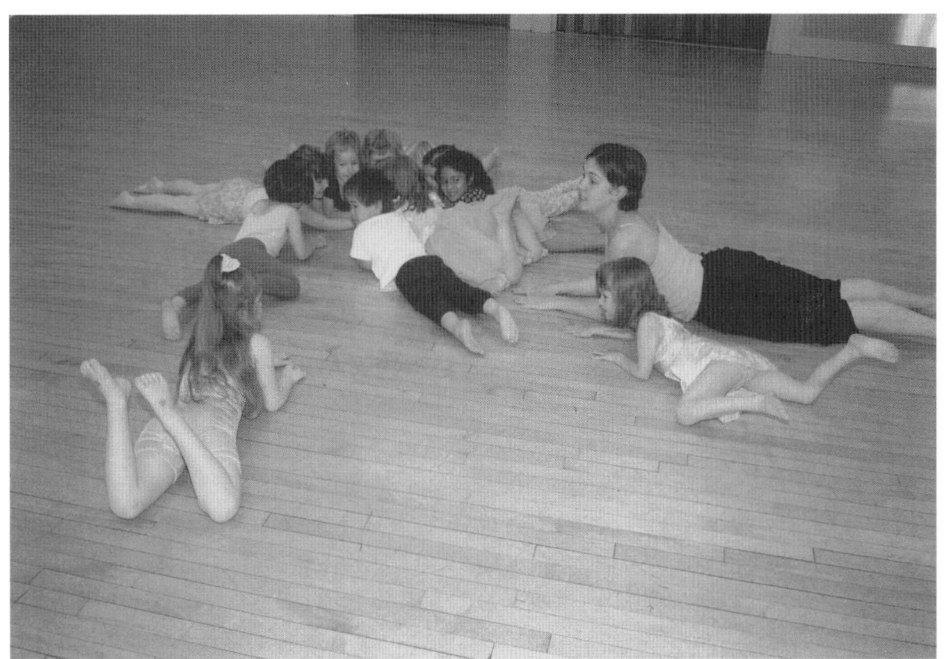

would **stop, stand very still and** then **twist** its long neck to the left and to the right, **shake** its mane and **shake** its tail. Then off it would **gallop,** around and around the field! Every day was the same! (Repeat actions above once or twice.)

"One day a big bird **flew** over the field (dancers change to birds and fly around) and **landed** on the fence (make balancing shape on tiptoes with arms reaching back like wings). The bird said to the pony, 'You silly pony! There are hundreds of horses over the hill and beyond the forest. **Leap** over the fence and follow me!' The pony was so excited that it **kicked** up its heels (**hitch kick** or **donkey kick**), **galloped** once around the field and **leaped** over the fence. Off the pony **galloped**. When the pony came upon the horses, it was so happy that it joined the herd and they formed a big family, all **connected** together!" End in a group shape.

This story can be repeated for three weeks by changing the bird into a frog that jumps, a snake that slithers and, finally, a flamingo that hops on one leg. Each change adds a new skill each week, keeps anticipation high and allows for continued practice on basic skills. Try to avoid saying "he" or "she" in mixed-gender classes.

Nature Stories

Because these stories are about environments and objects in nature, their focus is based on nonlocomotor skills. Skills practiced include swaying, floating, rolling, swinging, growing, shrinking, rising, sinking, poking and swirling.

"Once upon a time a small seed **lay** on the floor of a dark forest. (Dancers begin in ball shapes on the floor.) The wind **blew** it! (Seed rolls.) The rain **pelted** it! (Seed wiggles and shakes.) The sun shone on the seed and it began to **grow**! (Stretch and rise.) The sun **pulled** one branch forward (arm reaches forward) and **pushed** one branch backward (other arm reaches backward). The earth **twisted** one root sideways. (Leg twists to the side.) Leaves began to **sprout** on the branches. (Arms wiggle and shake.) There was a special golden leaf that **grew** to be very big. (Whole body expands.) One day, when a strong wind **blew** (tree rocks in the wind), the golden leaf **sailed** away (dancers fly through general space). It **swirled** and **swirled** in circles before **landing** in a rushing river, where it was **tossed** and **tumbled** over, under and around rocks and boulders! (Dancers can move on any level, leaping, rolling, jumping, turning.) Soon it **washed** up on shore and lay **resting** on the grass. A gentle breeze **picked** it up (rise) and the golden leaf **floated** through the air and landed right back on its mother tree." (Dancers end in a creative shape.)

Foot (or Hand) Stories

These stories work well in small spaces or during preschool circle time because they are performed sitting or standing in self space. Foot stories allow young dancers to work with the lower body in order to develop leg strength and flexibility without moving through space! Besides telling the story with the lower body, the upper body (hands, arms, head) may be used to depict the actions.

"Once upon a time there were two feet. (Dancers sit with feet in front of them. Hands can rest on the floor, arms slightly behind and supporting the upper body.) These two feet went **walking** down the street. (Walk feet in place on floor.) As they were **walking** down the street, whom should they meet? (You could name a character or the dancers could name something.) They met a horse! Off the horse **galloped,** with the feet right behind. (Feet gallop in place.) But the horse was too fast for the feet so off it went and the feet started to **trot** and then to **walk** and then they **stopped**! Who was standing in the path? A large rabbit! 'Come play with me,' called the rabbit and off the feet **jumped**! (Two feet jump on the floor.) But all of a sudden, the rabbit **jumped** down a big hole and the feet followed. It was very dark in the hole and the feet were afraid. (Feet **shake.**) 'How will I get out of here?' cried the feet. The feet **climbed** up and up and up (feet climb up imaginary wall) until they **fell** onto the grass and then started **rolling** downhill! (Feet roll around each other, as you would circle fists around each other.) Into a lake they **rolled**. But the feet were strong swimmers and they **swam** (swim in various ways – kicking, frog legs, heel-toe swivels, etc.) across the whole lake, **jumped** out, **shook** the water off one foot, **shook** the water off the other foot and **danced** (any movements) all the way home. The feet **yawned** very widely (feet stretch apart) and **melted** into bed, dreaming of the day's adventures!"

Toy Stories

These stories focus on toys that come to life. Many of the stories alternate between self and general space. At first the object is inanimate and can only move in its own space, but then magically dances around the room!

"Once upon a time there was an old toy store in a small village. In the dusty store lived many **broken** toys. (Dancers start in crooked shapes of their own choosing on different levels.) The toy maker was too old to fix them. Some of the toys had broken parts that moved in **jerky** ways. (Dancers move body parts sharply.) Other toys had parts that kept **twisting** from side to side. (Different body parts twist.) Some toys had parts that moved too **quickly**, while other toys had parts that moved too **slowly**! Every night when the toy maker fell asleep, the toys would dream that a new toy maker came to town and fixed all their broken parts. In their dreams, they would **march** up and down the shop in straight lines like soldiers. (Dancers march in straight pathways.) They would **twirl** like spinning tops. They would **gallop** like frisky ponies. They would **jump** up and down like bouncing balls. They would **float** almost without moving like brightly colored kites high in the sky. But as soon as the sun came up they would **look** around sadly and see that they were still **broken**!" (Dancers make crooked shapes.)

"But one day, a tall man came **striding** into the shop. (The teacher may play this role.) 'Why, what is wrong with all of these toys!' he exclaimed. 'Some move in **jerky** ways. Some move with **twisty** movements. Some move too **quickly** and others move too **slowly**!' (Dancer repeats movements from the beginning of the story.) 'I think I might be able to fix this terrible problem.' So he waved his magic wand and all of a sudden the toys began to **march** in straight lines...**twirl** like tops... **gallop** like ponies... **jump** like balls... and **float** like kites! (Repeat the general space section of the dance.) All the toys were so exhausted that they **melted** into a heap on the floor and **fell asleep**. But this time they knew their dreams had come true!"

Stories Based on Characters from Books or Movies

These stories use well-known characters from books or animated movies. Rather than reading the book as the dancers move to the words, create an original story based on a popular tale, while focusing on movement skills. Fairy tales, popular children's books such as Maurice Sendak's *Where the Wild Things Are* and animated movies might serve as springboards for these stories.

"Once upon a time there was a little fish. He lived in a huge ocean with lots of other creatures. One of these creatures was a big shark that wanted to eat him up. (Dancers **slither** on tummies as sharks.) There was also a deep-sea diver with a big net who wanted to catch him. (Dancers stand up and do a big, stomping, **body-side walk**.) He jumped, swam and swirled high and low through the ocean trying to escape the shark and the diver!" (Dancers move quickly, changing levels with **darting** and **swirling** movements.)

"But all of a sudden, the shark swam around the coral reef looking for the little fish. (Repeat **slithering**.) And here is the diver with the big net. (Repeat **body-side walk**.) The little fish **darted** through the water, trying to escape! (Repeat the **jumping** and **swirling** fish dance.) Oh, no! Here is that pesky shark again. (Repeat **slithering** for the third and last time.) Now the diver has returned. (Repeat **body-side walk**.) I know that the little fish will escape safely this time! (**Jump, swim** and **swirl**.) Oh, here comes the little fish's friend to help him get home." (Dancers find a partner and they **slide** together to the sides of the room.)

Instead of repeating the dance three times, change characters each time, bringing in turtles, jellyfish, starfish, etc. in order to practice more skills. This story works well with *Music for Creative Dance Volume IV,* #1. Change characters when the music changes speed. However, any ocean music or simply the voice is effective.

Shape Stories

The main character in shape stories has many adventures that cause it to change shape and move in a variety of ways. The shapes and actions are up to the teacher and the students within the lesson's concept. These stories, though rather silly and plotless, are still a fun way to practice skills. Here is one example that focuses on partnering.

"A long time ago there was a tiny town where pairs of tiny shapes lived quietly in little houses. One day a big wind **blew** the doors of the house open and **blew** the tiny shapes right out of the tiny houses. The shapes **rolled** and **rolled** away from each other until they each **fell** down their own giant hole. The shapes had to **stretch** very high to **climb** out of the holes. Then they **tiptoed** along the road, **looking** high and low for each other. Soon each shape was face to face with its friend! But every time one shape **changed** its shape, the other shape would **copy** it! After the first shape had **changed** three times, the second shape took a turn to make three shapes that its friend could **copy**.

" 'Let's stop this silliness,' the two shapes said, 'and **gallop** to the park.' So off they **galloped** together. They went around on the merry-go-round. (**Slide** in a circle holding hands.) They played on the teeter-totter (**tip** side to side holding hands) and they **swung** on the swings (hold hands and **swing** arms side to side and then **turn** up and over together). They even **crawled** under the bridge. (Take turns **crawling** under and through each other's legs.) By this time the shapes were very tired, so each pair of shapes **danced** its way back to its tiny house and **fell asleep** in a **connected** shape!"

Cinquains for All Ages

A cinquain is a modern poetry form that is useful for practicing dance skills. When using one in the Developing Skills section of the dance class, write one based on the lesson's concept and the skills for the dancers to practice. Compose the entire poem or omit one or two verbs for the dancers to add.

Read the cinquain in a dramatic or rhythmic voice while the dancers describe the words through movement. For a more brain-compatible experience, the dancers say the words as they dance. Pause between the words so the dancers have time to demonstrate each movement. I often take liberties with the pattern and repeat certain words when the performers need more support from my voice. Older dancers might memorize the poem and perform it to music without reciting it. Below are a few cinquains. Many more examples can be found in *Creative Dance for All Ages*.

Cinquain form:

- Noun
- Adjective, adjective
- Verb, verb, verb
- Four to five word phrase relating to the noun
- Synonym for the first noun or another noun

Cinquains:

Speed
Slow, fast
Creep, march, skip
Creating rhythms with our body
Time

Size
Near reach, far reach
Lunge, tiptoe, leap
Dancers stretch and curl
Shapes

Gravity
Strong, light
Press, float, ______
Dancing on the moon
Weight

Jack-O-lanterns
Round, hollow
______, rolling, ______
Candles create flickering faces
Halloween

Incorporating Motif Notation

Motif notation is useful for creating and documenting combinations for the Developing Skills section of the lesson plan. The dancers might notate the combination with the motif symbols, then read the combination as they practice the movements. The dancers might select four or five random cards with the symbols written on them or roll "dice" that have symbols on them to create a combination. They might use the symbols written on paper or a computer to notate a combination to practice outside of class. For more information on motif notation, refer to the article in the Appendices and the resources in the Bibliography. Following are three sample combinations.

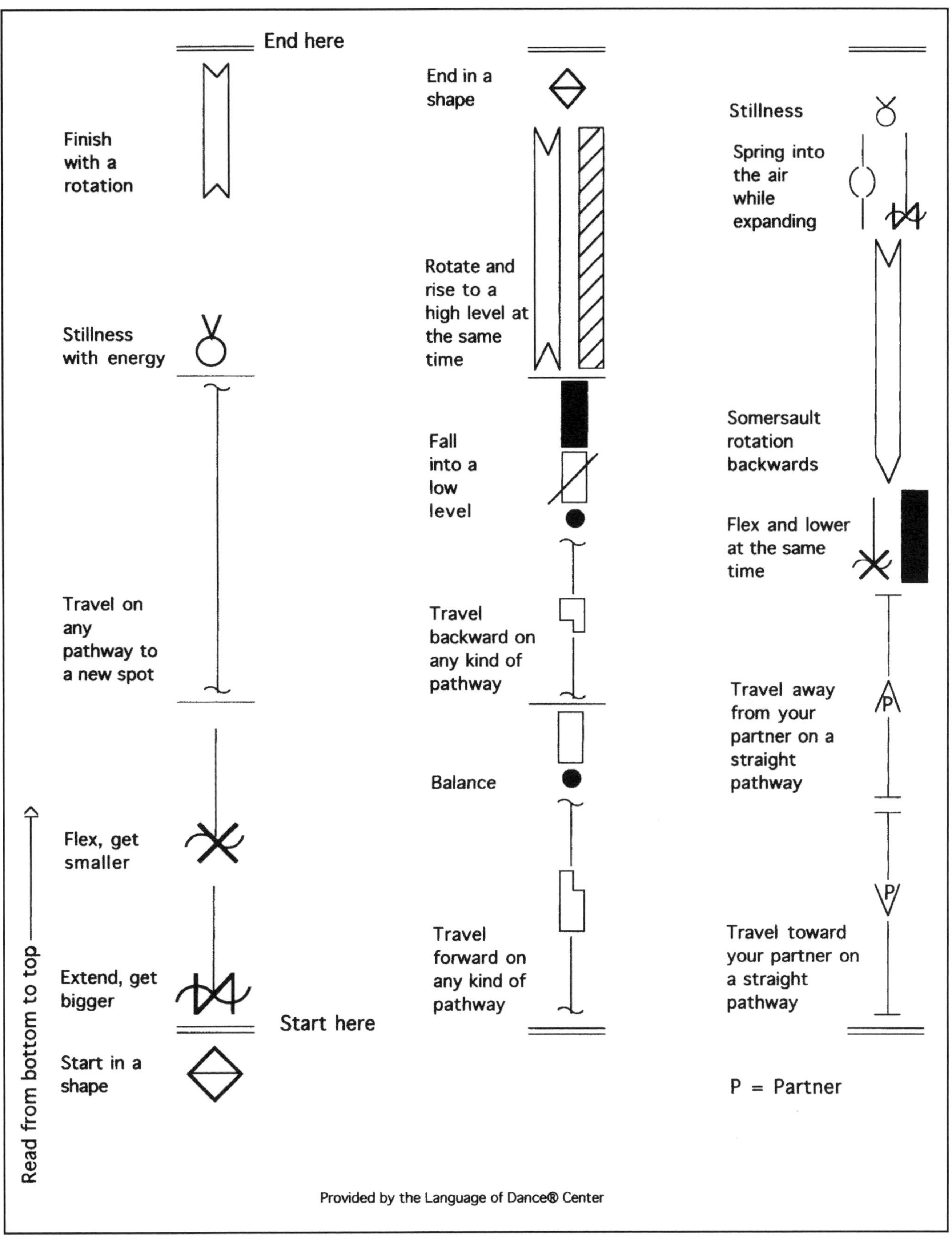
End here
Finish with a rotation
Stillness with energy
Travel on any pathway to a new spot
Flex, get smaller
Extend, get bigger
Start here
Start in a shape
Read from bottom to top
End in a shape
Rotate and rise to a high level at the same time
Fall into a low level
Travel backward on any kind of pathway
Balance
Travel forward on any kind of pathway
Stillness
Spring into the air while expanding
Somersault rotation backwards
Flex and lower at the same time
Travel away from your partner on a straight pathway
P
Travel toward your partner on a straight pathway
P
P = Partner
Provided by the Language of Dance® Center

Basic Circle Dances

These combinations are for infants through three-year-olds with adults, and ages four through eight with or without adults.

Basic circle dances have several benefits for children and adults:

- A sense of community is fostered (social skills).
- Sequencing and memory are developed through repetitive patterns.
- Moving to the pulse of the music refines beat competency (necessary for speaking, walking, cutting with scissors).
- Awareness of different cultures is acquired through hearing and moving to music from many countries.

It is easy to create basic circle or line dances for adult and infant, adult and toddler or adult and child classes. Form single circles with children between adults, all holding hands except for those children who prefer to be carried.

Circle dances are more difficult for young children without adults because of the complexity of moving in a circle while holding hands. With dancers ages three to six, do these circle dances in a scattered formation, with or without a partner.

To teach the skill of moving together in a circle, create an image of a magic ring. We want to keep the ring together so the magic will stay inside and help us dance well. Encourage dancers to lightly hold hands. Praise and encourage the dancers for working together as a team. When a dancer starts pushing, pulling or falling down, give the cue for everyone to let go and dance away. Continue the dance without holding hands if one or two dancers are pulling. Dance freely if many dancers are pulling and falling. Work on the circle dance for several weeks, improving the skill of holding hands or let it go for a few weeks. Return to it as the dancers gain more control of their bodies.

Although specific dance concepts for each circle dance are suggested here, others are easily substituted. The following dances can also be performed while holding hands, or in scattered formations as dance combinations rather than circle dances.

Circle Dance #1 - Energy

- Stamp feet sharply (16 counts).
- Clap hands sharply (16 counts).
- Walk smoothly backwards out of circle – use image of blowing up a balloon (16 counts).
- Walk into circle smoothly – let air out of balloon (16 counts).
- Poke fingers sharply (16 counts).
- Kick feet sharply (16 counts).
- Turn with your partner (or small group) smoothly (16 counts).
- Turn the other way smoothly (16 counts).

Repeat dance until music ends.

Suggested Music: *Best of Shenanigans' Dance Music, Volume 1,* "La Raspa"

Circle Dance #2 - Pathway

Hold hands in a broken circle or a line.

- Walk (or jog) in a curvy pathway - snake line (40 counts).
- Stop in self space and kick legs (8 counts).
- Clap hands (8 counts).
- Stomp feet (8 counts).

Repeat until music ends.

Suggested Music: *Best of Shenanigans' Dance Music, Volume 3,* "Savila Se Bela Loza"

Circle Dance #3 - Direction

- Slide (or walk) to the left (16 counts).
- Walk forward into the circle (8 counts).
- Walk backward out of the circle (8 counts).
- Jump up and down (4 counts).
- Turn to the right in self space or with a partner or adult (8 counts).
- Turn to the left in self space or with a partner or adult (8 counts).

Repeat, sliding (or walking) to the right.

Suggested Music: *Rhythmically Moving, Volume 5*, "Mayim"

Circle Dance #4 - Speed

- Walk to the right (16 counts).
- Walk to the left (16 counts).
- Walk forward into center, clapping hands (8 counts).
- Stay in center and stamp feet (8 counts).
- Walk backward away from center, clapping hands (8 counts).
- Stay in self space, stamping feet (8 counts).

Repeat from the beginning until music ends. Music gets faster and faster so that by the end everyone is running instead of walking.

Suggested Music: *Rhythmically Moving, Volume 2,* "Fjäskern"

Circle Dance #5 - Relationships

This Circle Dance is really a line or contra dance. Start in two lines facing each other. One child-and-adult pair stands across from another one in the opposing line. The two child- and-adult pairs form a couple. This dance is also done with a partner.

- Take four steps forward to greet the partner or couple across from you (8 counts).
- Take four steps backward away from your partner or couple (8 counts).
- Repeat forward and backward steps (16 counts).
- Two couples (or partners) come together, join hands and circle around (8 counts).
- Circle the other way and then go back to your place in the line (8 counts).
- Dancers in each line join hands and both lines slide sideways toward the end of the room (8 counts).
- All dancers slide back to their original places (8 counts).
- Head couples (the ones near the music) lead their own lines away from each other and down to the end of the line and then make an arch with their arms (16 counts).
- The other couples go under the arch and back to their places, now one place farther up the line (16 counts).

The dance commences with a new head couple (the prior head couple is now at the end of the line). This is a modified version of the Virginia Reel (see page 171). Do not worry about the counts with young children. Just feel the rhythm of the music and go with the flow.

Suggested Music: *Music for Creative Dance, Volume III*, #19

Circle Dance #6 - Size

- Clap four times (8 counts).
- Slide to the right (8 counts).
- Clap (or stamp, kick, punch) four times (8 counts).
- Slide to the left (8 counts).
- Take four giants steps into the center of the circle (16 counts).
- Run backwards with little steps out of the circle (8 counts).
- Spin (8 counts).

Repeat until the music ends. For older students, replace the claps with small and large movements such as poking and slashing, dabbing and punching, tiptoeing and kicking, etc.

Suggested Music: *Best of Shenanigans' Dance Music, Volume 2,* "Brown Jug Polka"

Circle Dance #7 - Weight

- Stamp strongly counterclockwise, then turn to face clockwise (16 counts).
- Tiptoe lightly clockwise (16 counts).
- Face the center of the circle and sway lightly (8 counts).
- Hold hands with your partner (or two to three couples) and walk in a small circle (24 counts).
- Walk in a small circle the other way (24 counts).
- Face the center of the circle and all hold hands (8 counts).
- Kick strongly into the center of the circle (8 counts).
- Stay in the center, kick or clap hands strongly (8 counts).
- Walk out softly and slowly with fingers to lips, making a shushing sound (16 counts).
- Repeat the kicking, shushing section (32 counts).

Repeat the whole dance two more times.

Suggested Music: *Rhythmically Moving, Volume* 6, "Fado Blanquita"

Circle Dance #8 - Balance or Focus

- Gallop clockwise (16 counts).
- Gallop counterclockwise (16 counts).
- Balance on one foot (or close your eyes for Focus concept) (8 counts).
- Walk (jump, tiptoe) into center and say, "Hello" (16 counts).
- Walk (jump, tiptoe) out and say, "Goodbye" (16 counts).
- Balance on the other foot (or close your eyes) (8 counts).

Repeat the dance until the music ends. Vary a section by circling with partner(s).

Suggested Music: *Music for Creative Dance, Volume II,* # 9

Each time the "sshhh" sound of the suggested music is heard the dancers make a balancing shape or close their eyes.

Circle Dance #9 - Flow

- Walk quickly (or run) with free flow one way around the circle (8 counts).
- Children (or girls) march with bound flow into the center and back out while adults (boys) clap (16 counts).
- Adults (or boys) march with bound flow into the center and back out while children (girls) clap (8 counts). This section is twice as fast as the previous section.
- Everyone spins alone with free flow (8 counts).

Repeat until music ends.

Suggested Music: *Best of Shenanigans' Dance Music, Volume 2,* "Ve' David"

Circle Dance #10 - Body Parts

- Gallop around the circle, holding hands with a partner (16 counts).
- Reverse directions, gallop counterclockwise (16 counts).
- Face partner, holding two hands, tip side to side (8 counts).
- Partners slide toward center of circle (8 counts).
- Tip side to side with partner (8 counts).
- Partners slide away from center (8 counts).
- Connect elbows with a partner; connect knees with a partner (16 counts).
- Connect shoulders with a partner; connect toes with a partner (16 counts).

Repeat the dance until the music ends. Older dancers connect more body parts within the 16 count phrase. Feel free to name other body parts than the ones suggested.

Suggested Music: *Best of Shenanigans' Dance Music, Volume 2,* "Doudlebska Polka"

Circle Dance #11 - Body Shapes

- Move around the circle clockwise with a choice of steps such as walks, slides, gallops, stamps, side steps, tiptoes, jogs, etc. (16 counts).
- Stop and form a curved shape and then a straight shape (16 counts).
- Move around the circle counterclockwise with any step for practice (16 counts).
- Stop and form an angular shape and then a twisted shape (16 counts).

Older dancers might form more shapes within the 16 count phrase. Feel free to name any shapes besides the ones suggested, such as wide, narrow, strong, tall, letters or numerals.

Suggested Music: *Best of Shenanigans' Dance Music, Volume 3,* "Cherkassia"

Circle Dance #12 - Level

- Slide counterclockwise (16 counts).
- Slide clockwise (16 counts).
- Stretch into a high shape (4 counts).
- Walk toward the center of the circle and say, "Hello!" (16 counts).
- Walk backward away from the center of the circle and say, "Goodbye!" (16 counts).
- Sink into a low level shape (4 counts).
- March counterclockwise (16 counts).
- March clockwise (16 counts).
- Stretch into a high shape (8 counts).
- Walk into the center, clapping hands and say, "Hello!" (16 counts).
- Walk backward away from the center, clapping hands and say, "Goodbye!" (16 counts).
- Make a high shape, a low shape, then a high shape (12 counts).
- Tiptoe counterclockwise (16 counts).
- Tiptoe clockwise (16 counts).
- Sink into a low level shape (8 counts).
- Repeat walking in and out (32 counts).
- Stretch into a high shape (4 counts).
- Repeat sliding counterclockwise and clockwise (32 counts).
- Form a favorite shape (4 counts).

It is easy to introduce different dance concepts and locomotor skills into this dance form.

Suggested Music: *Music for Creative Dance, Volume II, # 9*

Counts for the shapes are cued to the suggested music. When using other music, you may need to alter the number of counts for making shapes.

Movement Combinations for Ages Eight through Adult

Some of the combinations may be simplified for ages five through seven.

The following movement combinations serve as springboards for both the teacher's and students' creativity. To vary any of the combinations in this chapter:

- Focus on a different dance concept than the one suggested.
- Try other music selections for added inspiration.
- Change or reverse the order of the steps.
- Teach part of the combination one week and add on to the combination in subsequent lessons.
- Combine several combinations (or parts of combinations) for longer and more complex phrases.
- Replace basic movements with more difficult ones. For example, substitute a side fall for a melt. For younger or less experienced students, replace more difficult steps with easier movements. For example, do a slide instead of a grapevine step.
- Although counts are suggested, they serve only as a framework. Feel free to adjust the counts, letting some movements take more time, others less.
- Use repetition to create more complex forms. For example, repeat a short, well-known combination between phrases of new movement (ABACAD or ABBCBBD, etc.)

> ***Teaching Tip:*** *It is often easier for younger or novice dancers to learn combinations if the teacher says the names of the movements rather than the counts. For example, "Slide, slide, slide, slide, strrrreeeetch, turn once, turn again, wig-gle, wig-gle, wig-gle, wig-gle."*

Although a specific dance concept is paired with each combination below, other concepts may be substituted.

Combination #1 - Place

- Four slides through general space (8 counts).
- One big stretch in self space (8 counts).
- Two turns in self or general space (8 counts).
- Eight fast wiggles in self space (8 counts).

Repeat the combination several times.

Suggested Music: *Music for Creative Dance, Volume IV,* #5

Variations

- Ask students to change the timing of one or two sections (for example, two quick stretches and one slow stretch or two big slides and four fast turns).
- Substitute one or two movements for the ones suggested (slides become gallops, wiggles become pokes, etc.).
- Try the combination with a partner (slide together holding hands, stretch apart, turn away from each other, wiggle back together).

Combination #2 - Energy

- Slide (4 counts).
- Smooth arm movements (4 counts).
- Jump (4 counts).
- Sharp arm movements (4 counts).
- Gallop (4 counts).
- Smooth arm movements (4 counts).
- Hop on right foot (4 counts).
- Hop on left foot (4 counts).

Suggested Music: *Music for Creative Dance*, *Volume II,* #8

Variations

- Movements might be done for 8 counts each with younger or novice dancers.
- Try other locomotor skills alternated with upper body, axial movements.

Combination #3 - Body Parts

- Walk with still arms (8 counts).
- Swing arms and upper body to the right (2 counts).
- Swing arms and upper body to the left (2 counts).
- Swing arms and upper body in a full circle to the right (4 counts).
- Repeat swings starting to the left (8 counts).
- Run, do a fancy leap with special arms, freeze looking at a body part (8 counts).

Suggested Music: *Music for Creative Dance, Volume III,* #3

Variations

- Allow students to change the first or last 8 counts of the combination.
- A fun variation for partners is walking toward each other, holding hands on the swing section, then running and leaping away.

Combination #4 - Size

- Walk forward (or skip, gallop, leap) with big steps (4 counts).
- Fancy turn or walk in a circle with little steps (4 counts).
- Stretch into a big shape (2 counts).
- Shrink into a small shape (2 counts).
- Slide (4 counts).

Repeat several times. This is an easy pattern to do in a scattered formation.

Suggested Music: *Music for Creative Dance, Volume I,* #10

Variations

- A fun variation for duets or trios is moving toward one another for the whole combination. Repeat the pattern walking away from each other.
- Double the counts of each movement when working with young dancers.

Combination #5 - Direction

- Slide sideways to the right (8 counts).
- Tip side to side (8 counts).
- Gallop (or walk) backward (8 counts).
- Jump forward, backward, left, right (8 counts).

Repeat the combination sliding to the left. After dancers have learned the sequence, they add arm movements that reach in different directions.

Suggested Music: *Music for Creative Dance, Volume I,* #7

Play the slower version of the suggested music for younger dancers. Play the faster music that follows the slower one for older dancers.

Variations

- For younger students, try this combination with a partner: hold hands on the slide and tip, let go of hands and walk backwards, jump up and down (4 counts) and run forward to partner (4 counts).
- For older students, try the combination with partners, holding hands the whole time as one moves backward and the other moves forward. Partners take turns being the leader.

Combination #6 - Focus

- Twelve walks, changing direction and focus after every third step (12 counts).
- Two big swings down and up with whole body, with eyes closed (12 counts).
- Fast, curvy run, using multi-focus to look for the empty space (12 counts).
- Four shapes, changing focus with each shape (12 counts).

Repeat several times.

Suggested Music: *Music for Creative Dance, Volume III,* #14

Variation

- Rather than improvising movement, students set the combination to repeat it the same way each time.

Combination #7 - Speed and Level

- Eight fast runs in either a designated or improvised pathway (8 counts).
- One slow stretch (8 counts).
- Four fast turns (8 counts).
- One slow melt (8 counts).
- Several quick rolls at a low level (8 counts).
- One slow rise (8 counts).

Suggested Music: *Music for Creative Dance, Volume II,* #4

Variation

- Besides alternating fast and slow movements, explore changing the order. Begin with fast actions, end with slow ones (run, turn, roll, stretch, melt, rise). Start slowly and end quickly or mix slow and fast movements in a new order (run, turn, stretch, melt, roll, rise).

Combination #8 - Rhythm or Direction

- Twist to the right (3 counts).
- Twist to the left (3 counts).
- Turn to the right (6 counts).
- Twist to the left (3 counts).
- Twist to the right (3 counts).
- Turn to the left (6 counts)
- Four waltz runs forward (down-up-up, down-up-up, down-up-up, down-up-up) (12 counts)
- Swing upper body right, left, forward and backward (12 counts).

Suggested Music: *Music for Creative Dance, Volume II,* #6

Variation

- For younger students, skips might substitute for waltz runs and shapes for upper body swings.

Combination #9 - Flow or Level

- March forward (or change directions) with bound flow (8 counts).
- Make two bound shapes (8 counts).
- Spiral or melt to the floor (8 counts).
- Roll to the right and left like waves (8 counts).
- Rise to standing (8 counts).
- Fly and swirl like a leaf in the wind (8 counts)

Suggested Music: *Music for Creative Dance*, *Volume III,* #11

Combination #10 - Weight or Direction

- Lunge forward on right leg, pressing left arm forward (3 counts).
- Lunge forward on left leg, pressing right arm forward (3 counts).
- Lunge backward on right leg, pulling left arm backward (3 counts).
- Lunge backward on left leg, pulling right arm backward (3 counts).
- Float while moving forward or turning (6 counts).

Repeat several times, perhaps facing new directions in the room.

Suggested Music: *Music for Creative Dance*, *Volume III,* #14

Variation

- Try this combination with partner.

Combination #11 - Pathway

- Walk forward in a straight pathway with long strides and arms moving smoothly from low to high – arms down by sides, out to the side and then straight up (8 counts).
- Walk in a large circle to the right (curved path) with both arms carving around the circle. Return to original point on the circle (8 counts).
- Slide to the right forward diagonal with right arm reaching side right (2 counts).
- Slide to the left forward diagonal with left arm reaching side left (2 counts).
- Repeat right and left diagonal slides (4 counts).
- Pirouette (turn), run and leap (8 counts).

Repeat the pattern on the other leg so that you curve to the left.
Suggested Music: *Music for Creative Dance, Volume IV,* #10

Combination #12 - Relationship

- Four hinge slides. Hold one hand with partner and slide face to face, back to back, face to face and back to back. (8 counts).
- Turn away from partner (8 counts).
- Jump forward, backward, side right, side left (8 counts).
- Make two shapes (4 counts).
- Run and leap back to partner (4 counts).

Suggested Music: *Music for Creative Dance, Volume IV,* #9

Combination #13 - Energy or Direction

- Four smooth strides forward (8 counts).
- Two smooth strides backward (4 counts).
- Four sharp jumps turning to the right (4 counts).
- Two slashes with the arms (4 counts).
- Four sharp jumps turning to the left (4 counts).
- Two big gallops right and left (4 counts).
- Balance in a shape (4 counts).

Repeat several times.
Suggested Music: *Music for Creative Dance, Volume IV,* #11

Variations

- Move toward and away from a partner.
- Students design their own specific smooth and sharp arm movements.

Combination #14 - Weight

- Press and lunge with left hand and right foot (4 counts).
- Press and lunge with right hand and left foot (4 counts)
- Strong turn right (4 counts).
- Light turn left (4 counts).
- Shake whole body (8 counts).
- Hold still (4 counts).
- Flick four times with hands or other body parts (4 counts).

Repeat several times.

Suggested Music: *Music for Creative Dance, Volume IV,* #7

Combination #15 - Pathway

- Step hop-hop-hop on right foot in a straight path or turning to the right (4 counts).
- Step hop-hop-hop on left foot in a straight path or turning to the left (4 counts).
- Step-hop right, step-hop left, step-hop right, step-hop left in a zigzag pathway (8 counts).
- Swinging, either improvised or choreographed by students (16 counts).
- Run in a circle (8 counts).
- Four slashes with arms (8 counts).
- Repeat the swinging section (16 counts).

Suggested Music: *Music for Creative Dance, Volume III*, #10

Variation

- Arms are held at sides for step-hops and then released for swinging.

Combination #16 - Direction

- Walk four steps with arms reaching forward (4 counts).
- Jump four times, moving sideways right with arms "pushing" to the right (4 counts).
- Walk four steps with arms reaching forward (4 counts).
- Jump four times, moving sideways left with arms "pushing" to the left (4 counts).
- Repeat walks and jumps as above, walking and reaching backward instead of forward (16 counts).
- Two lunge steps forward (4 counts).
- Four running steps forward while kicking heels back toward buttocks with knees bent (4 counts).
- Repeat lunges and running steps (8 counts).
- Reach up (8 counts).
- Reach down (4 counts).
- Burst (4 counts).

Suggested Music: *Music for Creative Dance, Volume II,* #11

Combination #17 - Relationships

Begin several feet away from a partner.

- Four waltz runs toward partner; come together (12 counts).
- Revolving door turn right and left. Stand side by side with right sides together and walk in circle, "pushing" partner around as in a revolving door. (12 counts).
- One or two counterbalanced (or weight-sharing) shapes with partner (12 counts).
- Form one relationship shape (over/under, around/through) (6 counts).
- Run and leap away (6 counts).

Repeat, going to the same partner or a different one.

Suggested Music: *Music for Creative Dance, Volume I*, #2

Combination #18 - Energy

- Grapevine step to the right with smooth energy (8 counts).
- Hitch-kick front, hitch-kick back with sharp energy (4 counts).
- Attitude turn on right leg with smooth energy (4 counts).
- Stretch left leg forward with smooth energy (4 counts).
- Circle left leg around to back with smooth energy (4 counts).
- Slide back with left leg leading, then leap turn with sharp energy (8 counts).
- Move into a shape with smooth energy (or several sharp shapes), hold (8 counts).

Repeat. If using the suggested music, hold the last shape whenever the music pauses.

Suggested Music: *Music for Creative Dance, Volume IV,* #4

Combination #19 - Focus

- Four hinge slides, holding one hand with a partner (8 counts).
- Châiné turn away from partner, spotting (6 counts).
- One sharp shape looking at partner (2 counts).
- Creep backward toward partner, looking over shoulder (8 counts).
- Balance in a shape with eyes closed (4 counts).
- Dance back to partner (4 counts).
- Blind mirror, #1 leads (press palms together, follower closes eyes while leader guides through space) (8 counts).
- Blind mirror, #2 leads (8 counts).
- Dance far away from each other, using multi-focus (could be a directed step such as skip or boureé) (8 counts).
- Dance back together, using single focus (8 counts).

Repeat several times.

Suggested Music: *Music for Creative Dance, Volume IV,* #9

Combination #20 - Size or Pathway

Begin with the side of body to the line of direction.

- Big side step left as you reach left arm over head, drag right foot (count 1-2).
- Small step crossing right foot over left foot (count 3).
- Repeat big side step and small crossing step (3 counts).
- Small twists left and right (6 counts).
- Two big leap turns to the left (6 counts).
- Two waltz runs forward with arms moving in a figure 8 (6 counts).
- Four big skips in a circle (12 counts).
- Stretch into a big shape (6 counts).
- Curl into a small shape (6 counts).

Repeat.

Suggested Music: *Music for Creative Dance, Volume III,* #18

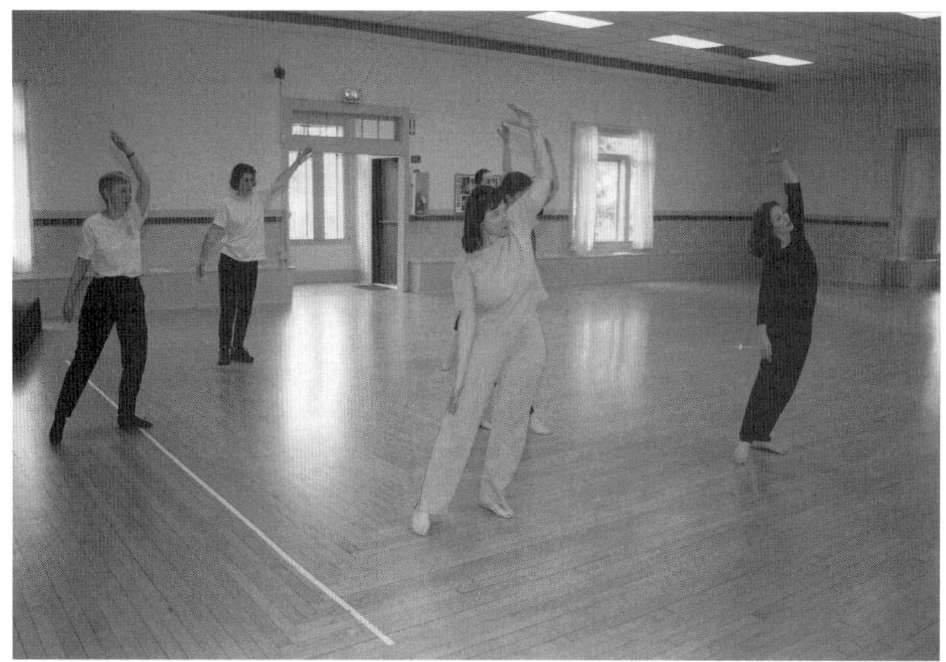

Combination #21 - Pattern

ABACADAE: A = chassé steps; B, C, D, E = jumps with varying hand movements.

- A: Chassé (slide forward) to the right (2 counts). Chassé left (2 counts).
- B: Two big jumps forward, pushing hands forward (4 counts).
- A: Repeat chassé right and left (4 counts).
- C: Two big jumps forward, clapping hands (4 counts).
- A: Repeat chassé right and left (4 counts).
- D: Two big jumps forward, slapping thighs (4 counts).
- A: Repeat chassé right and left (4 counts).
- E: Two big jumps forward, tapping knees (4 counts).

Suggested Music: *Music for Creative Dance, Volume II*, #2

Variations

- Practice locomotor steps such as pirouettes, step-hops, step-leaps or hinge slides, as well as chassés. When practicing the hinge slide, clap hands with each other to create different rhythm patterns.
- Ask dancers for ways to replace the jump pattern. Examples include balancing shapes, shapes with body parts connecting, spins and turns or different nonlocomotor movements.

Combination #22 - Body Parts

- Four long steps forward, starting on right while left index finger touches sternum and right index finger points to right on right step. Reverse arms on left step (8 counts).
- Kick legs, slash arms in karate-like fashion (counts 1-2, 3-4, 5, 6, 7, hold on 8).
- Different body parts lead randomly through space (8 counts).
- Right arm swings forward right diagonal with right foot step, right arm swings back left diagonal as left foot steps back, right arm swings all the way around. Chassé with the right foot (allow head to swing with arm). (8 counts).

Repeat several times. This combination uses the four Patterns of Coordination (Shape, Thrust, Hang and Swing) discussed in the Appendices.

Suggested Music: *Music for Creative Dance, Volume III, #17*

Variation

- Two lines face each other and pass through on the leading body part or chassé section.

Combination #23 - Weight or Relationship

Begin a few feet away from partner.

- Four steps toward partner with strong weight, with body-side walks (8 counts).
- Four step-hops with strong weight to meet partner (8 counts).
- Two counter balanced or weight-sharing shapes with partner (these may be designed by the partners or improvised) (16 counts).
- Balancing shape, connecting fingertips (8 counts).
- Dabbing over, under, around, through partner (8 counts).
- Light step-hops away from partner (8 counts).
- Floating turn to face partner (8 counts).

Repeat several times.

Suggested Music: *Music for Creative Dance, Volume III, #19*

Combination #24 - Balance

- Two waltz runs with swinging arms (6 counts).
- Two big skips with oppositional arms (6 counts).
- Repeat waltz runs (6 counts).
- Three jazzy, twisty jumps (3 counts).
- Balancing shape (3 counts).

Suggested Music: *Music for Creative Dance, Volume I*, #2

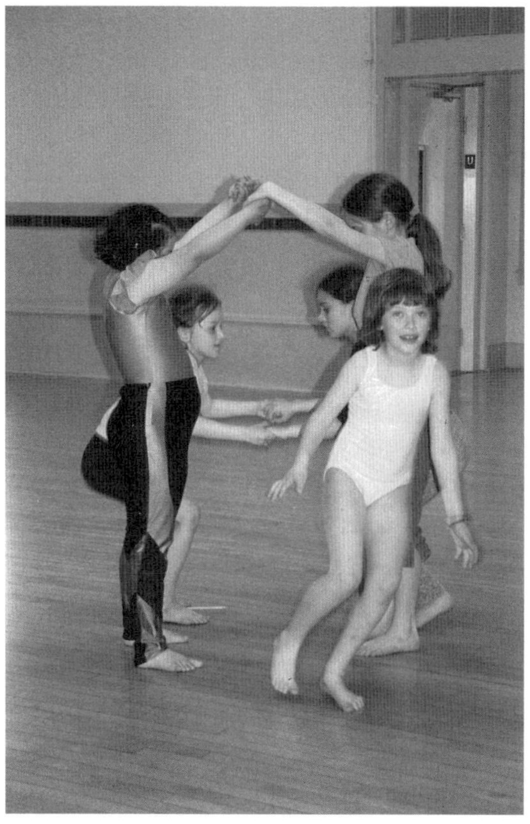

Variation

- Try this combination with a partner. Each moves toward the other and ends together in the balancing shape. Repeating the pattern, connect forearms and waltz run in a circle. Do big skips in a circle while still connected. Waltz run away from each other, do jazzy jumps and balance. Begin again with waltz run toward each other. Waltz runs together can be performed as a balancé.

Developing Combinations Over Four Weeks Using Dance Concepts

As part of the Creative Dance Center's visiting week, I often develop a combination over four weeks and then share it with parents on the fifth week. Repeating a pattern leads to mastery of skills while integrating the concept maintains students' attention. Below is an example of how one combination may be developed over several lessons through the conceptual approach.

Suggested Music: *Music for Creative Dance, Volume IV*, #2

Lesson #1 - concept is Place

- Gallop forward four times through general space (8 counts).
- Balance on left leg and press right leg and arm to right side in self space (4 counts).
- Balance on right leg, press left leg and arm to left side in self space (4 counts).
- Spin in self space with arms rising from low to high (8 counts).
- Skip through general space in a basic or fancy way, depending on age and experience (8 counts).

Lesson #2 - concept is Energy

- Gallop forward four times, adding swinging arms (8 counts).
- Balance on left leg and press right leg and arm to right side with smooth energy (4 counts).
- Balance on right leg and press left leg and arm to left side with smooth energy (4 counts).
- Spin in self space with shaky/vibrating arms rising from low to high (8 counts).
- Skip through general space, adding sharp arm movements (8 counts).

Lesson #3 - concept is Level

- Gallop four times, bending knees and staying low to the ground (8 counts).
- Balance in relevé on left leg and press right leg and arm to right side (4 counts).
- Balance in relevé on right leg and press left leg and arm to left side (4 counts).
- Spin in self space with shaky/vibrating arms rising from low to high (8 counts).
- Skip high with sharp arm movements (8 counts).
- Form a low level shape. Make a high level shape (8 counts).
- Spiral (or fall) to the floor and rise (8 counts).

Lesson #4 - concept is Balance

- Gallop forward four times (8 counts).
- Balance on left leg and press right leg and arm to right side (8 counts).
- Balance on right leg and press left leg and arm to left side (8 counts).
- Spin in self space with arms rising from low to high (8 counts).
- Hold in a balancing shape in stillness (8 counts).
- Four special skips forward (8 counts).
- Balance on left leg while moving right leg and both arms in floating movements (4 counts).
- Balance on right leg while moving left leg and both arms in floating movements (4 counts).
- Spiral (or fall off balance) to the floor and rise (8 counts).

Folk Dances

Folk dances are an excellent way to practice movement skills, develop sequencing, memorize patterns and practice transitional flow. They are fun, provide aerobic exercise and promote a sense of community. Because many folk dances are based on developmental movement patterns, they are brain-compatible. One might choose to teach the dances as movement combinations without a lengthy discussion of cultures. Using this approach, tell students the name of the dance, the country of origin and some information about the dance.

When teaching a folk dance for cultural awareness, it is valuable to show a video or DVD of dances from the culture of origin. Discuss the costumes, the instruments, the venue and the movement concepts that are emphasized. Discuss similarities and differences between this and other cultures and styles that are being studied. (See the Bibliography for world dance resources.)

Many dances described here may not be entirely "authentic" yet are created in the style of a culture. Many folk dances taught in schools today were choreographed in folk dance camps and festivals that started in the 1930s. European immigrants shared many of these dances from their homelands, while others were observed and recorded by teachers traveling abroad.

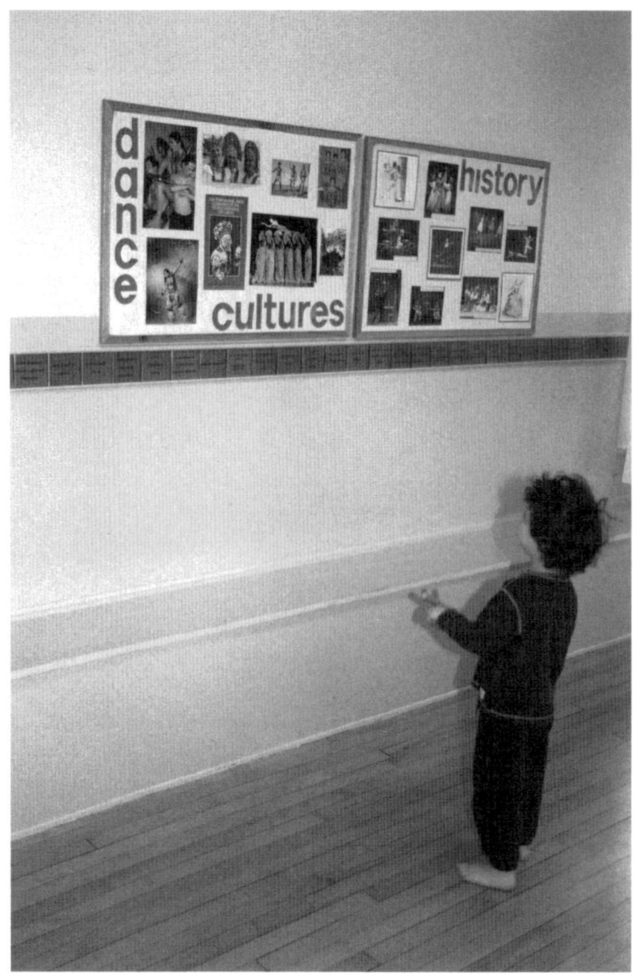

These dances are valuable beyond practicing steps and memorizing patterns. Every culture has a movement signature. When we try one different from our own, we gain a greater understanding of another culture. When we extend the dance experience through various resources about the culture – environment, clothing, music, food and customs – we appreciate the differences and similarities between the peoples of the world.

When teaching folk dance to beginners, do not worry about having them hold hands. Moving together in a circle is difficult. Teaching steps in a scattered formation or moving in a circle or line without holding hands is easier. Try both methods. Hold hands only when the students feel comfortable with the movement.

Think of a number of different cues, such as counts ("1-2-3-4-5-6-ready-go"), directional words ("forward, backward, side"), prepositions ("in, out, between, apart, together") and movements ("heel-toe, step-together-step"). Different students respond to different cues. Address several learning styles through a variety of cues. Students say the cues along with the teacher to better remember the steps.

Besides using folk dances to practice skills or to learn about different cultures, these patterns may serve as a springboard for improvisation and choreography. After teaching a folk dance in the Developing Skills section, have the students change a folk pattern or create a new dance during the Creating section of class. More ideas for choreographing folk dances will be discussed in the Creating chapter.

> ***Teaching Tip:*** *Start with circle and line dances, then add partnering dances. Make partnering fun instead of a problem. First, let friends be partners; on some days, ask boys and girls to be partners; on others request students to find someone with whom they have not yet danced. Change partners often during the lesson. Ask students to connect elbows with a partner by the count of five, stand back to back by the count of four or stand in a connected shape with a partner by the count of six. A dancer without a partner raises a hand and quickly finds another dancer raising a hand.*

In the following pages, specific folk dances are discussed. Try these ideas and then develop new dances with help from students. Included are some of my favorite and most successful dances. Feel free to make slight changes that stay within the style of the dance.

FJÄSKERN (Fee-**yes**-care-n) is a Swedish dance. The title means "hurry-scurry" or "this way and that way." The music gets faster each time the dance repeats. This excellent warm-up dance is a favorite with all ages.

Opening position: couples start side by side in a circle facing counterclockwise. They may hold hands in a cross-hand hold.

Section One

- Couples walk around the circle counterclockwise (16 counts).
- Walk clockwise (16 counts).

Section Two

- Partners face each other (hands may be placed on hips). Kick four times forward, touching the forward heel to the floor (4 counts).
- Clap hands once, then step forward three steps, passing right shoulders, changing places with partner. End facing partner again (4 counts).
- Repeat the heel and clap three more times. "Heel, heel, heel, heel, clap, change places," (24 counts).

Suggested Music: *Rhythmically Moving, CD 2,* "Fjäskern"

Variations

- Young dancers may do this dance without a partner in a scattered formation. During Section One, walk in various Pathways or Directions. During Section Two, clap hands four times and spin (4 counts). Repeat three more times.
- During Section One, partners shadow each other through general space (sixteen counts for each leader) and do Section Two as originally described.
- During Section One, practice locomotor movements other than walking (jump, skip, step-hop or slide).
- Practice different nonlocomotor movements during Section Two (twist, turn, swing, shake, float, punch or kick). The rhythm might be "twist, twist, twist, twist, clap, change places."
- In a scattered formation, have dancers practice a chosen locomotor movement toward a partner (32 counts of the first section). A couple might create a dance of two or more movements (32 counts of the second section).

SHOEMAKER is a Danish dance originally done by cobblers.
Opening position: Couples side by side in a circle.

Section One

- Roll fists around each other (winding the thread on the bobbin) (8 counts).
- Pull fists apart two times (breaking the thread) (4 counts).
- Pound fists together, one fist on top of the other (hammering the heel to the sole) (4 counts).

Repeat all of above (16 counts).

Section Two

- Polka with a partner (young children can slide with a partner, holding hands) (32 counts).

Suggested Music: *Music for Creative Dance, Volume III,* #19

Variations

- Perform the dance in a scattered formation without partners.
- Each time the music repeats, do the hand motions with a different body part such as head, feet, hips, elbows, knees, eyes. The dancers imitate the teacher's actions or create their own ways to wind, break and hammer. This variation is fun and an excellent whole body warm-up!
- During Section Two, the dancers improvise movements.
- During Section Two, call out directions relating to a specific dance concept. For example say, "dance on a high level" (16 counts), then say, "dance on a low level" (16 counts).
- During Section Two, call out steps such as backward jumps (16 counts) and skips with swinging arms (16 counts).

GREENSLEEVES is an English dance traditionally performed by the tailors' guilds. The last section depicts the needle sewing with the sleeve turned inside out to be sewn to the bodice.

Opening position: sets of two couples (four dancers), all facing counterclockwise in a circle.

Section One

- Couples walk forward in the circle (holding hands optional) (16 counts).

Section Two

- The four dancers in each set do a right hand star—reach right arms into center, touching hands, walk in small circle clockwise (8 counts).
- The four dancers in each set do a left hand star—reach left arms into center, touching hands, walk in small circle counterclockwise (8 counts).

Section Three

- The front couple in each set holds hands and moves backward under the arch made by the back couple (holding hands), who simultaneously move forward over the front couple (4 counts).
- This under/over movement is repeated three more times (12 counts).

Suggested Music: *Music for Creative Dance, Volume III*, #19

Variations

- Practice steps other than walking for Section One.
- In Section Two, substitute right and left elbow swings, do-si-do both directions and/or circle four. All four dancers hold hands and walk in a circle clockwise and then counterclockwise.
- Dancers substitute their choreography based on a dance concept such as Relationship (around and through, together and apart, beside and between) for one sixteen-count section.
- Introduce comparatives (big, bigger, biggest; tall, taller, tallest; strong, stronger, strongest). Have each quartet choreograph a comparative for sixteen counts. Substitute this choreography for Section Two.
- Make this dance a mixer: In Section Three, the back couple goes forward four steps on the last four counts (instead of going under the arch a second time) to become the back couple of the group ahead of them. The back couple in each quartet will go "Over, under, over and pass on to the next group."

VIRGINIA REEL was brought by the British Colonists to America in the early 1700s. Originally, the dance was known in England as "Sir Roger de Coverley."

Opening position: Contra dance formation. Four to eight couples facing each other.

Section One

- Walk forward to greet a partner and walk backward to one's place (8 counts).
- Repeat greeting (8 counts).
- Swing right elbows with partner, return to place (8 counts).
- Swing left elbows with partner, return to place (8 counts).
- Hold both hands with partner and circle around, return to place (8 counts).
- Do-si-do your partner, return to place (8 counts).

Section Two

- Head couple (the one nearest to the music or caller) slides down the middle and back to their place. Other couples clap (16 counts).
- Head couple casts off: they turn away from each other, each head dancer walks to the bottom of the line as the dancers in each line follow their leader (16 counts).

Section Three

- Form an arch and pass through: Head couple forms an arch with both arms. The other couples go around and under the arch, then walk to their new places (one spot farther up the line) for the beginning of the dance with a new head couple (16 counts).

Suggested Music: *Rhythmically Moving, CD 1,* "Soldier's Joy" or *Music for Creative Dance, Volume III,* #19

Variations

- Advanced version: Instead of head couple sliding down, they "reel the set." In this version, the head couple does a right elbow swing 1½ times around, a left elbow swing to next in line, right swing to partner, left swing to next in line, right swing to partner until reaching the end of the line. Then the head couple slides up the middle and casts off.
- Instead of having the head couple slide down the middle, each couple creates a special movement or pattern to perform as the head couple.
- When the head couple casts off, each leader dances in a special way. Each line copies the line leader.
- During the casting off, the teacher calls out movements such as high and low, strong and light, creeping, slashing, etc. Everyone does a version of the directed movement.
- By using the voice, a "caller" guides the dancers through a variety of steps. The caller switches the order of the calls in Section One to keep the dancers alert.

SCATTER SQUARE DANCE is based on American square dancing. Teaching basic square dance movements is easy and enjoyable with this variation created by physical educator Karen Hamilton Bafus.

When the teacher or caller says, "Hit that lonesome trail," the dancers move through the space in any direction and pathway. When the caller gives a specific call, the dancers find the people nearest them and perform as specified until the caller says, "Hit that lonesome trail" again.

Below are some possible calls. Add ideas or have students create new ideas and calls.

- "Promenade a partner." Move with a partner, in the handhold of the dancers' choice or a specified handhold.
- "Do-si-do a partner." Pass right shoulders, move around each other back to back and return to original position.
- "Swing your partner." Hook right or left elbows and turn around.
- "Horse and rider." One dancer is behind another with hands on shoulders.
- "Circle up four." Four dancers make a circle and walk clockwise or counterclockwise. "Go back the other way." Dancers walk in the opposite direction.
- "Right hand star." Touch right hands together and walk in a circle.) "Left hand star" Touch left hands together and walk in a circle. "Shoot that star." Raise arms, break apart and holler.
- "Go around the flagpole." Turn the partner around the other partner.
- "One goes down, the other goes around." One dancer kneels as the other goes around.
- "Circle up four and duck for the oyster and dive for the clam." Two dancers make an arch that the other two duck in and out of.
- "Follow the wagon train behind __________and__________." Couples form a line behind the leaders.
- "Covered bridge and all go through." One couple makes an arch with both hands. As each couple passes under the arch, they join the bridge, making an arch. Eventually, the dancers form a long line of arches or covered bridge. Couples continue to pass through the bridge until the caller says, "Hit that lonesome trail."
- "Circle up the wagon train, then all join hands in one big ring."
- "Circle left and circle right."
- "Face your partner and do a grand right and left." Shake right hands with a partner and pass right shoulders. Shake left hands with the next person and pass left shoulders. Continue the grand right and left until meeting the partner.

Suggested Music: *Rhythmically Moving, CD 1,* "Soldier's Joy" or other reels and jigs

BROWN JUG POLKA comes from Australia. This dance is known in America as the "Heel and Toe Polka."

Opening position: Couples face each other in a circle with one facing in and one facing out. Holding hands is optional.

Section One

- Touch heel to floor beside standing foot, touch toe behind standing foot. Repeat heel, toe (4 counts).
- Slide with partner counterclockwise (slide, slide, slide, slide) (4 counts).
- Repeat heel/toe pattern with the other foot (4 counts).
- Repeat slides clockwise (4 counts).

Section Two

- Partners clap right hands together quickly three times (counts 1 & 2). Clap left hands three times, clap both hands three times, slap thighs three times (8 counts).
- Partners swing with right elbows, then swing with left elbows (8 counts).

Suggested Music: *The Best of Shenanigans' Dance Music, Volume 2,* "Brown Jug Polka"

Variations

- Turn this dance into a mixer: in place of the left elbow swing, the inside dancers move to their left to find a new partner.
- Young dancers dance in couples in a scattered formation (rather than a circle).
- Students may dance alone. For Section One, jump or tap foot in place four times, then slide. For Section Two, dancers clap or tap different body parts, then spin to the right and left (instead of the elbow swing with a partner).

MAYIM (my-**yeem**) is an Israeli dance. Mayim means "water" in Hebrew. This dance emphasizes the importance of water in this desert country.

Opening position: single circle holding hands.

Section One

- Do grapevine step moving clockwise (16 counts).

Section Two

- Walk forward into the circle four steps, reaching arms above head (4 counts).
- Walk backward out of the circle four steps, lowering arms (4 counts).
- Repeat walking in and out of the circle with arm movements (8 counts).

Bridge: run clockwise four steps (4 counts).

Section Three

- Hop on right foot eight times while tapping left foot forward and side (8 counts).
- Hop on left foot eight times while tapping right foot forward and side, clapping hands as right foot touches in front (8 counts).

Suggested Music: *Rhythmically Moving, CD 5,* "Mayim"

Variations

- Simplify by substituting sliding or walking for grapevine steps, turning for hopping. Dancers do not need to hold hands in the circle.
- In Section Two, say the word "Mayim" four times while walking into the circle and make a "whooshing" sound while walking out.

VE' DAVID (vay da-**veed)** is an Israeli dance. The original title is Ve' David Y'Fey Enayim, meaning "And David of the Beautiful Eyes." David was a King of Ancient Israel.

Opening position: Single circle holding hands with partners (boy and girl) standing next to each other. See non-partner variation below.

Section One

- Walk eight steps counterclockwise (8 counts). This is a simplification of the original dance.
- Walk four steps forward into the circle while reaching held hands and arms up (4 counts).
- Walk four steps backward out of the circle while lowering held hands and arms (4 counts).

Section Two

- Girls alone walk into the circle four steps, reaching arms up and back out of the circle four steps, lowering arms while boys clap (8 counts).
- Boys alone walk into the circle four steps, reaching arms up, turn to face partner. Walk toward partner four steps while girls clap (8 counts).
- Boys swing girls with an elbow swing or an Israeli turn (Partners stand with right hips adjacent to one another. Hold partner around the waist with right arms. Left arms are held high) (8 counts).

Suggested Music: *The Best of the Shenanigans' Dance Music, Volume 2,* "Ve' David"

Variations

- Do the dance without partners. Spin alone for the last eight counts.
- In adult and child classes, have the children walk into the circle while the adults clap. Then adults walk into the circle while children clap. Adults spin children.
- Dancers partner with whomever they choose regardless of age or gender. Each couple decides who in the pair is #1 and who is #2. "Ones" walk into the circle as "twos" clap and vice versa.
- As a mixer the boys (or #2s) walk out four steps, moving to the girl (or #1) on the right of the former partner. Spin the new partner.

CHERKESSIYA (chur-kah-**see-**ya) is "…a dance for men from Circassia. They were followers of the Mohammedan faith, who sought religious freedom away from czarist Russia. They left southeastern Russia and migrated to Palestine and Syria. The Circassians were noted for their horsemanship. The rhythmic movement of the dance portrays either horses or riders."[1]

Opening position: single circle with or without hands held.

- Do grapevine step. Cross left foot stepping on right, step to side with left, step back on right, step to side with left clockwise four times, accentuating count one by stamping the right foot (16 counts).
- Kick forward, moving counterclockwise (16 counts).
- Repeat grapevine clockwise (16 counts).
- Kick backward, moving counterclockwise (16 counts).
- Repeat grapevine clockwise (16 counts).
- Do heel-toe swivel steps counterclockwise (16 counts).
- Repeat grapevine clockwise (16 counts).
- Prance counterclockwise (16 counts).
- Repeat grapevine clockwise (16 counts).
- Step-hop counterclockwise (16 counts).
- Repeat grapevine clockwise (16 counts).
- Do chug steps (low stamping with bent knees) counterclockwise (16 counts).
- Repeat grapevine clockwise (16 counts).
- Do side steps. Step side with right foot, crossing left foot behind right, bending knees as stepping on left, straightening knees as stepping on right foot) (16 counts).
- Repeat grapevine clockwise (16 counts).
- Do heel kicks. Hop from one leg to the other, placing heel on floor in front of other foot counterclockwise (16 counts).

Suggested Music: *The Best of the Shenanigans' Dance Music, Volume 3,* "Cherkessia"

Variations

- Younger dancers slide sideways or gallop instead of doing the grapevine step if it is too difficult.
- Students suggest other steps during the sections that alternate with the grapevine.

TROIKA (**troy**-ka) is a Russian dance. Troika means "three horses." The dance symbolizes three horses pulling a sleigh across the snowy Russian steppes.

Opening position: Sets of three dancers standing side by side, holding inside hands and facing counterclockwise in a circle like spokes of a wheel.

Section One

- Trios run forward in the circle with prancing steps or long leaping runs (16 counts).

Section Two

- Outside dancer in each trio prances under the arch of arms made by middle and inside dancers, then back to place. Middle dancer follows under arch and turns under his or her left arm. Dancers never let go of hands (8 counts).
- The inside dancer prances under the arch made by the middle and outside dancers, then back to place. Middle dancer follows and turns under his or her right arm (8 counts).

Section Three

- Three dancers hold hands to form a small circle. Run in circle counterclockwise, stamp feet three times on last three counts (16 counts).
- Trio circles clockwise and inside and outside dancers let go of hands to form a line. They are now ready to repeat the dance (16 counts).

Suggested Music: *The Best of Shenanigans' Dance Music, Volume2*, "Troika"

Variations

- Each trio creates a new pattern for Section Two. The dancers must stay connected through the sixteen counts.
- Practice a different movement for Section Three, such as skipping, step-hopping, kicking runs, hitch-kicks.
- Use a small scarf to connect the middle dancer to the partner on the left and another with partner on the right. These scarves serve as reins that make it easier for dancers to perform Section Two.
- On the last four counts, the middle dancer drops hands and runs forward four steps to join the trio in front. The two remaining dancers in each trio prance in place for four counts, then join hands (or scarves) with the new middle person. The dance is a fun mixer!

LA RASPA is a Mexican dance. "A rasp" is a file or scraping tool. During the hot summers in Mexico, the iceman used to scrape shavings off a big ice block for the children before giving the block to the mother for her icebox. The hand movements in the first section describe a filing or scraping motion.

Opening position: Couples face each other with both hands joined (or couples in single circle without hands joined).

Section One

- Leap from one foot to the other, placing opposite heel on the floor (right, left, right, hold). Arms are held in front in parallel with palms down, elbows bent. Right arm straightens as left arm bends with a scraping or sawing motion in opposition to the feet. Couples may also move while standing face-to-face and holding hands (4 counts).
- Repeat the first four counts seven more times (28 counts).

Section Two

- Right elbow swing with partner (8 counts).
- Left elbow swing with partner (8 counts).
- Repeat right and left elbow swings (16 counts).

Suggested Music: *Rhythmically Moving, CD 3,* "La Raspa"

Variations

- In Section One, dancers face center for first 16 counts, then face partner for second 16 counts.
- Dancers shake a shaker or maraca as they do the dance.
- Replace elbow swings with different locomotor steps (gallop, slide, skip).
- With young dancers, alternate feet in Section One without the pause (right, left, right, left).

SI, SEÑOR is a partner dance from Brazil. This dance is appropriate for ages ten and up.

Opening position: Couples in a circle face each other, with left or right side facing center. One faces clockwise, the other counterclockwise. Add a Latin flavor by adding hip and arm movements to the steps below.

Section One

- Take three steps toward center (step, close, step, hold, or step-together-step) then three steps away from center (8 counts).
- Repeat the steps in and out (8 counts).

Section Two

- Walk a complete circle around oneself (step-together-step, step-together-step) (8 counts).

Section Three

- Look at a partner and snap fingers, then twist to look at the person behind. Repeat. (8 counts).
- Face a partner, then take four steps past to meet a new partner (4 counts).

Suggested Music: *Folk Dances of Latin America,* "Si Señor"

FADO BLANQUITA (**fah** dough blahn **kee** ta) is a Portuguese-Brazilian dance. There is some controversy over the meaning of the name. Some say it means "little white father," referring to the missionaries who came to Brazil. However, Fado is a special form of music found only in Portugal, known as Portuguese "blues." The dance presented here describes the three main cultures in Brazil: Indian, African and Portuguese.

Opening position: A single circle with dancers standing in front of a partner, facing counterclockwise.

Section One represents the Indian culture in Brazil.

- Eight step-hops, keeping low to the ground, moving counterclockwise. Alternate bending the upper body forward for two step-hops, straightening spine for two step-hops. Arms are down by sides (16 counts).
- Repeat the eight step-hops, moving clockwise (16 counts).
- Bridge: sway to face partner (8 counts). On the last two counts change character while pressing right palms together with elbows bent and forearms touching.

Section Two represents the Portuguese culture in Brazil.

- Three schottische steps (step, step, step, hop three times) with partner, moving in a small circle counterclockwise. Dancer remains proud and upright, with focus always on the partner (12 counts).
- Change hands, schottische three times clockwise (12 counts).
- Repeat schottische steps counterclockwise and clockwise (24 counts).
- Bridge: sway to face center, changing character (8 counts).

Section Three represents the African culture in Brazil.

- Jump, then hop on the right foot, kicking left foot forward. Jump, then hop on left foot kicking right foot forward. Jump, then jump and turn to face out of circle, holding the last two counts (8 counts).
- Repeat the jump-kick pattern while facing out of the circle (jump, kick, jump, kick, jump, jump/turn, hold). End with the jump/turn facing into the circle (8 counts).
- Add rhythmic arm and torso movements.

Section Four returns to the Portuguese style. It reminds the dancers that Portugal was once a monarchy and how one bowed to the King and Queen.

- Take three slow, regal steps toward center of circle (right, left, right), extend left foot forward with slight bow (8 counts).
- Step backward out of circle (left, right, left), extend right foot back with slight bow (8 counts).

Section Five

- Repeat Sections Three and Four (32 counts).

Suggested Music: *Rhythmically Moving, CD 7,* "Fado Blanquita"

Variations

- In the second section, advanced dancers alternate three schottische steps touching right hand with partner, three schottische steps touching left hand with the corner, then back to partner and back again to corner.
- In the second section, younger dancers skip with a partner or by themselves. In the third section, they make up a jumping, kicking or turning pattern.

CHINESE FRIENDSHIP DANCE is traditionally danced by young children in a circle. One or two begin in the center. They choose partners and dance, while the others in the circle clap. Each time the dance begins, the dancers in the center choose new partners until everyone is dancing. Couples are scattered throughout the room. They either stay together or find a new partner before the chorus is repeated.

The chorus alternates with movements that promote strength, flexibility and coordination. The original music is no longer available. Select appropriate music from China and call out the dance steps to fit the musical phrasing.

Chorus

- Put right hand at angle over eyes and "look for a friend." Repeat with the left hand.
- Take four walking steps to your partner with a stylized walk (heel-ball-toe).

Section One

- Right elbow swing with partner while bending knees, kicking heels back. Left arm bends at elbow with fingers toward head in angular arm gesture.
- Repeat with a left elbow swing and angular right arm gesture.
- Wave good-bye with a sweeping arm (like a windshield wiper) and say, "Dzai-Jian" (z-eye jen).

Chorus

- Repeat the chorus movements described above.

Section Two

- Facing a partner, jump diagonally forward, end up side by side with right hips near with arms in a "V."
- Jump diagonally backward (facing each other again) with arms in a "W."
- Repeat jumping diagonally forward and backward. Alternate sides so that first the right side is next to a partner, then the left.
- Repeat several times, jumping forward and back with "V" and "W" arms.
- Wave good-bye and say, "Dzai-Jian" (z-eye jen).

Chorus

- Repeat the chorus movements described above.

Section Three

- Hold right hands with partner while standing face to face. Lunge away to the left side, making a strong angular counterbalance shape, with the left arm bent (as in Section One). Pull back to center to face partner.
- Change hands, lunge to right side with angular right arm.
- Repeat lunges to left and right.
- Wave good-bye and say, "Dzai-Jian" (z-eye jen).

Chorus

- Repeat the chorus movements described above.

Section Four

- Hold hands with partner and jump up and down like a see-saw. When one partner bend down, the other partner jumps up.
- Wave good-bye and say, "Dzai-Jian" (z-eye jen).

Variations

- Dancers create new movements for one or more sections.
- Each time the dancer "looks for a friend," walk to a new partner.

TANKO BUSHI (tan-ko boo-she, "Coal Miner's Dance") is a Japanese circle dance usually performed by young women at Bon Odori festivals in late summer. It is over one hundred years old and tells the story of coal mining.

Opening position: Single circle facing counterclockwise. Take small steps around the circle, keeping the arms fairly close to the body. Japanese dancers do not usually make large, sweeping motions.

"Dig the coal"

Tap ball of right foot, then step right. Make two digging motions with hands to the right. Repeat digging motions to the left while stepping with the left foot (4 counts).

"Throw the sack over your back"

Step forward on the right foot. Bring hands together with palms up to toss coal sack over right shoulder. Repeat on left side (4 counts).

"Shade the eyes"

Step back on left foot, shade right eye with back of right hand (sun is too bright). Repeat, stepping with right foot, shading eye with left hand. This movement also represents wiping sweat from the forehead (4 counts).

"Push the cart"

Step on right foot while pushing both hands forward as if pushing a coal cart up a hill. Step on left while pushing forward (4 counts).

"Call the man to get the coal"

Step forward on right foot, pushing arms to side. Step back on left foot. Bring right foot back to left while making a circle with arms, bringing palms together in front of chest (4 counts). Clap in this pattern: clap, pause, clap-clap, clap (4 counts).

Suggested Music: *Multicultural Folk Dance CD, Volume 1,* "Tanko Bushi"

Variations

- For young dancers, form a circle with dancers facing inward. Perform the arm gestures without the steps.
- Suggest other themes that relate to Japan, such as fishing, tea ceremony, gardening or calligraphy. Create hand and arm gestures to describe the new theme. Make them clear and easy.
- Create dances with basic gestures depicting a Haiku poem.

WEST AFRICAN DANCE is a dance I choreographed in the West African style. I recommend that your students watch a video or DVD of West African dancing before learning this dance. Several are listed in the Appendices.

Opening position: Single circle.

Section One

- Stamp right foot forward, tap left foot back. Stamp on left, tap right forward (4 counts). Arms, back and head alternate curving down to the ground, reaching up to the sky as feet stamp.
- Repeat three times (12 counts).

Section Two

- Walk backward, moving out of the circle. Touch right heel forward on count one. Step back on right on count two. Repeat left, right, left. Arms are bent at elbows and open and close as ribcage expands and contracts during heel-walks (8 counts).
- Repeat the heel-step, moving forward and back to place (8 counts).

Section Three

- Dancers create movements using rhythmic torso, head, arm and leg gestures that depict different kinds of work (drumming, digging, sowing, gathering, grinding, hunting, shucking or shelling, stirring a stew). Choose a different kind of work each time during the dance or repeat four patterns twice (16 counts).

Music suggestion: *Wongai: let's go*! "Soli"

Variations

- Think of different actions for the third section of the dance.
- Simplify the movements for Section One or Section Two.
- During Section Two, dancers enter and exit the circle while improvising new movements.

PATA PATA is from South Africa. Pata Pata stands for gently bumping hips with another dancer. **Opening position:** Dancers in lines or a scattered formation.

Section One
- Touch right foot to right side as arms open to the side with finger snap (1 count).
- Step right foot next to left foot, clap (1 count).
- Touch left foot to left side as arms open to the side with finger snap (1 count).
- Step left foot next to right foot, clap (1 count).

Section Two
- Turn toes out, raise bent arms with hands up and elbows down (1 count).
- Turn heels out, lower hands with elbows up (1 count).
- Turn heels in, raise hands with elbows down (1 count).
- Turn toes in, lower hands with elbows up (1 count).

Section Three
- Raise right knee in front of body, touch it with left elbow (1 count).
- Touch right foot sideward right (1 count).
- Raise right knee in front of body, touch it with left elbow (1 count).
- Step right foot next to left foot (1 count).

Section Four
- Kick left foot forward (1 count).
- Step left, jump a quarter turn right, clap. Quarter turn is optional for younger dancers (3 counts).

Suggested Music: *Rhythmically Moving, CD 6,* "Pata Pata" or any recording of "Pata Pata" by South African singer Miriam Makeba.

Variations
- Change arm movements in Section One. Arms move in and out, together and apart or side to side. dancers create their own patterns.
- After repeating the dance four times, do 32 counts of "Pata Pata" movement. Twice bump sides of hips together gently with a partner. Change sides or move around to different partners.
- After repeating the dance four times, the dancers create their own break dance, hip-hop or creative movements for 32 counts.
- During Section Four, experienced dancers create complex rhythmic patterns (polyrhythms) by clapping or slapping legs, feet, hands and so forth. A polyrhythm is a simultaneous combination of contrasting rhythms in music and dance.

In Summary

Students become more accomplished dancers by learning and practicing new steps and movements.

- Practicing basic skills through the lesson's dance concept makes learning skills engaging and meaningful.
- Dance skills may be taught through a multi-sensory, brain-compatible approach by using rhymes, motif notation, repeating patterns, dance concepts and a variety of formations and relationships.
- Practicing combinations of movement develops memory, sequencing and flow.
- Performing circle and folk dances develops collaborative skills and a sense of community.
- Viewing and learning dances from other countries develops an understanding of other cultures.

Having learned and practiced movement skills and patterns, the dancers are ready to create original dance studies and compositions during the Creating section of dance class.

Dance goes farther than the movement. ~ Anika, age 12

(Endnote)

[1] Pittman, Anne M. and Marlys S. Waller, Cathy L. Dark. *Dance A While: Handbook of Folk, Square, Contra and Social Dance*. 9th ed. San Francisco, CA: Pearson Education, Inc., 2005, p.339.

Chapter Four
Lesson Plan Section 4: Creating

In this chapter:

CREATING

IMPROVISING – playing with movements, structures and concepts in the moment
CHOREOGRAPHING – planning and arranging movements into a form with intent

DEVICES

Expansion	make the movements bigger
Diminution	make the movements smaller
Repetition	perform a movement or phrase several times
Canon	one dancer or group repeats the movement or phrase several counts later
Retrograde	perform a pattern and then "rewind"
Transposition	transfer the movement to a different or opposite body part
Accumulation	perform movement #1, then movement #1 and #2, then #1, #2, #3
Rhythm	vary the speed or change the rhythm of the movement
Opposite Actions	perform a movement, do the opposite and then connect the two
Concept Contrast	change the space, time or force of a movement

FORMS

ABA	a = one phrase or idea; b = a different phrase or idea
Suite (ABC)	three contrasting sections
Recurring Theme	theme in variation, ABACAD, ABBC, ABCDECFGC, etc
Abstract	non-representational, geometric form
Narrative	in the form of a story, representational
Broken Form	unrelated ideas, often illogical or humorous
Chance Dance	movement selected and defined but randomly structured

PRINCIPLES

Unity Contrast Harmony Balance Variety Emphasis Repetition

CREATING

Applicable National Dance Standards

The following standards from the *National Standards for Dance Education* will be achieved through the activities in this chapter:

- **Understanding choreographic principles, processes and structures**
- **Understanding dance as a way to create and communicate meaning**
- **Applying and demonstrating critical and creative thinking skills in dance**
- **Making connections between dance and other disciplines**

Chapter Introduction

After developing skills, dancers are ready to show you what they learned in the previous sections of the lesson by creating their own dances. They solve structured movement problems through improvisation or create set movement studies and dances through choreography.

Students are motivated to pay attention throughout the lesson knowing they have the opportunity to create their own work at the end of class. The Creating part of class is satisfying for students because it is a synthesis of the whole lesson. Exploring movement concepts and practicing skills sets the stage for original and meaningful student composition.

This part of class combines teacher-directed and student-centered work. Dancers solve structured movement problems in creative ways. This may seem similar to exploring a concept. However, in Exploring the Concept, the teacher constantly provides cues and suggestions, so the dancers will better understand and embody the concepts.

In the Creating section, the teacher becomes an observer and allows students to construct their own learning. Dancers work independently, but refer to the teacher for clarification when necessary. The teacher may give feedback during improvisation or choreography, but does not give specific cues or commands as in Exploring the Concept.

Creating may take only five to ten minutes for improvisation, but fifteen to forty minutes for choreography. The lesson length and goals will determine the amount of time for this section. In a thirty to sixty minute class, spend more time on improvisational structures than on choreography. The dancers might work with one choreographic project over a period of several weeks. They compose dances while the teacher utilizes the time to include all sections of the lesson plan for a brain-compatible approach. An important part of creating dance is sharing and assessing the creation. This happens in different ways during the last section of the Cooling Down lesson, explained in detail in the next chapter.

Improvisation

Improvisation is an excellent way for dancers of all ages to express themselves. It allows them to play with movement without the pressure of performance or creating a "correct" product. Improvisation can be a joyful, freeing experience, as well as a deeply moving and informative one. The dancers may play with and manipulate external stimuli such as props, partners, nature or art, or internal stimuli such as emotions, needs and thoughts. Improvisation can be an end in itself or lead to choreography through the generation of movement ideas that can later be used in creating dances.

Improvisation involves playing with movements, structures and concepts in the moment. Therefore, it usually takes less time than choreography. However, experienced dancers may delve deeply into the improvisatory experience, if that is a goal. To help students approach the concept in new and different ways, several improvisations, based on a singe theme or concept can be assigned within one class period.

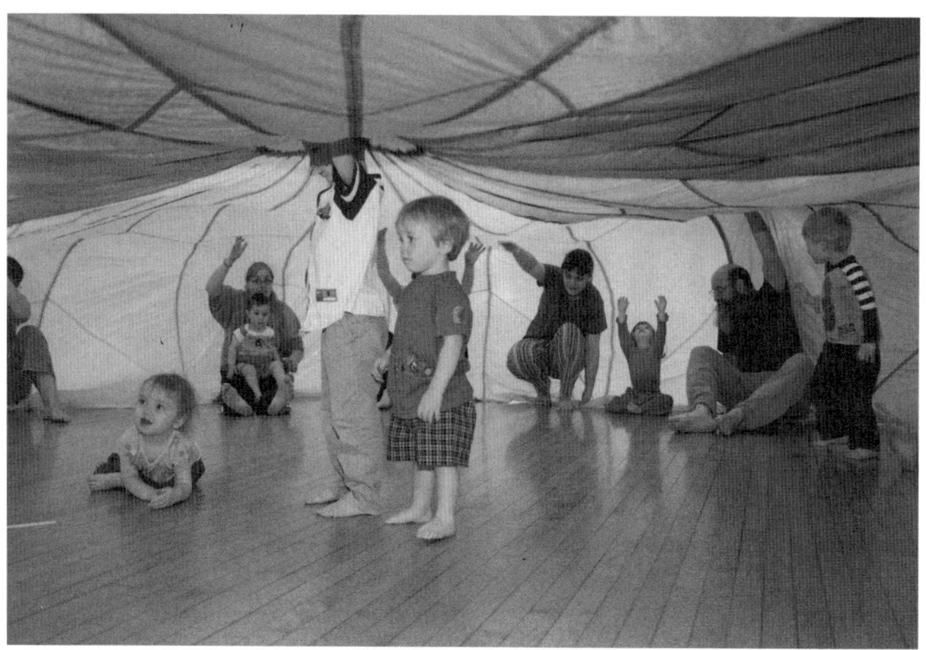

While young dancers love nothing better than "doing their own thing" and dancing freely, novice dancers or dancers who have been exposed exclusively to a teacher-directed approach may feel inhibited in the early stages of improvisation. It is important to structure the improvisation to assist the construction of the dancers' ideas. A conceptual structure is also important for young and uninhibited dancers because, through the structure, they are encouraged to delve deeply into the concept. Complete freedom leads to confusion while structure promotes creativity.

One way of supporting novice dancers during improvisation is to encourage them to copy someone else's movements for a short period of time. Another way is to say, "I see Medina galloping in curved pathways," "I see Todd stretching on low levels along straight pathways," "I see Hsai tracing curved pathways with the upper body while moving on straight pathways with the lower body," "I see several dancers moving with bound flow in zigzag pathways," "I see everyone moving in unique ways on all three pathways." This gives other dancers ideas and lets students know their creativity is appreciated.

Students' progress, as well as the teacher's success, can be assessed through improvisations. After giving students a simple structure or problem based on the lesson's concept, observe who has unique ideas, who embodies the concept and who uses the movement skills taught earlier. If the majority of the students understand the concepts and skills presented earlier in the lesson, then the class goals have been accomplished.

Most of the ideas found at the beginning of each concept chapter in *Creative Dance for All Ages,* as well as the ideas in Exploring the Concept in this book may be used for the Creating part of dance class. Below are additional suggestions for improvisation.

Free Dances for Infants through Age Six (Easily adapted for older dancers)

Most preschool and kindergarten dancers are not developmentally ready to create their own dances and remember them. Improvisations are more appropriate than choreography in parent and child classes when students are two months through three years old. Improvisation is an excellent way for dancers under the age of six to show what they have learned in class. In *Creative Dance for All Ages,* such improvisations are referred to as "free dancing," because young dancers freely express their feelings and ideas through the lesson concept.

With free dances, explain the structure for the improvisation, involving students in a quick demonstration if needed. Directions should be brief, as the structure is fairly simple. While students improvise, you, as the teacher, may dance with them for physical support or stand back and observe.

Young dancers are naturally self-focused, so sharing work with peers is not as important as it is for older dancers. However, it is important for dancers from ages three to six to feel their teacher is watching them. Acknowledge their creative dancing with smiles, eye contact and positive feedback through the "I see…" statements mentioned above. A quick and easy way to share free dances with ages four though six is to divide the class in half and alternate the roles of dancer and observer briefly three or four times.

While some structures specifically mention props, most of the following improvisations also include props when desired.

Plus and Minus Parts

Dancers begin improvising with one body part and slowly add others until the whole body is dancing. They subtract body parts in a different order than they added them, until just one is left moving. The teacher might name specific body parts for younger dancers.

Suggested Music: *Music for Creative Dance, Volume II,* #12

Antonyms

Dancers improvise pairs of antonyms named by the teacher, such as strong and light, wide and narrow, happy and sad. The lesson's concept usually dictates the antonyms used for the improvisation. This basic improvisation is more compelling when coupled with contrasting music and when both elements are explored using both sections of the music. For example, "Dance strongly on the strong music and lightly on the light music, then dance strongly on the light music and lightly on the strong music."

Suggested Music: *Music for Creative Dance, Volume I, II, III, IV* or *V (contrast pieces)*

Choose a Friend

Each dancer improvises alone until instructed to "Choose a friend." Then students dance to another person and both dance together. They alternate dancing alone and dancing with a different partner each time. The movements explored together and apart will depend on the lesson concept. For Balance, the dancers might dance off balance alone, then create balanced shapes together for half of the music. For the second half of the music, they might explore dancing on balance alone through general space, then tip off balance while holding hands with a partner.

Suggested Music: *Music for Creative Dance, Volume IV,* #15

Corner-Middle-Side

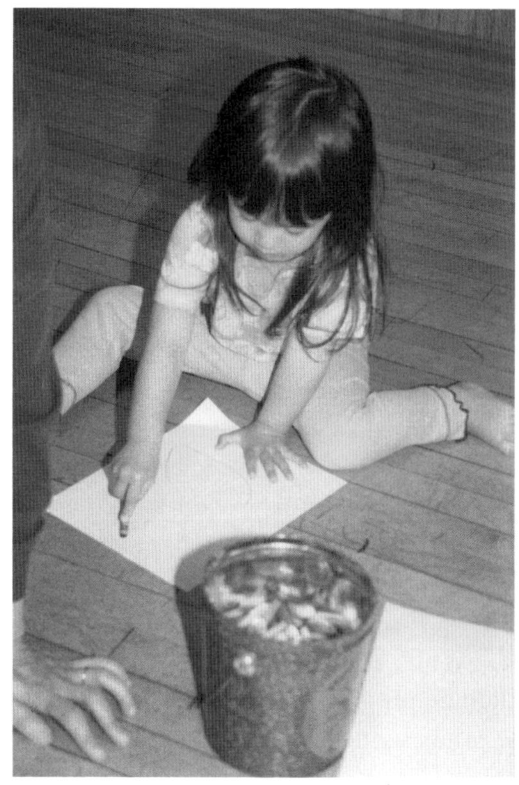

Dancers improvise movements to and in specific places of the room as directed. This excellent improvisation for Relationships may be used to explore any concept. When exploring Weight, for example, dancers may be directed to "press strongly to any side of the room…twist lightly on the sidelines…float to the middle…find a friend in the middle of the room and form a pulling shape together…dab lightly to a corner in a zigzag pathway…stamp in the corner…tiptoe quietly to the opposite corner…find a new friend and form a pressing shape together…glide backwards lightly to an adjacent corner…find two friends and form a strong shape together on a low level…move to the middle of the room, combining strong and light movements… end in a strong or light shape that shows your favorite way to move today." While this is a fairly structured improvisation, it is still excellent for free dancing. Everyone moves to his or her own timing and performs in a unique style. Some dancers will move quickly to the place named and then spend a longer time in that place doing the specified movements and vice versa.

Suggested Music: *Music for Creative Dance, Volume II,* #11

Drawing Designs

Play contrasting music while dancers draw the contrasts on paper (strong and light designs, curved and straight designs, self space and general space designs, balanced and off balanced designs, etc.). Then ask them to dance their drawings. Each dancer might put the drawing on the floor. As they improvise around all the drawings, they learn new ideas from other designs.

Suggested Music: *Music for Creative Dance, Volume I, II, III, IV* or *V* (contrast pieces)

Cinquains

A cinquain is used to motivate dancers to improvise (see Developing Skills). Dancers first listen as the poem is read and then improvise as it is repeated. Use a dramatic voice, varying the speed, pitch and volume to motivate a variety of movements.

Magic Scarves

Start with a pile of scarves in the middle of the room. Dancers bring the scarves to life by sprinkling imaginary magic powder with arms, legs and heads while moving around, toward and away from the scarves. Let each dancer pick a scarf and dance with it through the space. Alternate "awakening" the scarves and dancing with them. Focus on opposing elements in each section of the dance. For example, dancers might dance with isolated body parts in the "awakening" section and the whole body in the "scarf dancing." Dancers might dance on balance when awakening the scarves and off balance when dancing with them.

Suggested Music: *Music for Creative Dance, Volume IV,* #1

Gypsy Dance

Place small piles of instruments (or scarves) around traffic cones scattered throughout the room. The cones represent gypsy campfires. Dancers form groups around the cones and dance around them, focusing on one element of the lesson concept (slow, big, strong, smooth, etc.). Then they pick up instruments, dancing and playing in the space, focusing on the opposing element (fast, small, light, sharp, etc.). Dancers return their instruments to a different cone and begin the improvisation again.

Suggested Music: *Music for Creative Dance, Volume III,* #8 or *Volume I,* #9

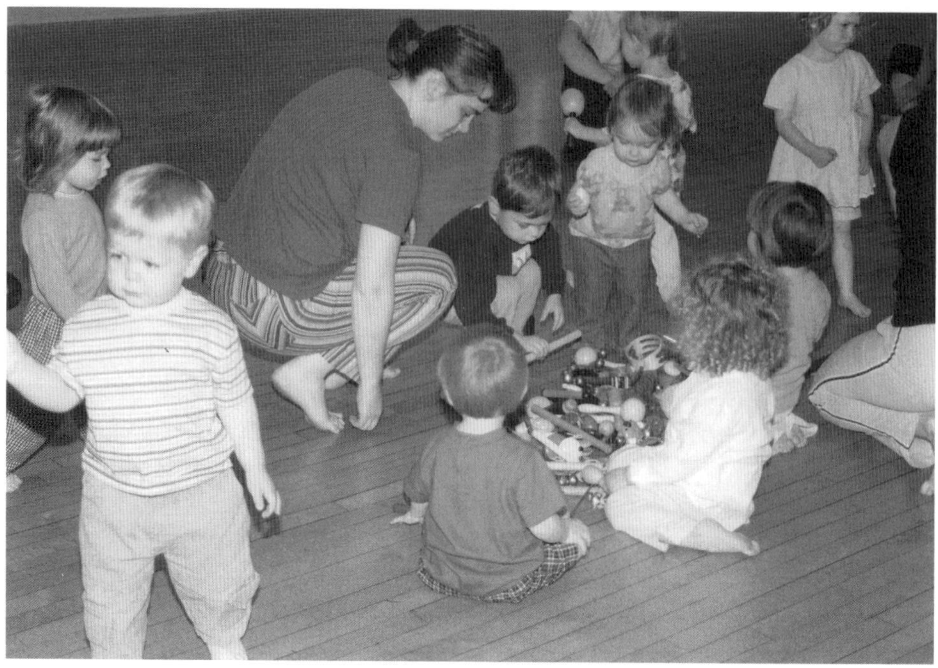

Paint Brushes

Push small scarves into one end of the foam sticks to act as paintbrushes. If foam sticks are not available with holes in the ends, use small, hand held scarves. Dancers alternate painting the space and themselves (excellent tactile stimulation), while focusing on the lesson concept (Level, Pathway, etc.). Dancers may paint with both the scarf and stick end.

Suggested Music: *Music for Creative Dance, Volume IV,* #12

Structured Improvisations for Ages Seven through Adult

Older or experienced dancers benefit from improvisation because they learn to think quickly and work in the moment. The spontaneous response to external or internal stimuli keeps the senses active and the brain synapses firing. Improvisation is literally brainstorming. It is an excellent way to keep creative juices flowing when the stress of tests, work and everyday living keep dancers' brains overwhelmed or confused! Not dealing with competition or production is liberating. It opens new avenues of thought and emotion. Improvisation generates ideas and is therapeutic.

With these dancers, the teacher's role during improvisation is primarily that of observer rather than participant. The structures are more complex with fewer cues. Older or experienced dancers learn from observing each other and enjoy the exchange.

While some structures mention specific props, many improvisations described below may also include props.

Art Works

Hold up a work of art such as a Calder or Matisse print. Cards and posters can be found at local art museums, over the Internet or in art books from the library. Ask the dancers to improvise movement based on the designs, shapes, lines, colors, relationships or spatial elements used by the artist.

Connect the improvisation to the lesson concept. For example, when the concept is Pathway, the use of line by the artist will motivate the dancers. Show one work of art, two or three by the same artist or several by different artists.

Suggested Music: *Music for Creative Dance, Volume III,* #12; *Volume II,* #10; or *Volume IV,* #7 (depending on the artwork)

Photos

Choose two dynamic photos from dance calendars, books, posters, etc. Display the two photos in PowerPoint, tack them on the wall or hold them up. Each dancer will choose one photo to inspire the beginning shape of a dance and the other photo the ending shape. The dancers improvise based on the photos while keeping in mind the following questions: "If the dancer(s) in the photo came to life, what movement would be next? How would the movement need to change for the dancer to end in the second shape? When would the transition happen? How would the dance differ if you switched the order of the photos?" Longer improvisations can be introduced through a series of three or four photos.

Suggested Music: *Music for Creative Dance, Volume I,* #8 or #5

Word Cards

Choose a card from a pile of locomotor and nonlocomotor word cards and one from a pile of concept words. Call out the pair of words (i.e., jump low, skip strongly, twist slowly, float off balance). Dancers improvise the word pair until the teacher calls out a new one. To focus on the lesson concept, the dancers add an element of the concept to each word pair. For example, if the concept is Pathway, one dancer might jump low in a curved pathway, skip strongly in a straight pathway, twist slowly in a straight pathway and float off balance in a zigzag pathway. Another dancer might choose a different pathway for each pair of words.

Suggested Music: *Music for Creative Dance, Volume I,* #10

Motif Notation

Select four to five motif symbols (found in the Appendices). Display one at a time and ask the dancers to improvise at least four different ways to move. Sometimes say, "change," as a signal for dancers to find a new way of exploring the symbol. Other times count from one to four slowly while the dancers vary their movements after each count. Display two symbols at the same time to generate more complex or specific movements.

Suggested Music: *Music for Creative Dance, Volume I,* #16

Textures

Allow dancers to touch several objects with different textures, such as sandpaper, silk, bubble wrap, toothpicks, stones, sponges and golf tees. Call out three or four of the objects one at a time for the dancers to describe through improvisation. They can add sounds to create a textured sound score.

Maps

On a piece of paper each dancer draws three geometric shapes to represent cities, then three pathways to connect the shapes. Each trades maps with another dancer and dances the new maps. "Where will they start? What nonlocomotor movements will they do in each city? How will they travel to the next city?"

Suggested Music: *Music for Creative Dance, Volume III,* #13

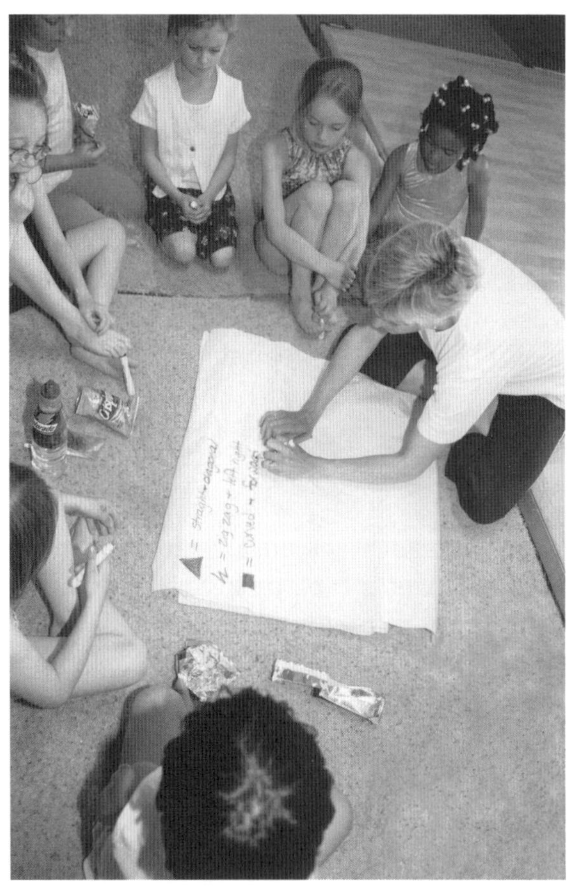

Poems

Read or display a short poem (cinquain, haiku or couplet) for improvisation. Read the poem first while the dancers listen and then while the dancers improvise. Use a dramatic voice, varying tempo, pitch and volume to inspire a variety of movements. Experienced dancers may prefer to read or write the poem themselves, then create their own timing and phrasing.

Suggested Music: *Music for Creative Dance, Volume II,* #18 (for haiku)

Combinations

Dancers base their improvisation on the dance combination they practiced in the Developing Skills section of class. After referring to the choreographic devices chart found in this chapter (expansion, diminution, retrograde, etc.), they vary the combination. To structure the improvisation for novice dancers, call out different choreographic devices at intervals so dancers explore different ways to revise the combination with the same device. This allows dancers to get new ideas from each other.

Suggested Music: *Music for Creative Dance, Volume III,* #10 (4/4), #17(6/8), #18 (3/4) or #19 (2/4)

Synonyms

Dancers improvise the subtle differences between similar words such as "burst," "pop," "explode," "expand" and "erupt." How does the dancers' size, level, direction, energy, weight or flow change from word to word? Ask the dancers to prepare a list of synonyms for dance class.

Suggested Music: *Music for Creative Dance, Volume IV,* #4

Enter/Exit

Dancers stand around the edges of the space. They enter at random (or when the teacher calls their names) in relation to the lesson concept. They move in and through the space, relating to others if desired. They exit using opposite movement from which they entered. When exploring Focus, for example, dancers enter with multi-focus, dance by focusing on another dancer and exit while focusing on one of their own body parts. When the concept is Level, dancers enter on a low level, play "Level Boogie" in the space and exit on a high level. Encourage dancers to observe each other and to play off the energy and rhythm of the dancers entering and exiting the space. Constantly change level so they are never on the same level as other dancers.

Suggested Music: *Music for Creative Dance, Volume III,* #16

Minimalism

Give dancers different problems to solve with specific parameters. For example, they move in all directions and levels while constantly facing toward one wall; they move smoothly in self space with the upper body (the lower body is frozen) and sharply in general space with the lower body (the upper body is frozen). They move as a group starting at a high level in one corner of the room and ending in a low level in the opposite one.

Suggested Music: *Music for Creative Dance, Volume IV,* #10

Sounds

Each dancer or the teacher writes a sound on an index card such as "whoooooosh," "click," "sshhhh," "buzzzzzzz" and "tchtchtch." The teacher or student selects random cards and reads the sound on the card (or holds up the card). The dancers repeat the sound as they improvise it. Move through many sound cards quickly with novice dancers or spend a longer time on five or six sounds with experienced dancers. These cards may be used later with choreography. An added challenge is to think of sounds that reflect the lesson's concept (sharp and smooth, high and low, curved and straight).

Flocking

Dancers organize themselves into three to six groups, with four to six dancers in each group. Each group starts in a corner (or side, for six groups). The leader of group #1 dances from the corner into the center and then freezes in a shape. The rest of group #1 moves into the center as one group (or flock), copying the leader's movements. Then the leader of group #2 dances into the center and group #2 copies the leader's movements. As the leader of group #3 dances into the center, group #1 slowly backs away from the center and returns to their corner. The improvisation continues with new leaders for each round until everyone has been a leader. Encourage leaders to keep their movements simple and clear so their flock can copy them as one body. This is an excellent improvisation for practicing ensemble dancing.

Suggested Music: *Music for Creative Dance, Volume I,* #15

Suites (ABC)

Suites are improvisations with three sections that explore three elements of a concept such as curved/straight/zigzag pathway, low/middle/high level, sagittal/vertical/horizontal planes, single/multi/internal focus or off/on/counterbalance. Dancers might also explore two opposing elements of a concept during the first two sections; the third section of the suite as a combination of elements (A = sharp, B = smooth, C = sharp and smooth).

Suggested Music: *Music for Creative Dance, Volume III,* #16

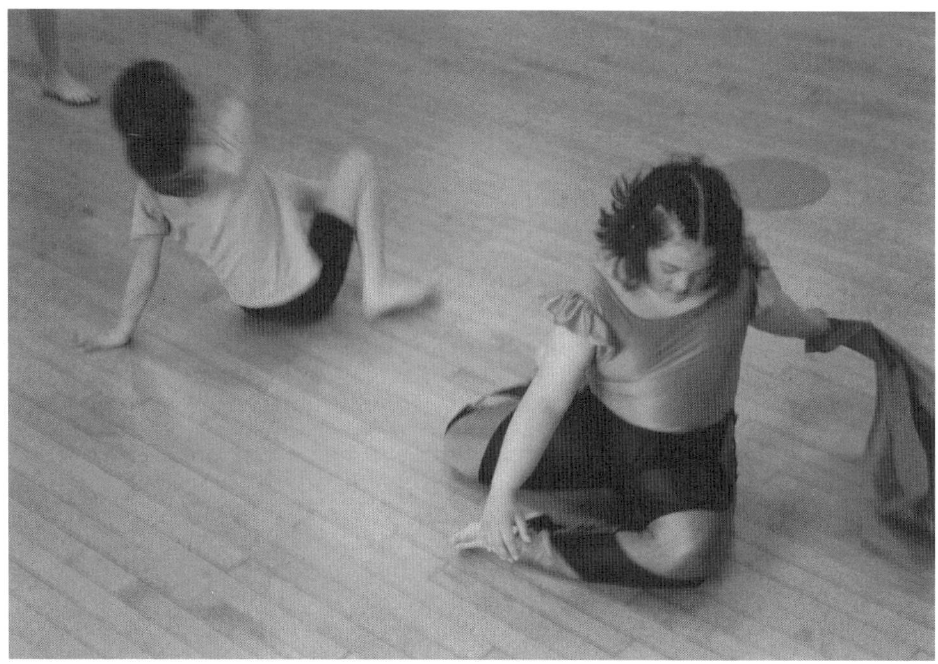

Repetition

For ABA improvisations, dancers explore one element of a concept (far reach), then the opposing element (near reach) and repeat the first element again (far reach). For ABACA improvisations, dancers explore one element of a concept repeatedly (A), alternating with different elements (B and C). For example, A = smooth energy, B = sharp energy, A = smooth energy, C = swingy energy.

Suggested Music: *Music for Creative Dance, Volume IV,* #6

Four Movements

List four movements and assign a number to each (i.e., 1 = turning, 2 = running, 3 = stillness, 4 = floating). Prepare slips of paper for all students in the class times four. Write the numeral 1 on as many pieces of paper as there are students in the class. Continue with 2, 3 and 4. Dancers choose four slips of paper and improvise according to the numbers they picked. Direct the dancers to do the movements in the order the numbers are picked or they may rearrange the order. For example, a dancer may pick the numbers 1, 1, 4, 3, and improvise different ways of turning (relating to the lesson concept) until a signal is given, do more turning until the second signal, float until the third signal and finally be still. While this dancer improvises, another may run, float, turn and run, following the sequence of numbers chosen.

Suggested Music: *Music for Creative Dance, Volume IV,* #18

Focus Fun

Dancers choose a focus (internal, single or multi) for each section of the improvisation. They may also pick a card with a focus on it. For internal focus, dancers move in self space. For single focus, dancers copy the movements of others who may or may not be aware they are being copied. Dancers then use multi-focus to relate to many dancers in any way they choose. This structure often results in humorous improvisations. Even though this improvisation uses Focus, other concepts are easily included. When exploring Size, dancers may choose small movements in the internal focus section, large movements in the single focus section and both large and small movements when relating to everyone in the multi-focus section.

Suggested Music: *Music for Creative Dance, Volume I,* #13

Roll the Die

Choose three themes such as movements, concepts and emotions. Assign a different movement to each number on a die, then a different concept to each number and, finally, a different emotion. Each dancer rolls the die once to discover the movement, a second time to discover the concept, a third to discover the emotion to be danced. The dancers then improvise their movement-concept-emotion combinations (run-slowly-excited, turn-off-balance-bored, press-low-level-angry). The dancers find these chance combinations challenging but fun to explore. Dancers exchange combinations with other dancers for more exploration. Other themes might include body parts and environments (float-legs-scared, jump-mud-lightly).

Suggested Music: *Music for Creative Dance, Volume III,* #21

Balloon Bounce

Alternate holding the balloon (or a ball) in different ways (in one hand, with both hands, between knees, cradled in one arm) and dancing while tapping, kicking, bouncing, dabbing or punching the balloon with different body parts. This is excellent for eye-hand and eye-foot coordination. A similar idea is to balance a beanbag, spot or streamer on different body parts while dancing and then dance in different ways with the object.

Suggested Music: *Music for Creative Dance, Volume I,* #1

ShapeScape Suite

Dancers improvise many ways of dancing inside a stretchy band by creating a variety of shapes with the band and their bodies. Next, they hold the stretchy band in one or both hands and dance with it as they might with a scarf. Finally, dancers place the stretchy band on the floor in different shapes and dance inside, outside, over and around the shapes.

Suggested Music: *Music for Creative Dance, Volume IV,* #14

Nature Dances

Students improvise outdoors as they relate to and dance with natural objects (trees, plants, flowers, stones, shells, twigs, etc.), and manmade objects (statues, benches, signs, etc.). A portable sound system, voice, musical instruments or the natural and manmade objects may provide accompaniment.

Dance Making: The Art of Choreography

Choreography is the art of organizing movement into a form of communication. It requires planning, unlike the spur-of-the-moment art of improvisation that, though sometimes highly structured, is more open-ended than choreography. A choreographer's purpose ranges from pure movement (abstract) to telling a complex story (narrative), but form must be present for movement to be choreography.

Form is of the essence, but many choreographers today lack an understanding of the importance of this element. The best post-modern works that broke with tradition had form. Choreography without form leaves the audience without feeling, just a sense of random movement. Of course, more goes into a well-choreographed dance, but it is an important and often forgotten ingredient.

Students introduced to choreographic forms, devices and principles in the Creating section of class learn to become skilled choreographers. The age and experience of students, as well as the amount of time available, will determine how deeply a subject is presented. Choreography involves planning and practice; this takes time. Choreography often requires collaboration. This is valuable for the development of interpersonal intelligence, but also requires time. Sharing and reflecting on choreography (discussed in the next chapter) can be time consuming as well. However, learning about all aspects of choreography and having the opportunity to create dances is so valuable for students that class time must be organized in a way that makes this learning experience possible. Understanding and using the principles of choreography may strengthen students' writing skills and establish a foundation for understanding other art forms.

Choreography is best suited for dancers ages six through adult. Each week give novice dancers a different problem to solve that relates to the lesson concept, while introducing a new choreographic form or device. In the later part of the year, students might spend four or five weeks on a chosen choreographic project.

When introducing choreographic forms, devices and principles to young or novice dancers, have the whole class create a study with the teacher's help. After the dancers practice a few times, divide them in half – one for performance and one for observation. This is an easy way to introduce the elements of choreography. After four or five classes working as a whole, they usually gain enough experience to create their own studies in small groups.

Available class time and student experience determine which choreographic studies are appropriate. Novice dancers need less time to choreograph because they have fewer skills to draw upon. They are more successful when given simple, well-structured movement problems. Experienced dancers cope with complex, open-ended choreographic assignments and enjoy having adequate time for a project. Experienced dancers also benefit when asked to work quickly when time is limited. I call this "power choreography."

***Teaching Tip**: I am often asked about accompaniment. Students age eight through adults at the Creative Dance Center are fortunate to have live music. The accompanist improvises as dancers share their studies. When I teach without live accompaniment, I choose from several alternatives:*

- *The dancers accompany their own compositions with words, sounds or silence.*
- *The observers accompany dancers on instruments, when available.*
- *As DJ, I ask each group which music they prefer (bouncy, lyrical, fast, slow, etc.). I then play recorded music and fade it as the dance ends.*
- *I select music at random and the dancers move with or against the rhythm .*
- *When dancers work on a choreographic project over several weeks, each group selects or creates its own music with my approval.*

Choreographic Studies for Ages Seven through Adult

Many of the following studies require organizing students into groups of three to five, depending on the size or experience of the class. Less experienced dancers work better in smaller groups. Refer to the list on "Ways to Group Students" for different grouping techniques. It is important to vary the method of grouping, so students do not always pick the same people to work with. Creating dances with different dancers each week exposes students to new ideas and strengthens collaboration skills.

After the dancers are grouped, explain the choreographic structure. Outlining the criteria for the dance on the board or chart paper is helpful. Sometimes the whole group improvises a short dance based on the structure before choreographing in small groups. Let the dancers know how much time they have to plan their studies and always give them a two-minute warning before time is up. Occasionally, have a dress rehearsal near the end of the allotted time. All the groups run through their pieces at the same time. Check to see that everyone is on the right track. When the time is up, the studies are shown and an opportunity for reflection is provided (discussed in the following chapter).

While the dancers are working in small groups, observe and help with problems that arise. When groups spend too much time talking, the teacher may have to help dancers begin the process by

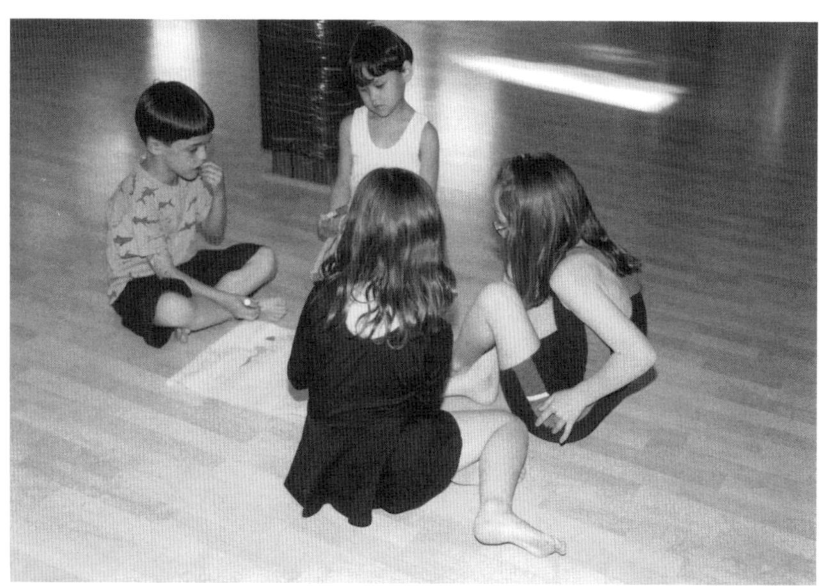

reminding them that improvising is a wonderful way to generate ideas. Suggest they draw designs on paper, list words or images for describing through movement or combine two locomotor actions and two nonlocomotor actions into a phrase and then use a choreographic device to vary the phrase.

When groups have trouble collaborating (when there are too many "bosses"), discuss the problems, ask for suggestions to solve them and encourage solutions. If they have no solutions for collaboration, suggest several options. For example, if a movement is too difficult for someone, that person can adapt it. They can divide into smaller groups (i.e., two duets) to work on sections and then put the parts together. Dancers might create an improvised section where everyone works on their own movement, then include a short section in which they work together. The teacher confidently reinforces the students' ability to resolve their differences and then walks away.

Groups do not always finish their studies at the same time. Ask those who finish quickly to show their dance. One might ask, "Did you meet all the criteria for the study?" "Are there ways to make the movement or meaning clearer?" "Are the transitions smooth?" "Is there a clear beginning and end?" Usually the dancers have more work to do. Remind the groups who do not complete their study before the sharing that it is a work in progress. They will need to improvise any unfinished parts when performing. This is a wonderful learning experience.

Ways to Group Dancers

If groups are uneven, ask for volunteers to join other groups or make your own alterations.

- **Birthday months**: Group dancers according to the months in which they were born (For four groups: January-March, April-June, July-September, October–December).
- **Birth dates**: Group dancers according to the days on which they were born (1-7, 8-15, 16-22, 23-31 or 1-5, 6-10, 11-15, 16-20, 21-25, 26-31).
- **Initials of first (or last) name**: Decide how many groups are needed and group letters accordingly. (A-F, G-K, L-P, Q-U, V-Z for 5 groups. Adjustments may need to be made.)
- **Coordination Patterns**: Group dancers according to their Home Pattern. (Hang, Swing, Shape, Thrust. See the Appendices for more information.)
- **Pick of the cards**: Use one or two decks of playing cards or make original number cards. Divide the total number of dancers by the number of groups desired (i.e., twenty-four dancers divided by six groups equals four cards in each group). For this example, combine four aces with four twos, four threes, four fours, four fives and four sixes. Each dancer picks one card and then joins the group with the dancers holding the same number. (Also use picture or symbol cards.)
- **Color of clothing**: Group dancers according to the primary color of their clothing (blue, green, black, etc.).
- **Mixed ages**: Group dancers according to their ages. Ask each dancer to join someone from each age group to form a new group.
- **Quartets**: Dancers find a partner, then find another pair to form a quartet.
- **New friends/Old friends**: Dancers form a shape with someone they have not danced with today. Now find another pair with someone you have danced with today.
- **Mixed genders**: Girls form pairs (or trios) with girls, boys with boys. Now boy-pairs connect with girl-pairs to create mixed-gender quartets (or trios and pairs join to create a group of five).

Choreographic Devices and Forms

Choreographic devices are useful for manipulating and modifying movement practiced earlier in the lesson. Each device is explored individually through improvisation or introduced into any of the choreographic structures described in this chapter. Understanding and incorporating devices into improvisation and choreography leads to the creation of unique and layered compositions.

Choreographic Devices

- **Expansion**: Make the movements bigger.
- **Diminution**: Make the movements smaller.
- **Repetition**: Repeat a movement or phrase several times.
- **Canon**: Repeat the movement or phrase several counts after the previous person or group begins it.
- **Retrograde**: Perform a pattern and then "rewind" (jump, turn, roll; roll, turn, jump).
- **Transposition**: Transfer the movement to a different or opposite body part.
- **Accumulation**: Perform a movement once (1), then do it again adding a second movement (1, 2), then do the first two movements and add a third movement (1, 2, 3).
- **Rhythm**: Vary the speed or change the rhythm of the movement.
- **Opposite Actions**: Perform a movement (float), do the opposite (slash) and then connect the two (float and slash).
- **Concept Contrast**: Change the space, time or force of the movement.

Composing dances gives students experience with and an understanding of the various forms that choreographers use. In *Creative Dance for All Ages*, many choreographic exercises are described for each dance concept. In this book, studies for each choreographic *form* are described on the following pages. Although compositional ideas are categorized under specific forms, many ideas may be used to create dances in other forms. Teachers are encouraged to mix and match ideas with forms.

Choreographic Forms

- **ABA**: A= one phrase, theme or concept; B= a different phrase, theme or concept
- **Suite** (ABC): Three sections, often with a moderate beginning, slow middle, fast ending
- **Recurring Theme**: Theme and variation, rondo, ABBC, ABCDECFGC, etc.
- **Abstract**: Nonrepresentational, geometric form; movement for movement's sake
- **Narrative**: A story line or representational (i.e., a dance about nature)
- **Broken Form**: Unrelated ideas, often illogical and humorous
- **Chance Dance**: Movement selected and defined but randomly structured through the chance roll of dice, draw of a card, etc.

ABA Dances

Concepts (for solos, duets, trios or small groups)

Dancers create studies based on the lesson concept in an ABA form (i.e., high-low-high or low-high-low dances). They decide which element will be illustrated in the A section and the B section. Ask the dancers to perform an ABA dance with a "twist." When the A section is repeated, the dancers may add a slight variation. Young dancers particularly enjoy creating surprise endings!

Suggested Music: *Music for Creative Dance, Volumes I-V* (Play the first three sections of any contrast song that has an AB form.)

Photos (for solos, duets, trios or small groups)

Choose two dynamic photos from dance calendars, books, posters, etc. Display the two photos by using PowerPoint, tack them on the wall or hold them up. Each group will choose one photo to inspire the A section of the dance and the other photo for the B section.

Images (for trios or small groups)

In the A section, dancers choreograph unison movement focusing on one element of the lesson's concept (i.e., strong weight). In the B section, the dancers choose different images that reflect the opposite elements and choreograph solos reflecting those images. Section A will demonstrate unison group movement. Section B will demonstrate solo dances reflecting movements that contrast with A. Light weight images include balloons, feathers and snow. For section B, all images (balloons, feathers and snow) are represented in the contrasting solos.

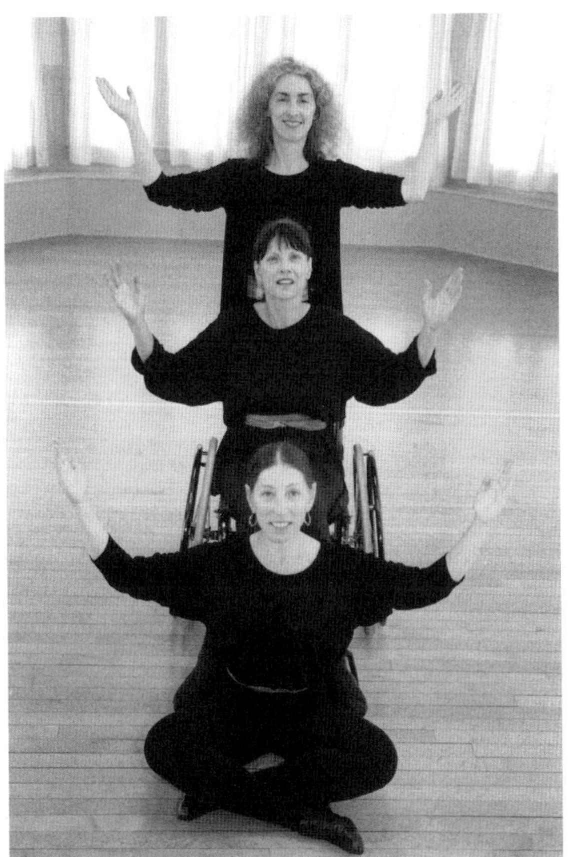

Totem Poles (for trios, small or large groups)

Organize dancers into groups of three to six. It is helpful to show pictures of totem poles if students are unfamiliar with them. For the A section, dancers create a totem pole with shapes relating to each other on different levels. For the B section, dancers travel through space depicting movements of fish, birds or other animals. The dancers repeat the A section.

Suggested Music: *Music for Creative Dance, Volume III,* #1 or *Volume IV,* #13

Variations

- For the A section, dancers move in self-space within the totem pole formation.
- For the B section, all dancers create a creature (eagle, salmon, bear) and dance in unison, then break apart into many creatures.

Natural Disasters (for small or large groups)

Groups create dances about blizzards, hurricanes, volcanoes, tsunami, forest fires, earthquakes, tornadoes, etc. Assign a different disaster to each group or assign the same disaster to all groups. This study is appropriate for teaching the concepts of Weight, Energy, Relationships, Balance or Flow. For example, the dance may begin with bound flow, move to free flow and end again in bound flow. Props may be added for visual effect. Dancers might also create their own sound effects with instruments, body or voice.

Geysers (for solos, duets, trios or small groups)

This idea is based on a lesson by Ann Hutchinson Guest.

Prepare strips of paper that can also be used for other studies. Cut long strips of blue paper for the geysers (1" by 6"), shorter strips of white paper for stillness (1" by 3") and squares of brown paper for boiling mud surrounding the geysers (1" by 1"). Each group of dancers selects pieces from each pile and places them on the floor to create a pattern in the ABA form. For example, A= white, brown, brown, brown, brown; B = blue, blue, white, blue, blue; A= white, brown, brown, brown, brown. Then the dancers create a "geyser dance" based on their pattern. The blue strips (water) inspire smooth, slow, free flow, off balance or high movements (depending on the lesson's concept) and the brown squares (mud) might inspire the opposite element of the lesson's concept (sharp, fast, bound flow, on balance or low movements). Stillness (the white pieces) is an important concept in choreography. Dancers might accompany their movements with appropriate sounds. Other images might be used, such as water fountains and drips, wind and rain or rivers and rocks.

Unison and Contrast (for trios or small or large groups)

For the A section, the dancers create together a dance phrase to be performed in unison. For the B section, each dancer or pair of dancers choreographs a solo or duet phrase. Encourage the dancers to make smooth transitions between sections. The class might suggest signals to communicate with each other on when to change sections during the dance.

Suite (ABC) Dances

Cycles (for small or large groups)

Select one type of cycle for all groups or assign a different cycle to each group. Suggestions include the water cycle; life cycle of frogs, butterflies, fish, birds, other animals or plants; the seasons and the earth's rotation (morning, afternoon, evening). For the water cycle, the first section might show different bodies of water evaporating, the second section, condensation and cloud formations and the third section, various forms of precipitation.

Variation

- Find pieces of cloth, printed with fish, birds, leaves or clouds. Give each group a large piece relevant to the cycle and have them incorporate it into their dance.

Textures (for solos, duets, trios or small groups)

Choose three objects with different textures such as sandpaper, silk and a sponge. It is helpful to have a set of textured objects for each group to touch and manipulate. Let the dancers arrange the objects as they choose and then compose a texture suite. Encourage them to make the transitions between sections clear. An additional challenge is to do the first section at a medium tempo, the second at a slow one and the third fast. For accompaniment, the dancers might make appropriate vocal or body sounds that describe the textures.

Concepts (for solos, duets, trios or small groups)

Dancers create suites based on three different elements of one concept, such as curved-straight-zigzag pathways, upper-middle-lower body parts, off-on-counterbalances, forward-backward-sideways directions and pulse-pattern-breath rhythms. Each section focuses on a different element. Groups select the order for performing the elements.

Three Places (for solos, duets, trios or small groups)

Dancers choose three different areas of the "stage" for each section of the suite, such as downstage right, upstage left and center stage. They compose a movement phrase for each section and decide on a transition to move them from place to place. All dancers move from place to place as one group. Or pairs and trios within a group may travel to and dance in different places.

Matter (for small or large groups)

Each section of the suite represents one state of matter (solid, liquid, gas). Dancers decide whether to start with solids or gas. In the solid section, they dance close together; in the liquid section, they move farther apart; in the gas section they use the entire space. Dancers may choose specific objects (ice-water-steam) to represent the three states of matter.

Three Verbs (for solos, duets, trios or small groups)

Give each group a card with three verbs; ask dancers to pick their own verb cards or have groups brainstorm a list of verbs and select three for their suite. The verbs may be action words (leap, twist, crawl) or verbs related to dance concepts such as rise, hover and fall (Level). Occasionally request dancers to choose one locomotor word (jump), one nonlocomotor word (push) and create a new verb ("jumpush").

Emotions (for solos, duets, trios or small groups)

Suites based on emotions may be created in several ways. First, the dancers choose three contrasting emotions on which to base their dance. Second, give each group three cards: two of the cards have faces describing emotions and the third card is blank. The dancers choose an emotion and draw it on the blank card. Then they create a dance based on the three facial expressions depicted on the cards. Third, give trios three blank cards and ask each dancer to draw an emotional face on each card. Fourth, give groups sets of three emotional verbs to be described through movement (i.e. search, find and lose). For any of these studies, the dancers may put the three contrasting emotions into any order they wish.

Rhythms (for solos, duets, trios or small groups)

Dancers create suites based on three different meters or dance styles. These can include 6/8 meter-3/4 meter-2/4 meter, polka-waltz-march or jazz-ballet-flamenco.

Folk Dances (for small or large groups)

After students have practiced an ABC form folk dance in the Developing Skills section, ask them to re-choreograph one section or create an entirely new dance based on the style or music of the original folk dance. For example, "Mayim" is a dance about water. Students choreograph dances using the structure of "Mayim," illustrating the elements of air, fire or earth.

Dances in Nature (for solos, duets, trios or small groups)

Students create dances outdoors that relate to natural and manmade objects (trees, benches, statues, plants, ponds, bugs, etc.). Choose three different objects as motivation for the suite or relate to one object in three different ways. Voice, musical instruments, a portable sound system or objects found in nature can be used as accompaniment.

Enter/Center/Exit (for solos, duets, trios or small groups)

Dancers choreograph a phrase to enter the stage space, focusing on one element of the lesson's concept (fast pulse when the concept is Rhythm). They choreograph a second phrase (a rhythm pattern) to perform in the center of the space. They exit the stage in a movement that is opposite from their entrance (slow pulse).

Ideas for other concepts include:

- **Focus:** Enter focusing on a partner, dance center stage focusing on a particular object, exit focusing on the audience.
- **Pathway:** Enter in a curved pathway, dance center stage in zigzag pathways, exit in a straight pathway.
- **Planes:** Enter moving in the sagittal plane, dance center stage in the horizontal plane, exit with movement in the vertical plane.

Recurring Themes

Refer to the chart on "Choreographic Devices" for ways to vary movement phrases.

Body Parts (for solos, duets, trios or small groups)

Dancers create ABACAD dances that focus on body parts. For section A, dancers choreograph a repeatable phrase that uses the whole body. For section B, dancers compose a phrase emphasizing one part, such as an arm. They choose other body parts for sections C and D.

Colors (for solos, duets, trios or small groups)

Cut three or four different colors of paper into strips. They may be 1.5" to 2" wide and 3" to 4" long. Dancers lay them on the floor in a pattern; one color represents the theme and the other colors the variations. Dancers choreograph a phrase and then employ choreographic devices to modify it. For example, dancers may vary the phrase (indicated by the green strip), using expansion to make the movement bigger. This variation might be indicated with a yellow strip. Then they use diminution to make the movement smaller and indicate it with a blue strip. For this example, the pattern of paper strips is green, yellow, green, blue, green. The dancers perform the original phrase (green paper), the phrase performed with expanded range (yellow paper), the original phrase (green paper), the phrase performed with smaller range (blue paper), ending with the original phrase (green paper).

New Concept/Old Concept (for solos, duets, trios or small groups)

Dancers create a phrase based on the lesson's concept and then vary it by combining a new concept with previously studied ones. If the lesson's concept is Weight, the dancers create a movement phrase combining strong and light movements. They vary the weight phrase by performing it on a different level and then in a different tempo.

Rhythm Patterns (for solos, duets, trios or small groups)

Dancers create patterns on the floor with the paper strips from the "Geyser" study. Dancers may arrange the paper strips to describe canons or rounds or repeat a pattern with slight variations in the design. Dancers choreograph studies based on the pattern.

Folk Dances (for small or large groups)

Groups vary the movements in one or two sections of a folk dance learned earlier. Each group teaches others their variation so every time the folk music is repeated the whole class performs a new variation.

Motif Notation (for solos, duets, trios or small groups)

Dancers write a short movement phrase with motif symbols. Then they exchange these phrases with one another or with another group. They practice the new phrase and choose a choreographic device to vary the phrase. After practicing the variation, they perform the phrase and its variation for the original writers of the phrase. Dancers enjoy this exchange!

Synonyms (for solos, duets, trios or small groups)

Dancers choreograph a study that shows the subtle differences between three synonyms. Some synonym triads include burst, explode, pop; contract, deflate, wither; rise, reach, climb; corral, surround, squeeze; scatter, throw, dispense; squirm, wiggle, writhe.

Comparatives

Dancers choreography studies inspired by comparatives such as big, bigger, biggest; slow, slower, slowest; strong, stronger, strongest; silly, sillier, silliest; straight, straighter, straightest; smooth, smoother, smoothest.

Narrative Dances

Literature (for solos, duets, trios or small groups)

Legends, myths and fairy tales provide excellent material for narrative dances. To avoid pantomime when using literature for choreography, it is helpful for dancers to use the movement concepts in their narrative studies. For example, many stories are based on journeys. The dancers might begin with Pathway. What pathways do the characters take to reach their destination? What happens along the way? How might they dance on these pathways? What energy is needed to portray different characters? On what level do they travel? Selecting one action-oriented part of the story to recreate keeps the focus on dance, rather than mime.

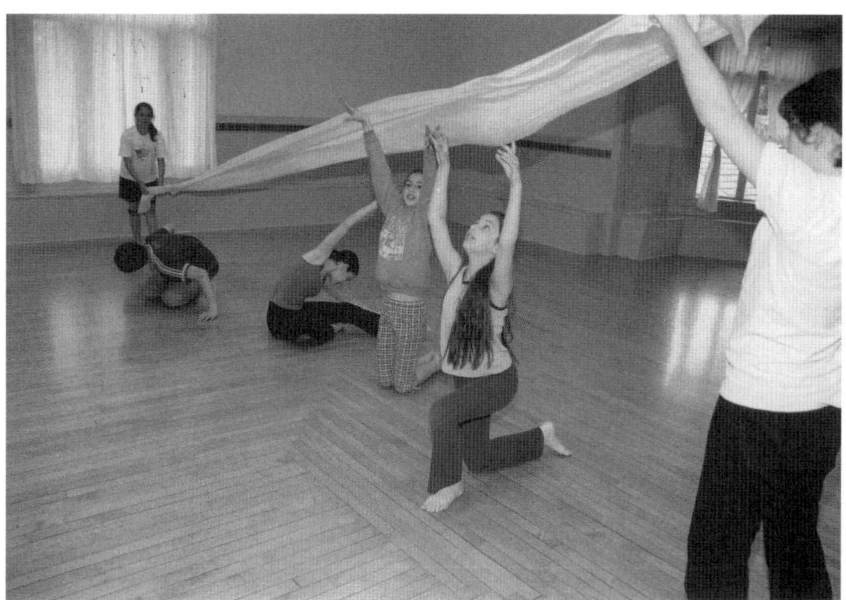

Poetry (for solos, duets, trios or small groups)

When looking through a poetry anthology, find one or more poems relating to each movement concept. There are poems about strong winds and gentle breezes (Weight), shadows (Relationships), winding roads (Pathway), jugglers (Focus) and marching soldiers (Body Parts). Select poems that relate to the lesson's concept. Pairs or groups might choreograph dances based on the same poem. If the poem has several stanzas, each group might work on one stanza and then the entire class performs the poem, one stanza at a time.

Cinquain (for solos, duets, trios or small groups)

Dancers or the teacher writes a cinquain that tells a story. The poem inspires the choreography. The dancers read the poem as they dance or make vocal or body accompaniment. Use this form:

Noun	Witches
Adjective, Adjective	Crooked, Spry
Verb, Verb, Verb	Swoop, Cackle, Fly
Four word phrase	Broomsticks cross the moon
Noun or synonym	(On) Halloween

Diamante (for small or large groups)

A diamante combines two cinquains with opposing ideas. The poem begins with a noun and ends with its antonym. Below are two examples, one that is complete and one that each dance group completes themselves.

Noun	**Conflict**
Adjective, Adjective	Angry, Disconnected
Verb, Verb, Verb	Slash, Stamp, Scream
Two nouns relating to noun, two to antonym	War, Divorce, Peace, Community
Verb, Verb, Verb	Breathe, Care, Listen
Adjective, Adjective	Calm, Connected
Antonym	**Resolution**

Prey
Small, Weak
Run, Quiver, Hide
________, ______, ______, _____
Hunt, Catch, Eat
Big, Strong
Predator

Haiku (for small or large groups)

These Japanese poems provide excellent structures for narrative dances. Choose haiku with lots of action words and a clear story. Dancers also enjoy writing their own haiku. Have dancers vocalize the haiku in different ways as they dance. Speak the haiku before, during or after the dance; speak only certain words of the haiku as they dance. Repeat certain words as a sound score for the dance. Japanese flute music provides an inspiring accompaniment for the choreography.

Silly Situations (for solos, duets, trios or small groups)

Write nouns, adjectives, verbs and adverbs on index cards or have the dancers write some to share with each other. There should be one part of speech on each card. Groups select six to ten cards to create a narrative dance. The dancers may need to fill in some missing words. One example is, "(The) crooked, lazy scarecrow jumped slowly (along the) bumpy river." The dancers extend this silly situation into a short narrative dance.

Yoga Positions (for solos, duets, trios or small groups)

Select four or five yoga positions that the dancers know or quickly teach them. The dancers create narrative dances based on the meaning of the poses. The dancers form the positions in self space, creating transitions that move through general space from one pose to another telling the story. Or the poses come to life and move through space to tell the story.

Emotional Music (for solos, duets, trios or small groups)

Select music with dynamic changes that tells a story or evokes strong emotional responses. As the music plays, the dancers create a story. They draw designs, stick figures, symbols, faces depicting emotions, etc. as they listen or exchange ideas in groups. The dancers then use their designs or ideas to compose narrative dances. Many classical compositions work well for this study. There are also two music selections written especially for story dances on Eric Chappelle's *Music for Creative Dance* CDs *(Volume II,* #20 and *Volume III,* #13*)*.

Short Stories (for solos, duets, trios or small groups)

Write simple story plot cards for dancers to select and use as motivation for narrative dances. Here are some ideas borrowed from literature: "You are controlled by a puppet master, but yearn to break free; you fall down a rabbit hole to discover a new world; you find yourself piloting a little submarine deep on the ocean floor; you are turned into a scarecrow and try to figure out how to become human again."

Folk Dances (for small or large groups)

Many cultures tell stories through dance. "Tanko Bushi" from Japan tells the story of coal miners at work. After learning a story dance or viewing a video from one of these cultures, the dancers choreograph a narrative dance in the style of the culture of origin.

Antonyms (for solos, duets, trios or small groups)

Write pairs of verbs that are antonyms on index cards or have dancers create their own. Examples include meet and part, search and find, conflict and resolve, advance and retreat, wake and sleep, climb and fall or open and close. Dancers create scenarios based on the words that illustrate their antithetical pair.

Biographies (for solos, duets, trios or small groups)

Dancers research a famous dancer or other historical figure using books, videos or the internet. They select four to eight verbs from their research and several adverbs and adjectives. This vocabulary is used as motivation for a dance depicting one or more important aspects of the person's life. The narrative dance may be expanded through further research. Several biographies of dancers are listed in the Bibliography.

Abstract Dances

Art Cards (for solos, duets, trios or small groups)

Give each group a postcard of an abstract work of art. They may be bought at museum stores. Choose art works that have clear shapes, pathways or energy such as works by Matisse, Calder, Jacob Lawrence and Australian Aborigines. Dancers create abstract dances based on these artworks.

Stones (for duets, trios or small groups)

The teacher will need a container of small stones. Each dancer selects two to five stones depending on how many dancers are in a group. Groups form small circles and each dancer in a group takes a turn placing a stone in the center of the circle. The placing of stones should be a quiet ritual. Stones may be placed on top of other stones, next to, near or far from other stones. Continue until all are used and a design is created. The groups then create dances motivated by the designs. Instead of stones, other natural objects such as twigs, shells, wood blocks and leaves may be used.

Paper Strips (for solos, duets, trios or small groups)

Take paper strips from the "geyser" activity described earlier in the chapter. Dancers place the strips randomly to create a dance based on the lesson's concept. The blue strips represent one element (free flow, strong weight, smooth energy, forward direction, off balance, curved pathway, etc.), the brown squares represent the opposite and the white strips represent stillness. Dancers create an abstract dance inspired by their pattern, adding vocal or body accompaniment.

Sounds (for solos, duets, trios or small groups)

Dancers choose three to five vocal, body or instrument sounds. They match movements to the sounds to create an abstract dance. Encourage dancers to create sounds that vary in tempo, rhythm, pitch and volume to inspire a variety of movements. Sounds can be written on cards for selection by novice dancers.

Word Cards (for solos, duets, trios or small groups)

Dancers select four or five cards with a locomotor or nonlocomotor movement or a concept element written on it. They arrange the cards randomly as a dance phrase, considering what word makes an effective beginning and what makes an effective ending. For example, "twist, low level, spin, backwards, roll," may be selected to compose an abstract dance. The dancers decide how to perform each word and create transitions between the actions.

Movement Maps (for solos, duets, trios or small groups)

Dancers create movement maps by drawing roads (pathways) connected to cities (geometric shapes). Consulting their maps, the dancers perform nonlocomotor movements or form shapes in the cities and travel along the roads using different locomotor movements. Groups decide whether to choreograph dances in unison with all members moving together from city to city or independently from city to city. These maps are made simple or complex by adding legends, speed limits, rivers, mountains, compass directions, etc. Dancers choreograph their maps or exchange maps with others for map reading practice.

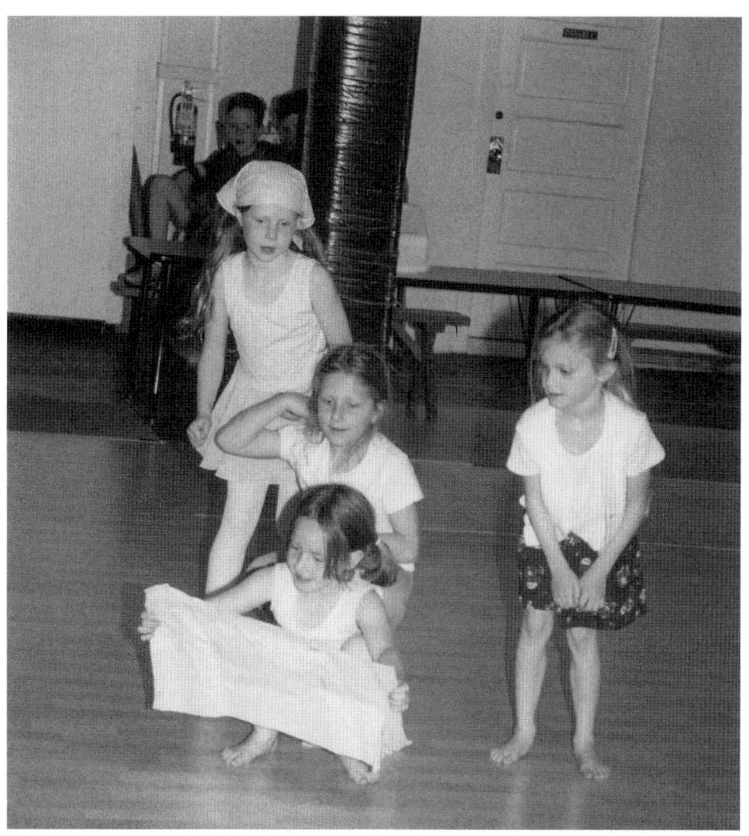

Designs (for solos, duets, trios or small groups)

Dancers draw abstract designs to inspire abstract dances. They are based on the lesson's concept so designs are drawn with strong and light, curved and straight, sharp and smooth or fast and slow strokes.

Symmetry/Asymmetry (for duets or small groups)

Dancers make symmetrical designs by folding paper in half and cutting a shape or drawing on folded paper towels or napkins with food coloring or permanent pens. When the paper is unfolded, dancers will see beautiful symmetrical designs to inspire their dances. An easy way to choreograph symmetrical designs is for pairs or groups to mirror each other's movements. Dancers improvise or choreograph an asymmetrical section for contrast.

Motif Notation (for solos, duets, trios or small groups)

Dancers write a movement phrase using motif symbols on paper or a computer or arrange cards written with symbols into a combination. They create a dance using their notation as a springboard. Dancers also enjoy creating one or two new symbols to notate special actions or emotions in their compositions.

Computer Dances (for solos, duets, trios or small groups)

Dancers choreograph dances on computers in their classrooms using Life Forms or LabanWriter programs. The dances may be set on dancers in the studio or assessed on the computer. Dancers may exchange compositions with classmates for further practice in reading notation and choreographing.

Geometric Shapes

Dancers compose dances with geometric shapes. They can use body parts, relationships to other dancers or props such as stretchy bands, streamers, ribbons or Chinese jump ropes. Transitions between shapes should be included in the choreography.

Props

Dancers explore how many ways they can manipulate a prop (a piece of newspaper, an apron, a chair, a scarf, a hula hoop, a box, a balloon, a large ball, a hat, etc.) Encourage them to use choreographic devices as well as the movement concepts to discover a variety of ways to dance with their prop. After dancing with the prop, dancers select three or four ideas generated through improvisation and compose a prop dance.

Combinations

Dancers may vary combinations learned earlier in class to create new abstract dances. This is a quick way to choreograph, because the dancers already have a phrase from which to work. They do not have to create completely new material. Dancers should be encouraged to use the choreographic devices or dance concepts to "tweak" the old combination into a new dance.

Dance History

Dancers watch a video of a work by a dance pioneer or living choreographer such as Martha Graham, Hanya Holm, Doris Humphrey, José Limón, Paul Taylor, Alwin Nikolais, Alvin Ailey, Twyla Tharp, Chuck Davis, Jiri Killian, Savion Glover, Anthony Tudor or George Balanchine. The dancers discuss the concepts and choreographic devices used and the purpose of the choreography. They then create studies in the style of the choreographer. Alternatively, dancers compare and contrast two choreographers and create contrasting dances. These dances may not always represent the abstract form. Resources for dance videos may be found in the Appendices.

Chance Dance

Several chance dances are described in the section on improvisation. Chance dances are often improvised. By performing studies together in a random fashion, choreographed phrases may also be performed in the chance form. After choreographing any of the studies mentioned above, several individuals, duets or trios perform their compositions at the same time. This is an excellent way to generate ideas for choreography and to see choreographic devices occur by chance when groups relate unexpectedly. Observers reflect upon these moments and remember them for future compositions.

Broken Form

Broken form occurs when the choreographer abruptly " breaks" the structure of the dance. For example, in the middle of a narrative dance, the choreographer may insert an abstract phrase that does not fit into the story. This "breaks" the form and startles the audience. It is a non sequitur and often humorous. It may have the reverse effect and be alarming, which may be the choreographer's goal. Dancers may choreograph in one style and then break into another. They may work with a somber subject and then break into children's playful songs or games. The composition might be fanciful and inventive and then robotic and pedestrian. Students of all ages use broken form naturally as they solve other choreographic problems. Discuss the concept and the feelings this form generates.

Combining Improvisation and Choreography

Combine improvisation and choreography by giving dancers a problem to solve that involves a section to be choreographed and one that can be improvised. It saves time and allows for different learning styles. Some individuals enjoy setting and rehearsing steps and others prefer working spontaneously. When combining choreography and improvisation, each dancer has the opportunity to do what is comfortable and also learns to take risks.

Any of the choreographic studies described in this chapter may be modified to include improvisation. Similarly, the ideas for improvisation may include a short choreographed phrase. Below is one example used with dancers of all ages.

Ocean Dance (ABC form)

Dancers work in pairs. Each pair choreographs a three-part phrase that (1) travels towards each other, (2) involves mirroring each other and (3) incorporates turning around or with each other. (Other three-part structures may be used.) For section A, dancers improvise movements in their scattered self spaces that are slow, flowing, change levels and have characteristics of ocean crea-

tures or plants. For section B, dancers perform their three-part choreography. When using the suggested music, this occurs during the first 24 measures of the metered music. For section C, the dancers improvise blind mirroring (pairs press palms together and take turns being blind and being the leader). When using the suggested music, the dance repeats and the blind mirroring section is longer the second time through. The structure can be adapted to any music or performed in silence.

Suggested Music: *Music for Creative Dance, Volume II,* #1

Designing Choreographic Projects with Ages Nine through Adult

Some class structures allow students to create dances over a period of three to six weeks or longer. In these situations, dancers have more time to work on a project as well as evaluate and revise their compositions. Use the acronym below as a format for composing dances.

CREATE

Choose a topic, purpose or message; identify the inspiration.

Research the topic by reading, discussing, observing, brainstorming; identify key points.

Explore movement possibilities for key points. Experiment with dance concepts.

Augment movements and develop dance phrases.

Tie phrases together into a cohesive dance, integrating any music, sound, text or props.

Evaluate the dance and make revisions if necessary.

As an example, one group chooses the topic of "Autumn."

For **research**:

- Listen to different pieces of music with an autumnal atmosphere.
- Read poems about Autumn.
- View Autumn scenes in books, calendars, etc. (leaves, bonfires, football games, etc.).
- List eight words that describe Autumn.
- Describe four feelings associated with Autumn.

To **explore** movements for the topic:

- Improvise to the music.
- Find the verbs in a poem, create movement for them.
- Connect each scene to a concept such as Energy, Flow or Relationships.
- Choose four of the eight words from a list and describe them through movement
- Form two shapes describing each of the four feelings.

To **augment** the movements explored here, dancers develop four to six movement phrases incorporating the verbs, shapes and concepts from their exploration.

Dancers select a form for their composition and **tie** the phrases together with transitions that compliment chosen music or text. The dance may be videotaped or performed for peers. It is **evaluated** and revised.

Checklist for Creating and Revising Dances

Another format that helps student choreographers is the "Six Traits for Writing Compositions." Jackie Conrad, dance educator in the Vancouver, Washington school district, adapted these traits into a checklist for choreography. They are slightly changed here.

Ideas: The dance has an idea, purpose or message. This may be based on curriculum (literature, art, history), social skills (respect, trust, friendship), emotions (hate, sorrow, joy), dance concepts (Shape, Rhythm, Weight), etc.

Organization: There is a beginning, middle and end demonstrating rising action, climax and resolution. The dance demonstrates a clear progression through these parts.

Voice: The dance demonstrates individuality and invention. It does not copy music videos. It acknowledges the audience: "What is the choreographer saying?" It creates an atmosphere, "How does the dance make the audience feel?"

Fluency: The dance is unified and has transitional flow: "Are the dancers stopping to think between phrases or does the piece flow?" The dance has stylistic control: "Was that fall planned? Is the dance a jumble of styles? Do the phrases fit together?"

Word Choice/Movement Choice: The dance includes contrasts in space, time, force, movement and use of the body. Artistic choices support the idea through the use of various pathways, levels, energies, timing, relationships, actions, etc.

Conventions: The dance includes controlled punctuation such as pauses (commas), stillness (periods) and energy shifts (exclamation points). The dancers plan entrances and exits, bows, etc.

Choreographic Principles

The basic principles that apply to all the arts apply to choreography. Choreographers keep these principles in mind as they create and revise dances.

- **Unity**: Did you create a unified dance with a consistent style and theme?
- **Contrast**: Did you use contrasting elements or is the dance all on one level or at one speed?
- **Harmony**: Are all movements of the dance compatible? Is there a feeling of accord?
- **Balance**: Does the whole piece feel balanced or off balance? Is there a beginning and middle, but no ending? Is there too much contrast, but not enough repetition?
- **Variety**: Are concepts from space, time, force and body included?
- **Emphasis**: Is there a purpose or meaning to the movement? What elements, ideas or themes have you accentuated?
- **Repetition**: Were phrases, movements or themes repeated?

A Personal Note

Young dancers ages eight to fifteen in my dance company, Kaleidoscope, spend two hours per week for six weeks creating group dances for their Winter Concert. They use both checklists described above throughout the six weeks. I serve as a facilitator, moving from group to group, asking questions to help them clarify the purpose of their dances, reminding them to refer to the "Six Trait" checklist. During the fourth week, I videotape their dances. They use the checklist to assess their choreography while watching the tape. They have the fifth week to make necessary revisions and the sixth to polish their dances, share them with peers and practice.

The dancers create sophisticated, well-crafted dances because they have experience with and understand many choreographic skills. They also have weekly practice improvising and creating short studies in their regular dance classes. The ability to collaborate with their peers to create meaningful work is an important skill they will use throughout their lives. I believe that similar opportunities should be available for *all* young people.

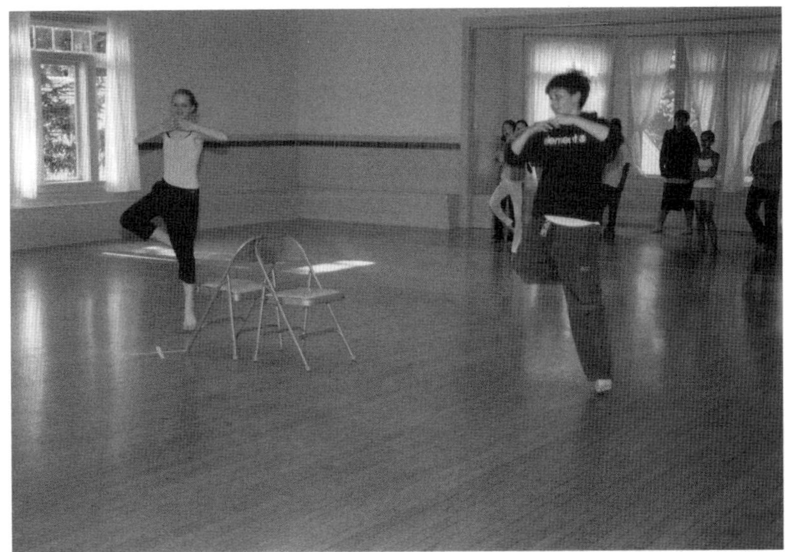

In Summary

In this chapter, we have explored the definitions and benefits of both improvisation and choreography:

- Improvisation is the art of generating and playing with movement in the moment.
- Improvising encourages dancers to take risks and expand their range of movement choices.
- Choreography is the art of planning and organizing movement into a form with intent.
- Dancers learn to organize movement and develop critical thinking skills as they make appropriate movement choices to communicate ideas through choreography.
- Dancers use choreographic devices, forms and principles to compose dances.
- When creating dances, students combine creative and technical skills to communicate ideas and feelings.
- Working with others to compose dances strengthens social skills.
- Choreography and improvisation may be used for assessment.

Now that the students have improvised or created dances, they are ready to share and assess their creations. The Cooling Down section of the lesson provides an opportunity for dancers to review concepts and bring closure to dance class.

Choreograph what you want to see. ~ Danielle, age 13

Chapter Five

Lesson Plan Section 5: Cooling Down

In this chapter:

Vocabulary Poster: Cooling Down Flow Chart

Applicable National Dance Standards

Chapter Introduction

Cooling Down for Infants through Age Five

Cooling Down for Ages Six through Adult

- **Relaxation Exercises**
- **Reflecting on Key Concepts**

Cooling Down for Ages Six through Adult following Improvisation or Choreography

- **Performance Skills**
- **Audience Skills**

Dance Talking: The Art of Evaluating Dances

- **Recording Compositional Work**

Performances, Recitals and "Informances"

In Summary

In Closing

Cooling Down Flow Chart

If you are teaching	*and your Creating activity was*	*your Cool Down may be*
infants with adults	free dance	social or interactive time
toddlers through age three with adults	free dance	goodbye dance and/or stamps
ages three to five without adults	free dance	goodbye dance and/or stamps
ages six through adult	improvisation or choreography without sharing	relaxation exercises and/or reflection
ages six through adult	improvisation or choreography with sharing	simple feedback
ages six through adult	choreographic projects	complex feedback and/or recording dances

COOLING DOWN

Applicable National Dance Standards

The following standards from the *National Standards for Dance Education* will be achieved through the activities in this chapter:

- **Identifying and demonstrating movement elements and skills in performing dance**
- **Understanding choreographic principles, processes and structures**
- **Understanding dance as a way to create and communicate meaning**
- **Applying and demonstrating critical and creative thinking skills in dance**
- **Making connections between dance and healthful living**

Chapter Introduction

After creating, bring closure to dance class by providing a transition for leaving the dance space or moving on to another subject area. The content for the Cooling Down section depends on what was presented in the Creating section, as well as the age of the students. When teaching classes for infants through age five, a closing ritual that reviews the lesson's concept is recommended. This section may also include encouraging comments to each dancer along with rubber stamps on hands and feet.

When older dancers improvise or choreograph during the Creating section, it is beneficial for them to share and evaluate their compositions during the last section of class. This provides an opportunity to develop performance, observation and audience skills. If the choreographic studies are not ready for sharing, or sharing improvisations is not a goal for the class, dancers can stretch, review the lesson concept, reflect on what they learned during the class or do relaxation or visualization exercises.

Concluding class with review and reflection helps the brain synthesize information presented earlier. Observing classmates' compositions provides a visual reminder of the concepts and skills learned in class. Sharing verbal or written feedback with peers strengthens other neural pathways. This multi-sensory cool down makes the last part of class an integral part of a brain-compatible lesson.

Cooling Down for Infants through Age Five

End dance class for infants and adults with infant massage. Allow babies to play with props, practice their developmental movements and socialize as the adults interact with their infants or talk to each other. It is also important to allow time for changing diapers or nursing. At this time, discuss the importance of movement, as well as current articles on early childhood education.

For ages walking through three with adults, class ends with a "goodbye dance." The children dance or run across the room to give their caregivers a big hug. This may be repeated two or three times. An additional way to end class is to stamp the young dancers' hands or feet with a picture related to the day's concept (i.e., a kite for free and bound flow) while giving them positive feedback about their dancing.

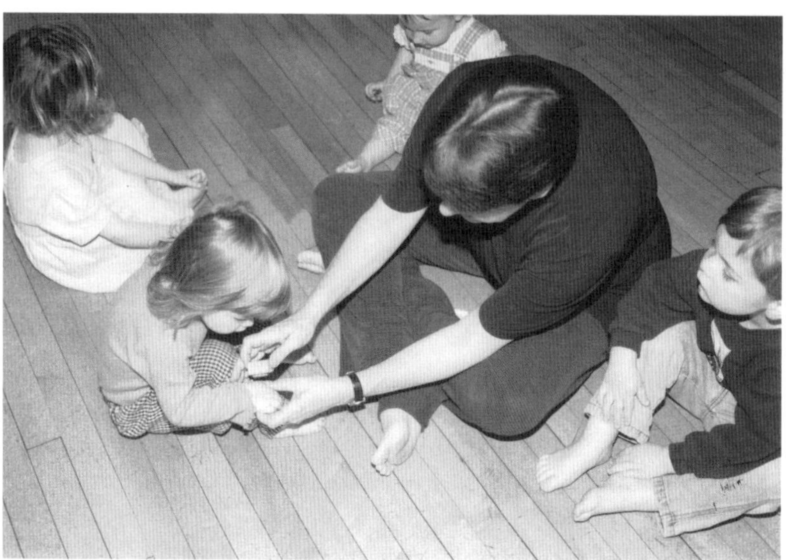

For ages three to five without adults, end class with a conceptual "goodbye dance." The children dance across the room individually, in pairs or groups (depending on the class size) reiterating the lesson's concept (i.e., a growing, shrinking dance about Size). Another idea is to divide the class in half, with each part taking turns improvising for the other. At this age, keep the improvisations short and alternate the roles of dancer and observer three to five times. The quick alternation of roles will keep the young dancers' attention while providing each child opportunities for dancing and observing. After sharing, ask dancers to show their favorite shapes, elements or movements from the day's lesson. They may also discuss a special moment they remember, but keep discussion brief at this age or each child will give a life history!

If not sharing improvisations, end with stamps, positive comments for each dancer or a relaxation exercise. Breathing deeply while lying on the floor and listening to calming music is an excellent way to cool down. Some teachers sing a special goodbye song. Ending with a descriptive comment for each child ("I saw you dancing high and low today" or "I am proud of the way you listened today") makes each child feel special.

***Teaching Tip**: In sixty-minute classes, for toddlers through four years with adults, provide a rest time for the adults after thirty minutes of dancing. Lower the lights and play quiet music for about three minutes. During this time, look after those children not resting with parents. They may sit near you or quietly move about. Encourage adults to breathe slowly as you offer tips for relaxing.*

In sixty-minute classes, for ages three to seven without adults, provide rest and alignment time for children after thirty minutes of dancing. Work quickly with each child while the others lie quietly. Focus on alignment by moving each dancer's arms and legs gently in upper-lower, body-side and cross-lateral patterns. Play calming music to help the children relax.

Suggested Music: *Music for Creative Dance, Volume I,* #8; *Volume II,* #10; *Volume III,* #7; *Volume IV* #17 or favorite lullabies.

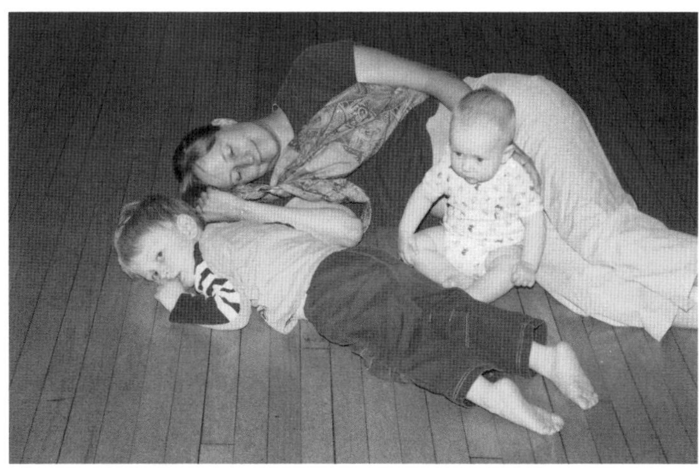

Cooling Down for Ages Six through Adult

If the lesson does not include sharing and observing improvisation or choreography, end with stretching, relaxation exercises or reflection on key concepts learned in class. Classes ending with sharing and observation may also include a quick relaxation exercise or review question as time allows.

Relaxation Exercises

Mirroring

The teacher or leader moves in slow motion, using the lesson's concept (i.e., moving in all six Directions) as the students follow. This may be done sitting or standing.

Suggested Music: *Music for Creative Dance, Volume III,* #18

Mirroring in Groups

Divide the class into two groups facing each other. The leader stands behind the first group and moves in slow motion, so that the second group faces the leader and follows the leader's movements. The leader moves behind the second group, who now become the observers. The observers enjoy watching the movers change energy, speed and level.

Suggested Music: *Music for Creative Dance, Volume III,* #1

Seated Blind Mirror

Partners sit face to face. They press palms together and close their eyes. Leader #1 moves hands slowly in different directions in curved and straight pathways with big and small movements as the partner follows. Alternate leadership several times.

Suggested Music: *Music for Creative Dance, Volume I,* #8

Blind Mirror and Dance Away

Partners stand face to face and place palms together without interlocking fingers. Leader #1 moves Leader #2, who has eyes closed, slowly in self space. At the signal, Leader #2 opens eyes. Both dancers dance in slow motion away from each other. Partners return to each other at a second signal. Leader #2 becomes the leader.

Suggested Music: *Music for Creative Dance, Volume II,* #10

Blind Mirror in Self and General Space

Partners stand face to face and place palms together without interlocking fingers. Leader #1 moves Leader #2, who has eyes closed, slowly in self space. At the signal, Leader #1 moves Leader #2 slowly through general space. At the second signal, Leader #2 will be the leader and Leader #1 will close eyes and be moved in self and general space.

Suggested Music: *Music for Creative Dance, Volume III,* #17

Drawing Designs

Partners sit one in front of the other facing the same direction. The dancer in front closes his or her eyes. With fingertips and appropriate touch, the dancer behind draws designs on the partner's back that reflect the lesson's concept. For example, when the concept is Energy, the drawer will draw with a smooth, then sharp but gentle touch. When the concept is Level, the drawer draws on the upper then lower back or create designs that rise and fall. Partners switch roles at the teacher's signal or cue in the music. This is an excellent way for the dancers to review the lesson's concepts both kinesthetically and visually.

Suggested Music: *Music for Creative Dance, Volume IV,* #17

Hook-Ups

This position, described by Dr. Paul Dennison[1], is particularly useful in public schools where time for relaxation is limited. Standing, sitting or lying, dancers cross one ankle over the other. They then stretch their arms forward with backs of hands together and thumbs pointing down. Lifting one hand over the other (preferably the hand on the same side as the top foot), they interlace fingers and clasp palms. Then they roll the hands down, in and up toward the body with clasped hands on the chest with elbows pointing down. Now they rest their tongues on the roof of their mouths behind their teeth. Dancers should remain in this position for two minutes. This exercise activates both brain hemispheres and integrates the mid brain with the frontal lobes. It is excellent for relaxation, concentration and focus. Students use it to self-regulate behavior when they are over stressed or stimulated.

Constructive Rest

Dancers lie on their backs in constructive rest position (CRP) as described by Mabel Todd and named by Lulu Sweigard. The knees are bent with feet flat on the floor. The knees may fall inward or use a belt or tie to hold them together so the legs may fully relax. The hands rest on the stomach or arms are folded across the chest. Individual dancers should find which position is most relaxing. In CRP, dancers concentrate on their breathing, giving extra attention to tight or misaligned body parts. Dancers might also use imagery to work through alignment problems or stress.

Suggested Music: *Music for Creative Dance, Volume II,* #1

Visualization

Dancers lie on the floor with the lights lowered. The teacher leads them through a visualization that calms and centers them. A student-favorite exercise is the "Golden Light" or "Favorite Color." The dancers think of a golden light or another favorite color that they inhale. Exhaling, they visualize the color and breath swirling around their bones, muscles or body parts, that are named one by one. They breathe the color in and out, warming and relaxing their bodies. Other visualizations focus on favorite places to relax (the beach, a sunny meadow, a bed), sensations (bubbling water, vibrating strings, warm oozing mud) or relaxing music.

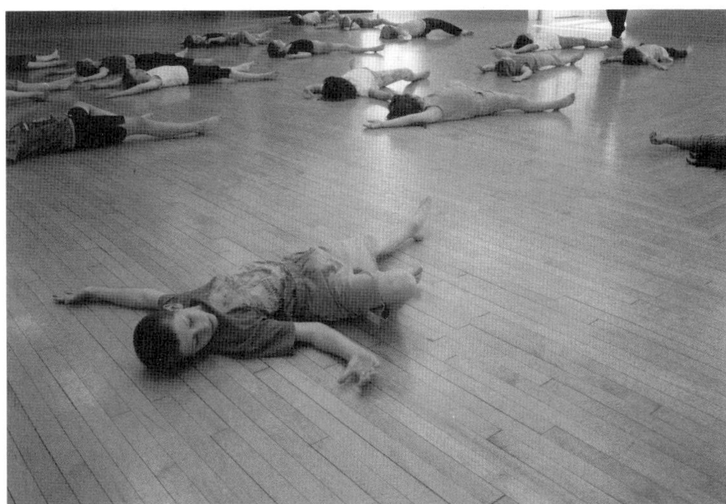

Suggested Music: *Music for Creative Dance, Volume IV,* #17

Alignment

Dancers lie on their backs. The teacher or peer carefully and slowly lifts, bends, stretches and jiggles another dancer's arms and legs in correct alignment. The head may also be moved very carefully. The dancers release all muscle tension as they are being guided.

Suggested Music: *Music for Creative Dance, Volume I,* #15

Reflecting on Key Concepts

Another brain-compatible ending to class is asking dancers to reflect on what they learned or felt during class. Below are possible questions you might ask, as well as various modes students use to respond.

Reflection Questions

- What new concept did you explore during this class?
- What new movement or step did you learn in this class?
- How did you improve?
- How do you need to improve?
- What is your favorite part of class and why?
- What is your least favorite part of class and why?
- What excites you about dance class?
- What scares you about dance class?
- Do you like dancing alone or in pairs or groups?
- Do you like choreographing alone or with others?
- What motivates you to work harder?
- What motivates you to learn new ideas, steps or concepts?
- How do you learn best? By moving, listening, reading and writing or by drawing and watching?
- What part of dance class is easy?
- What part of dance class is hard?
- If you were the teacher, what changes or additions would you make?

Techniques for Responding to Reflection Questions

Mapping: Dancers create visual maps to review key points learned in class.

Journaling: Students write their feelings and thoughts in a journal.

Pair Share: Partners review and discuss ideas and concepts they learned.

Conversation Webs: Groups of five to six dancers sit in a circle with a ball of yarn. One dancer holds the ball and shares an idea or feeling and then tosses it to the next speaker while maintaining a hold on a strand. At the end of the reflection, all dancers are connected by the yarn web.

Talking Stone: Small groups sit in a circle. Each dancer takes a turn holding a smooth stone while answering the reflection question presented by the teacher, then passes it to the next dancer.

Time: Each dancer has thirty to sixty seconds (depending on the number in class) to share feelings and ideas with a partner or group. The teacher calls "next" or rings a chime when it is time for the next person to talk.

Drawing: Dancers draw designs that reflect new ideas discovered in class. Young dancers might draw faces that mirror their feelings about dance class.

Four Squares: Each dancer folds a paper into quarters. On the first square, one writes a key concept learned. On the second square, a question that still remains unanswered. On the third, an affirmation about some part of class in which one excelled. On the fourth, note an area to be improved. In the middle of the paper, one writes one's name. Dancers exchange papers with friends to help each other solve the question.

Cooling Down for Ages Six to Adult Following Improvisation or Choreography

After structured improvisation in the Creating section, dancers briefly share the improvisations during the Cooling Down section. This exercise develops performance, audience and observation skills. Depending on the class size, divide it in half or in several smaller groups. Have each group "perform" briefly for the others and ask the observers to offer feedback.

After dancers finish choreographing, dances may be shared and evaluated. Sharing choreography and responding is an important part of dance class. In the beginning, only positive feedback should be given. When encouraged, dancers will take risks and grow. As dancers become more experienced and confident, observers may give more detailed evaluations.

When dancers share compositions, performance skills are strengthened. When they observe dances, audience skills are strengthened. When they respond to what they observe, they learn to evaluate dances articulately.

Performance Skills

These skills are practiced when sharing dances in class.

- Begin by taking several deep breaths.
- Start with a moment of stillness, indicating to the audience that the students are ready to perform.
- Use nonverbal cues (eye contact, breath, touch) to communicate with fellow performers.
- Continue dancing (improvising when necessary) when steps or sections of the dance have been forgotten.
- Maintain decorum despite mishaps or other complications.
- Use appropriate focus and expression to communicate the purpose of the dance.
- Hold in stillness or exit to signal the end of the composition.
- If appropriate, bow when the dance is completed.

Audience Skills

The four A's of audience behavior are practiced when sharing dances in class.

Attend: Give performers full attention by imagining that the whole body is covered with eyes, that all the eyes are watching the dancers. It is helpful for everyone to take a deep breath before the performance to aid attention.

Allow: Allow choreographers to create art in their own way, whether it surprises, confuses, pleases or upsets the audience. Maintain an open attitude.

Applaud: Applaud performers when the dance is finished. Applause can be clapping, thumbs up, silent clapping or some other form.

Appreciate: Appreciate the performance by giving descriptive and constructive feedback. Discuss with the performers and choreographers the concepts, forms and devices that were used as well as the skills that were displayed.

Dance Talking: The Art of Evaluating Dances

Observing improvised or choreographed movement and responding to it is an important part of any dance class. Through this exercise, students hone their observation and aesthetic valuing skills. They learn to recognize concepts that are emphasized, various choreographic devices and forms employed by the dancers and choreographers, what choreographic choices made the dance unique and how these choices made them feel and respond to the dance.

When facilitating feedback, ask the performers to sit in front of the "audience," who talk directly to the dancers. Request that the comments focus on the choreography rather than on any one dancer. For example, "I saw many levels in the dance that made it exciting to watch," rather than, "I thought Sean did the most interesting movements."

Encourage every observer to make at least one reflective comment during this time of sharing and responding. If a dancer does not know what to say, tell her or him to think about it and ask again later. If a dancer "likes everything," ask for one concept or movement that is remembered. If someone "liked the ending," ask "Why?" It is important in dance class that dancers become critical and articulate thinkers. Encourage them to use the dance vocabulary they learn in class to give detailed and meaningful feedback to peers. Also ask the performers to comment on their experience. Ask the choreographers to comment on the choices they made.

***Teaching Tip**: Discussing choreography can be time consuming. Below are a few ways to streamline it:*

- *Only the group that is going to perform next gives feedback to the group that just performed.*
- *Call on three to four dancers to speak after each group performs. Select different speakers each time.*
- *Pairs or trios in the audience share ideas with each other and then ask one person in each group to comment on the performance and choreography.*
- *When half the group is performing for the other, have each observer pair up with one performer for discussion.*
- *Each observer thinks of only one or two words to share. These may be called out individually or shared simultaneously.*
- *Observers write or draw feedback on paper to give to performers and choreographers.*

Simple Reflection Questions Following Improvisation or Choreography

Time constraints may limit the discussion to just one question or activity suggested below. Feedback may be shared on the spot or collected and given to each choreographer or choreographic group to review and discuss. Responders include self, peers, teachers and guests or outside observers. Feedback is given through oral, written, kinesthetic and visual modes.

- What did you see?
- Did the dancers meet the criteria established for the study?
- How did you (or the dancers) solve the choreographic problem?
- Name one choreographic device the dancers (or you) employed.
- Tell me one thing about the end (or beginning of this dance).
- Name one or two concepts or movements that stood out most.
- What is the one part you remember best? What is the part you enjoyed performing most?
- Describe one similarity and one difference between two dances.
- Solve the "mystery" by guessing the missing verbs the dancers chose for their cinquain, what natural disaster was depicted, which work of art they chose to choreograph, etc.
- Name the prominent concept in this dance (Body Shapes, Relationships, Focus, Rhythm, etc.)
- If you could make one addition or revision for this dance, what would it be?
- Draw one to three shapes you saw in the dance.
- Draw the pathway (energy, relationship, rhythm or use of space) you saw in the dance.
- Draw how the dance made you feel.
- Write three dance elements (i.e., light, backward, sharp) that describe shapes and movements in this dance.
- Write two things the dancers did that made the piece exciting or memorable.
- Write two or three adjectives that describe this piece.
- Write a title for this dance, then call it out when I give a signal.
- Write three verbs describing movements you saw, then chose one to do through movement.
- Make a shape that you saw in the dance.
- Try to replicate a movement that you thought was unique.

Detailed Evaluation

When dancers work on choreographic projects over a longer period than one class, it is useful to provide detailed feedback. The observers consult the "Six Trait Writing Composition" checklist in the previous chapter for ways to evaluate choreography more deeply than through the basic methods outlined in Simple Reflection Questions.

The following steps also provide deeper discussions of choreography. In addition, these questions may serve as a checklist for choreographers as they evaluate videotapes of their own compositions.

Step 1

The Facts: Describe what is seen in the dance. "What kind of…did you see?"

- **Spatial concepts:** Place, size, level, direction, pathway, focus.
- **Rhythmic concepts:** Pulse, pattern, grouping, breath.
- **Force concepts:** Energy, weight, flow.
- **Body concepts:** Body parts, shapes, relationships, balance.
- **Movement skills:** Locomotor and nonlocomotor movements.
- **Devices:** Expansion, diminution, repetition, retrograde, transposition, accumulation.
- **Form:** ABA, suite, theme and variation, abstract, narrative, chance.

Step 2

The Design: Look at the way the facts are put together.

- **Unity:** Does the piece feel whole with a beginning, middle and an end?
- **Contrast:** Do some elements contrast (i.e., changes in levels, directions or speed)?
- **Harmony:** Does the choice of concepts create a harmonious or jarring feeling?
- **Balance:** Do the concepts balance one to another (spatial, rhythmic, etc.)?
- **Variety:** Are there various movement choices or just one or two?
- **Emphasis:** Is there a dominant theme to the dance?
- **Repetition:** Does the repetition of movements and themes create a satisfying form?

Step 3

The Meaning: What is the purpose or meaning of the work? How did the choreographer combine the facts and design to create meaning and purpose?

- Is the choreographer mostly interested in expressing an emotion?
- Is the choreographer primarily concerned with imitating nature?
- Does the dance deal with abstract ideas such as shape, space, time, force or form?
- Does the choreographer tell a story?
- Does the title tell you the dance's meaning or purpose? If there is no title, what might you call it?
- Make a short list of words or phrases that describe the meaning of the dance (loneliness, conflict, simplicity of design, interest in rhythm, playful, adventure, peace, friendship, etc.).

Step 4

The Evaluation: Evaluate the dance and performance.

- The meaning or purpose of the dance was clear__ not clear __.
- The dance contained unique elements: many __ some __ few __ none __.
- Did the choreographer(s) meet the criteria of the dance? All__ some__ none__.
- What were the strong elements or parts? Why?
- What were the weaker elements or parts? Why?
- The accompaniment was appropriate __ or inappropriate __.
- What do you suggest for revision?
- The dancers were always focused __ often focused __ unfocused __.
- The dancers danced with clarity __ no clarity __.
- The transitions were smooth __ fairly smooth __ rough __.

Evaluating Dances through ORDER

Dance educator Larry Lavender outlines a philosophy of dance observation and evaluation for college students and adults in *Dancers Talking Dance* (Human Kinetics, 1996). He uses the acronym ORDER to help students remember a system for evaluating dance compositions.

ORDER

Observation: Students carefully observe the work with open minds.

Reflection: Observers reflect silently, then record their impressions on paper for several minutes.

Discussion: Observers share and discuss reflections with each other and the choreographer(s).

Evaluation: Share aesthetic judgments (description of the work's merits and flaws as perceived by the viewer).

Recommendations for Revisions: Observers recommend revisions to the work.

The value of this approach is that the observers record their ideas before hearing others' comments. All observers are engaged in the feedback process because everyone has the opportunity to write down comments before being swayed by the comments of their peers.

A Modification of the ORDER Process for Dancers Ages Nine through Sixteen

Lavender's ORDER for younger dancers is modified here.

Observation: Students carefully observe the work with open minds.

Reflection: Observers reflect silently, then record their impressions on paper for several minutes.

Discussion: *Choreographers* discuss their thoughts and feelings about their work. Then observers discuss with each other and the choreographers.

Evaluation: *Choreographers* evaluate peer responses.

Revision: *Choreographers* choose which revisions are to be made (with some input from the teacher when appropriate).

With this age group, the choreographers first discuss the strengths and weaknesses of their composition, then observers share their recorded observations. The choreographers may determine whether many people made the same suggestion (a point that needs revision) or only one or two people made a suggestion (a point that likely does not need revision). Choreographers revise their work based on their peers' evaluations, their aesthetics and sometimes teacher input. This process may be repeated several times until a dance is ready for public performance. When young choreographers take the lead in the evaluation process, they feel encouraged and gain confidence to improve choreographic skills.

Recording Compositional Work

When dancers work on a project for several weeks, they might record their work for possible changes and revisions. It is also helpful for portfolio assessment. The Cooling Down section of class is an excellent time to do this. There are many ways for choreographers to record their work.

- **Video**: The choreography may be filmed.
- **Photographs**: Polaroid or digital photographs of the beginning, middle and end of a dance help dancers remember phrases.
- **Mapping**: Dancers map out the spatial designs of each section of their compositions.
- **Notation**: Dancers notate dances through systems such as motif notation, Labanotation, Benesh Movement Notation, etc. or symbols they create themselves.
- **Narratives**: Dancers write the stories of their dances.
- **Diagrams**: Dancers draw diagrams that illustrate their dances.

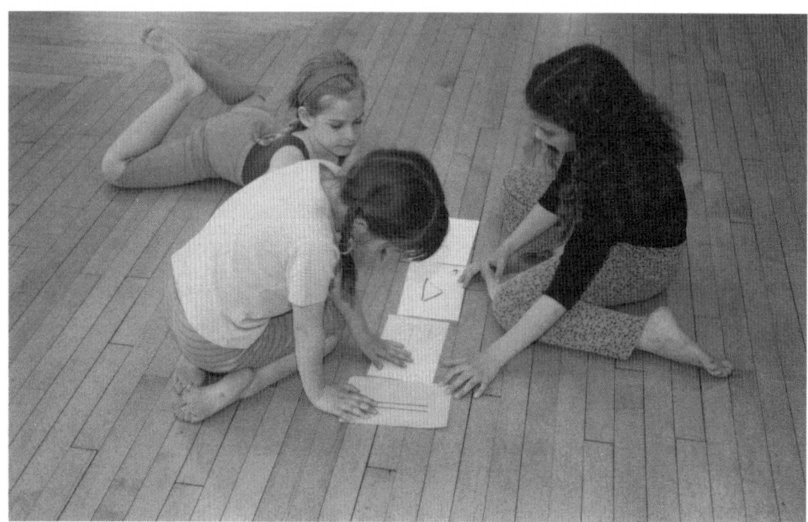

Performances, Recitals and "Informances"

Dancers need to share their works beyond the classroom or studio. It is also appropriate to conclude a residency, quarter or year of classes by sharing concepts and skills with family, friends and the community. The dancers' accomplishments may be shared in several different ways.

Performances are public showings of student work. Students should spend time in dance classes exploring dance concepts, honing technique and creating compositional studies. They should not spend valuable class time rehearsing for concerts. However, it is appropriate for dance studios or schools that have performance groups to present formal concerts. These groups should have rehearsals outside of class. Formal performances are not only motivational but educational as well. Formal performances teach dancers theater etiquette, how to care for costumes, proper make-up techniques, how to perform in front of lights and more! Positive performance experiences provide dancers with confidence that carries over into other areas of their lives.

Recitals are usually presented at the end of the year by private studios. It is recommended that they spend more time on learning how to dance than on the production of one dance performed at the year-end recital. An "informance," as described below, is more brain-compatible than a recital. Exploring all dance concepts, practicing many steps and combinations of movements, collaborating with others and creating dances is so much more valuable to students than many months of practice on a dance created by the teacher. Because recitals are the norm for dance studios, many dance educators wonder how to move beyond this tradition. Start by educating parents, who only want the best for their children, about brain-compatible dance education. Offer dance informances as an alternative to formal recitals. If possible, start a special performance group of motivated students who are able to spend time outside of regular dance classes to choreograph and rehearse for formal performances.

"Informances" are informal and informative performances of student works. Informances might be arranged during the school day to share dance works with other classes, in the evenings or on special visiting days for parents and friends. The teacher or selected students introduce the dancers' choreography. They discuss the choreographic process, dance concepts learned, choreographic forms or devices used and any other pertinent details. Informances are an excellent way to educate parents and the community about the values of a brain-compatible approach to dance education.

Helpful Hints for Informances:

- Explain the process the dancers went through to create their work, how the classes were organized, what concepts they learned, etc. Older students discuss their choreography and what they learned in dance class.
- Explain the time the dancers spent in class (one class a week during a four-week residency, thirty minutes a day for two weeks, once a week for ten weeks, etc.). Also mention the time spent creating the dance (ten minutes each class, two classes before the informance, one hour a week for ten weeks, etc.).

- Design the whole program so there is contrast between dances. Mix age groups, styles and moods of pieces. Introduce each dance by explaining the concepts and skills to be demonstrated or special things to look for.
- Always be proud and positive and never apologize!
- If the program is long, involve the audience. They might mirror or echo your movements in their seats, come out on the floor or up on the stage to participate in a move-and-freeze dance.
- Spend time in class teaching the concepts of dance, not drilling a recital piece. Incorporate the explorations and dance combinations from class into a choreographic structure that were put together the last few classes. For example, alternate a short combination with brief periods of structured improvisation or present a longer movement combination followed by student choreography.
- Create simple costumes for everyone, such as one color T-shirts with contrasting tops and pants; add a sash or let everyone "do their own thing!"
- Your most important job is to provide each student with the knowledge and skills necessary to perform confidently in front of an audience.

Dance educators often say they have no time at the end of their class for cooling down. (I understand this problem very well!) However, this is an important part of a brain-compatible lesson. The time spent cooling down varies considerably from class to class and week to week, but time taken is well spent. Answering one reflection question, doing one short relaxation exercise or commenting on the choreography helps the brain synthesize information learned during the class. Even taking three deep breaths as the dancers review the lesson's concept is beneficial.

It is amazing how few dances, movies, books, television shows and plays have satisfying endings. Ending class in a satisfying way is as important as creating an opening ritual. Please take time to do so.

In Summary

An ending ritual provides a smooth transition between dance class and other activities:

- Stretching and relaxing are healthy ways to cool down.
- Reflecting on key concepts learned in class aids memory and comprehension.
- Sharing improvisations and choreography strengthens performance and audience skills.
- Evaluating dances develops critical thinking and aesthetic valuing skills.
- Dancers become articulate, knowledgeable speakers and writers through the feedback process.
- Informances are a positive, appropriate way to share concepts and skills learned in brain-compatible dance classes.

In every dance you watch, there is a good thing and something that needs to be worked on.
~ Kelly, age 11
Unless you have somebody give you feedback on your choreography, the dance is never complete. ~ Jacob, age 11

(Endnote)

[1] Dennison, Paul E., and Gail E. Dennison. *Brain Gym*. Ventura, CA: Edu-Kinesthetics, Inc, 1992.

In Closing

A dance educator has an important job. People need to move joyfully and meaningfully to develop strong brains and bodies. Teachers have the power to change lives – to help people think as well as to feel better. To do the job well, take a moment to review your mission statement. Employ some of the techniques to reflect on personal planning and presentation of lessons. If you are stuck for an idea or solution to a problem, do the BrainDance, laugh and breathe so that the brain starts working again.

Teaching brain-compatible lessons is not as daunting as it may seem. Make gradual changes in planning and presentation. Do not try to overhaul the curriculum all at once. Remember the mantra "Patience and Practice." Be patient with the learning curve of yourself and your students. It takes patience and practice to modify any teaching style. It takes patience and practice for students to gain the knowledge and confidence to create well-crafted dances, to dance skillfully. Remember that students mirror the teacher's attitude and manner. If we are stressed, our students will be too. If we smile, so will they. Having fun is the most brain-compatible approach, because students learn when they are emotionally engaged in a positive way.

Being an exemplary dance educator requires lifelong learning. Take risks and teach students to do the same. Write articles about dance, then teach the students to write. Reflect on your teaching, teach the students to be reflective. Sharpen your visual skills, then teach students how to observe with objectivity and clarity. Become familiar with dance concepts to teach students a language that goes beyond steps so they have the knowledge to create. Break down the boundaries between dance cultures, styles, disciplines, the private and public sectors, theorists and practitioners.

Dance educators in all arenas need to work together. If we continue using a brain-compatible approach, we will reach all learners. We will change the bodies and minds of our students as well as our own. We will become a culture that dances, thinks, feels, creates and fully expresses our humanity!

Appendix A

Neurological Development and Appropriate Dance Content

Understanding brain development helps teachers choose appropriate content for brain-compatible dance classes. Ages are approximate. Stages overlap due to individual differences. Neurological information is based on material from Carla Hannaford's *Smart Moves.*

Lower Brain Development: Conception to 18 months

Basic survival needs
Motor development
Sensory development

Dance classes include:

- Motor activities such as developmental movement patterns, crawling and creeping and basic movement skills.
- Vestibular activities such as swinging, rocking, spinning, tipping on different levels and in different directions while being held by an adult.
- Sensory activities with props of different textures and colors; variety of musical meters and styles, instruments and sounds; obstacle courses; exploration of dance concepts through an adult's touch and support.

Mid-Brain Development: 15 months to 5 years

Social development, understanding self and others
Emotional development
Language exploration
Gross motor proficiency
Memory development
Imagination

Dance classes include:

- Partner work (adult and child with ages 15 months to 3 years, peers with ages 4-5), group circle dances, moving together and apart; and connecting with others.
- Expression of feelings through movement.
- Verbalization of the dance vocabulary, singing songs and repeating rhymes and chants.
- More practice with basic locomotor and nonlocomotor skills.
- Appropriate imagery (coming from the children), story dances and exploration of the dance concepts.
- Moving with a variety of props to develop eye-hand-foot coordination and receive tactile stimulation.
- Music with words and instrumental music with a clear pulse in a variety of meters and styles.

Upper Brain Development (Gestalt Hemisphere): 4 to 7 years

Whole picture processing
Sense of rhythm and flow
Language comprehension
Discovers similarities
Spontaneous
Free with emotions
Intuitive
Now-oriented
Egocentric

Dance classes include:

- Partner work, moving together and apart and connecting with others.
- Expression of feelings through movement.
- Opportunities to embody the dance concepts through verbalization and movement.
- Appropriate imagery (coming from the children), story dances and dance "games."
- Rhythmic activities with instruments exploring pulse and pattern.
- Learning and practicing more advanced locomotor and nonlocomotor skills such as hopping, skipping, balancing, lunging, melting, etc.
- Repetition of patterns and movement phrases that include stillness.
- Composing simple dances as a group with teacher facilitation with ages 4-5 and in pairs with ages 6-7.
- Sharing dances with half the class performing and the others watching, followed by simple reflection.
- Positive and descriptive feedback by teacher.
- Visual art activities such as drawing the concepts and simple movement maps or notation.
- Music accompaniment with a clear pulse and variety of tempi.
- Energetic activities that flow together smoothly.
- Improvisation with props.

Upper Brain Development (Logic Hemisphere): 7 to 9 years, (Frontal Lobe Elaboration): 8 years

Language refinement
Reading and writing skills development
Linear math processing
Technique/skill development
Fine motor development
Control of social behavior through inner speech
Visualizing sequence of operations
Logical thinking about concrete objects

Dance classes include:

- Collaborative activities in duets, trios and small groups.
- Expression of feelings through movement and words.
- Opportunities to embody the dance concepts through verbalization, movement and reflection.
- Complex dance "games" and structures.
- Rhythmic activities using voice, body and instruments to explore pulse, pattern, and grouping.
- Learning and practicing more advanced locomotor and nonlocomotor skills such as grapevine, hinge-slide, dodging, contracting, etc.
- Repetition of longer patterns and movement phrases which include rhythmic variation.
- Creating and sharing solo, duet or small group dances followed by simple reflection.
- Notation of dances through motif, mapping, drawing, etc.
- Positive and detailed feedback by teacher.
- Simple feedback from peers.
- Variety of musical styles and meters.
- Occasional exploration with props.

Increased Corpus Collosum Elaboration and Myelination: 9 to 12 years

Whole brain processing
Ability to reverse thoughts and operations
Performing mental transformations
Developing complex patterns of logic

Dance classes include:

- Collaborative activities in duets, trios, small and large groups.
- Opportunity for students to choose partners and groups as well as to work in teacher-directed groups.
- Expression of feelings of self and group through movement and words.
- Activities that alternate high and low energy.
- Discussions of further complexities of dance concepts, body-mind connections and proper alignment.
- Opportunities for students to invent new dance "games" and structures.
- Rhythmic activities using voice, body and instruments to explore pulse, pattern, grouping, and breath.
- Combining and practicing more advanced locomotor and nonlocomotor skills such as polka, schottische, leap-turns, falls and spirals.
- Learning cultural, folk and historical dances.
- Composing dances in a variety of forms based on meaningful themes.
- Opportunity for independent practicing, rehearsing and revising dances.
- Notation of dances through motif, mapping, drawing, etc.
- Sharing solo, duet or small group dances followed by detailed reflection.
- Instrumental music in a variety of styles, cultures and meters.
- Positive and detailed feedback by teacher.
- Peer coaching.
- Journaling.

Hormonal Emphasis: 12 to 16 years

Learning about self, others, community, and meaningful living through social interaction
Understanding abstract principles
Considering hypothetical possibilities

Dance classes include:

- Collaborative activities in duets, trios, small and large groups.
- Opportunity for students to choose partners and groups.
- Opportunity to express deep and meaningful feelings about life issues through movement, discussion and writing.
- Discussions about healthy living, career opportunities and connections between dance and brain function.
- Clear improvisational structures and support through cueing of dance concepts.
- Simple lessons in anatomy and kinesiology.
- Rhythmic activities using voice and body to explore pulse, pattern, grouping and breath.
- Repetition of complex patterns and ensemble movement phrases.
- Introduction of different dance styles and dance pioneers through videos, movement and literature.
- Composing, critiquing, and revising dances.
- Opportunity for independent practicing and rehearsing.
- Notation of dances through motif, Life Forms, LabanWriter, mapping or invented symbols.
- Sharing small group dances followed by detailed peer and personal reflection.
- Positive and detailed feedback by teacher.
- Peer coaching.
- Journaling.

Refining Cognitive Skills: 16 to 21 years

Whole mind-body processing
Social interaction
Future planning
Complex structures of thinking and perceiving

Dance classes include:

- Fun and meaningful content focusing on dance concepts, skills and forms.
- Opportunities to embody the dance concepts through verbalization and movement.
- Collaborative activities in duets, trios, small and large groups.
- Opportunity for students to choose partners and groups while being encouraged to work with the opposite sex.
- Opportunity to express deep and meaningful feelings about life issues through movement and writing.
- Opportunity to analyze dance concepts, research career opportunities and make connections between dance and brain function.
- Analyzing and using complex rhythmic structures in dance improvisations and compositions.
- Hands-on experiences in anatomy and kinesiology, information about nutrition.
- Collaborations with musicians, understanding music concepts.
- Challenging and complex movement patterns and phrases in different dance styles.
- Learning and practicing different dance techniques such as contact improvisation.
- Experiences with dance history and dance production.
- Composing dances in a variety of forms.
- Exploration of multimedia in choreography.
- Performing, critiquing and revising dances.
- Opportunity for independent practicing and rehearsing.
- Notation of dances through motif and other notation systems.
- Positive and detailed feedback by teacher.
- Peer coaching.
- Journaling.

Elaboration and Refinement of the Frontal Lobes: 21+ years

Insight
Refinement of emotions
Global/systems thinking
Refinement of motor skills

Dance classes include:

- Fun and meaningful content.
- Opportunities to embody the dance concepts through verbalization and movement.
- Collaborative activities in duets, trios, small and large groups, as well as solo work.
- Information about proper alignment, exercise and nutrition.
- Opportunity to express meaningful feelings about life issues through movement.
- Discussions about connections between dance, brain function and healthy living.
- Clear improvisational structures and support through cueing of dance concepts.
- Rhythmic activities using voice, body and instruments to explore pulse, pattern, grouping, and breath.
- Practice with all locomotor and nonlocomotor skills.
- Repetition of patterns and movement phrases alone and with partners.
- Structured group "folk" dances focusing on community and flow of movement.
- A combination of improvisation and choreography.
- Composing simple dances based on clear structures.
- Sharing solo, duet, or small group dances followed by positive and descriptive reflection.
- A variety of musical styles, meters and tempi.
- Occasional exploration with props.
- Positive and descriptive feedback by the teacher.

Appendix B

Assessment

The Why and What of Assessment

Why? The Value of Assessment
Students evaluate and improve their work.
Teachers evaluate the effectiveness of their instruction.
Teachers clarify and improve instructional strategies and curriculum.
Teachers determine where to go next with their instruction.
Parents, teachers and students receive documentation of student learning and achievement.
Community learns which schools and school districts provide quality instruction in dance.
Schools create appropriate standards.

What? The Content of Assessment in Dance
Dance vocabulary – understanding and using the concepts of dance.
Dance skills – demonstrating movements, steps, forms and styles.
Dance making – improvising, choreographing, collaborating.
Dance performance – communicating, sharing improvisations and compositions in informal and formal settings.
Dance response – responding to artistic works with an understanding of the concepts, form, context and potential expressiveness of a piece of choreography or sample of cultural dance, with informed aesthetic judgment.
Dance inquiry – reflecting on self and others through the study of culture, history, society and philosophy.

When? The Appropriate Time for Assessment
In every class through meaningful feedback.
At the end (and sometimes beginning) of a unit, course, quarter, semester, year.
As mandated by school districts (such as at the end of 4th, 8th and 12th grades).
When a student desires to move to the next level (in a dance studio), to a new school or changes grade levels or programs.

Where? The Place of Assessment
Dance studio/space
Classroom
Stage or performance venues
Home

Who? The Constructors and Evaluators of Assessment
The teacher
The student
Peers
Outside observers
Consultants
The School Personnel
The Studio Personnel
The School District
The State Board of Education
The Federal Government
Dance organizations
Parents

How? The Tools of Assessment
Rubrics
Rating scales
Video and photos
Anecdotal comments
Performances, presentations, demonstrations
Journals and logs
Checklists
Conferences
Reports
Sketchbooks, illustrations, notation, maps, idea webs
Reviews, interviews
Questionnaires
Reflections
Objective tests

Two Categories of Assessment

Conventional Assessment:
- Includes short answer or multiple choice, paper and pencil fact-based tests.
- Involves assessment of book and school work.
- Focuses on what a student can recall and comprehend.
- Is norm referenced.
- Does not involve students in evaluation.
- Assesses one type of learning.

Alternative Assessment:
- Focuses on application, analysis, synthesis and evaluation.
- Involves self-evaluation, meaningful tasks and problem solving.
- Shows work through portfolios, projects and/or performances.
- Is doing-based and connected to life beyond the schoolroom.
- Is tied to standards and outcomes.
- Focuses on what students know, do and value.
- Assesses multiple ways of learning.

Types of Alternative Assessment

Authentic Assessment:

- Implies tasks are meaningful and valued.
- Extends beyond class work into real-life settings.
- Demonstrates accomplishments and quality products which are valued beyond the assessment.
- Involves dialogue between teacher and student which includes self-evaluation and justification.
- Is based on clear standards.
- Takes place repeatedly and anytime during the learning process.

Performance Assessment:

- Involves direct, systematic observation of student performance.
- Involves rubrics and/or rating scales.
- Is judged by trained raters (i.e. dance specialists should judge dance students).
- Is ongoing.
- Includes creation of products.
- Is based on clear goals, purpose and performance criteria.
- Pays attention to extraneous interference such as cultural biases, language, etc.
- Involves interaction between student and teacher.

Portfolio Assessment:

- Is a summary of individual progress and accomplishments created by the student.
- Requires portfolio documents be kept in a container such as a box, folder, large envelope, etc. and added to over the school year or years.
- May include works in progress and "best" products.
- Entries are chosen by the student, although pieces may be chosen by teacher and student.
- Tells a story of student learning through videos, journals, interviews, reviews, photos, notation, reports, rating scales, etc.
- Involves self-assessment as well as teacher and parent input.
- Indicates broad spectrum of abilities and skills.

How Can We Assess Art?

One of the problems with assessment in dance is that it does not often get at the heart of the art form, which is about those fleeting moments that really touch us personally. How can evaluators agree on scores for levels of expression, intention, creativity, and meaning – those intangibles that make a particular dance work or performance special to one's self? Perhaps the best that assessment in the arts can and should do is to focus on the artist's craft. Assessments may indicate that students had the opportunity to be exposed to the vocabulary, concepts, history and experiences afforded by dance education. It may reveal their comfort with the medium and their mastery of the craft. However, I do not believe that one's artistry can or should be assessed. Noted author and educator Dr. Robert Sylwester agrees:

> *...precise assessment of the arts is a hopeless enterprise, since the arts can't be narrowly defined, easily measured, and precisely reproduced. You can't box something that allows the human spirit to soar.*
>
> *...Arts performance and products obviously can be and are evaluated. Critics do it all the time. But their criticism is subjective, and two critics may differ considerably on their assess-*

> *ment of the same artistic performance or product. The value of such critical assessment is thus dependent on the experience and credibility of the critic, and not on some external objective true/false measure.*
>
> *...I've always viewed the arts as an exploratory enterprise that allows our brain to reconstruct the ordinary elements of our life and world into something extraordinary—a celebration of the ordinary. For those who purport to be human, what's more important in life and school than that?*[1]

Many dance educators have expressed similar feelings and concerns about the need, value, and even logistics of assessing dance. However, assessment has been taking place in quality dance programs for many years through feedback.

If we think of authentic assessment as central to learning and not something that occurs after learning has taken place, then feedback is the most authentic form of assessment. Remember that feedback is not only general praise but, more importantly, useful information about what happened. Therefore, the most meaningful feedback comes from the students themselves as they solve problems, learn new skills and create dances while making adjustments in their processes in order to achieve quality products. The immediate feedback that comes from movement and through reflection helps students achieve mastery.

The teacher's role in assessing through feedback is to offer constructive advice to the students to help redirect and guide their learning to facilitate greater mastery. Thus, a feedback loop is created in which a student performs a task, makes adjustments based on personal and peer feedback and guidance from the teacher, performs again, makes readjustments and continues in this upward spiral until mastery occurs. This is an easier assessment system and it also teaches students that learning is lifelong.

However, dance educators are fully aware of the mandate by the federal government to create standard-based assessment tools. In order for dance to take its proper place in public education alongside assessable content areas like reading and math, dance educators must clarify the skills and learnings inherent in dance. Many books have been written on assessment philosophy and techniques that dance educators may find helpful. I include some in the Bibliography. Review the reflection and feedback tools discussed in Chapters Two, Four, and Five of this book. Below are a few examples of assessment tools not included in *Creative Dance for All Ages.*

Samples of Assessment Tools

The Offices of Education and Instruction in many states have formed teams of arts specialists to write classroom-based performance assessments for the arts. I suggest checking with this office to see if voluntary or mandated performance assessments exist in your state to which you can refer.

Most dance specialists agree that rubrics, rating scales, checklists and journals are the most useful forms of assessment. One of the most difficult problems in assessing students in brain-compatible dance classes is the focus in these classes on collaboration and group activities. Because school assessment tries to isolate an individual's progress, it is sometimes difficult to assess each individual accurately during group activities and projects.

Consider asking students to create rubrics and checklists with your guidance. These may be shared with the class and comprehensive and fair assessment tools might be created through this team effort.

Rubrics

A rubric is a scoring guide that aims to delineate criteria and measure a student's ability to meet the criteria. Intended to be as clear and objective as possible, scoring according to rubrics remains subjective. While trained scorers work hard to establish a normed perspective, an individual scorer invariably sees through one's own eyes. Rubrics have several components. These components include one or more dimensions on which performance is rated, definitions and examples that illustrate the attribute(s) being measured, and a rating scale for each dimension.

It is better to have shorter scales (three to four points) than longer scales. As each point has to be well defined, it is more difficult to create longer scales. Dance educators often have 100 to 800 students to assess, so shorter scales are more efficient. A scale with four points is considered beneficial because it forces the assessor to score toward one end of the scale or another. There is no middle score as with a three- or five-point scale.

The scoring rubric rating scales may be qualitative and/or numerical. Qualitative rubrics may have scale points with labels such as the examples described below. Note that the language in the earlier examples is more accessible for young students who may be using the scoring rubric themselves.

Yes, Partially, No
Great, Okay, Needs Work
Not Used, Used Some, Used A lot
Not yet, Developing, Achieving
Quality Work, Satisfactory, Needs Improvement
Always, Most of the time, Less than half of the time, Never
Strongly Agree, Moderately Agree, Moderately Disagree, Strongly Disagree
Strongly Present, Present, Not Present
Outstanding, Adequate, Lacking
Novice, Apprentice, Proficient, Distinguished

Below are examples of a combination of qualitative and numerical scales:

3 Complete evidence of a variety of Pathways
2 Partial evidence of a variety of Pathways
1 Minimal evidence of a variety of Pathways
0 No evidence of a variety of Pathways

4 Consistently moves safely through space
3 Moves through space safely most of the time
2 Occasionally bumps into other dancers
1 Constantly bumps into other dancers

Sample Rubrics

Rubric for Creating a Solo Dance Study

The task requires the student to create a solo dance study in ABA form. A consists of a 24-count phrase, B consists of a 16-count phrase. The focus of the dance study will be on changing Levels.

4 Study clearly demonstrates ABA form, level changes and correct phrasing.

3 Study clearly demonstrates two of the three criteria (form, level changes, phrasing).

2 Study clearly demonstrates one of the three criteria (form, level changes, phrasing).

1 Study is a random combination of movements and demonstrates none of the criteria clearly.

Rubric for Evaluating a Solo Dance Study

The task requires the student to state what his dance partner did well in creating a solo dance study and to explain why.

4 Identified dance concepts and choreographic processes and explained with details why it was good.

3 Identified a few dance concepts and choreographic processes, explained with little detail.

2 Identified one dance concept or choreographic process, offered no explanation.

1 Could not identify or explain at all.

Checklists

Checklists consist of skills or tasks that are checked (✓) off when observed by the teacher or peer, or performed by a student.

Teacher Checklist for Partner Skills

Student Name	Touches partner appropriately	Responsible leader	Responsive follower	Offers ideas & listens to others
Toya	✓		✓	✓
Samuel		✓	✓	
Misha	✓	✓	✓	✓
Kyung	✓	✓	✓	
Serena	✓	✓		

Student (or Teacher) Checklist for Movement Skills

Name_________________________ Grade or Age___________ Date___________

✓__ I can crawl across the floor on my belly using four limbs in a cross-lateral pattern.
✓__ I can skip across the room.
✓__ I can leap in a curved pathway.
___ I can spin three times to the left and to the right.
✓__ I can run, stop quickly and hold a shape for five counts.
___ I can balance on one leg for eight counts.
✓__ I can perform four movements in a row with smooth transitions.
___ I can fall safely to the floor and rebound.

Rating Scale

A rating scale is another form of assessment that many dance educators use. This is a combination of a rubric and a checklist. Some educators call this a performance critique. The scoring scale you use is determined by the tasks being assessed and who is doing the assessment. The scale can be qualitative and/or numerical.

Title/Task: **ABA Solo Study**
Person Assessing ________________ ___self ___peer ___teacher ___guest
Date __________ Location ______________________
Choreographer(s) ____
Performer(s) ____

What to look for in the performance:

	Seen A Lot (3)	**Seen (2)**	**Not Seen (1)**
Specific Criteria			
(smooth level changes)	____	____	____
(clear phrasing)	____	____	____
(clear form)	____	____	____
General Criteria			
Clear beginning	____	____	____
Clear movements	____	____	____
Flow between movements	____	____	____
Developed theme	____	____	____
Clear ending	____	____	____
Unique voice/ideas	____	____	____
Clear visual focus	____	____	____
Polished performance	____	____	____

Total Score (if using numerical scale)____

Other comments:

Journals

Journals provide another useful assessment tool as they reflect thoughts and feelings of the students as they grow and develop their skills, knowledge and understanding of dance.

As well as written entries, journals may contain drawings, sketches, movement maps, idea webs, invented or learned notation and faces that describe emotions. The age and level of your students determine the content of their journals. Provide students with a few questions to stimulate their reflection. You may ask one or two questions each week or offer a list of questions from which to choose over a course or year. After individual reflection through journaling, it is beneficial to have partners or small groups share journal reflections with each other.

Possible Journal Questions:

What key concept(s) did you learn this week?
What new vocabulary did you learn?
What was your favorite part of class and why?
What was your least favorite part?
What became easier for you this week?
What was most challenging?
In what area do you want to improve?
How was your focus and concentration?
How would you describe your participation?
Did you prefer to work alone or with others? Why?
What question about dance would you like to find the answer to?
What does the word "dance" mean to you today?

Grading

In schools where dance is part of the curriculum, grades or some sort of scoring system is usually required. This is one of the objectives of assessment. My belief is that when marks are required, students should receive scores in two areas:

1) Participation and cooperation
2) Understanding and demonstration of dance concepts and processes (how students perform, respond, and create)

These marks may be followed by a brief anecdotal comment. Needless to say, all marks and feedback should be justified through a variety of assessment tools.

(Endnote)

[1] Sylwester, Robert. Excerpts from "A Celebration of the Ordinary: The Key Role of the Arts in Educating a Brain." October 2002. www.BrainConnection.com

Appendix C

Motif Notation

The motif symbols are derived from Labanotation, the system for recording movement originated by Rudolf Laban. The Bibliography contains a variety of resources for motif notation. Below is one description of motif notation, identified as the Language of Dance® by Ann Hutchinson Guest.

Language of Dance®
By Tina Curran, Director, Language of Dance® Center (USA)

Language of Dance® (LOD) with its integration of motif symbols is a fresh and original way of looking at dance and understanding the basic movements of which it is composed. It explores building blocks of movement from their basic components to more subtle and complex combinations.

Created by the world-renowned movement educator, Dr. Ann Hutchinson Guest, the LOD approach provides all practitioners – be they non-dance specialists or specialists – with a sound framework for exploring and experiencing dance.

LOD facilitates this movement understanding through the basic *Movement Alphabet*. It includes exploring, creating, observing and analyzing movement and provides the opportunity to record movement in symbols. The experience extends boundaries for dance and movement professionals; for any individual it opens up the world of physical movement and illustrates its use in dance, sport and other recreational movement activities. Powers of appreciation, interpretation and evaluation of material are developed through observation with the accessibility of an available and clear vocabulary.

LOD is a powerful tool for the dance educator for motivating, transforming, and assessing the making of dances by children and adults. Integrating motif symbols into dance classes in creative, kinetic, and exciting ways supports literacy, critical thinking, multiple intelligences approaches and assessment.

Divergent thinking and exploration is promoted by incorporating a language of symbols that is inclusive of all cultures and creative potential. Diversity of interpretation and performance is encouraged and celebrated within the structure of the symbolic dance language.

Language of Dance:

- Provides a clear and sequential framework, beginning with the universal elements of the Movement Alphabet and developing progressively in complexity.
- Integrates the written language of Motif Notation into the movement experience to connect the physical experience with cognitive understanding.
- Establishes a common vocabulary for talking and writing about dance while providing multiple entry points to promote creative and critical thinking.
- Is accessible to and inclusive of all learners, including age, skill level, cultural background and movement domains.

The Language of Dance® approach identifies a list of basic actions in the *Movement Alphabet*. These LOD® symbols provide a visual link to the conceptual dance vocabulary used throughout this book. Language of Dance® is brain-compatible when used in conjunction with the concept vocabulary because it provides a multi-sensory approach: the vocabulary is visualized through symbols as well as read, spoken, and written.

This Movement Alphabet is encountered first through the movement experience. In a creative movement class, each action is physically explored and the understanding reinforced through the introduction of the movement terminology and symbol. While a selected element from the alphabet is chosen as the focal point for a lesson, there is freedom in how that concept is interpreted, allowing individual choice and promoting creativity.

The elements are further explored utilizing the written form on symbol cards arranged in a sequence to create "phrases" and "dances" by teacher and student. Different orders, combinations and juxtapositions call on different movement skills and create variation in expression. A wide range can be embodied even when dealing with only a few elements.

The building of these elements into phrases leads eventually to choreography at a mature and enriched level. Powers of appreciation are developed through observation, interpretation and evaluation of material through the benefit of a common vocabulary. The experience gained leads to an understanding of how these prime actions and their variants build in complexity and are used in established movement techniques and genres. Integrated in the technique or repertory class, LOD supports skill building and enhances range of movement development. This approach transforms what is often implicit learning into explicit understanding leading to generative use of knowledge.

Language of Dance® benefits multiple learning styles at the elementary, secondary and higher education levels in the dance field as well as the general community. It benefits educators by providing an accessible, clear and sequential framework with a universal language to communicate and create movement for students of all ages and abilities in any movement domain.

LOD provides a structure without boundaries. To learn more, please visit the Language of Dance website at: www.lodc.org or contact the following:

Language of Dance Center, Inc (USA)
Tina Curran
tinalodc@aol.com
212-366-6850-phone/fax

Corporate Address:
1972 Swan Pointe Dr.
Traverse City, MI 49686

Language of Dance Centre (UK)
info@lodc.org
44-207-229-3780-phone/792-1794 -fax
17 Holland Park
London W11 3TD , UK

LANGUAGE OF DANCE®

THE MOVEMENT ALPHABET

The prime actions ('verbs') and concepts of which movement is comprised.

Symbol	Name	Description
	Any Action	Movement of some kind, a change
	*Stillness*	Suspension of motion, sustainment of inner energy
	*Any Flexion*	Contracting, folding, closing in, making smaller, narrowing
	*Any Extension*	Lengthening, reaching out, enlarging, opening out
	*Any Rotation*	Any revolution, turn of the body-as-a-whole, or of parts of the body
	*Any Traveling*	Any path (straight or curved) moving from one location to another
	*Any Direction*	Axial movement up, down, to the right, left, forward, backward, etc.
	Support	An action ending in a new support, transference of weight, a step
	*A Spring*	Any aerial step leaving the ground and returning to it.
	*Balance*	Equilibrium, centering of center of gravity over a static or moving support.
	*Falling*	Center of gravity moves beyond the base of support
	*Destination*	Statement of ending situation, position or state to be reached, designated aim
	*Motion Toward*	Approaching, moving toward a person, object, direction or state of being
	*Motion Away*	Leaving, withdrawing from a person, object, direction, or state of being

Also Included:

Any Still Shape
The movement aims to produce a shape

Any Form of Relating
The aim of the movement is to produce a relationship of some kind.

Notes

Appendix D

Patterns of Coordination

In 2001, I was introduced to Coordination Pattern Theory through dance colleagues, Ingrid Hurlen and Krista Harris. The theory immediately resonated with me because of the focus on the mind/body connection. I invited Betsy Wetzig, Coordination Pattern theorist, to come to Seattle to present workshops for the Creative Dance Center faculty and the community. Since that time, I have been playing with the material in different ways and with different populations. I find the Coordination Pattern Theory to be very accessible and useful for all ages and learning situations. My students enjoy exploring and using the patterns for coordination, creativity and communication. The teachers I train find the information invaluable for understanding multiple learning styles and planning lessons that engage these multiple styles.

I feel that the material is so valuable that I asked Betsy Wetzig if I could share some of the information on Patterns of Coordination with my readers. She very generously agreed to my request.

The information in this Appendix has been excerpted or adapted from handouts and articles by Elizabeth Wetzig. It includes information on learning styles and creativity from Wetzig's work with Dr. Patricia Pinciotti, Chair of the Early Education Department at East Stroudsburg University in Pennsylvania.

What is Coordination Pattern Theory?

Coordination Pattern Theory explains and elaborates the impact of movement on learning, communication and creativity by making movement a window to the mind's work. This framework is based on an understanding of the body's four essential neuromuscular patterns and their tension scale, the psychomotor components of each pattern, and the mind/body connections that cause and facilitate learning and creativity. An understanding of the Patterns enables teachers to physically see the mind's work by observing students' movement and its consequences. Even a basic understanding of the Patterns and their functions will make it possible for a teacher to more fully engage each student's whole body and whole brain in the learning experience.

If we were all neurologically the same, there would be one dominant and subdominant coordination pattern for perceptions and awareness for each and every one of us. With only one dominant pattern or style, we could communicate completely every time we made a statement. We would all experience and report the same events in the same way. But since we are not neurologically the same, we have different patterns for perception, relaxation, and creative thought and we therefore have and like different styles of learning and creativity. We "see" and describe the world in different ways. To truly communicate, we must understand these basic differences in human nature.

Coordination Pattern Theory highlights the kinetic (moving) and kinesthetic (sensing movement) elements of learning that are often overlooked in the classroom. Artistic explorations provide a natural opportunity to see the unique relationship between moving and the processes of thinking, feeling, sensating and intuiting as students actively and creatively solve problems. When students are given access to and have experience with, all four Patterns of Coordination, they bring their full potential to the learning experience.

The four basic Patterns of Coordination, SWING, THRUST, SHAPE, and HANG, designate the four ways a person's muscles, nervous system and brain organize themselves. Each Pattern uses a different set and order of muscle contractions to create a specific kind or quality of movement, trigger center and alignment of the body. The mental aspects of the Patterns can be seen as embedded in their physical aspects and vice versa. (For more detailed information, see descriptions of each Pattern further on in this article.)

As a focusing mechanism, the Pattern or Patterns we are "moving in" determine the aspects of reality we see, feel, hear and think about and are therefore the movement Patterns of our "attention." Moreover, each Pattern has characteristics that are evidenced both physically and mentally. Such characteristics include types of awareness and reasoning, perception mode, affective and social behavior, personality, organizational approach, task orientation, sequentiality and randomness, directness and indirectness, rhythmic structure and balance of design.

One of the four Patterns is an individual's dominant or "Home" Pattern, the pattern of their lowest tension level. This Home Pattern is thus the individual's pattern for relaxation, alpha brain wave activity and creativity.[1] This Home Pattern is the pattern of "I" or "Self," and should be in one's primary mode or style of functioning. This is the pattern we are born with, perhaps genetically encoded with. When an individual is in one pattern, he/she is in a "state," such as a state of meditation or a state of extreme agitation. Being in a pure state is relatively rare. Most of our lives are spent in a "style," that is, a combination of two Patterns, usually our Home Pattern and one other pattern. The use of style augments our basic Home Pattern, giving us the opportunity to access all the characteristics of all the patterns. Through competence in a variety of styles we give ourselves a freedom of access to all four Patterns and thus to the functions of all four Patterns and to the talents of our whole mind and body.

By mentally and physically knowing how to access and use all four Patterns well and how other people access and use them, individuals can work from a Home Pattern strength to communicate and work effectively in a variety of styles. Such individuals are usually described as eclectic, flexible and well-integrated or possessing harmony with themselves and others.

It is possible to improve the use of one's own pattern of relaxation, perception and creativity while learning to understand and improve our use of the other three patterns. This gives us a greater freedom and flexibility to respond to our environment (and the people in it) in a positive way. This flexibility helps us to learn from and teach those who "see," "hear," "feel" and "experience" the world in a different way without being threatened or frustrated by their differences.

Since the other patterns can be connected to our Home Pattern through style, potentially we can all do, think, learn in and from all four Patterns. This stylistic learning or awareness process is just the same as in any creative activity such as an artist's use of a variety of styles. In such cases the Home Pattern remains the dominant part of the styles. Training in the Four Patterns can make us better coordinated and thus improve our self-image and athletic abilities. The patterns also have an important effect on learning. The patterns are organizing forces in our nervous system and brain. They are the primary media of our kinetic and kinesthetic memory and awareness, and so significantly effect our learning.

Since these patterns also create different qualities and ways of acting on the environment, they combine to create our cultural differences. One can see the effects of these human movement patterns in the creation of religious rites, business styles, governmental organization, parenting styles and language structure to name a few. The interrelationship between an individual's "home" pattern and the dominant pattern of his culture is an important aspect of any learning experience.

There is a great deal we can find out about the learning process by studying the coordination patterns, their perceptions and kinetic components, and their affinities of brain modes, personality types, awareness processes and so forth. The following are a few of the basic correlations and affinities of one's "home" coordination pattern.

Movement Qualities and Effects of Each Pattern

Swinger

This pattern has the effect of rocking and swinging with a strong tendency to move laterally. The muscles that trigger Swing movement are around the naval. The pathway of Swingers meanders in "S" curves. A movement that is done on one side of the body tends to be repeated on the other side. A similar relationship tends to happen to movement done with the upper and lower parts of the body as in African dance. The Swing Pattern moves with a heaviness and lightness because of the momentum nature of the swing. It is the dominant movement pattern of belly dancing, José Limón and Swing Jazz. It loosens one's joints. It gives endurance. It is necessary in jumping, swinging bats and golf clubs, long distance running and dribbling in soccer and basketball. Lack of ability to use the swing pattern is usually described as athletic ineptitude in playing ball games or stiffness.

The Swingers are practical, strongly interactive, usually people persons and often nurturing. They tend to be loyal and supportive cheerleaders to those people and ideas they like. They usually prefer to deal with sensated data at a very practical level. Yet, their use of image to connote meaning is often humorous and body-oriented like Chaucer's and Swift's. They use their environment (the world, people, ideas, etc.) as pieces that can be weighed against one another to reach understanding. They tend to deal with the "whole as just another piece to be weighed." They understand that everything is a part of something else.

They often do two things at a time better than one. Many Swingers tend to watch what's happening, get involved and then get out again. This way of functioning contributes to their talents as hosts, therapists and salespeople. They tend to pay more attention to the practical application of their endeavors. Yet their practicality does not get in the way of their need to embellish and deal tactilely with their environment. Swing children are talkative and humorous and enjoy interactive activities and collaboration. Many doodle and are better at multi-tasking than doing one thing at a time.

By its nature, a Swinger's rocking leads to emotional interaction and group activity. When rocking, one comes in and out of relationships, a little interaction with the person on the right, a little with the left. Group interaction tends to be sought after by a Swinger and is used for learning and creating. Even inanimate objects are often described and thought of as having social/interactive values. Swinging can help an introvert prepare for a party!

Thruster

In Thrust, there is always a counter pull in the body. The movements in Thrust tend to be asymmetrical and travel on diagonals through the body. The muscles that trigger Thrust movement are just above the pubic bone. The pathway of Thrusters tends to move in sharp, straight, and often diagonal lines. It is the dominant pattern of the Martha Graham technique and karate. It is necessary in the sprint run and split leap in dance. Lack of ability to use the Thrust Pattern is generally described as a lack of quickness or ability to use strength.

The Thrusters are hands-on, now learners. They tend to be involved in structuring or restructuring their environment. They are interested in the practical skills that make the world go, often gravitating toward technical processes in science and art. The Thrusters preference to see the part, in light of the whole (which is helped by their right brain mode Gestalt abilities), also contributes to their tendency to reorganize data.

They seek the structuring essence as in a haiku or in dialectical logic. In Thrusters, form follows function and because of their "sensating" attitude toward life, they have an affinity for the use of the "medium as the message."

Thrusters act "onto" their environment. They are task-oriented doers. Their aptitude for manipulation includes themselves and draws them to such skills as visualization techniques. Pinpointed and specific, they tend to dislike generalizations. They seek clarity and precision, especially of ideas and definitions. They prefer concrete concepts of a Gestalt perception. They work directly toward mastery of their chosen skills and mastery of their environment through skills. Thrust children are often interpreted as strong and assertive. They enjoy working on skills and tasks as a way of understanding and they want clear and visual instructions.

Shaper

The Shape pattern has the effect of making shapes. It holds and places weight and tends to move the body vertically through space. The muscles that trigger Shape movement are located in the area of the diaphragm. The path of this pattern tends to be forward from your place or where you are. It is the dominant movement pattern of classical ballet and yoga. This pattern holds the body parts together in a clear shape. The movements tend to be symmetrical and balanced. The Shape Pattern is necessary in shooting a basketball or doing school figures in ice skating and dressage. Lack of ability to use the Shape Pattern is usually seen as lack of form, clarity and consistency in movement.

The Shapers are placed persons, thinkers who like to figure out the best way to do something and then repeat that pattern as consistently as possible (to be correct). They tend to hold onto ideas and to have a propensity to "apologize" their position. They have a strong affinity for the "formal" and "classical." Shape children are able to sit still and listen and, therefore, do well in traditional school settings. They ask questions and respond well to auditory directions. They want to learn one way of doing things and prefer to do something the same way every time. They have trouble accepting change.

Shapers have a strong understanding of character (i.e., "the shape of a person"). They are often interested in character development and stories. The novel was essentially created by Shapers. They have a talent for knowing where objects (even people) belong. Shaper cultures such as the Victorian include a sense of one's position in society, of class and of propriety.

These "placement" talents are very useful to people in management and counseling positions. Such positions often attract Shapers. They also have a talent for seeing and remembering shapes, which comes in handy when attempting such tasks as spelling and finding lost items. The mind-body state of Shapers has balance and symmetry. Shapers are interested in the correct sortedness of things. They are thinkers. They use their thinking first; that is why they ask questions. Because arithmetic is about shape, Shapers are good at computational math.

Hanger

This pattern has the effect of hanging, falling, flowing (not Laban's definition of flowing) or flailing. It is a going with, sequentiated activity that tends to move randomly or in the direction of fall. The muscles that trigger Hang movement lie at the fulcrum of momentum and therefore the trigger center for this pattern moves around the body as one moves in the Hang Pattern. The pathway of hangers tends to move randomly or in ovals or figure eights. It was the dominant movement pattern of Isadora Duncan and Doris Humphrey. It has the effect of connecting body parts sequentially. It is necessary in tumbling, sliding into base, falling and rolling with a fall and evasive movements. Lack of ability to use the Hang Pattern is generally described in terms of ungraceful or rigid movement.

The Hangers are connective, "go with the flow," kinetic, flexible and enjoy variety, spontaneity and random changes in energy and movement. Such randomness facilitates the Hanger's affinity for making new connections and seeing how a variety of divergent things actually share "sameness" or associations. In seeing how things are the same, they understand how things hang together and what the whole really is.

For Hang children or children in a Hang stage of development, their flexibility and connectiveness can take on a mimetic, even chameleon-like, behavior. Mothers and teachers can often tell with whom the children have been because of their ability to so completely take on the playmate's persona. Usually the children are unaware they have done so and for adult Hangers, such mimetic behavior may suddenly show up in "copycat" phrases and gestures they did not fully intend to use. Actually, this mimetic behavior is a process of getting to really know someone and understand the meanings of their idiosyncrasies.

Hangers keep attending to the whole. It is a major part of their view and understanding of reality. This preferred whole conceiving can interfere with their desire, and at times, their ability to deal with the part before the whole. This whole seeing often includes the movement and energy components of reality.

Hangers collect ideas and associate them in strings of thought, much like Walt Whitman's poetry. They are often very collective of things, especially organic things such as shells, stones, fibers, etc. Going with the flow, they prefer to follow and find concrete concepts – to seek the essence of what is. They tend to structure or "act on" the environment as little as possible. These flexible, Hanger behaviors and thought processes are very useful in nomadic and herding type cultures. Interest in infinity, the ends, where things go or the ultimate comes from the reaching kinetic experience involved when Hanging towards something. A Hang teacher is a challenger, challenging people to be themselves.

SOME COORDINATION PATTERN MIND/BODY ELEMENTS

Research on the neurological patterns and other brain-based studies indicates that our muscles, nervous systems and brains are organized according to these four different Patterns of Coordination. Each of the four Patterns (Swing, Thrust, Shape, Hang) use a different set and order of muscle contractions that lead to a distinct quality of movement, body alignment and ways of perceiving, thinking and feeling. They coordinate our mind and body.

PATTERN:	**SWING**	**THRUST**	**SHAPE**	**HANG**
PERCEPTION MODE:	MIXED (ALL 3)	VISUAL	AUDITORY	KINETIC
PERSONALITY TYPE:	FEELING	SENSATING	THINKING	INTUITING
MOVEMENT EXAMPLE:	HULA, BOUNCING	KARATE, PUSHING	BALLET, PLACING	TAI CHI, MEANDERING
PROCESSES INFORMATION BY:	PLAYING, IMAGINING	REORGANIZING, PIN-POINTING	FORMALIZING, QUESTIONING	CONNECTING, SEEKING ESSENCE
WORKING MODE:	INTERACTIVE, FUN	INDEPENDENT, STAY ON TASK	ONE TO ONE, BEST/RIGHT WAY	ONE OR MANY, IMPROVISE
MOVEMENT CONCEPT:	FLOW	WEIGHT	SPACE	TIME

A Pattern can be stimulated mechanically, chemically by an act of will or with an environmental stimulation such as music, art, dance or drama. One can also block a Pattern by using another Pattern to consciously or unconsciously "override" it. A Pattern override can freeze out our feelings and other mental processes, block energy and even cause injury.

However, for short periods of time overrides are useful and even necessary, for our survival. For example, if you had to enter a burning building to save a child, the Shape and Thrust overrides would allow you to think clearly and act quickly while shutting out feelings.

Overrides may be caused by parents, teachers, stress, injuries, improper training or the environment. A Shape parent who has a Hang child may try to "Shape-up" the child, causing conflict and overrides. We are creatures of habit and often, over time, our overrides can become our nature. When this happens, overrides can take away our freedom to move and function at our full potential. Our society now uses medications to override problems that may be better helped through movement and dance. We are a society that uses phrases such as "mind over matter" and "no pain, no gain." However, research shows that listening to our mind/body system and working with movement as a function of the mind, as well as the body, can help us have a richer, fuller and healthier life!

Interaction Guide

This brief guide introduces you to some of the positive ways in which you can interact with each Coordination Pattern, as well as some of the behavior that limits our interactions.

With a SWINGER **do:**
- be playful
- be loyal
- let them daydream
- let them doodle
- let them make a mess
- let them interact
- applaud them often
- encourage sense of responsibility

With a SWINGER **don't:**
- be too hurried
- attack them personally
- expect them to stay on task
- demand exact copies
- let them be walked on
- totally control them
- leave them alone for too long
- ignore loyalty

With a THRUSTER **do**:
- be logical
- be brief and to the point
- be friendly but not gushy
- support their independence
- be organized and orderly
- give them space and time
- encourage their sense of honor

With a THRUSTER **don't:**
- take their arguments seriously
- demand feelings
- seem weak
- ignore their skills
- forget to show them how
- engage in power games
- ignore order

With a SHAPER **do:**
- answer their questions
- respect them
- be sequential
- let them do one thing at time
- give them some undivided attention
- be correct
- encourage their sense of duty

With a SHAPER **don't:**
- put them down
- assume they're okay
- be rude or impolite
- make them work in large groups
- forget to give them clear directions
- be too critical
- ignore rules

With a HANGER **do:**
- be physically present
- enjoy their energy
- help them organize
- be flexible and open
- look for and praise their connections
- help them find words for thoughts and feelings
- encourage sense of service

With a HANGER **don't:**
- put down their movement
- put down their enthusiasm
- totally isolate them
- put down their individuality
- expect them to know where things are
- forget their impulsive creativity
- ignore fairness

Note: A teacher, parent, partner or colleague who can work, think, play and be in each Pattern will be utilizing many of the "do" behaviors. When students, children, partners or colleagues react negatively to what you have just done or said, you have set up a roadblock to positive interactions. Look for the Pattern cues!

Teaching, Learning, and Creating Cycle

I have found the work by Wetzig and colleagues to be quite valuable in a variety of educational settings. The cycle below can be used when planning or teaching a lesson or unit of study, to learn new information, and/or to choreograph and compose. You can start anywhere in the cycle that seems most appropriate and then move once or several times around the cycle until the task is completed.

When I choreograph a dance, I often start in Hang where I improvise and get new movement ideas. Then I might go to Swing, adding layers and exploring other possibilities. I then move to Shape where I plan the sequence and create a form for the dance. The final pattern is Thrust. I teach the dancers the movements and then the dance is presented in performance or for evaluation, in which case we would move through the cycle again to explore revisions for the dance. When planning a lesson, I often follow a cycle of Shape, Swing, Hang and Thrust. When teaching, I move back and forth and around the cycle several times. Think about your own experiences. Do you usually work from your Home Pattern strength and stay there or move around the cycle? Do you start in different patterns depending on the task at hand? Does your teaching style allow your students to move and learn in all four patterns?

Another way to look at this cycle is to think about group dynamics. Your students will form groups for problem solving, composing dances or developing projects. When they are aware of the Coordination Patterns, they can form groups that have all styles present. Creating a team with all four Coordination Patterns allows the gifts of each pattern to be expressed and valued. If groups contain only Hangers, the task may remain in the improvisation stage. A group of all Swingers may spend too much time playing to complete the task. A group of Shapers may argue about who has the correct way of doing things and the group of Thrusters may complete the task so quickly that quality or depth is compromised. Because each Pattern has an important part to play in a group, the groups will be more successful in completing quality work when each person is allowed and encouraged to use their Home Pattern in a constructive way. Of course, the idea of understanding group dynamics through Coordination Patterns can also be applied to Teacher Associations, Non-profit Boards, PTA's, classrooms, and families!

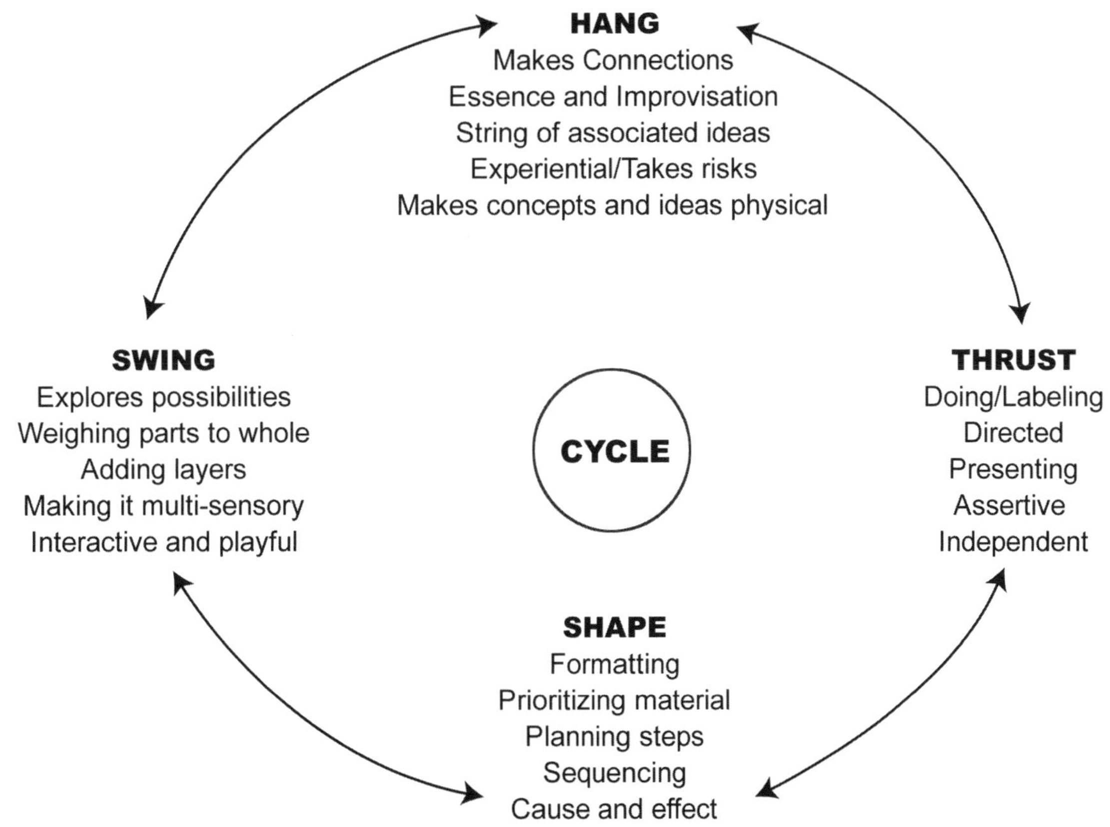

The Coordination Patterns can be used for:

COMMUNICATION

The Coordination Patterns coordinate the way we move with the processes of our brain. For example, when you are being assertive, your muscles have a thrusting or pushing quality. They even affect the development of personality and style. Research shows that typically 80-90% of what we are communicating actually is expressed through our body language not our words. Movement is the language of our right brain. Coordination Patterns hold the syntax of this language. Coordination Pattern Training™ gives you a deeper understanding of your body's language and how the Patterns of the body language effect musculature. For example, through such training, you can see how one's typical expression of anger or fright can block learning, as well as contribute to an injury. Moreover, understanding the Coordination Patterns makes movement a window to the mind's work and to our stylistic differences. It gives you insight into some of the most basic processes of communication. You can learn to recognize when others are thinking, feeling, sensating or using their intuition. You understand the effects (both positive and negative) of movement signatures and styles.

CREATIVITY

Understanding and accessing all four Patterns of Coordination leads to greater creativity. Instead of being stuck in one style, using all four styles helps one move through a cycle of creativity. One might start with Hang to gather ideas, move through Swing to embellish those ideas, Thrust to physically master the movements and then Shape the ideas into a form. Exploring all four patterns will also increase one's movement styles, which will lead to new creative movements and ideas.

CHANGE

Understanding Coordination Pattern Theory will keep us from repeating the same stress and holding patterns of the mind and body which move us towards tonic muscles, misalignment and injury. Because of their centrality to the whole process of movement, improving the Coordination Patterns improves breathing, gait, relaxation, flexibility, strength, range of motion and in fact, everything that movement does. Coordination Pattern Training™can be integrated into any dance, therapy, body work or movement exercise system. It can help change the misused Coordination Patterns, which cause injury and misalignment, into Patterns that support a healthy mind/body system.

About Elizabeth (Betsy) Wetzig

Elizabeth M. Wetzig is a movement researcher, choreographer, dancer and educator. Elizabeth began her Coordination Pattern work in 1971 based on research on the Neuromuscular Tension Patterns discovered by Dr. Josephine Rathbone at Columbia University in the 1930s and on the work of Dr. Valerie Hunt, who discovered the Tension Pattern Scale in the 1960s. Elizabeth first applied this knowledge and improvement of coordination to her New York City dance company throughout the 1970s, as well as to a group of improvisational dancers and musicians called Sound Shapes. She then began working with educators studying the effects of the Coordination Patterns on learning styles. In the 1980s, this educational work led to workshops for Full Potential Learning with Dr. Patricia Pinciotti at East Stroudsburg University. In the mid-1980s Elizabeth began doing body work and research with practitioners of and therapists from Trager, Feldenkrais, St. Johns Neuromuscular Therapy and Hellerwork, as well T'ai Chi Chuan, Yoga, and Laban's Effort Shape. Having taught dance and movement at the college level since 1971, she currently teaches at Cedar Crest College and at the MS Wellness Program at Good Shepard Hospital in Allentown, Pennsylvania and conducts workshops nationally on Coordination Pattern Theory. Elizabeth is co-authoring a book with Dr. Ginny Whitelaw of CDR International that focuses on the Coordination Patterns in business practice.

Contact Elizabeth Wetzig for book and workshop information at H2OZIG@aol.com or through her website at http://www.symmetricalenergyarts.com.

(Endnote)

[1] This information is based on the work of Dr. Josephine Rathbone and Dr. Valerie Hunt.

Appendix E – Three Articles

Toward Best Practices in Dance Education Through the Theory of Multiple Intelligences

By Anne Green Gilbert

Reprinted with permission from *Journal of Dance Education*, Volume 3, Number 1, (2003): 28-33.

The push for standards and assessments in the field of education has caused us to look at how we teach. Many books about brain research and how this might affect teaching practice have been written over the last two decades. Perhaps no book has so affected the world of arts education as that of Howard Gardner's *Frames of Mind,* written in 1983. Arts educators were thrilled with the Theory of Multiple Intelligences (MI theory) because they felt that is was proof that the arts are not just talents but intelligences – ways to learn and know and therefore, the arts should be part of core curriculum.

We are still fighting the battle to make dance a part of every child's education. Why is this when we have so much research pointing to the essentialness of movement to basic learning? Perhaps dancers and dance educators have either not been exposed to this research or have had trouble translating the research into material meaningful to their teaching situations. This research is in fact very valuable and can help us be better teachers. If our dance classes incorporate the multiple intelligences and brain research, I believe that parents and principals will be clamoring for dance in the schools! The few existing dance programs might not be the first to be cut and gyms might be filled with dancers instead of being turned into computer labs.

What does brain research tell us? Below is a list of how students learn best or in a "brain compatible" manner. (Jensen 1998, Brandt 1998, Wolfe 2001) We learn best:

- Through a multi-sensory approach (hear, see, say and do);
- When the material is authentic and meaningful to us;
- When we are emotionally engaged and given opportunities for reflection;
- Through social interaction and collaboration;
- When the material is challenging but achievable;
- When the feedback is positive, specific, timely and learner-controlled;
- Through novelty and repetition;
- When the material is developmentally appropriate and student-centered;
- When the material is presented sequentially and holistically rather than randomly and in sub-parts; and
- Through a variety of teaching strategies.

When I consider the list above and reflect on the rote, mimetic and often negative way I was taught dance, I am surprised that I continued my studies! Unfortunately, I still view many such dance classes around the country and talk with students who have had similar experiences and have not continued their dance studies! Could the way we teach dance be why there is so little dance in public education? Could the way we train dance teachers or the very lack of dance education courses for dancers be a problem? It is easy to blame administrators, economics, the constant and often conflicting changes in school reform, and other related problems for the absence of dance in education. It is much harder to take a long look at our profession and demand that we, ourselves, do a better job of teaching.

I believe that focusing on the seven intelligences in every dance class can help us create brain-compatible dance education and encourage best practices in dance teaching (Table 1).

Bodily-Kinesthetic Intelligence

As dance educators, we may not give this intelligence too much thought because we feel that as we are teaching dance, we obviously are strengthening this intelligence. But there is more to developing this intelligence in our students than just teaching steps. For me, the bodily-kinesthetic intelligence is about understanding and embodying the concepts of movement and dance: space, time, force, and body. The locomotor and nonlocomotor actions are not concepts, but simply the steps we use to move us in and through space. If we just focus on steps, we teach dance in a rote method that has little meaning. The research clearly shows that little will be remembered with this approach (Jensen 1998). I am not sure that many of the researchers, including Howard Gardner, fully understand the bodily-kinesthetic intelligence. I say this because the researchers that are the proponents of movement often give lectures and include little movement in their own teaching. However, current research discussed in books by Eric Jensen, Carla Hannaford, Patricia Wolfe and Marilee Sprenger does state that movement is a crucial component of the learning process. As dance educators we can use this research to underscore the importance of our programs. However, we need to be sure that we are in fact teaching to the bodily-kinesthetic intelligence, not just mindlessly moving. To strengthen this intelligence in our students we give them ample opportunity to become fully aware of their bodies through positive structured and improvisation activities. They learn how to move safely and with ease. This means that we need to understand anatomy and alignment and what exercises are developmentally appropriate for what ages.

Proper nutrition should be part of this discussion – what we put into our bodies to make them work efficiently. While some young people starve themselves, becoming addicted to nicotine and other drugs, others have a problem with obesity! The balance lies with understanding the importance of protein; healthy fats which help build myelin (the fatty substance that insulates axons); less sugars and carbohydrates; and plenty of water and oxygen, essentials for the brain and body (Hannaford 1995).

Another way to strengthen this intelligence is through many and varied movement experiences. This seems fairly obvious, but I have observed many dance classes in which the material is either repetitive to a fault or extremely random. When students explore dance concepts in a sequential way their understanding of movement is greatly deepened and the balance between novelty and repetition, so important for brain development (Jensen 1998), is assured. Focusing on a different dance concept each week will provide the variety. Following the same lesson plan format each week will provide the repetition. Building on familiar movements and patterns will provide the sequencing.

When practicing familiar movements, the kinesthetic intelligence can be deepened by exploring these movements through the other six intelligences. For example, you might explore the skill of turning in this manner:

- Listen to and select a variety of music compositions that "sound like" turning and/or create your own turning sound score with vocal, body and instrument sounds (musical intelligence).
- Turn with external focus, internal focus, eyes closed, "spotting", in one place, through general space, around objects or people, holding a prop and/or observe dancers turning and draw pictures or designs of the different turns (visual/spatial intelligence).
- Explore and understand the physics of turning and centrifugal force. Create a repetitive pattern using two to three different turns, or practice computation by counting the number of turns you can do and the number of turns done by all the dancers divided by the number of minutes it takes to do the turns (mathematical/logical intelligence).
- Speak and write the word "turn" in different languages and through symbols such as motif or pictographs (linguistic intelligence).
- Explore ways to turn with a partner, in a trio, or quartet. Learn turns from others, and teach turns to others (interpersonal intelligence).
- After turning and observing others turning, reflect on your feelings about turning (intrapersonal intelligence), then share these feelings with peers (interpersonal intelligence).

Remember, when practicing skills it is important for all the dancers to be moving as much of the class time as possible. I have observed dance classes where the movement time is less than optimum for developing the bodily-kinesthetic intelligence. Dancers stand more than is necessary while waiting for turns in lines. They sit to listen to directions that could be shorter and clearer. They must wait for all their peers to be perfectly quiet or while the teacher works with one of them and ignores the rest. In large classes, try different formations when moving across the floor so that students do not have long waits in lines (i.e., scattered, oppositional lines that pass through each other or two horseshoes). Instructors should demonstrate new ideas and movements quickly with simple, clear directions and should repeat or enlarge upon the directions while the dancers are moving. Students will often pick up the ideas better through their visual and kinesthetic senses than their auditory senses.

Musical Intelligence

While music is often an integral part of dance classes, I think it is sometimes not used in a brain-compatible way. Do all dance educators understand music concepts? Music and rhythm are very powerful ways to enhance memory (Sprenger 1999). If teachers and students sing or chant simple rhymes to accompany exercises and movement patterns (rather than counts), these patterns will be much better remembered and enjoyed. Counting in "eights" does not really constitute musicality. Most of us could probably benefit from a simple course in music for dancers.

We all have our music preferences just as we have our movement preferences. Are we using a variety of styles, meters and instruments? Is the music developmentally appropriate for the age group? Younger students respond better to music that is medium fast, has a strong beat and contrasts in dynamics. Music with words may sometimes be too directive or inappropriate for older and younger students. Younger students can easily respond to 4/4, 3/4, 2/4 and 6/8 meters, while older students can be challenged with 5/4, 7/8 and other more uncommon meters. Dance educators could share music from many cultures with their students. If live accompaniment is used, teachers should try alternating live accompaniment with recorded accompaniment to provide the variety that will give your students the right support for the movement and the variety needed to motivate and educate. A steady drumbeat can be helpful during some parts of class, but a steady diet of drumbeats may not provide the variety needed for a full exploration of the musical intelligence.

Building an appropriate music library takes time and effort. Dance teachers could seek the advice of music specialists, other dance educators and borrow music from the library for listening at home before spending money on inappropriate music. We all have our favorite pieces that we play over and over. Teachers should try to add at least three to five new ones to your repertoire each year.

Spatial Intelligence

A multi-sensory environment in which a student is offered the opportunity to "see, hear, say and do" the curriculum results in a 90%-95% retention rate (Jensen 1998). Students need to use the spatial intelligence for more than just copying your movement style. In my experience, mirroring and mimicking only the teacher's movements will result in little learning because this does not engage the social or emotional intelligences the interpersonal and intrapersonal intelligences.

Creating posters for the students to look at with the very rich dance vocabulary of all the elements of space, time, force, body and movement is a first step. Posters of skeletons, muscles and brains help dancers visualize what they are moving and using (models are even better). Photographs of dancers in action provide impetus for choreography and movement phrases. Dance explorations that involve copying peers' movements such as shadowing and mirroring cannot be underestimated. By copying many people's movements, students enlarge their movement vocabulary and gain practice in using their spatial intelligence.

Seeing is also a wonderful way to gather instant feedback for students and teachers. Timely feedback is the most brain-compatible (Jensen1998). When teachers want students to learn from each other, they should encourage multi-focus activities. Encouraging students to copy others or to "try on" other movement signatures during explorations helps the most inhibited students move with ease.

Watching dance videos of many dance styles, cultures and historical periods also increases our knowledge and understanding of the world. Observing classmates' compositions sharpens the visual sense and helps students see not only dance performances with more intelligence and acuity but also architecture, sculpture, paintings and other performing arts. Moving in pathways over, under, around and through other dancers and objects strengthens spatial intelligence.

The spatial intelligence can be further strengthened through art activities such as drawing movement maps, creating different designs, collages and sculptures as choreographic motivators through such activities as using famous works of art as an impetus for compositional studies and improvisations.

Linguistic Intelligence

There can be many opportunities in a dance class for students to engage the linguistic intelligence. When you teach dance conceptually, the lingusitic intelligence will be strengthened when the students are presented with new concepts and dance vocabulary. Exploring dance concepts (space, time, force, body) in each class provides vocabulary and tools that not only offer a structure for creating, performing and responding, but also connect to life, making dance class meaningful. It is important to make sure the dancers say the vocabulary as they embody it. When you "say and do" vocabulary simultaneously the brain remembers it better. In 1977, I conducted a research project in the Seattle Public Schools. Third grade students studied language arts concepts through dance activities. The students involved in the study increased their MAT scores by 13% from Fall to Spring, while the district-wide average showed a decrease of 2% (Gilbert 1979).

When assessing choreography, students should be encouraged to use the dance vocabulary so that their evaluations are clear and constructive. Besides speaking and reading dance vocabulary, teachers can make an effort to share the learning principles of brain research and MI theory with students. Let them know how important movement is to the brain. Explain how your classes allow them to experience all the intelligences. Provide journals in which they can write new vocabulary, poems, thoughts and questions. Encourage discussion by providing time for students to share questions with each other because students learn best through social interaction.

A quick way to include the linguistic intelligence is to have a brief reflection after an improvisation. For example, after a partner activity ask the dancers who preferred being a leader to sit down and those who preferred being a follower to stand up. Then ask each student to think of only one to two words why she or he made this choice and speak those words aloud. As an extension, the dancers could write down all these words for a further discussion, or write a story about what makes good leaders or followers during their language arts class. Through these exercises, linguistic intelligence can easily be integrated into dance classes so that a balance of bodily-kinesthetic and linguistic intelligences exists.

Logical-Mathematical Intelligence

Through improvisation, choreography and technique, we work with actual math concepts. For example, consider the simple computation of Section A = 16 counts, Section B = 24 counts, Section C =16 counts, then how many counts for the whole composition? We have 25 students and I want to have 6 different groups working on dances so how will that work out? The math concepts of symmetry, asymmetry and geometric shapes can be explored through improvisations using props or body parts. Repeating patterns and sequences can be developed through a variety of movement combinations. Students can also gain an understanding of the logic of physics concepts (such as momentum, force and gravity) when they are explored through dance.

When the dance educator considers the logical-mathematical intelligence, it should be a reminder to include some repetitive techniques, skills and patterns in every class as well as novelty through the addition of problem solving exercises. As mentioned earlier, a combination of repetition and novelty is very brain compatible (Jensen 1998). This intelligence reinforces the importance of repetition of skills, which builds myelin, the fatty substance that insulates our axons and creates faster and smoother communication between brain cells. Repetition of skills also provides low stress activities that allow dancers to notice their growth and development. By including improvisations and compositional studies, we offer dancers novelty and the opportunity to logically solve problems, which is another way to strengthen this intelligence.

Interpersonal Intelligence

Social interaction is very important to learning. We often learn best when working with others (Brandt 1998). The limbic brain (social/emotional brain) is becoming neglected in America because of the increase in technology (Hannaford 1995). Because of this, we are noticing an increase in our society in behavior problems, anti-social behavior and violence. When we sit in front of televisions, video games and computer screens, we have little time for socialization. When young people are forced to be in so many structured situations such as school and after-school activities, they do not have time for free play with friends, which is such a valuable time to strengthen the interpersonal intelligence.

People with strong interpersonal intelligence are so important to a successfully functioning society. This intelligence will not be nurtured in dance classes where students stand in self space at the barre and move in isolation in lines across the floor. It will not be nurtured through dance competitions.

Teachers can include social interaction in the dance class by alternating structured skill activities with improvisation and exploration and by doing a lot of partner and small group work. Shadowing, mirroring, shape museums (see Table 1) and similar activities strengthen the interpersonal intelligence. There are several other strategies in which dance can include the interpersonal intelligence:

- Exercises in which students change partners frequently, even several times during one activity (especially when working with mixed sexes and special needs students).
- Vary groupings for choreography using random ways to select these groups.
- Vary group numbers by using trios, duets, quartets, quintets and so forth. When doing combinations across the floor, work often as partners. After a partner or trio activity, ask the dancers to share with each other ways they could work together better or new ways to collaborate positively.
- Young dancers enjoy holding hands, older dancers enjoy meeting and passing, counter balance movements and weight sharing.
- Include activities that encourage appropriate touch such as "Sculptor and Clay" and "Action/Reaction."
- Include peer coaching in your classes by pairing more experienced dancers with less experienced dancers and having students teach each other phrases they have created themselves. When a student becomes a teacher for a peer, learning is greatly increased (Jensen 1998) and social skills are strengthened.

Intrapersonal Intelligence

Emotional engagement is another key to learning. Emotional involvement is very important for memory (Sprenger 1999). How many facts or steps do we forget yet how many "special" teachers and favorite dances do we remember? If dance class is fun and joyful our students secrete serotonin, a "feel good" and self-esteem producing chemical. Descriptive positive reinforcement, smiles, encouragement and validation go a long way to creating a positive emotional environment where learning and memory flourish. Of course, an engaging lesson plan is essential! A little stress also increases emotional involvement so challenging and complex, but appropriate, activities are recommended. However, too much stress causes the body to secrete excess cortisol, a chemical that can be harmful to the brain and body (Sprenger 1999).

To promote the development of the intrapersonal intelligence, after dance explorations and improvisations students could be asked to reflect on how the movements or experience made them feel. They can do this simply by standing to show one way or sitting to show another feeling. ("If you enjoyed moving with sharp energy the most, sit down. If you enjoyed moving with smooth energy the most, stand up.") You might leave it at that or ask each student to explain his or her reaction in one or two words such as "challenging," "more creative," "easier," "more exciting," "calming" and so forth. They can also express their feelings about dance class or certain aspects of class in journals, to a friend or draw a face showing their emotions. It is important to have at least one self-reflection opportunity in every class. Remembering to include activities that strengthen the intrapersonal intelligence will ensure that students are emotionally engaged.

Conclusions

Including the multiple intelligences can be more than just providing a variety of random arts activities in your studio or classroom. From the examples above, it can be seen that dance can engage and nourish all seven of Gardner's multiple intelligences; as an activity, dance is not restricted to just the bodily-kinesthetic realm. Applying the concept of multiple intelligences to the practice of teaching can be a powerful tool for encouraging learning beyond simple dance technique. When the number of dance educators using "best practices" increases, our student base will increase, our job opportunities will increase and more importantly, a greater number of people will have the opportunity to have a holistic, multi-intelligence, quality education.

Resources:

Brandt, Ron. (1998). P*owerful Learning.* Alexandria, VA: ASCD.

Gilbert, Anne Green. (February 1979). "Learning Language Arts Through Movement." Paper presented at *Dance as Learning Conference,* Claremont, CA.

Hannaford, Carla. (1995). *Smart Moves.* Arlington, VA: Great Ocean Publishers.

Jensen, Eric. (1998). *Teaching With The Brain in Mind.* Alexandria, VA: ASCD.

Sprenger, Marilee. (1999). *Learning and Memory: The Brain In Action.* Alexandria, VA: ASCD.

Wolfe, Patricia. (2001). *Brain Matter: Translating Research into Classroom Practice.* Alexandria, VA: ASCD.

Table 1: Brain Compatible Dance Lesson Using Multiple Intelligences

Warming-up

"Walk Through the Concepts of Dance" (Bodily-Kinesthetic Intelligence)

Introduce and walk through all 15 dance concepts of Space, Time, Force and Body.

Suggested Music: *Music for Creative Dance, Volume I,* #15

Exploring the Concept (Relationships to people, objects)

1. "Pulse/Rhythm"(Musical Intelligence)

Stands back to back with a partner and clap a steady pulse directed by the teacher. Bend knees up and down to the pulse and feel the beat in each other's backs. Try medium, slow and fast pulses when keeping the steady beat. When the music stops, freeze and then move around the room, creating your own rhythms with body claps and slaps. Alternate your own rhythms with keeping the steady pulse of the teacher.

Suggested Music: *Music for Creative Dance, Volume III,* #2

2. "Puzzle Shape Museum" (Visual/Spatial Intelligence)

Half the class forms statue shapes with lots of negative (empty) space. The other half moves around the shapes each making a shape fitting into a statue like a puzzle piece but without touching. Then the statue comes alive and moves to another statue to create a new puzzle piece, and so forth.

Suggested Music: *Music for Creative Dance, Volume IV,* #17

Developing Skills

"Dance of Eights" (Logical-Mathematical Intelligence)

Walk eight steps while counting to 8. Step backward and snap fingers every two counts while counting to 8 in twos (2,4,6,8). Stretch wide while counting to 4, curl small while counting 4 more (5,6,7,8). Turn for 7 counts and make a shape on count 8! Improv 16 counts smooth and 16 counts sharp. Repeat counting dance, ending with a turn for 6 counts and a shape on 8. Improv 16 counts slow and 16 counts fast. Repeat counting dance, ending with a turn for 5 counts and a shape on 8! It is important for all the dancers to count out loud (hear, say, do). Try dances of 6, 10, 12, and so forth.

Suggested Music: *Music for Creative Dance, Volume I,* #10

Creating

"Cinquain" (Linguistic Intelligence)

Create a cinquain (a five line poem) about a subject or concept you are studying (animals, nature, climate, electricity, geometry, etc.). The poem can be created as a group or individually. Have the students dance the poem as they speak the words.

Noun	Water
Adjective, adjective	High, Low
Verb, verb, verb	Evaporating, Condensing, Precipitating
Four word sentence	Water gives us life
Noun or synonym	Cycle

Closure/Cooling Down

"Blind Mirror" (Interpersonal Intelligence and Intrapersonal Intelligence)

Partners press palms together. Follower closes eyes and leader guides follower through space slowly. Reverse roles and change partners if time allows. Discuss with each other your feelings as leader and follower.

Suggested Music: *Music for Creative Dance, Volume II,* #1

The Male Myth

By Anne Green Gilbert

Reprinted courtesy of *Dance Teacher* magazine, Volume 25, Number 2, February (2003): 72-75.

I teach teachers all over the world and they always ask me the same question, "How can I get more boys into my dance program?" I have been teaching dance to boys (and girls) for over 30 years. In that time, I have thought a lot about this so-called problem. When I teach creative dance in public schools grades K-6, all the boys are fully engaged! When Kaleidoscope, my dance company of children ages 8-14, performs in schools, the boys in the audience are the ones asking how they can join! This leads me to strongly believe that boys are not resistant to dance. So why do we think they are? And why aren't more boys dancing in the private studios? I believe that the way we teach dance and the stereotypes surrounding dance are the roots of the problem.

Thinking Outside the Barre

The way we train dancers in the traditional studio model may be a reason why many boys are not drawn to dance. Standing at a barre for long periods of time, learning steps through a rote method and receiving negative criticism are not conducive to productive learning for either gender. However, young girls may be willing to put up with conventional methods for a time if they dream of becoming a ballerina. Boys, on the other hand, will not, because they have not been encouraged to pursue dance in the first place.

I teach modern and creative dance based on the principles of Rudolf Laban. I have adapted these principles into 15 movement concepts, most of which are pairs of antonyms, such as high-low levels, strong-light weight, and curved-straight pathways. These concepts are effective because children learn easily through opposites. Each dance lesson focuses a movement concept, rather than on movement skills, a theme or story. The students find these concepts meaningful and engaging. They love learning the movement vocabulary, that relates to the other arts, to school subjects and to their activities.

This vocabulary of concept pairs also forces me, as the teacher, to move out of my personal movement signature. A movement signature, in short, is the way a person prefers to move. In general, many boys prefer movement that is sharp, strong, fast and on a low level (close to the ground). Many girls prefer movement that is smooth, slow, light, and on a high level. My movement signature may be opposite of many boys' movement signatures. When we explore all 15 movement concepts, we, teacher and students together, move with strong and light force, sharp and smooth energy, fast and slow tempo, free and bound flow, single- and multi-focus, in curved and straight pathways, on and off balance, over and under each other, together and apart, floating and punching, swinging and shaping, rising and falling, growing and shrinking and much more. Who could resist dancing in so many wonderful ways?

Along with a conceptual approach, I have designed a lesson plan format that alternates teaching dance skills with improvisation and choreography. This format encourages students to grow and develop as they learn new ways of moving. Students find this format emotionally engaging because they are empowered to construct their own learning.

Boys are not resistant to dance; they are resistant to the way we often teach dance. I believe that if we teach dance in the studios and schools in a brain-compatible way, boys will be fully engaged. I say this because everyday I see the boys in my classes jumping for joy and asking for more! When teaching in a brain-compatible way:

- provide a safe environment where feedback is timely and positive;
- engage the emotions through joyful and meaningful dance experiences;
- provide the tools for creative dance making;
- encourage social interaction;
- provide challenging but achievable goals;
- present developmentally appropriate activities;
- offer experiences for all types of learners – kinesthetic, visual, auditory and read/write;
- allow the students to construct their own learning.

The Value of Dance For Boys

Brain-compatible dance education can be a positive alternative to highly pressured competitive sports that are not fun and can actually be harmful. When a person is in stressful situations, the brain releases a chemical called cortisol. This chemical destroys brain cells. However, when a person moves with ease and joy in an engaging dance class, the brain releases serotonin, a chemical that produces a feeling of well-being and self confidence!

On the other hand, dance classes can be an excellent complement to sports activities. One of my student's mother was telling me a story about her son's soccer practice. The coach was trying to describe some complicated plays when finally my student said, "Oh! You mean we move through the general space in a curvy pathway and then we hold our position in self space." The coach looked at him and said, "Yeah, I guess that's right." This helped my student, as well as the other boys, execute the play properly. He had a movement vocabulary learned in dance class that his teammates understood. He also had lots of practice, moving his body in many different ways that complimented and reinforced his soccer skills. He was already a step ahead of the boys who did not dance. Being involved in brain-compatible dance classes enhances all other physical activities by making us aware of our movements.

In his book, *Real Boys: Rescuing Our Sons from the Myth of Boyhood* (1998), William Pollack discusses the problem we have in America of not allowing our boys to cry, show tender feelings, or discuss emotions. These boys feel alienated from society and are unable to share their problems with others, leading them to confusion, anger and often violence. Daniel Goleman, author of *Emotional Intelligence* (1995), writes about the importance of understanding and using our often-ignored emotional intelligence. According to Eric Jensen's *Teaching with the Brain in Mind* (1998), "the affective side of learning is the critical interplay between how we feel, act and think. There is no separation of mind and emotions." While our logical side tells us to "set a goal," it is our emotional side that gives us the passion to achieve that goal.

Dance classes boost emotional intelligence. When boys explore *all* movement concepts and reflect upon them, they become whole and healthy individuals with many varied movement possibilities with which to deal with life. Exploring movement concepts, creating dances and working collaboratively with a diverse group of people has a very humanizing effect on our boys. Creative dance brings balance to a boy's life and schedule.

Beyond Stereotypes

Several years ago, I asked a Seattle-area choreographer, Tom Truss, to work with the nine boys in Kaleidoscope on a new piece about boys in dance. These boys participate in a two-hour dance class at the Creative Dance Center (of which I'm the artistic director) once a week, and also have a two-hour company rehearsal. The company performs every three weeks or so for elementary schools and presents public concerts four to five times a year. These boys have also traveled abroad to perform at international dance conferences. Tom encouraged the boys, ages 7-1/2 to 14, to talk and write about their experiences and feelings about being a dancer. Their writings and discussions were very informative and the dance that Truss created with them was very powerful.

Most of the boys had been teased by their classmates. Very few of their peers had heard of modern dance and wondered if they had to wear tutus. Only one of the boys, who was home-schooled, had not been teased. The boys had different reasons for wanting to dance: exercise, a creative outlet, an alternative to highly competitive sports, to become better at sports, to meet interesting people, a love for performing. Because they had each other as a support system, the boys were not bothered too much by the teasing. The boys encouraged their friends to attend concerts and started a process of educating them. Once their friends attended a Kaleidoscope concert, they were very appreciative of the boys' talents. Occasionally, one would ask to join the group.

My two sons, who were also in Kaleidoscope, had a different experience because I volunteered to teach dance in their elementary school classes weekly from Kindergarten through fifth grade. All their peers had creative dance classes from ages 5 to10 and thought dance was great and quite the norm, so my sons were never teased. Several of the boys in my sons' classes even wanted to join Kaleidoscope, but most parents would not allow them because their sons were already busy with competitive sports or because they felt that dancing was not an appropriate activity for boys.

These stories and our own experience show us that, sadly, stereotypes about boys in dance deter the boys and their parents from enrolling in private studios. I have found that there needs to be a critical mass of boys in any one class to attract other boys. Many years ago I taught a "Just Boys" class to bring more boys into the studio. But after a few years, I realized that I taught these classes exactly as I taught a coed class. I did not want to discourage the important social aspects of boys and girls playing and collaborating together. Why should we continue to alienate the sexes? Why do we want girls to have grace and boys to have strength? Why can't boys and girls have strength and grace?

Rather than offer boys-only classes, I decided to embark on a campaign to educate parents. I wrote articles in our studio newsletter, spoke with parents and sent boys' parents free tickets to Kaleidoscope concerts. Although I reached a few parents, I believe that the majority of parents in the U.S. do not get the message or do not believe it. But although my studio classes are still filled primarily with girls, boys in my public school classes are clamoring for more dance. It is the boys themselves who have experienced good dance classes who will ultimately change our society's beliefs.

How Exercises Help Struggling Readers In School

By Katie Johnson

Katie Johnson is the author of three books on reading and writing. She has been teaching across the United States for thirty-five years at the elementary and university level. She currently teaches in the Shoreline School District in Washington and for Lesley University.

Introduction

When seven-year-old Benjamin first tummy-crawled across the tiled section of my reading classroom, he could not keep his stomach on the floor. My eyes widened as I watched him move slowly across the ten feet of tile *on his right side*, using both arms and both legs more like a beetle on its back. "No wonder he's having so much trouble reading," I thought.

Reading and Movement. What is the connection? Ben's first tummy crawl occurred in the fall of 1999, when I was in my second year of combining reading instruction and "neurodevelopmental" exercises with my public school students, grades K-4. "Neurodevelopmental" is an adjective referring to the process of the neurological development of the human child from the first breath to walking, involving the lower parts of the brain. (The word "lower" refers to the position of these parts of the brain, closer to the brain stem than the cortex, which is the top of the brain.)

Ben's demonstration was the most extreme of unfinished neurodevelopment I had yet seen in my work as a reading teacher. I was beginning to see two things: 1) that the children who made the best gains in reading also make the best gains in their movement activities; and 2) that my understandings of brain development and movement and their connection to learning was at the most beginning stage. Since then, I have learned more every day and also know that there is much more to learn!

Now, when I am working with small groups of readers in grades K-6, I include some exercises for brain development in the time that we have. Sometimes it is only five minutes, perhaps two or three exercises; sometimes it is fifteen minutes with five or six exercises. How much and how often we do it depends on what I think the children need. Every group is different; every child is different. I enter the picture when a child is not learning to read as readily or as efficiently as the school or the teacher or the district expects the child to learn – the standards change pretty often these days! Like all teachers, I use any and all methods, materials, technology, tricks, plans, cons, combinations and even rewards to nudge, teach and push and pull children into reading. As I am able (and required) to assess what each one's needs are in reading, so too I assess each one's needs in neurodevelopmental terms.

If a child is interrupted in the development of the brain between the ages of 0 and 3, physical, emotional and sensory balance will not be achieved because the work of the midbrain will be unfinished. Later, when the child is trying to learn in school, these ragged edges will be interfering with learning.

Fortunately, unfinished neurodevelopment can be completed through exercises designed to replicate the brain's early patterns. The BrainDance encompasses all of these patterns; my exercise routines focus on a few more deeply. All the children in my school, K-3, do Anne Green Gilbert's BrainDance almost every day, except for the days of bus fire drills and early morning assemblies. This habit is now in its third year and it is a wonderful habit. The children I work with, though, often need a little more, more of the same kind of work and so I do exercises. Often I can spot the children who "need more" by watching them in BrainDance; more often, I choose the children who need help in reading and then do a rough neurodevelopmental screening and other vision tests having mostly to do with eye-tracking. (See the end of this chapter for more about vision exercises.)

This year, 2003-2004, is the second year that I have begun my day with a small group. During the first half of the year before the December winter break, I had seven children in this group, five boys and two girls from first and second grade with a fifth-grade boy as my assistant. (Last year, my assistant was a second grader and the children were all K and 1.) We did these exercises:

- Knee Smacks
- Breathe-and-Blow
- The Scarecrow
- The Lizard
- Eyeballs

And, sometimes,

- Spins
- Sensory Work in Partners

These correspond roughly to the Cross-Lateral/Vestibular, Breath, Body-Side, Cross-Lateral, Body-Side, Vestibular and Tactile sections of BrainDance. Since it often seems to happen that the children I work with have not had much experience with Body-Side and Cross-Lateral movement, we mostly do those. I would like to do a survey of my students to learn how much car seat and video game time they have had.

Knee Smacks

The first year I did knee smacks, 1999-2000, I asked the first graders and the second graders to stand in one spot and smack their knees with the palms of their hands, right hand on left knee, left hand on right knee. When I do this, I automatically bring my knee off the ground so it will meet my approaching hand as my hand crosses my midline. (For more on crossing the midline, see the end of this chapter.) Many in this first group could not balance on one foot, another big red flag indicating that neurodevelopment is not finished. Ben always fell over, so I made sure he reached down to his knees, keeping both feet on the floor. Even so, he sometimes had trouble keeping his balance. We tried to do ten of these; sometimes I counted 1-10, sometimes 10-1. I also asked the children to follow the movement of their hands with their eyes, so that they looked at the right knee as their left hand hit it and so on. (The next year, I taught them to skip and knee-smack at the same time, which should be twice as hard, but does not seem to be. If you can do the right-hand-to-left-knee and vice versa, it does not seem to matter if you do the exercise standing still or in forward motion.)

This year and last, the small group of children knee-smack around the two large tables in the room, counting as they go from 1 to 25. It is almost like a march and music is as useful here as in BrainDance. I watch to see

- Whether they are smacking the *opposite* knee;
- How energetically they smack the knee;
- If they can keep track of the counting for themselves;
- If they can stay balanced.

Many of them begin "homolaterally," that is, smacking the right knee with the right hand. As they watch the others and as they begin to balance more successfully on one foot, they become more cross-patterned and more confident, beginning to really zip around the tables. (Because they are doing other eye-tracking activities during my time with them, I do not worry about having them look at the knee they are smacking.)

The ones I really worry about are those who are merely limply touching a knee with a few fingers, whether cross-laterally or not. These are the ones whose sensory and tactile development is unfinished. Brett, for example, barely tapped his knees in September with one finger; then for quite a few weeks he touched his knees with his four fingers flat, carefully; by Thanksgiving he was smacking fairly consistently and grinning as he did so. Gari traced a similar path through those months, although he never grins.

Breathe and Blow

This exercise is stolen directly from the Toddler BrainDance. The children each have a "spot" in the room that they go to after their knee-smacks. My assistant calls out "Breathe...Blow" six times while I cock my ear toward each one to be sure he or she is taking a big breath. On "Blow," the children propel themselves backward about a foot, exhaling loudly as they go. They think this one is a riot. All smiles, they lie down for the "Scarecrow."

Scarecrow

The exercise the children call the "Scarecrow" replicates some very early patterning in the brain. (Its real name is Asymmetrical Tonic Neck Reflex.) To do the "Scarecrow," the children lie down on their backs on the floor. They bend the left leg so that the knee makes a triangle flat on the floor with the foot resting against the inside of the knee of the other leg. They bend the left arm so that it, too, makes a triangle flat on the floor, the third side of which is the left side of the head. They turn the head to the right, the right cheek on the floor, looking at the fingers of the right hand, which is stretched out straight, flat on the floor. The right leg is lying straight down.

When the children are in this position, they listen for the cue (I use counting backwards) whereupon they reverse everything. So on "Ten" the left leg straightens, the left arm straightens and points to the left, the right arm and leg become triangles and the head is turned, cheek to floor, so that the child is staring at the fingers of the left hand. Then on "Nine," they switch back and so forth.

This movement has several purposes, not least of which is horizontal tracking. As you switch sides, your eyes move with the movement of your head, looking completely to one side's outstretched fingers and then to the other side's outstretched fingers. The "Scarecrow" replicates the earliest tracking the infant does, moving its head from side to side looking for the approaching Person With Food. It also practices homolateral movement, where the same-side arm and leg move together; this is a precursor to cross-lateral or cross-patterned movement.

While the children are doing the "Scarecrow," my assistant and I watch to be sure that they are switching correctly, focusing on the outstretched hand and keeping the straight leg straight. The essential achievement here is a smooth movement, as smooth as achieved by a champion swimmer, so that the head starts to turn and the arms and legs switch without any jerk or delay. Then I will know that this child is ready to move on to another floor pattern further along the developmental trail.

When the "Scarecrow" count gets to zero, everyone gathers at the end of the linoleum for the lizard.

The Lizard

The Lizard (Anne's name – I occasionally forget and call it the Gecko) is the cross-patterned self-propelled tummy crawl. A child who can do this movement effortlessly and consistently has probably fitted all the pieces into place. Barring serious eye convergence problems (see section on eyes below) unusual sensory integration or bonding attachment issues or truly awful parenting, such a child will be able to work to the edge of his or her abilities.

Tummy crawling requires the traction available only on hardwood floors or linoleum. Carpet does not provide it. For my exercise groups, I use a ten-foot length of linoleum that my assistant lays out over the carpet when the children come in. Early in the school year, I see all kinds of tummy movements – most you could not dignify by the title of crawl. The most incomplete and the scariest are like Benjamin's, where the tummy does not come near the floor; some children can move themselves along the linoleum using both arms and legs, but they do not use both legs – one always drags and they usually pull themselves with both arms at once. Some propel themselves with enormous effort in one of three ways:

- Use their elbows to drag themselves along, both elbows together in a pull-and-wait rhythm – the wait is to get their elbows back out in front again;
- Use their elbows in that together way, but also push with the toes of their feet (requiring the same wait-time to bend up again for the next move);
- Pull with their hands instead, squeaking the linoleum and occasionally lifting up their midsections like inchworms.

I have come to recognize that these locomotion methods are stages in the development of the finished cross-patterned crawl. Of all of them, the "sidewinding" is the least developed and the one-legged one the most. What they are working toward is a regular cross-patterned crawl, where one arm and the opposite leg are bent and reaching/pushing at the same time, alternating with the other combination as they traverse the space, with their eyes looking side to side as they move each hand forward. This is what they missed, for whatever reason, as developing infants and it is through this stage that they must pass.

It may seem a little odd that we are practicing, in my small group, the earliest pattern and the last pattern back-to-back. I think the justification is that we are in a remediating situation. It is important to remember, too, that the child continues to move in many earlier-patterned ways even as one develops new skills – it is not as if we never add again once we have learned to multiply.

Spins

The vestibular system is perhaps the most basic of all and perhaps still the least well understood. How many children have you ever played with who want to do "bounce-on-Grampa's-knee" games or beg to be whirled around in a circle over and over and over until you are nearly worn out or say "Again!" a million times when you are pushing a swing? These children want and need to be *out of* balance so that their brains can work to get them *into* balance, thereby increasing their ability to maneuver in the world. Children must have a clear sense of where they are in their world. The vestibular system keeps them there. I think of it in terms of balance and, in fact, that is one of the screenings I use to determine a developed vestibular.

Grownups generally say they will not spin, they do not like it, it makes them dizzy. They smile regretfully when I tell them that it is good for them to be dizzy. Children, thank goodness, are not usually so fearful. If they can spin, they like to show off; if they cannot, they like to fall down. Fortunately. So at the end of our time we sometimes spin, just a whirl on one foot, a "zoom around in a circle" on one foot and then the other. "Go the other direction," I say and sometimes they can and sometimes they cannot. Skipping is another vestibular activity as well as a cross-lateral one.

Eyeballs

Last, because it is calmer, we do eyeballs. Each child has a paper eyeball about an inch and a half across, colored by the child, glued to the top of a strip of tag – or it could be cardboard – about 8 inches long. The child's task is to hold the strip, moving it slowly across his or her field of vision, at eye level, following it with the eyes, not the head. Some children get better at tracking across a page of print by doing this simple thing every day; some do not and require more serious vision therapy.

Then the time is up and these children go back to their classrooms to begin the day.

Movement Activities For Learning

I adhere to the theory of teaching, which can be summarized in the old adage, "If at first you don't succeed, try, try again," with the additional refrain, "And try as many things as you can think of!" So with the first graders, I read aloud, read with the children, have the children read what they can to me and to each other; make pictures of important parts of stories in various ways and media; act out stories, words, letters, sounds and anything else that fits; sing; and, of course, work through the phonics of English so they will have internalized some strategies to decode written text. In first grade, the phonics elements in play are the sounds of the consonants and the sounds of the short vowels.

Teaching short vowels is a long process in first grade. As the reading teacher in the building, my job is to focus on the children who are not having success with reading in the regular classroom, who are not able to do the work as quickly, or who do not remember letters and sounds consistently, who cannot, in a word, read the text. (Reading the pictures is much easier.) Movement is both a foundation and a method for this phonics work.

We can use movements and our bodies to plant phonics skills more deeply into our brains because we use the kinesthetic track as well as the auditory and visual tracks. The flip of this is that doing ANY movements that help make the pathways of the brain automatic, may more effectively help the brain assimilate and learn the elements of phonics and reading – no matter how they are presented.

So movement works both ways for phonics. It is a kind of a "two-fer."

Letter Recognition

A very simple way to use the kinesthetic connection to learning to read is with a chalkboard and a shallow bowl of water. As you are teaching a letter, ask the children to put their first two fingers into the water and make the letter on the blank chalkboard. (The clean-up advantages to this activity are clear!) It will vanish almost at once and you say another letter and this game can go on for a long time. It is important to use the first two fingers of (what you hope is) the child's dominant hand because those two fingers will be the ones to grasp the pencil. (See further on about those two fingers and the use of clay.) Later, or with slightly older children, use a fat paintbrush instead of fingers. The disadvantage of the paintbrush is that it is not grasped in the same way a pencil is grasped. On the other hand, it is quite fun.

Clay

The teacher may use clay or Play-Doh (Hasbro, Inc.). I use this substance for a million phonics-related exercises and for comprehension, too. It is gratifying to many children, almost all ages – even adults. Clay is easy to make and to keep; if you use a plastic zipper bag for each child, no one should be accused of spreading germs.

Getting the Fingers Ready

There are a few children who lack fine-motor control, a phrase that always makes me think of matchbox cars. It is not funny, though, when the muscles in small fingers are simply not ready to take on the many printing tasks of even the kindergarten day. So we play "The Pizza Game," which can also be called the tortilla or cookie or pancake game. It is about muscles, though, not food.

Give each child a piece of clay about the side of a small plum or a large walnut. Demonstrating, ask them to roll it on the table with the palm of their hands until it is a fairly smooth ball. Then, using only the first two fingers, "smush" the ball down in small "smushes" until it is fairly evenly flat. This is pretty difficult, so praise imperfect cookies at first.

As they are working, give each one a much smaller blob of clay about the size of a cherry tomato and show them how to pinch off bits between their thumb and forefinger so they have six (or however many they are old) bits. Then, still demonstrating (you will have a pizza, too!), ask them to roll small balls between their first two fingers and thumb. These are the chocolate chips or the sausages or the peppers or the bacon. When they have placed these balls on the flat piece, then they get to flatten them into the pizza (or whatever) with their thumbs. This last part has nothing but energy!

The point of this is the strengthening of the muscles in the fingers used to hold pencils. That is it. Any additional growth in tactile or sensory abilities is a gift.

Letter Formation

Using a chunk of clay about plum-sized again, each child makes a snake about the size of a pencil as even as possible. "Even" gets better with practice. Then you simply say, "Make a T," or another letter and they do it. When I have children who are either bossy or not very confident, I give each one a different letter to make so they cannot copy or compare themselves. This is about letter formation and, of course, letter names. I do three or four at the beginning of a lesson, then put it away and go on to something else less exciting. You can also have a designated letter-chooser, so Anna, for example, gets to tell the others what to make on Tuesday, Sally on Wednesday and so on.

Consonant Sounds

After a few weeks, we begin working on sounds. One way to make this more complex is to use riddles. Once again each child makes a snake and I say, "Make the letter that starts 'book.' " After many of these, we go to, "Make the letter at the end of 'sat.' " After a few hundred of those and both of those mixed up, we begin, "Make the letter that starts the word that means 'a bright round star in the sky in the daytime,' " or 'the last sound in the name of what's covering the floor' or 'the letter that begins the number that comes after eight.' " The possibilities are endless.

Meanwhile they are getting better at clay manipulation and thinking about sounds so we can do rhymes. For this, each child must make three snakes so their bags of clay are a little fatter. I get to make three snakes too, when we begin rhymes.

Rhyming Families

First, I make the letters "c," "a" and "t." I talk about them. "First I am going to make a 'c.' Who can tell me what sounds this letter makes? Yes, that 'k' sound. Isn't English fun? Now I am going to make a letter we use a lot ... think about apples and alligators. Yes, an 'a.' Last, I am going to make the sound at the beginning of 'teacher.' Yes, it's a 't.' Now look at these letters when I line them up together... Yes! You all know that word, it's 'cat!' "

They then each make "c-a-t" on the table. Everyone puts his or her pointer finger under the "c" and we blend the letters to make the word "cat!" There are success and pride here, a good place to begin any lesson.

"Okay, " I say, "now I'm gonna make this harder!" On a good day, everyone smiles and sits up straighter at these words. On an ordinary day, the children keep fiddling with their letters.

We change the word from "cat" to "can" to "cap" to "map" to "mat" to "sat" and so on. Probably we can do three or four changes in a sitting. This is very empowering work and it requires quite a lot of fairly complicated understanding of sounds – what is at the beginning, what is at the end, which letter is which, which letter is where and then, always, using the pointer finger under the first letter and blending the letters to make the word. All this repetition and manipulation and especially the combination, reinforces the tracks the axons are making in their brains and the "myelination" of those tracks is building.

All of the suggestions so far have had the children perched at or near a table, sometimes in chairs, sometimes standing, depending on how much they control their wiggles or their wiggles control them, or how tall the table is compared to how short they are. The arms, hands and fingers largely perform the activities of the movement – on purpose, certainly, in the case of the pizza. But, of course, children learn phonics with their whole bodies as well!

The first graders are accumulating vowel sounds, the short ones that are the most difficult. We attack short vowels in many ways, these sixes and I – and I use the war metaphor deliberately, as it feels quite appropriate to me. This work is a struggle, if not truly a battle.

Many children are not developmentally ready to analyze words, sounds and written language at this age and, of course, by definition the children I work with are less ready than the average child to do nearly anything with language except speak it. The school assembly line is set up, however, so that first graders must learn the letters and sounds of English and be able to use them to decode their reading.

I have made 43 million vowel games during my teaching life and any one of them could be turned into a movement activity. Here are a few.

Body Letters

Begin with the first letter of someone's name or the letter "T." Make one, by standing straight and tall and holding your arms out straight to the sides. "What's this letter?" Answers will not, we hope, vary. Ask the children to make a "T." They will do this, imitating you and giggling. Then put them into partners and ask them to make a "T," using both their bodies. Rejoice when a pair gets down on the floor to do this and you do not have to suggest that – but if you have to, do. Praise every single pair's "T," no matter what it looks like. Then ask who has another letter to try?

Clearly, the sky is the limit. Some clever child will tell you that two people are not enough to do "M," or "Z" or "I." Rejoice again and ask, "What strategy would be good to use then?" You only want to do a couple of these every day, at the start of a lesson, so that you will always end the game with them still wanting to "do another letter!" If you want to keep track, you can designate a child to write the letter you have done on a chart so that you will not do "T" every day. After playing this any-letter game for many days, you can begin to challenge them to only make a letter if it is a vowel. Then practice only the vowels for a while.

Body Words

When the children are working with the three-letter rhyming word families ("cat," "hat," "mat," etc.), they can make the words with their bodies. Divide the group into sets of three and call one set the Beginnings, one set the Endings and one set the Vowels. Ask them to make "c-a-t" with their bodies, for a test run. Then ask them to make other words in that rhyming family. If you can, have them write their words on a chalkboard or a small lapboard each time they have created one. You can do the same ones as in the clay game described above.

Five-Vowel Sort

We have five pictures drawn on pieces of paper – a cat, a pen, a fish, a dog and a duck. (You might think that a pen is an odd choice for young children, but in fact they are always eager to use a pen. It is an item they covet, mostly because they are not often allowed to use one.)

I set these down on the floor in an array at one end of the linoleum.

We have a set of cards with words written on them, such as "fan," "bat," "men," "leg," "brick," "hop," "nut," etc. We also have a set of cards with pictures on them of things that are recognizable that have short vowel sounds, such as "drum," "cap," "moth," "puppy," "elephant," "bib," etc.

I attach a picture or a word card to each child with a clothespin. The children tummy-crawl down the linoleum one at a time and deposit their cards on the appropriate picture. Then they walk back, get another card attached and do it again. We do this three times or until we are tired of it, whichever happens first. Then we gather around the pictures and see if the cards have the same short vowels.

Silent-E Dance

When we have outgrown short vowels and begun to talk about long vowels, one of the first things we talk about is the magic-E phenomenon of English. For a wonder, most – really, a majority – of the words that end in silent-E in English do have a long vowel in that syllable. Not all, of course – this is English, impossible, rule-breaking English. One of the many activities for learning what silent-E does is the dance of the same name.

Give all but two of the children in the group a word card with a short-vowel word on it –you can use the same ones you used in the crawling exercise above – and give the other two a card with an "e" on it. Sing, or use a tape, so there is music. When it stops (after about five seconds), the "e" dancers must connect to one of the word dancers and they must figure out what the word they have made says. We share, word people become "e" people, the remaining dancers get a new word and you do it again. You can, of course, give a dancing direction on top of the phonics direction, such as "Move in general space in a straight pathway," or "Slide in a zigzag pathway until the music stops" or any number of other possibilities.

If it feels safer to you, put the words on string or yarn necklaces instead of in their hands.

Spelling

As an extension of any of these activities, use the tried-and-true body-part-spelling routine from Anne Green Gilbert's first book. Simply choose a body part for spelling in the air—I like elbows best—and then ask for a volunteer to choose the next body part to spell with and so on. I am finding this particularly useful this week with the second graders and that dreadful arsenal of w-words, for which visual discrimination is a weak reed at best: "what," "went," "when," "want," "were," "where," "how," "who." Anything that can put these into kinesthetic memory is worth doing!

Eyes and Vision, Too

"So, Alexandra, this reading stuff is still not so easy, is it?" I asked the second grader with sympathy as we met to do the mid-year reading test.

"No," she sighed. "I mean, I mostly get it but sometimes I just can't figure out the words."

"Yeah," I agreed, hoping I sounded supportive, which I was and not as discouraged as she seemed to be, which I also was. I did not understand why reading was so hard for Alexandra. She had a good brain and a good understanding of any text that was read to her or, after much agony, she decoded herself. She made good connections, inferences, summaries and all the rest of the comprehension clutter. Her problem was creating words out of the letters on the page. Decoding.

And even there, she was a puzzle. When we – Alexandra and I and the other Title I-supported second graders – worked on consonants or vowels or rhymes or inflections or compounds and all the rest of the decoding pieces, she did fine. Usually we did this orally, as well as on the chalkboard, with games, in writing and the occasional worksheet and Alexandra always "got" the phonics or spelling concept.

And her mother read with her every night since nearly conception and discussed the stories as well as I could have done myself.

So what was going on? She could hear, she could think, she could see, she could converse and she had all her neurodevelopmental pieces in place, as far as I could tell. She just could not read.

So I handed her the little book she was supposed to read to me for this mid-year test and, as one more idea, asked, "Since the print in this booklet is a little darker than some of the books we read, do you think that will make a difference? Let me know if you think it does."

She shook her head no, then answered very seriously, taking my breath away. "Whether the words are dark or light, they move the same."

Blink. Stay calm, I told myself. I scrambled in my mind for how to ask the next question. "So how do the words move?" I asked, hoping to match Alexandra's calm tone.

"Well, mostly they move just across the page, you know and into the middle where the staples are." She pointed. I was speechless. I was thinking hard unpleasant thoughts.

Why had I not checked her eyes?

Now it may seem that checking eyesight is not part of a reading teacher's job and it is true that I had only vaguely made it my concern since the previous spring. Until that moment with Alexandra, I was not thinking about checking everyone's eyes.

The year before this, a second-grade boy named Josh was a puzzle to his mother and his teacher, but was not having trouble reading so I did not work with him. After the March conference, his teacher asked me what I thought about his doing some exercises. I told her to refer mom to the Developmental Movement Center's free screenings, which she did. About two months later Josh's mom raced into my room, breathlessly laid a piece of paper on my desk and said, "Eyes! It's his eyes! This woman is fabulous! You should look into it!" And she flew out again.

"This woman" was Nancy Torgerson, a developmental optometrist. What with one thing and another, I did not manage to get in touch with her until almost the end of the year, when I called and asked her what I should be doing to check on eyes. Sometimes I am astounded by what I get away with.

Right at the end of the year we met. She came to school, in an almost unheard of gesture of interest in what I was doing. "Dr. T." is one of the busiest people in the world. I did not know then how honored I was.

She did not know anything about me, either. We sat down and talked non-stop for about two hours and she left me with a couple of very quick diagnostic tools and two new words: tracking, which I vaguely knew already; and teaming, a.k.a. convergence, which was brand new and, apparently, the key to many eye problems that were otherwise puzzling.

Tracking

Tracking comes in two directions, horizontal and vertical. You scan (and read) English text across a page, horizontally, from left to right and if your eyes are not able to do that efficiently and smoothly, they wobble or jump halfway across and your reading wobbles or jumps too. It is very easy to see the eyes actually twitch. I test for this routinely now with every child I see by asking him or her to follow a pencil I move slowly in front of their eyes from left to right and back again. With the youngest children, fives and sixes, I put a sticker on the eraser of the pencil for them to focus on; for the older ones I make a pen dot on the side of the eraser.

More than once, I have moved the pencil across the child's field of vision and the eyes do not follow it at all – the head follows it! The child has fixed her eyes onto the pencil and moves her whole head instead of her eyes. Several things may be happening here, I have learned: one, she cannot tell that her eyes are not moving because she has never tried to move them independently from the movement of her head; two, she is only using one of her eyes and has to move her head so the usable eye can see the pencil; three, the idea of focusing anywhere but straight ahead is brand new and incomprehensible because she has been looking only straight ahead from her baby seat, car seat and at the television all her life.

If the eyes can move smoothly, we are way ahead; helping the head to stay still is much easier than fixing the jerky tracking.

Tracking vertically is less obvious, but it is also easy to see when you are looking for it. The child who skips whole lines as she is reading is not tracking vertically. She leaves the right side of the page and jumps down too far on the left side. The easiest way to check for this is to ask a child to "read" a series of letters, numbers, or shapes from the top of a piece of paper to the bottom, perhaps twenty or so symbols. They should be big enough to see, a little bigger font than this, but in a straight row vertically. A child with vertical tracking problems will not be able to name the symbols quickly and steadily.

It also seems to be true that most children who are inefficient vertically are also inefficient horizontally; it does not always seem to follow the other way around.

Fortunately, these tracking abilities are functions of the neurodevelopment of the infant and toddler and can be addressed by exercises. Teaming, on the other hand, is much more complex. Unfortunately, issues of convergence cannot be resolved by exercises (although they certainly do not hurt).

The more I work with children now, since my introduction to developmental optometry, the more I see eyes that do not track; the more I can help children to track more efficiently, the more easily those children read. I do not mean to suggest that I do not continue to teach phonics, fluency, comprehension strategies, vocabulary and responding in writing. I do. I do not mean to suggest that tracking is the only thing that can be amiss with children's eyes. It is not. But when the children and I do "eyeballs" and other small, less-than-five-minute eye activities, their tracking, focus, ability to see foreground distinct from background and spatial perception can improve.

Eyeballs

Take a one-inch circle of ordinary paper and ask the children to color it as an eye. Glue it to the end of a one-inch by eight-inch strip of tag and you have a tracking-practice device. All the children I work with have one. Most of them need it and they all use it every day in reading group. I just say, "Eyeballs." They get them out, they start moving them across their fields of vision about ten inches away from their faces and I watch each one in turn. When I have watched everyone do at least two passes, the eyeballs are put away. (Sometimes, with the "squirreliest" ones, I give them a small sticker to attach to the eyeball strip. This is not a reward for doing it; it is merely an acknowledgment that they have done it.)

Neva, in fifth grade now, still cannot keep her head from moving as she reads; when she moves her eyeball device, I sometimes put my hand gently on top of her head (always telling her that I am about to do this) for a line or two so that she will try to remember. For a while, I used a small beanbag instead of my hand until another teacher said one day, "What about lice?" The beanbag has just enough weight to keep the head still and the cloth has just enough traction to keep from slipping (that is why the obvious solution, put it in a plastic bag, does not work) so it was not at all invasive. Brett, in fact, keeps asking for it still. (Eye exercises do not have any effect on children who perseverate!)

Toilet-Paper Rolls, Paper Clips and Other Exotic Tools

The next hardest and related, skill is focusing. It is related to tracking, but different in that the target you are trying to focus on is not connected to a book or an eyeball. Being able to stop your eyes as they move from one point to another is an essential skill for school.

Nicky, for example, has learned to track; but when I move his eyeball myself, stopping it at random as it goes across his vision, his eyes keep on going and then have to slide back to where we stopped. The toilet-paper roll is used with a small straw and a partner to practice focusing. One child holds the roll at chin height, about eight inches in front of his chest, hole pointing toward his partner. The other child puts the straw into the tube and quickly pulls it out; the tube-holding child moves the tube about four inches to the left, the other inserts the straw again. After four inserts, they trade jobs. Repeating this twice is a round of this game.

There are many more games with several purposes. This year's first graders are particularly fond of pickup sticks played with ten straightened-out paper clips. This is another focus activity that also serves eye-hand coordination and the ability to perceive an object against a background.

Conclusion

If the only help that movement gives was getting wiggles out, it would be useful. If, as I believe, deliberate movement activities and routines such as these can help the child's process of brain development, then I must use them. On a good day, when everyone is smiling and moving well, I like to think that I can hear the myelin oozing along those dendrites. I am helping to build not only readers and writers, but also complete human beings.

Appendix F

CREATIVE DANCE CRIB SHEET

CONCEPTS
Place
Level
Size
Direction
Pathway
Focus
Speed
Rhythm
Energy
Weight
Flow
Body Parts
Shapes
Relationships
Balance

BRAINDANCE
Breath
Tactile
Core-Distal
Head-Tail
Upper-Lower
Body-Side
Cross-Lateral
Vestibular

GROUPINGS
alone (solo)
pair (duet)
trio
quartet
small group
large group
half group
whole group
leader/group

STRUCTURES
or Motivators
shadow
mirror
opposite lands
back to back
zombie & magician
sculptor & clay
shape museum
machines
shape fences
connected counts
chopsticks
props
instruments
8 counts
folk dances
stories
chants/rhymes
songs/poems
cinquain
diamante
haiku
picture cards
motif notation
art works
photos
paper strips
enter/exit
flocking
totem poles
nature objects
dance history/
culture
Coordination
Patterns (Swing,
Thrust, Shape, Hang)

FORMATIONS
scattered
single lines-
shoulder to
shoulder
opposing lines
crossing lines
follow leader lines
passing through
lines
single circle
double circle
small circles
triangles
diamonds
half space
third space
quarter space

CHOREOGRAPHY
Form
ABA
Suite – ABC
Recurring Theme
Narrative
Abstract
Chance
Broken form

Devices
Expansion
Diminution
Retrograde
Transposition
Repetition
Canon
Rhythm
Contrasts
Accumulation
(1; 1,2; 1,2,3)

Principles
Unity
Contrast
Harmony
Balance
Variety
Emphasis
Repetition

REFLECTION
Attend, Allow,
Applaud, Appreciate

SKILLS
Locomotor
crawl
creep
roll
walk
run
jump
hop
leap
gallop
slide
skip
prance
tiptoe
fly
slither
waltz run
grapevine
schottische
step-hop, etc.

Nonlocomotor
bend
twist
stretch
swing
shake
turn
lunge
curl
kick
poke
melt
float
glide
press
wring
slash
punch
dab
flick, etc.

Notes

Appendix G – Lesson Plan Form, Formats and Examples

Introduction

James Zull, in *The Art of Changing the Brain,* writes about the biology of the brain in connection with learning. All parts of the brain must be engaged for deep learning to take place. A balanced brain not only receives knowledge, it is also able to use that knowledge to generate new ideas. Learning involves a cycle of sensory input, to make connections and take action. Deep learning begins with a concrete *experience* that engages the sensory cortex. Then the back integrative cortex is engaged during *reflection* to help one remember relevant information and analyze the experience. The engagement of the frontal integrative cortex, responsible for short-term memory, problem-solving and making judgments, allows one to generate *abstractions* and create new ideas. To complete the learning cycle the motor cortex is engaged and one *actively tests* new ideas through speaking, writing or moving.[1]

How does the learning cycle relate to the study of dance? Do traditional technique classes encourage students to move through the entire learning cycle? Do they encourage a balanced and deep learning experience? Can we ask the same questions about choreography and improvisation classes?

In traditional technique classes, students primarily engage only the back cortex of the brain; moving back and forth from *sensory experience* to *reflection,* they learn and replicate steps, receive analytical feedback from teachers, and replicate more steps. The front cortex is seldom engaged. The students know a lot of steps and patterns but have trouble improvising and creating or talking and writing about dance.

Students in choreography and improvisation classes primarily engage only the frontal cortex of the brain, moving back and forth from *abstraction* to *taking action*. They are very good at solving problems, generating new ideas and creating dances and papers, but there may not be substance behind the movement or writing. Without *concrete experiences* and *reflection,* these students lack the skills and knowledge to make their actions meaningful.

The sample lesson plans in this Appendix are designed to create a balance between experience and abstraction, between receiving knowledge and using knowledge. As you plan your own lessons, continue to reflect on how you might provide a balanced and profound learning experience for all your students, using the brain-compatible techniques presented in this book.

Sample Lesson Plan Form

Date:

Age, Level, or Grade:

Objectives:
1.
2.
3.
4.

Dance Concept:
Thematic Concept (optional):

Equipment/Music:

Warming-up:
  1.
  (2.)

Exploring the Concept:
  1.
  (2.)
  (3.)
  Reflection:

Developing Skills:
  1.
  (2.)
  (3.)

Creating:
  1.
  (2.)

Cooling Down:
  1.
  (2.)

Lesson Plan Format for Infant Dance Classes – age 2 months to pre-walking

Warming Up

Quick warm-up: Move to waltz music while holding the infant in different positions. Swing, sway and turn forward and back, right and left, up and down. Pause in stillness. Relate to other couples.

BrainDance: Do simple exercises, stretching infant's arms and legs unilaterally, bilaterally and cross-laterally. Sing and chant nursery rhymes for accompaniment. Include circling, bending, twisting and stretching. Do exercises with infant on back and stomach. Work with the infant balancing on small therapy balls. Do simple exercises for adults, working on core support, arm, leg and back strength and stretches. Refer to the Warming Up chapter for ideas.

Exploring the Concept

Concept Exploration: Focus on a different dance concept every class. Dance with infant while exploring high and low movements, sharp and smooth movements, fast and slow movements, etc. Refer to the exploring the Concept chapter for ideas.

Relating: Clap or touch infant's feet and hands to another infant's feet and hands; mirror and shadow infant and adult pairs; dance together and dance away. Focus on the dance concept.

Rhythm Instruments: Play appropriate instruments with, around and on (tapping) infant. Keep a steady pulse in slow, medium, and fast tempi. Explore different meters with infant in adult's lap: bounce gently to 4/4 meter, sway and rock to 3/4 meter, bounce faster to 2/4 meter, bounce in galloping fashion (uneven) to 6/8 meter. Allow infants to explore instruments. Make sure instruments are safe with no small parts that may end up in infants' mouths. This is also a nice time for adults to do their own exercises while infants play with instruments and socialize with other infants.

Developing Skills

Folk Dance: Perform simple "circle" dances while holding the infant in various positions. Move sideways, come together and have infants relate, go apart and turn around. Try different movements such as marching, sliding, galloping and bouncing. Refer to the Developing Skills chapter for many examples.

Creating

Sensory Activity: Play peek-a-boo with scarves and silk; swing infants in pieces of cotton or lycra material; pat, rub, tap infant gently in different ways; pull around on sheets or large scarves; roll balls around; bounce and roll infant on therapy balls. Encourage adults to get down on the floor and practice crawling and creeping with their infant. Great for infants AND adults!

Cooling Down

Relaxation: Adults breathe deeply and slowly while sitting or lying quietly with infant or they may give infant a gentle massage. Mothers may nurse infants.

Lesson Plan Format for Parent and Toddler Classes – walking through age 2

Warming Up

Quick Warm-up: Dance with small scarves (one for each hand) while exploring the concept.

BrainDance: Perform toddler version with rhymes.

Exploring the Concept

Concept Exploration: Explore the lesson concept through contrast and pause songs.

Shaping: Alternate forming shapes alone or together and dancing through general space. Explore shaping with props such as stretchybands or scarves.

Waltz: Adult waltzes while holding the child or while holding hands with the child for bonding and vestibular stimulation. Vary directions in space. Vary ways of holding the child. Add stillness for fun. Add relationships: two couples come together and go apart for socialization and eye-tracking.

Rest: Adults lie down on the floor in constructive rest position. Children can rest with adult or socialize quietly with each other.

Developing Skills

Instruments: Play instruments focusing on pulse while sitting on the floor. Allow children to explore various instruments. Encourage adults to keep a steady pulse. Play a second piece of music, cueing everyone to explore the lesson concept while practicing simple locomotor skills.

Combining Movements: Perform a simple circle dance (see Developing Skills chapter) that relates to the concept and includes appropriate locomotor and nonlocomotor skills.

Obstacle Course: Create an obstacle course with various objects and props. Vary the pathway and line of direction.

Creating

Free Dance: Explore a different prop each week while focusing on the lesson concept or alternate dancing with a parachute on odd numbered weeks, improvise with a prop on even numbered weeks.

Cooling Down

Toddlers sit near you as you rubber stamp their hands and feet, giving each dancer positive feedback.

Lesson Plan Format for Parent and Child Classes – ages 2 1/2 to 4 years

Warming Up

Quick warm-up: Dance with small scarves (one for each hand) while exploring the concept.

BrainDance: Perform toddler or preschool version with rhymes.

Exploring the Concept

Concept Exploration: Explore the lesson concept through contrast and pause songs.

Shaping: Alternate forming shapes alone or together and dancing through general space. Explore shaping with props.

Circle Dance: Perform a simple circle dance (see Developing Skills chapter) that relates to the concept and includes appropriate locomotor and nonlocomotor skills.

Rest: Adults lie down on the floor in constructive rest position; children can rest with adult or socialize quietly with each other.

Developing Skills

Instruments: Play instruments, focusing on pulse while sitting on the floor. Allow children to explore various instruments. Encourage adults to keep a steady pulse. Play a second piece of music, cueing everyone to explore the lesson concept while practicing simple locomotor skills.

Combining Movements: Introduce and practice appropriate locomotor and nonlocomotor skills through rhymes, stories or simple movement combinations. Refer to the Developing Skills chapter for ideas.

Obstacle Course: Create an obstacle course with various objects and props. Vary the pathway and line of direction.

Creating

Free Dance: Explore a different prop each week while focusing on the lesson concept or alternate dancing with a parachute on odd numbered weeks, improvise with a prop on even numbered weeks.

Cooling Down

Children sit near you as you rubber stamp their hands and feet, giving each dancer positive feedback.

Lesson Plan Format for Technique Classes

For Ballet, Modern, Jazz, Tap, Flamenco, Social, etc.

Warming Up

Technique/BrainDance: Move through the eight developmental movement patterns of Breath, Tactile, Core-Distal, Head-Tail, Upper-Lower, Body-Side, Cross-Lateral and Vestibular, introducing and integrating the lesson's dance concept (i.e. Level, Direction, Size, Pathway, Focus, Balance, Energy, etc.). The BrainDance may be performed lying, sitting and/or standing. Integrate appropriate technique into the patterns in the style of dance being taught.

Exploring the Concept

Concept Exploration: Explore the lesson concept through a short improvisation. Refer to Exploring the Concept chapter for ideas.

Reflection: Students reflect on the exploration through a reflection question. Refer to Exploring the Concept chapter for examples.

Developing Skills

Technique: Teach a new step (assemblé, split fall, step-ball-change); practice familiar skills; do barre or center floor work.

Combining Movements: Practice or add on to a familiar combination or start a new combination. Bring novelty to familiar phrases by changing formation or relationships and integrating the lesson's concept. Refer to Developing Skills chapter for sample combinations.

Creating

Choreography/Improvisation: Individual dancers (or duets, trios or small groups) rechoreograph one part of the combination above or choreograph 8-16 counts of new material to add to the combination. Alternatively, dancers improvise for two-three minutes relating to the lesson's concept and in the style of dance being taught. Refer to the chapters Exploring the Concept and Creating for ideas.

Cooling Down

Dancers share choreography with the whole class or with several other individuals or small groups. Then ask dancers to reflect on what they observed. After improvisation, dancers might stretch muscles as they reflect with a peer on what they learned or how they improved.

Examples of Brain-Compatible Lessons

The following pages contain:
Five sample lessons for ages 4–8 that are designed as a cohesive five-week unit.
The lessons may also be taught separately.
1. Place
2. Focus
3. Weight
4. Relationships
5. Flow

Five sample lessons ages 9–Adult that are designed as a cohesive five-week unit.
The lessons may also be taught separately.
1. Place
2. Focus
3. Weight
4. Relationships
5. Flow

Preschool Class on Level

Technique Class on Balance

Energy and Emotions

Dancing Math

Music and Dance

Visual Art and Dance

The following lessons are appropriate for a variety of settings from public schools to private studios. In conservatory settings use the 30-minute lesson plan ideas and increase time spent on technique and skills to create a 60-90 minute lesson.

Lesson Plan #1 on PLACE
Ages 4–8

National Dance Content Standards: 1, 2, 3, 4, 5, 6, 7

Ages: 4–8
Grades: PreK–3rd

Length: 30 minutes (For a 60-minute lesson, add the activities suggested.)

Objectives

Students will:

- Identify and demonstrate elements of the concept PLACE.
- Move safely in and through space.
- Work cooperatively with others.
- Remember and repeat a combination of movements.
- Respond to music cues.
- Reflect on the experience.

Equipment: CD player; *Music for Creative Dance, Volumes II* and *III*; whiteboard or chart paper on which to write conceptual vocabulary; rhythm instruments (optional); objects to leap over (optional).

Warming-up

1. BrainDance: Students perform the BrainDance with rhymes, sitting in self space for the first four patterns (Breath, Tactile, Core Distal, Head-Tail) and traveling through general space for the last four patterns (Upper-Lower, Body-Side, Cross-Lateral, Vestibular).

2. Introduce the Concept: Students "hear, see, say and do" the concept of Place (self space and general space).

Exploring the Concept

1. Body Halves: Dancers freeze lower half of body and dance with upper half in self space then freeze upper half and dance with lower half through general space. This is a good time to introduce other concepts by suggesting specific movements, such as "Try big arm movements with arms stretching far from one another. Now try little arm movements with arms dancing close to each other. Now legs can dance with big and small movements." Each time the music pauses make a new movement suggestion (fast and slow arms and legs, strong and light, sharp and smooth, forward and backward, etc.).

Suggested Music: *Music for Creative Dance, Volume II,* #3

Reflection: "If you liked dancing in self space the most, sit down. If you liked dancing in general space stand up. Look around and see who likes moving the same way you do."

For a 60-minute lesson, add the following two activities:

2. Puzzle Shapes: Pairs of dancers form shapes together in self space that look like two puzzle pieces (related but not touching). On the teacher's signal they dance away through general space. On a signal, they reform into new puzzle shapes. This continues to the end of the music. Encourage dancers to change Levels, Size, and Direction.

Suggested Music: *Music for Creative Dance, Volume II,* #5 (Music pauses every 8 counts so dancers have to form shapes quickly and then dance briefly away from each other. This does work with young children, providing an exciting challenge!)

3. Rhythm: Dancers stand back to back with a partner in self space while bouncing knees and clapping or tapping the teacher's pulse. Then they dance away from their partners through general space to their own pulse or anyway they choose. When the music pauses alternate "Back to Back" and "Dance your own way through general space." Dancers can be directed to find a new partner each time. Rhythm instruments may be substituted for clapping. Preschool children may keep the pulse in self space without a partner.

Suggested Music: *Music for Creative Dance, Volume III,* #2

Developing Skills

1. Folk Dance: Direct dancers through the "Shoemaker" dance found in the Developing Skills chapter under "Folk Dances." In self space, the students perform gestures illustrating winding thread, breaking thread, pounding nails. They may do this with hands or upper body parts, such as head, shoulders, elbows, arms, etc. Through general space, students practice appropriate locomotor skills such as galloping, sliding, jumping, hopping, etc. Older students may practice different ways of moving with a partner.

Suggested Music: *Music for Creative Dance, Volume III,* #19

For a 60-minute lesson, add the following activity:

2. Leaping and Turning: Set up a leaping course with milk cartons or cones and spots. Dancers move through the course leaping over the cartons or cones. When they come to a spot, they run around it or spin once next to it.

Suggested Music: *Music for Creative Dance, Volume II,* #11

Creating

1. Cinquain: Dancers and teacher create a cinquain together about Place (ask dancers for ideas for the three action words).

Place
Self, General
(Twist), (leap), (float)
Move and stop
Space

Suggested Music: Say the words in a dramatic voice as the dancers move. Repeat each action word three times or repeat "We move and stop" three times with varying speeds.

Cooling Down

1. (2.) Mirroring: Dancers mirror the teacher's slow movements in self and general space.

Suggested Music: *Music for Creative Dance, Volume III,* #7 (Play the music for about one minute.)

For a 60-minute lesson, do the following activity before or instead of Mirroring:

1. Sharing and Reflecting: After practicing the cinquain, half of the dancers perform the cinquain for the other half and vice versa. They reflect briefly on what they observed and/or what parts they enjoyed performing. Encourage students to use the 4 "A's" of audience behavior (Attend, Allow, Applaud, and Appreciate).

Lesson Plan #1 on PLACE
Age 9–Adult

National Dance Content Standards: 1, 2, 3, 4, 5, 6, 7

Ages: 9–13 (This lesson may be adapted for age 14–Adult.)
Grades: 4th–8th (and beyond)

Length: 45 minutes (For a 60-minute lesson, add the activities suggested.)

Objectives

Students will:

- Identify and demonstrate the elements of PLACE.
- Learn and perform a combination of movements
- Work cooperatively with others to create a movement phrase.
- Respond to music cues.
- Reflect on their experiences.

Equipment: CD player; *Music for Creative Dance, Volumes 1, II,* and *III*; one chopstick for every two students; whiteboard or chart paper on which to write conceptual vocabulary.

Warming-up

1. BrainDance: Students perform the BrainDance, standing in self space and traveling through general space. You may include some dance technique with experienced dancers.

2. Introduce the Concept: Students "hear, see, say and do" the concept of Place (self space and general space).

Exploring the Concept

1. Chopsticks: Partners balance one chopstick between flat palms and dance together through general space. When the music changes, Leader #1 holds the chopstick and makes shapes in self space while Leader #2 copies the shapes (or creates connected or relational shapes). With novice dancers, suggest shapes such as high, low, strong, backward, upper half wide/lower half narrow, etc. Alternate leadership several times or change partners after each student has been the leader and repeat the improvisation.

Suggested Music: *Music for Creative Dance, Volume I,* #1

Reflection: "Share with your partner which was your favorite part and why: moving together with the chopstick or making shapes. Now discuss which you preferred and why, being the leader or the follower."

For a 60-minute lesson, add the following activity:

2. Symmetry and Asymmetry Shape Museum: Half the dancers are scattered through the room, forming symmetrical shapes. The other half dances around the statues through general space, stopping at a statue to move one to two body parts so that the statue becomes asymmetrical. The sculptor then copies the statue, which frees the statue to dance away and sculpt another statue. Symmetrical shapes should be changed to asymmetrical shapes and vice versa.

Suggested Music: *Music for Creative Dance, Volume III,* #3

Developing Skills

1. Skills: Practice square dance movements such as do-si-do, elbow swing, promenade, etc.

2. Folk Dances: Perform "Scatter Square Dance," described in the Developing Skills Chapter under "Folk Dances."

Suggested Music: *Music for Creative Dance, Volume III,* #19

OR

1. Combining Movements: Introduce a Movement Combination with skills appropriate for your students. Select a combination from the Developing Skills chapter under Combining Movements.

2. Leaping and Turning: Two dancers at a time leap over objects (cones) spread apart along both sides of the space, they spin across the far end of the room toward each other and then slide down the middle of the room (face to face). Practice specific leaps appropriate to your age group and/or encourage specific arm shapes while leaping.

Suggested Music: *Music for Creative Dance, Volume II,* #11

Creating

1. Ocean Dance: Dancers work in pairs. Each pair choreographs a three-part phrase that (1) travels towards each other, (2) involves mirroring each other, and (3) incorporates turning around or with each other. (Other three-part structures may be used such as traveling sideways toward each other, moving over and under, and weight-sharing). For the A section, dancers improvise movements in their scattered self spaces that are slow, flowing, change levels and have characteristics of ocean creatures or plants. For the B section, the dancers perform their three-part choreography. (When using the suggested music, this occurs during the first 24 measures of the metered music.) For the "C" section, the dancers improvise blind mirroring in self or general space. (Pairs press palms together and take turns being blind and being the leader.) When using the suggested music, the dance repeats and the blind mirroring section is longer the second time through.

Suggested Music: *Music for Creative Dance, Volume II,* #1

Cooling Down

1. Sharing: Half the pairs share their work during the first half of the music and then the other half shares during the second half of the music. After performing, ask each couple from the first half to find a couple from the second half and have them reflect together briefly on the use of Place and unique elements they noticed about each other's choreography.

For a 60-minute lesson:

2. Stretching or **Journaling:** Lead dancers in a short series of stretching exercises or allow time to write in journals.

> ***Teaching Tip**: Another option for "Creating" is to begin a choreographic project with the "Ocean" theme. Dancers may begin researching the flora and fauna of the ocean, the difference between how vertebrates and invertebrates move, the effect of weather on the ocean, etc. The class could then end with a quick improvisation to ocean music or sounds, stretching, blind mirroring or constructive rest. The dancers continue this project for four or five weeks, developing material, practicing, and sharing their final dances on the fifth or sixth class. See the chapter on Creating for ways to structure choreographic projects.*

Lesson Plan #2 on FOCUS
Ages 4–8

National Dance Content Standards: 1, 2, 3, 4, 5, 6, 7

Ages: 4–8
Grades: PreK–3rd

Length: 30 minutes (For a 60-minute lesson, add the activities suggested.)

Objectives

Students will:

- Identify and demonstrate elements of the concept FOCUS.
- Move safely in and through space with a prop.
- Work cooperatively with others.
- Remember and repeat a combination of movements.
- Respond to music cues.
- Reflect on their experiences.

Equipment: CD player; *Music for Creative Dance, Volumes I, II,* and *III*; whiteboard or chart paper on which to write conceptual vocabulary; spots (optional).

Warming-up

1. BrainDance: Students perform the BrainDance with or without rhymes. Explore different types of focus (single and multi-focus as well as eyes closed) throughout the BrainDance.

2. Introduce the Concept: Students "hear, see, say and do" the concept of Focus (single focus and multi-focus).

Exploring the Concept

1. Zombie and Magician: Dancers find a partner. The Magician moves a prop (plastic, scarf or streamer) in many different ways. The Zombie moves the way the prop makes him or her feel. If necessary, provide support during the activity by suggesting the use of other concepts such as changing Levels, Size and Energy. Change roles.

Suggested Music: *Music for Creative Dance, Volume I,* #9

Reflection: "If you liked being the Magician sit down. If you liked being the Zombie stand up. Tell your partner (or the whole class) why you made that choice."

For a 60-minute lesson, add the following activity:

2. Erosion Pairs: Change partners from the activity above. Dancers take turns being a mountain shape or wind/water. Wind/water dances around the mountain shape (who has eyes closed), then stops and moves one (body) part of mountain shape to make it smaller and lower (erosion). The wind/water dancer then copies the new mountain shape and the mountain shape becomes wind/water. The mountain shape keeps eyes closed until the wind/water dancer has finished "eroding" the shape. When both dancers are little shapes on the floor (erosion is complete), they stand up and mirror each other through the sequence they just went through.

Suggested Music: *Music for Creative Dance, Volume I,* #15

Developing Skills

1. Folk Dance: Review the "Shoemaker" dance from the first lesson. Dancers look at (focus on) the body part they are moving in the first section. In the "polka" section, dancers might practice galloping, sliding or hinge-sliding with a partner while focusing on each other.

Suggested Music: *Music for Creative Dance, Volume III,* #19

For a 60-minute lesson, add the following activity:

2. Leaping: Each dancer places a spot in a self space in the room. For about 24 counts, dancers explore jumping, leaping and hopping over their spot using single focus. Then they move through the room using multi-focus to leap over as many spots as they can until the signal is given to return to their spot. Keep alternating self and general space with single and multi-focus.

Suggested Music: *Music for Creative Dance, Volume III,* #6

Creating

1. ABC Dance:

A - Dancers dance around, over, near and far (not too far) from their spot while always focusing on the spot.

B - Dancers dance around all the spots while focusing on the other dancers while using multi-focus.

C - Dancers dance on the spot while focusing on a secret object (a body part, the ceiling or floor, something on the wall, etc.)

Suggested Music: *Music for Creative Dance, Volume II,* #12 (play three sections for a short dance or six sections and repeat the dance), or *Volume III,* #16 *(*a piece with three longer sections).

Cooling Down

1. Sharing: After practicing the ABC Dance, half the dancers perform the dance for the other half and vice versa. Ask dancers in one half to pair-up with someone in the other half and tell each other which section was their favorite and why. They might also try to guess each other's secret focal point. With PreK students, use the music from *Volume II* and have the dancers switch the roles of audience and performer several times. Then ask a few simple reflection questions or have them get into A, B, or C groups to show which was their favorite section to perform (or watch).

For a 60-minute lesson, do the following activity:

2. Blind Mirror: Pairs sit down facing each other. They both have their eyes closed and finger tips touching. Leader #1 moves the arms in a variety of slow movements and then Leader #2 leads the movement.

Suggested Music: *Music for Creative Dance, Volume II,* #10 or *III,* #7 (Fade the music down and up as a signal to change leaders. Change leaders several times.)

Lesson Plan #2 on FOCUS
Age 9–Adult

National Dance Content Standards: 1, 2, 3, 4, 5, 6, 7

Ages: 9–13 (This lesson may be easily adapted for age 14–Adult.)

Grades: 4th–8th (and beyond)

Length: 45 minutes (For a 60-minute lesson, add the activities suggested.)

Objectives

Students will:

- Identify and demonstrate the elements of FOCUS.
- Be responsible leaders and followers while using props.
- Work cooperatively with others to create two short movement phrases.
- Remember and repeat a combination of movements.
- Respond to music cues.
- Reflect on their experiences.

Equipment: CD player; *Music for Creative Dance, Volumes I and II*; one chopstick for every two students; whiteboard or chart paper on which to write conceptual vocabulary.

Warming-up

1. BrainDance: Students perform the BrainDance shadowing and/or mirroring a partner. Direct which leader leads which pattern. (For example, "Leader #1, Breath…. Leader #2, two types of Tactile," etc.). Integrate dance technique if appropriate.

Suggested Music: *Music for Creative Dance, Volume II,* #21

2. Introduce the Concept: Students "hear, see, say and do" the concept of Focus (single focus and multi-focus). You might also discuss internal and external focus.

Exploring the Concept

1. Chopsticks and Trios: Three dancers balance three chopsticks between three palms to form a triangle (advanced dancers might balance the chopstick between shoulders, feet, hips). The dancers move together without traveling, but by changing levels, etc. At the signal or when the music changes, each of the three holds one chopstick, and Leaders #2 and #3 copy Leader #1's movements through general space (shadowing). Alternate the two sections; dance in one spot with chopsticks, then follow the leader through general space.

Suggested Music: *Music for Creative Dance, Volume 1,* #16

Reflection: "Turn to your partners and tell them which part you thought was most challenging, focusing on the chopstick or focusing on the leader and why. Which part was more enjoyable during the shadowing part, being the leader or follower?"

For a 60-minute lesson, add the following activity:

2. Comparative Fence Shapes: "Everyone come to the end of the room. I will ask one dancer to start the fence by forming a big shape. When your name is called, dance along the path of the fence line, focus on the shapes that are already in place, then connect to the last person in the fence by making the next shape in the trio of comparatives. For example, the second person would make a shape bigger than the first. The third person would make the biggest shape. The fourth person would make a big shape and so on. When all the dancers are connected, the first dancer in line will break away from the fence, dance along the fence and reconnect at the end of the line of shapes. Hold your shape in the fence until the person you're connected with breaks away from the fence. Then dance down the fence again and make the appropriate sized shape at the end of the line." If you have a large group, divide the class into two or more separate fences.

Suggested Music: *Music for Creative Dance, Volume I* ,#3

Reflection: "Did you notice a shape that you had never seen before as you traveled along the fence? If so, try to form that shape. Could you clearly see the pattern of comparatives or not? What made this game difficult or easy for you?"

Developing Skills

1. Folk Dance: Review "Scatter Square Dance," perhaps introducing several new steps. The dancers will be required to use multi-focus and single focus throughout this dance. Another option is to teach "Si Senor," described in the Developing Skills chapter. This dance is also a fun Focus dance.

OR

1. Combining Movements: Continue to practice the movement pattern from the first lesson on Place, bringing in the concept of Focus. You might have the students perform the pattern toward and away from a partner, close eyes for a section of the phrase, explore internal and external focus or add on a new part that shows a strong use of Focus.

Creating

1. ABC Chance Dance: Partners create a movement phrase for A and for B.

A - Focus on your partner as you enter and dance in the space.

B - Focus on a secret object (i.e., elbows, ceiling, audience, floor, back wall). Students might pick a card on which a special focal point is written or they may choose their own object. Dancers in the pair should focus on the same object.

After they have created their A and B sections, tell them that section C will be an improvisation that involves the use of multi-focus to improvise with other pairs that will also be performing with them. To make the dance even more of a chance dance, play three short sections of music. The dancers transition to the next section during the pause in the music.

Suggested Music: *Music for Creative Dance, any volume,* "Pot Pourri" or contrasting short selections from any instrumental CD.

Cooling Down

1. Sharing: Half the pairs perform, then the other performs. After performing, ask each couple from the first half to find a couple from the second half and have them reflect together briefly on the use of single and multi-focus. They may also try to guess each other's secret object.

For a 60-minute lesson, add the following activity:

2. Visualization or **Journaling:** Lead dancers in a short visualization exercise with their eyes closed or allow them time to write in journals or create drawings, illustrating the Comparative Fence dance.

Lesson Plan #3 on WEIGHT
Ages 4–8

National Dance Content Standards: 1, 2, 3, 4, 6, 7

Ages: 4–8
Grades: PreK–3rd

Length: 30 minutes (For a 60-minute lesson, add the activities suggested.)

Objectives

Students will:

- Identify and demonstrate elements of the concept WEIGHT.
- Move safely in and through space with a prop.
- Work cooperatively with others.
- Remember and repeat a combination of movements with rhyming words.
- Respond to music cues.
- Reflect on their experiences.

Equipment: CD player; *Music for Creative Dance, Volumes I, II* and *III*; whiteboard or chart paper on which to write conceptual vocabulary; one prop for every student such as plastic, scarves or foam sticks.

Warming-up

1. BrainDance: Students perform the BrainDance with or without rhymes. Perform the patterns using strong and light touch and movements.

2. Introduce the Concept: Students "hear, see, say and do" the concept of WEIGHT (strong and light). Refer to the chapter Exploring the Concept for an explanation of this concept.

Exploring the Concept

1. Strong and Light Land: In one land (one half of the room), dancers move lightly. When the music changes they dance to the other land and move strongly. Suggest a variety of images such as snow, gentle breezes, feathers, etc. for "Light Land" and giants, hurricanes, dancing through mud, etc. for "Strong Land."

Suggested Music: *Music for Creative Dance, Volume I,* #14

Reflection: "Think about how you move during the day. If you move mostly with strong weight, make a strong shape. If you move mostly with light weight, make a light shape. Notice who made the same type of shape as you and who made the opposite type of shape."

For a 60-minute lesson, add the following activity:

2. Bridges: Dancers dance through the space with light movements. On a signal, they find a partner and form a bridge by pressing palms together with strong weight, leaning into each other (sharing weight). They hold the strong bridge shape until the signal to press away and dance lightly. Encourage dancers to find a new partner every time they make bridges.

Suggested Music: *Music for Creative Dance, Volume III,* #4

Developing Skills

1. Combining Movements: Perform this simple pattern to the tune of "Brother John."

"Walking strongly, walking strongly; skip, skip, skip; skip, skip, skip.
Running, running lightly, running, running lightly; tip, tip, tip; tip, tip, tip!
Sliding strongly, sliding strongly; jump, jump, jump; jump, jump, jump.
Running, running lightly, running, running lightly; bump, bump, bump; bump, bump, bump!
Turning strongly, turning strongly; hop, hop, hop; hop, hop, hop.
Running, running lightly, running, running lightly; now we stop; now we stop!"

Feel free to exchange other skills for the ones mentioned above that are appropriate to the level of your students. Use a dramatic voice as you sing or chant the song and change volume on the strong and light movements. Repeat the song several times as dancers change Speed or Direction or add arm movements.

For a 60-minute lesson, add the following activity:

2. Leaping and Turning: Create a leaping course in a horseshoe formation with small and big cones, or spots and milk cartons. Dancers leap lightly over the small/low objects (placed along one side of the room) and strongly over the big/high objects (placed along the other side). The dancers perform turns across the top of the horseshoe. The pattern might be light leaps, turns, strong leaps. More advanced students could practice different patterns such as strong leap, light leap, light leap, turns, light leap, strong leap, strong leap.

Suggested Music: *Music for Creative Dance, Volume II,* #11

Creating

1. Props: This activity may be done with any prop such as scarves, plastic or foam sticks. Dancers dance lightly with the prop. When the music changes, they dance strongly. Suggest different actions to motivate a variety of light and strong movements. For example, flick, dab, float, glide, tiptoe, whisper, sway and punch, press, wring, slash, kick, jump, pull.

Suggested Music: *Music for Creative Dance, Volume III,* #15

Cooling Down

1. Reflecting: Half the dancers make a shape (or do an action) to demonstrate their favorite way of moving strongly or lightly. Then the other half makes a shape or action they just observed. Repeat the reflection with the second half of the dancers performing and the first half observing/forming shapes.

For a 60-minute lesson, add the following activity:

2. Blind Mirror: Pairs stand facing each other with palms pressed firmly together. Leader #1 has eyes open and moves the arms of Leader #2 (who has eyes shut) in different Directions and with changes in Speed and Size. Then Leader #2 opens eyes and becomes the leader.

Suggested Music: *Music for Creative Dance, Volume I,* #8 (Fade the music down and up as a signal to change leaders. Change leaders several times.)

Lesson Plan #3 on WEIGHT
Age 9–Adult

National Dance Content Standards: 1, 2, 3, 4, 5, 7

Ages: 9–13 (This lesson may be easily adapted for age 14–Adults.)
Grades: 4th–8th (and beyond)

Length: 45 minutes (For a 60-minute lesson, add the activities suggested.)

Objectives

Students will:

- Identify and demonstrate the elements of WEIGHT.
- Work cooperatively and safely with others to create weight sharing shapes.
- Remember and repeat a combination of movements.
- Relate to natural disasters through movement.
- Reflect on their experiences.

Equipment: CD player; *Music for Creative Dance, Volume IV*; whiteboard or chart paper on which to write conceptual vocabulary.

Warming-up

1. BrainDance: Students perform the BrainDance. Perform the patterns using strong and light movements and touch. Integrate dance technique if appropriate.

2. Introduce the Concept: Students "hear, see, say and do" the concept of WEIGHT (strong and light). Refer to the chapter Exploring the Concept for an explanation of this concept.

Exploring the Concept

1. Weight Share: Partners explore weight sharing shapes, such as pressing both palms together, pulling apart, pressing backs together, pressing sides together, pulling apart with one hand and then the other. Explore pressing and pulling on different levels in different directions and with various body parts. Partners press or pull with strength and then press or pull into lightness before moving on to find a new partner for further exploration.

Suggested Music: *Music for Creative Dance, Volume IV,* #17

Reflection: "Discuss with your last partner your feelings about this activity. What did you enjoy about it? What was difficult for you? What was easy? Do you think the height or size of your partner makes a difference?" (It should not.)

For a 60-minute lesson, add the following activity:

2. Shape Museum: Everyone has a partner. Half of the couples begin as statues in the museum, forming a weight sharing shape with the partner. The other couples enter the museum, dancing together with light movements. Dancing couples copy weight sharing statues. Statue couples dance away lightly to copy a new statue pair. An option is to have dancers change the weight sharing shape after they have copied the statue.

Suggested Music: *Music for Creative Dance, Volume IV,* #12

Developing Skills

1. Folk Dance: If you taught "Si Senior" in the Focus lesson, you might review the dance by discussing the use of Weight and emphasizing strong lower body and light upper body movements. Instead of the finger snap, dancers might do a double hand clap with partner. If you reviewed "Scatter Square Dance" in the previous lesson, you might introduce "Fado Blanquita." This dance contains interesting weight shifts and variations in strong and light movements.

OR

1. Combining Movements: Continue to practice the movement pattern from the first and second lesson. Discuss the use of Weight in the pattern and emphasize strong and light movements for the appropriate sections or steps. If appropriate, add a weight sharing shape at the beginning, end or in the middle of the combination.

Creating

It is helpful before doing this activity for the students to have some knowledge about natural disasters.

1. Natural Disaster Improvisation: Dancers improvise movement about blizzards, hurricanes, volcanoes, tsunami, forest fires, earthquakes, tornadoes, etc. Call out a different disaster every 30 seconds. (Name three to four contrasting disasters.) Props could be added for visual effect. Dancers could also create their own sound scores with body or vocal sounds. Dancers should use a variety of strong and light movements to depict their natural disaster. This activity may not be appropriate if a natural disaster has recently occurred in your area. On the other hand, it may serve as a springboard for a therapeutic discussion.

For a 60-minute class, you might have time for choreography instead of improvisation:

1. Natural Disaster Choreography: Groups of dancers create short dances about blizzards, hurricanes, volcanoes, tsunami, forest fires, earthquakes, tornadoes, etc. Assign a different disaster to each group or assign the same disaster to all the groups. Props could be added for visual effect. Dancers could also create their own sound scores with instruments, body or vocal sounds. Dancers should use a variety of strong and light movements to depict their natural disaster.

Cooling Down

1. Sharing: Review the 4 "A's" of audience behavior (Attend, Allow, Applaud, Appreciate). Following improvisation, divide the class in half. Every dancer in one half performs a brief improvisation about a disaster of choice. Reverse roles of observers and performers. Following choreography, groups share their dances with the whole class or another group. Observers guess the disaster and then discuss the use of strong and light movements, the beginning and ending, unique ideas or other concepts that were emphasized.

Lesson Plan #4 on RELATIONSHIP
Ages 4–8

National Dance Content Standards: 1, 2, 3, 4, 7

Ages: 4–8
Grades: PreK–3rd

Length: 30 minutes (For a 60-minute lesson, add the activities suggested.)

Objectives

Students will:

- Identify and demonstrate elements of the concept RELATIONSHIP.
- Move safely in and through space.
- Work cooperatively with others and a prop.
- Remember and repeat a combination of movements using rhyming words.
- Respond to music cues.
- Reflect on their experiences.

Equipment: CD player; *Music for Creative Dance, Volume I*; whiteboard or chart paper on which to write conceptual vocabulary; one prop for every student such as plastic or scarves; rhythm instruments (optional).

Warming-up

1. BrainDance: Students perform the BrainDance with or without rhymes while focusing on Relationship words such as "near," "far," "above," "below," "in front," "behind," "on," "off."

2. Introduce the Concept: Students "hear, see, say and do" the concept of RELATIONSHIP (over, under, around, through, beside, between, on, off, in, out, etc). Refer to the Exploring the Concept chapter for an explanation of this concept.

Exploring the Concept

1. Zombie and Magician: Review this dance game from Lesson #2 with the variation described here. Pairs – the Magician moves the whole prop (plastic or scarf) over, under, around, behind, in front, etc. The Zombie moves the way the prop moves. When the music changes, the Magician moves small parts of the prop to represent body parts moving near, far, together, apart, beside, etc. For example, moving just the top of the prop in a circle may indicate circling of the head. Moving the lower part of the prop up and down might suggest feet jumping off and on the floor. Moving the two ends of the prop together might suggest upper and lower body parts moving together and apart. If necessary, provide support during the activity by suggesting different Relationships. Dancers change roles several times. With preschool children, you might be the Magician for the whole class.

Suggested Music: *Music for Creative Dance, Volume I,* #1

Reflection: "Name two or three different relationships that your magician made you create." Students might call out words at the same time, share with a partner or speak when you call their name.

For a 60-minute lesson, add one or the other of the following activities:

2. Touch Shape Museum: Statues stand inside the museum in a neutral position (not in a shape). When the music begins, each dancer outside the museum enters and dances through general space around, between, in front of and behind the statues and stops in front of a statue. The dancer lightly touches three body parts (one at a time). When the statue is touched that body part moves into a shape in relation to the other parts (over, around, in front). After three body parts have been touched and the statue has created a new shape, the dancer copies the shape and the statue is free to dance away. If your students have trouble with appropriate touch, they might use a prop to touch body parts. After the shape is copied, the statue takes the prop and dances away.

Suggested Music: *Music for Creative Dance, Volume I,* #5 or #15

OR

2. Instruments: Each dancer has one rhythm stick or one cymbal. The dancers move through space while moving the instrument over, under, around, through, beside body parts. On a signal, dancers find partners and keep a pulse by tapping two instruments together. If instruments are not available, the dancers might come together and clap hands.

Suggested Music: *Music for Creative Dance, Volume I,* #3

Developing Skills

1. Combining Movements: Review the pattern below from Lesson #3, adding Relationships (pairs dance side by side, shadow, and/or come together and apart).

"Walking strongly, walking strongly; skip, skip, skip; skip, skip, skip.
Running, running lightly, running, running lightly; tip, tip, tip; tip, tip, tip!
Sliding strongly, sliding strongly; jump, jump, jump; jump, jump, jump.
Running, running lightly, running, running lightly; bump, bump, bump; bump, bump, bump!
Turning strongly, turning strongly; hop, hop, hop; hop, hop, hop.
Running, running lightly, running, running lightly; now we stop; now we stop!"

Feel free to exchange other **skills** for the ones mentioned above that are appropriate to the level of your students or other **concepts** ("walking backward"). Repeat the song several times as dancers practice different Relationships with their partners.

For a 60-minute lesson, add the following activity:

2. Leaping and Turning: Create a leaping course in a double horseshoe formation. Name two dancers at a time. They start apart on the far sides of the horseshoes and leap over objects. The dancers perform turns across the top of the horseshoes and come toward each other. They leap side by side along the near sides of the horseshoes back to the beginning of the course.

Suggested Music: *Music for Creative Dance, Volume I,* #6

Creating

1. AB Dance: Say the directions for each section as the dancers perform.

A – Dancers move in self space forming relationships with individual body parts. Call out Relationship words if dancers need suggestions.

B – Dancers move through space relating to other people by moving around, between, beside, over or even copying another dancer's movements. With novice dancers, you will need to offer suggestions as the dancers move.

Repeat the dance several times for deeper exploration (ABABABAB).

Suggested Music: *Music for Creative Dance, Volume I,* #16

Cooling Down

1. Reflecting: "In the last dance, if you enjoyed moving in self space relating to yourself, make a shape with body parts close together. If you enjoyed moving through general space relating to other people, make a shape with body parts far apart."

For a 60-minute lesson, add the following activity:

2. Sharing: After practicing AB dances several times, one half performs for the other half (AB), then roles switch. Change roles two or three times so that each group as the opportunity to observe and perform several times. This alternation gives dancers the chance to observe new ways of moving and then explore those ideas themselves.

Lesson Plan #4 on RELATIONSHIP
Ages 9–Adult

National Dance Content Standards: 1, 2, 3, 4, 5, 7

Ages: 9–13 (This lesson may be easily adapted for age 14–Adults.)
Grades: 4th–8th (and beyond)

Length: 45 minutes (For a 60-minute lesson, add the activities suggested.)

Objectives

Students will:

- Identify and demonstrate an understanding of the elements of RELATIONSHIP.
- Work cooperatively and safely with others to create a Totem Pole Dance.
- Remember and repeat a combination of movements.
- Reflect on their experiences.

Equipment: CD player; *Music for Creative Dance, Volumes I and III* or *IV*; whiteboard or chart paper on which to write conceptual vocabulary; pictures or models of totem poles (optional).

Warming-up

1. BrainDance: Students perform the BrainDance while focusing on Relationship words such as "near," "far," "above," "below," "in front," "behind," "on" and "off." If chairs are available, try the chair variation of the BrainDance. Students discover new movements when working with a chair. Integrate dance technique if appropriate.

2. Introduce the Concept: Students "hear, see, say and do" the concept of RELATIONSHIP (over, under, around, through, beside, between, on, off, in, out, etc). Refer to the Exploring the Concept chapter for an explanation of this concept.

Exploring the Concept

This exploration is enjoyed by all ages. The process is the same, but the "product" will be different depending on your students' level of experience.

1. Zombie and Magician: Pairs – the Magician moves the whole prop (plastic or scarf) over, under, behind, in front, etc. The Zombie moves the way the prop moves. When the music changes, the Magician moves small parts of the prop in different ways to represent body parts moving near, far, together, apart, etc. For example, moving just the top of the plastic may indicate head movements. Moving the bottom part might suggest dancing feet. Moving the two ends of the plastic together might suggest upper and lower body parts moving together and apart. If necessary, provide support during the activity by suggesting different relationships. Change roles.

Suggested Music: *Music for Creative Dance, Volume I,* #1

Reflection: "Discuss with your partner which role you preferred today and why, Magician or Zombie?"

Developing Skills

1. Folk Dance: If you taught "Fado Blanquita" in the Weight lesson, you might review the dance by emphasizing the different Relationships. For example, moving as individuals but part of a community in the first and last sections and relating to a partner in the second section. Dancers also move behind and in front of others, dance around each other, and move together and apart. You might want to add the variation in which the couples do the schottische step first with their partner and then with their "corner." This creates a new and more challenging Relationship.

If you are ready to introduce a new dance, "Greensleeves" also emphasizes a variety of Relationships.

OR

1. Combining Movements: Continue to practice the movement pattern from the three previous lessons. Discuss the use of the Relationship of body parts to body parts to bring more clarity to the movements in the pattern. For example, do arms stay apart or move over or under; do legs come together and apart; what is the head-tail Relationship? Add new movements that focus on new Relationships. Perform the pattern in relation to other dancers by dancing side by side, apart and together, in trios, etc.

Creating

For a 45-minute lesson, the dancers may need to improvise the B section.

For a 60-minute class, the dancers may have time to choreograph the B section.

1. Totem Pole dances (ABA form): Organize dancers into groups of three to six. It is helpful to show pictures and briefly discuss totem poles if students are unfamiliar with what they are and look like. For the A section, dancers create a totem pole by forming shapes relating to each other on different levels. For the B section, dancers travel through space depicting movements of fish, birds or other animals. Then the dancers repeat the A section. Dancers should emphasize Relationships within the totem pole and as they move through space.

Dancers may choose to incorporate the following ideas: for the A section, dancers move in self space within the totem pole formation. For the B section, dancers create a creature together (eagle, salmon, bear) and dance in unison, then break apart into many creatures.

Suggested Music: *Music for Creative Dance, Volume III,* #1 or *Volume IV,* #13

Cooling Down

1. Sharing: If time allows, each group may perform their dance one after the other in a ritual, without applause between dances. Then everyone applauds and a discussion about the dances takes place. See the Creating chapter for suggestions of reflection questions. If time is short, several groups might perform at the same time. Observers might then each form a shape they saw in the dance.

> ***Teaching Tip:*** *Totem pole dances make exciting choreographic projects. Introduce this theme in the first lesson on Place. Dancers do research in the library and on the Internet on the history and meaning of totem poles. Lesson #2 introduces the importance of Focus in the totem pole dances. Lesson #3 introduces variations in the use of Weight during the B section. Lesson #4 introduces the idea of Relationships within the totem pole and the relationship of the totem pole to the community. Lesson #5 is the culmination of the project with performance and evaluation. Music and Art are easily integrated through the creation of sound scores and totem pole models, drawings or costume pieces.*

Lesson Plan #5 on FLOW
Ages 4–8

National Dance Content Standards: 1, 2, 3, 4, 5, 6, 7

Ages: 4–8
Grades: PreK–3rd

Length: 30 minutes (For a 60-minute lesson, add the activities suggested.)

Objectives

Students will:

- Identify and demonstrate elements of the concept FLOW.
- Move safely in and through space.
- Respond to music cues.
- Use haiku poetry to motivate new movements and ideas.
- Reflect on their experiences.

Equipment: CD player; *Music for Creative Dance, Volumes I, II,* and *III*; whiteboard or chart paper on which to write conceptual vocabulary; one prop for every student, such as plastic, scarves; several haiku; objects to leap over (optional).

Warming-up

1. BrainDance: Students perform the BrainDance with or without rhymes. Perform the patterns focusing on the elements of Flow. For example, perform some of the patterns with bound, measured, controlled movements and others with free, more uncontrolled movements. Briefly discuss the difference. While performing the patterns discuss the flow of blood and oxygen. Explore holding breath and breathing freely. How does this effect movement?

2. Introduce the Concept: Students "hear, see, say and do" the concept of FLOW (free flow, bound flow). Refer to the Exploring the Concept chapter for an explanation of this concept.

Exploring the Concept

1. Water and Ice: Dancers move with free flow movements as rivers, waves, whirlpools and waterfalls. When the music begins to "freeze" the dancers move with bound flow until they are frozen in shapes that represent icebergs (solo shapes) or glaciers (group shapes). Responding to the music, the dancers alternate free flow movements with bound flow movements and shapes. This exploration might also be done as "Water and Ice Land." See the Exploring the Concept chapter for a full explanation.

Suggested Music: *Music for Creative Dance, Volume I,* #4

Reflection: "If you found it easier to move with free flow, make a big shape. If you moved more easily with bound flow, make a small shape. Look around the room and see who feels the same way you do."

For a 60-minute lesson, add the following activity:

2. Rhythm: Direct the dancers to move with free flow through general space. Then direct them to stop on a spot (imaginary or real) and follow your pulse by clapping and tapping body parts (or using rhythm instruments).

Suggested Music: *Music for Creative Dance, Volume III,* #2

Developing Skills

1. Folk Dance: Teach "Tanko Bushi," a Japanese folk dance described in the Developing Skills chapter. In this dance the upper body moves with some free flow while the lower body is bound. Discuss briefly some of the elements seen in Japanese dance. In a 60-minute class, show a brief sample of Japanese dance on video (see Bibliography for World Dance Resources). In general, traditional Japanese dances use more self space than general space. Upper body movements are very important and gestures are used to tell stories and connote meaning. Movement is performed in a bound kinesphere. Very large movements that stretch far from the body are not generally performed.

OR

1. Leaping and Turning: Create a leaping course in a horseshoe formation. One side of the course is Free Land and the other side is Bound Land. In Free Land, the dancers leap over objects without stopping and with flowing arm movements. In Bound Land, they leap over one object and then freeze on a spot. This might be repeated three times (run leap, run freeze, run leap, run freeze, run leap, run freeze). This is difficult for young students. Remind them to freeze on the spot for about three counts. The dancers practice turning at the top of the horseshoe between the two lands. Allow the dancers to move through the leaping course two to four times. The second or fourth time reverse directions by starting with the opposite land.

Suggested Music: *Music for Creative Dance, Volume II,* #11

Creating

1. Haiku: Read a haiku (a Japanese poetry form) and discuss it briefly. Then read it again as the dancers improvise with free and bound flow movements to bring the poem to life. If time allows, have students improvise movements to another haiku.

Suggested Music: *Music for Creative Dance, Volume II,* #18

For a 60-minute lesson, alter the previous activity:

With Preschool and kindergarten students, choose one haiku for which the whole class will create movement. Read the haiku and ask for movement ideas to use to portray the poem. When should bound flow be used? When should free flow be used? What other concepts can be used to depict the haiku? Choose students to demonstrate ideas, then create a haiku dance together. Older students may work in pairs, trios or quartets. Dancers work together to choreograph a haiku dance using free and bound flow. All the dancers could work with the same haiku or a different haiku might be assigned to each group.

Cooling Down

1. Sharing and Reflecting: Half of the class performs for the other half. Change roles. Observers might share a favorite movement or moment with the class or a friend.

For a 60-minute lesson, alter the previous activity:

1. Sharing and Reflecting: Each group shares their haiku dance. If all groups are using the same haiku, several groups might perform at the same time. After a group has performed, the observers draw a simple line design on a small piece of paper that depicts the dance (or a moment in the dance) and presents the design to the performers. This continues until all groups have shared.

Lesson Plan #5 on FLOW
Ages 9-Adult

National Dance Content Standards: 1, 2, 3, 4, 5, 6, 7

Ages: 9–13 (This lesson may be easily adapted for age 14–Adults.)
Grades: 4th–8th (and beyond)

Length: 45 minutes (For a 60-minute lesson, add the activities suggested.)

Objectives

Students will:

- Identify and demonstrate the elements of FLOW.
- Move safely in and through space.
- Remember and repeat a combination of movements.
- Work cooperatively together to create dances based on haiku.
- Reflect on their experiences.

Equipment: CD player; *Music for Creative Dance, Volumes I and II;* several examples of haiku; whiteboard or chart paper on which to write conceptual vocabulary.

Warming-up

1. BrainDance: Students perform the BrainDance focusing on the elements of Flow. For example, perform some of the patterns with bound, measured, controlled movements and others with free, more uncontrolled movements. Briefly discuss the difference. While performing the patterns, discuss the flow of blood and oxygen. Explore holding breath and breathing freely. How does this effect movement? Include dance technique if appropriate.

2. Introduce the Concept: Students "hear, see, say and do" the concept of FLOW (free flow, bound flow). Refer to the Exploring the Concept chapter for an explanation of this concept.

Exploring the Concept

1. Water and Ice: Dancers move with free flow movements as rivers, waves, whirlpools, and waterfalls. When the music begins to "freeze," the dancers move with bound flow until they are frozen in shapes that represent icebergs (solo shapes) or glaciers (group shapes). Responding to the music, the dancers alternate free flow movements with bound flow movements and shapes. Encourage dancers to take risks and move off-balance with free flow and then be very controlled during the bound flow sections. If the class is large and the space is small, you might divide the group in half and have the icebergs form around the edges of the room. The other half melts into free flow while the icebergs hold still. As the music changes, the dancing half starts to move to the sides of the room and freeze. The other half melts into free flow. Continue this alternation.

Suggested Music: *Music for Creative Dance, Volume I,* #4

Reflection: "Find a partner and share your feelings about free and bound flow. Which flow do you use mostly in school? Which flow do you use after school? Which flow do you use on vacation? Which flow did you find most challenging in that activity?"

Developing Skills

1. Folk Dance: Teach "Tanko Bushi," a Japanese folk dance described in the Developing Skills chapter. In this dance the upper body moves with some free flow while the lower body is bound. Discuss briefly some of the elements seen in Japanese dance. In a 60-minute class, show a brief sample of Japanese dance on video (see Bibliography for World Dance Resources).

In general, traditional Japanese dances use more self space than general space. Upper body movements are very important and gestures are used to tell stories and connote meaning. Movement is performed in a bound kinesphere. Large movements that stretch far from the body, are not generally performed.

OR

1. Combining Movements: Continue to practice the movement pattern from the four previous lessons. Discuss the use of the Flow to add more clarity to the movements in the pattern. For example, which movements should be performed with more bound flow and which with more free flow? Dancers might add a new section that has improvised free flow movement or eight counts of free flow movement followed by a leap and stillness to end the combination. Half the students might perform the combination for the other half and vice versa. Briefly discuss how the pattern has developed over five lessons or weeks and how the level of performance has improved through repetition and practice.

Creating

1. Haiku: Read a haiku (a Japanese poetry form) and discuss it briefly. Then read it again as the dancers improvise with free and bound flow movements to bring the poem to life. If time allows, have students improvise movements to a different haiku.

Suggested Music: *Music for Creative Dance, Volume II,* #18

For a 60-minute lesson, alter the previous activity:

Dancers work in pairs, trios or quartets to choreograph a dance based on a haiku with free and bound flow. All groups might work with the same haiku or a different haiku might be assigned to each group.

Cooling Down

1. Sharing and Reflecting: Half of the class performs for the other half as you read the haiku. Change roles. Observers might share a favorite movement (or moment) with the class or a friend.

For a 60-minute lesson, alter the previous activity:

1. Sharing and Reflecting: Each group shares their haiku dance. If all groups are using the same haiku, several groups might perform at the same time. If the groups are using different haiku, ask each group to read their haiku before they perform or during their performance as a sound score. After a group has performed, the observers draw a simple line design on a small piece of paper that depicts the dance (or a moment in the dance) and presents the design to the performers. This continues until all groups have shared.

Lesson Plan on LEVEL for Preschoolers

National Dance Content Standards: 1, 3, 4, 7

Ages: 2–4
Grades: Preschool (This lesson may include parents or caregivers.)

Length: 30 minutes (For a 60-minute lesson, add the activities suggested.)

Objectives

Students will:

- Demonstrate the elements of LEVEL.
- Move safely in and through space.
- Remember and repeat a combination of movements and rhyming words.
- Respond to music cues.

Equipment: CD player; *Music for Creative Dance, Volumes I and II*; whiteboard or chart paper on which to write conceptual vocabulary; objects for an obstacle course (optional); paper and crayons (optional).

Warming-up

1. BrainDance: Students perform one of the short versions of the BrainDance for young children described in the Warming Up chapter. Perform the first four patterns sitting and the last four standing.

2. Introduce the Concept: Students "hear, see, say and do" the concept of LEVEL (high, middle, low). Refer to the Exploring the Concept chapter for an explanation of this concept.

Exploring the Concept

1. High and Low: When the music is pitched high, the dancers dance on a high level. For low- pitched music they dance low; middle pitch they dance at a middle level. When the music is sustained they hold still and listen for the pitch of the music. Suggest different ways of dancing on different levels as the dancers are moving.

Suggested Music: *Music for Creative Dance, Volume I,* #11

Reflection: "Make a high shape if you like to dance high. Make a low shape if you like to dance low."

For a 60-minute lesson, add the following three activities:

2. Elevator Shapes: Dancers make shapes moving from low to high and back down to low in self space. Very young dancers might copy your shapes or you might suggest specific shapes such as curved, straight, strong, wide, twisted, narrow, tipping, etc. Use the image of going up and down in an elevator, stopping on each floor to make a shape on a new level. Go up and down several times, and stop on different levels for different amounts of time. Use your voice to indicate high, middle and low levels.

3. Circle Dance: Choose a simple circle dance from the Developing Skills chapter and perform holding hands with adults if available. Do not have students hold hands if adults are not present. If the space for dancing is small, have the dancers perform the steps in a scattered formation.

4. Rest: Dancers breathe lying or sitting quietly.

Suggested Music: *Music for Creative Dance, Volume II,* #10 (fade the music when rest time is over).

Developing Skills

1. Combining Movements: Chant the words as the students and you do the movements.

"Gallop, gallop, gallop, gallop, **mop! mop!** (low level movements)
Turn, turn, turn, turn, **pop! pop!** (high movements)
Slide, slide, slide, slide, **flop! flop!** (low movements)
Jump, jump, jump, jump, **stop! stop!"** (middle level shapes)

Feel free to exchange other skills for the ones mentioned above that are appropriate to the level of your students and the amount of space available for dancing. Use a dramatic voice as you sing or chant the song, changing pitch on the high and low movements. Repeat the song several times changing speed or adding arm movements.

For a 60-minute lesson, add the following activity:

2. Obstacle Course: Create an obstacle course with any objects available that make dancers change levels such as tunnels, mats, and benches. Use cones of different heights or stack cartons to create low, middle and high objects for leaping over.

Suggested Music: *Music for Creative Dance, Volume II,* #11

Creating

1. Story Dance: Tell a simple movement story that inspires the dancers to move on different levels. There are several examples of stories in the Developing Skills chapter. If the dancing space is small, the dancers could sit in self spaces and tell the story with feet and arm movements. Remember that feet may dance high, arms may dance low and vice versa.

OR

1. High and Low Land: Divide the space into High Land and Low Land. When the music is soft dancers dance in Low Land. When the music is loud, they dance in High Land. Suggest different ways of moving high and low or comment on movements that you see as the dancers move. If the room is small, half the class may sit around the edges and watch while the other half dances. Change roles several times without stopping for discussion.

Cooling Down

1. Mirror: Dancers mirror your movements for 30 to 60 seconds. (Move slowly in self space changing levels.)

Suggested Music: *Music for Creative Dance, Volume I,* #8

For a 60-minute lesson, you might have time to add the following activity:

2. Reflecting: Dancers draw objects on paper that are different heights (levels) such as dancers crawling and jumping, mountains and hills, houses and skyscrapers, children and adults, lizards and giraffes, squares and rectangles, tall ovals and short ovals, etc.

Sample Brain-Compatible Technique Class

> ***Teaching Tip:*** *The following lesson may be adapted for any style of dance such as ballet, contemporary, jazz, tap, hip-hop, flamenco, etc.*

National Dance Content Standards: 1, 2, 3, 4, 6

Ages: 9–adults
Length: 60–90 minutes
Objectives

Students will:

- Identify and demonstrate the elements of BALANCE.
- Identify and demonstrate skills in performing dance technique.
- Work cooperatively and safely with others.
- Remember and repeat a combination of movements.
- Reflect on their experiences.

Equipment: CD player; *Music for Creative Dance, Volume IV*; whiteboard or chart paper on which to write conceptual vocabulary.

Warming Up

1. Technique/BrainDance: Move through the eight fundamental movement patterns of Breath, Tactile, Core-Distal, Head-Tail, Upper-Lower, Body-Side, Cross-Lateral and Vestibular by introducing and integrating the concept of balance by moving on and off balance within each pattern. You might also discuss how working in each pattern separately balances and integrates the whole body. The BrainDance may be performed lying, sitting and/or standing. Appropriate technique in the style of dance being taught is integrated into the patterns. Discuss the use of balance in that style. Dancers identify helpful tools for balancing on one body part such as core support, correct alignment, single focus, use of breath and counterbalancing.

Exploring the Concept

1. Concept Exploration: Dancers demonstrate various types of balance as they move "on balance" with controlled movements, "off balance" with tipping and falling movements and with "counterbalance" by forming balancing shapes on one body part with or without a partner. Dancers change the type of balance on your verbal command.

Suggested Music: *Music for Creative Dance, Volume IV,* #18

Reflection: "Share with another classmate which type of balance (on, off, counterbalance) is most challenging for you and one way you might improve that skill."

Developing Skills

1. Technique: Teach a new step (assemblé, split fall, step-ball-change); practice familiar skills; do barre or center floor work. Focus on the elements of Balance.

2. Combining Movements: Practice or add on to a familiar combination or start a new combination that contains elements of Balance. Refer to the Developing Skills chapter for sample combinations.

Creating

1. Improvisation: Dancers work in pairs to create Illusion Shapes by forming balancing shapes together that appear to need each other to remain balanced. However, when one dancer dances away, the partner remains balanced as if by magic. A new shape is formed and the other dancer dances away to see if the partner can balance alone. Encourage the use of Levels, Size, and Weight as the dancers create complex balanced shapes. Dancers dance away from the partner in the dance style of the technique being studied. Refer to the Exploring the Concept chapter for a more detailed explanation of this improvisation.

Suggested Music: *Music for Creative Dance, Volume IV,* #3

Closure

1. Reflection and Stretching: Dancers stretch in pairs and share with each other one new idea they learned about themselves, regarding the concept of Balance.

Energy and Emotion

National Dance Content Standards: 1, 2, 3, 4, 6, 7

Ages: 5–11
Grades: K–6th
Length: 45–60 minutes
Dance Concept: Energy
Thematic Concept: Emotions

Vocabulary that may be used in this lesson includes happy, sad, shy, bored, angry, scared, proud, confused, excited, nervous, pleased, frightened, furious, jubilant, loved, stressed, jealous, worried, envious, terrified, hopeful, embarrassed, guilty, curious.

Objectives

Students will:

- Identify and demonstrate the elements of ENERGY.
- Identify and demonstrate various EMOTIONS.
- Work cooperatively and safely with others to display a range of emotions.
- Remember and repeat a combination of movements.
- Reflect on their experiences.

Equipment: CD player; *Music for Creative Dance, Volume IV*; about 18-20 cards with a face drawn on each one that depicts an emotion (emotions may be duplicated and students could create their own cards); whiteboard or chart paper on which to write conceptual vocabulary.

Warming-up

1. BrainDance: Students perform the BrainDance relating to various emotions. For example, students may breathe as they do when angry, then when happy. Each tactile movement might be associated with a different emotion. Students may perform Core-Distal movements with bursting and shrinking energies and feelings.

2. Introduce the Concept: Students "hear, see, say and do" the concept of ENERGY (sharp, smooth, shaky, swingy). Refer to the Exploring the Concept chapter for an explanation of this concept.

Exploring the Concept

1. Planets: Dancers glide or float smoothly through space on the smooth music. When the music changes, call out a specific energy (sharp, shaky or swingy). Dancers imagine landing on a planet where only that type of energy is used when moving. As they dance with that energy, they associate feelings with it and call out those emotions or remember them for reflection time. In the suggested music, the smooth section alternates with bouncier music three times so that all four energies may be explored. Remember to suggest that dancers explore new ways of moving with Energy by integrating other concepts such as Direction, Level, Size and Pathway.

Suggested Music: *Music for Creative Dance, Volume IV,* #6

2. Emotion Shape Museum (Adapted from Helen Landalf.)

Statues "inside the museum" make small, round, low shapes scattered through the space (like seeds). Dancers outside the museum enter and "water" a statue by gently stroking the back of the statue three times. The "seed" grows slowly into a full-body shape that describes an emotion. Students imagine that the emotion starts growing in the toes and fills the whole body until one is standing in a clear shape. The dancer who watered the seed then copies the emotion statue, and the statue dances away. The new one shrinks to a seed and waits to be watered, and the cycle begins again. Encourage dancers to use facial expressions as well as body language. Young dancers may do this in pairs facilitated by teacher directions.

Suggested Music: *Music for Creative Dance Volume VI,* #10

Reflection: (Choose two or three questions.) "Who tried on a new emotion, or one that you seldom feel? What was that emotion? Form a shape that demonstrates it. How did it feel to copy someone else's emotion? Share your feelings with a friend. Were the emotions clear? How did it feel to let go of your emotion and dance away? What energy did you use when dancing away? What was your favorite part of this exploration?"

Developing Skills

1. Combining Movements: Students perform the combination of movements they are currently practicing, but in different emotional states. For example, they perform the combination as if they were angry, happy, frightened, sad or depressed. Discuss how the energy changes with the emotion. Do the movements also change Size, Level and Weight? If the students are not currently practicing a combination, choose two locomotor and two nonlocomotor movements and put them together into a phrase such as walk, turn, run, stretch. Perform them in three emotional states as described above.

Creating

1. Emotion Suites: Dancers form trios and choose three cards with faces drawn on them that depict emotions. They put them into an ABC order and choose an energy for each section. Dancers create abstract movement for each part with smooth transitions between sections. With young children, facilitate a whole group dance depicting three emotions chosen by the class.

Cooling Down

1. Sharing and Reflecting: Groups share dances individually or two or three groups at a time share. Observers guess the emotions or draw faces for the emotions portrayed. Discuss the contrasts in Energy, Level, Speed, etc. and magical moments that happen by chance when two or three groups perform together.

Dancing Math Lesson

National Dance Content Standards: 1, 2, 3, 4, 5, 7

Grades: 1st–8th
Length: 45–60 minutes
Dance Concept: Shape
Thematic Concept: Geometry

Vocabulary that may be used in this lesson: triangle, circle, square, rectangle, vertical, horizontal, diagonal, intersecting, acute angle, obtuse angle, right angle, hypotenuse, parallel, perpendicular, radius, circumference, diameter, parallelogram, pentagon, hexagon, congruence.

Objectives

Students will:

- Identify and demonstrate the elements of SHAPE.
- Identify and demonstrate the elements of simple GEOMETRY.
- Remember and repeat a combination of movements.
- Work cooperatively and safely with others to demonstrate geometric shapes and concepts.
- Reflect on their experiences.

Equipment: CD player; *Music for Creative Dance, Volume 1V*; whiteboard or chart paper on which to write conceptual vocabulary.

Warming-up

1. BrainDance: Students perform the BrainDance by forming and naming parallel and perpendicular lines and obtuse and acute angles. Dancers also form geometric shapes and move on different planes throughout the BrainDance patterns. Introduce or review vocabulary appropriate to age and experience of students.

2. Introduce the Concept: Students "hear, see, say and do" the concept of SHAPE (straight, curved, angular, twisted, symmetrical, asymmetrical). Other vocabulary may be introduced such as cone, sphere, pyramid. Refer to the Exploring the Concept chapter for an explanation of this concept.

Exploring the Concept

1. Geometry Vocabulary: Dancers move through space, tracing geometric shapes on the floor and in the air with different body parts. When the music pauses, call out a geometry concept such as "acute angles." Dancers quickly find a partner, trio or small group and demonstrate acute angles with fellow students. Deeper learning occurs when the dancers repeat the vocabulary verbally several times as they demonstrate it through movement. Continue in this way until eight to ten geometry words, appropriate to level of students, have been named and demonstrated. Remind dancers to change Levels, Directions, Speed and Energy as they dance through space.

Suggested Music: *Music for Creative Dance, Volume IV,* #18

Variations:

- Dancers shadow in pairs or trios through space and then form the geometry concept together. Students may find new partners half way through the exploration.
- Instead of tracing shapes, dancers move through space, shape shifting into different shapes, lines, and angles.

Developing Skills

1. Symmetry Shape Museum: Half the students form **symmetrical** shape statues "inside the museum." When the music begins, dancers outside the museum enter and dance to a symmetrical statue. Carefully, using appropriate touch, a dancer moves one or two body parts of the statue to create an **asymmetrical shape.** The dancer copies the asymmetrical statue, and the statue dances away. The asymmetrical statue waits for a dancer to change it back to a symmetrical statue. Dancers must use their spatial intelligence to look at the statues carefully! If the statue is symmetrical, it must be changed to an asymmetrical shape. If the statue is asymmetrical, it must be made symmetrical. Statues can be reminded to hold their shapes until someone changes **and** copies them. Then they are free to dance away. The concept of "congruence" may be introduced during this activity. Two shapes are congruent if laid one upon the other and match in all respects. When a dancer copies a statue, the two shapes should be congruent (matching).

Suggested Music: *Music for Creative Dance, Volume 1V,* #10

Reflection: "Form a symmetrical shape if you find that type more challenging to create. Make an asymmetrical shape if you find that type more challenging. Which was more challenging to recognize? Form that one."

Creating:

1. ABC Geometry Dances: Students work together in small groups to create short dances that demonstrate knowledge of geometric terms and concepts.

A – Dancers in the group form three shapes, together or individually, that depict three terms such as acute angles, obtuse angles, right angles.

B – Dancers in the group create a movement phrase that clearly demonstrates the concept of diameter (or circumference or radius). Terms may be assigned to groups or be freely chosen.

C – Dancers in the group form an ending shape that depict intersecting lines (or another concept).

> ***Teaching Tip:*** *With primary grade students, create one ABC dance as a whole group under your guidance or have students work in pairs with appropriate vocabulary.*

Cooling Down:

1. Sharing and Reflecting: Groups share dances. Observers guess the geometric terms depicted.

Younger dancers might be divided into two groups for sharing. Observers may draw the geometric designs depicted in the dances.

Music and Dance Lesson

National Dance Content Standards: 1, 2, 3, 4, 6, 7

Grades: K–8

Length: 45–60 minutes
Dance Concepts: Speed, Rhythm
Music vocabulary: pitch, tempo, meter, accent, phrasing, staccato, legato

Objectives

Students will:

- Identify and demonstrate the dance elements of SPEED and RHYTHM.
- Identify and demonstrate music vocabulary.
- Work cooperatively with others to create a staccato and legato dance.
- Respond to music cues.
- Reflect on their experiences.

Equipment: CD player; *Music for Creative Dance, Volumes I* and *III*; two inch wide paper squares, rectangles, and circles; whiteboard or chart paper on which to write conceptual vocabulary.

Warming-up

1. BrainDance: Students perform the BrainDance patterns with varying speeds and rhythmic patterns. For example, they breathe slowly and quickly and then in a pattern of slow breath, quick breath, quick breath, slow breath.

2. Introduce the Concept: Students "hear, see, say and do" the concept of SPEED (slow, medium, fast) and RHYTHM (pulse, pattern, grouping). Refer to the Exploring the Concept chapter for an explanation of these concepts.

Exploring the Concept

1. Pitch: Dancers respond to the varying pitches in the music by dancing on a high level when the pitch of the music is high, low level when the pitch is low, and middle level when the pitch is between high and low. As the last note of each section is held, the dancers freeze in a shape and listen for the next pitch.

Suggested Music: *Music for Creative Dance, Volume I,* #11

2. Tempo: Dancers match the tempo of the music with isolated body part and whole body movements. When the music pauses, dancers freeze and listen for the next tempo. Older dancers may do this activity by shadowing a partner or shadowing in a trio or quartet. Leadership changes during the music pause.

Suggested Music: *Music for Creative Dance, Volume III,* #9

3. Pulse and Pattern: Dancers stand back to back with a partner and bounce knees and clap the pulse directed by the teacher. They may also keep the pulse by slapping or tapping body parts or playing rhythm instruments. When the music pauses, dancers freeze. When the music continues, the dancers move away from the partners, dancing by themselves, clapping or tapping rhythm patterns by combining fast, slow and medium pulses. Dancers alternate keeping the teacher's pulse while standing back to back with a partner and clapping rhythm patterns through general space.

Suggested Music: *Music for Creative Dance, Volume III,* #2

Developing Skills

1. Grouping: Dancers respond to the grouping of beats (meter) with appropriate movement. When the music is 2/4, they march, walk, jump in different directions and add arm movements. When the music is 3/4, they swing, sway, twist, turn. Encourage them to make a strong or forceful movement at the beginning of each grouping (accent).

Suggested Music: *Music for Creative Dance, Volume III,* #4

2. Phrasing: Dancers practice a familiar folk dance or combination of movements. They focus on the phrasing of the music rather than counts or verbal cues.

Creating

1. Staccato and Legato: Put a pile of paper squares, rectangles and circles on the floor. The paper shapes should be about 2" wide and three different colors. Squares represent quick, staccato movements. Rectangles represent slower, legato movements. Circles represent stillness. Solo dancers, small groups (or the whole class together) create a staccato and legato pattern by laying the shapes on the floor in a sequence.

Example: circle, square, square, square, rectangle, circle, square, square, rectangle, circle. Translated into movement this is stillness, quick move, quick move, quick move, sustained movement, stillness, quick move, quick move, sustained movement, stillness.

Staccato and legato vocal and body sounds may be added to accompany the movement.

Cooling Down

1. Sharing and Reflecting: Staccato and legato dances are shared and discussed.

Visual Art and Dance Lesson

National Dance Content Standards: 1, 2, 3, 4, 5, 6, 7

Grades: K–8

Length: 45 minutes (For a 60-minute lesson, add the activities suggested.)
Dance Concepts: Pathway and Energy
Thematic Concepts: Line and Texture

Objectives

Students will:

- Identify and demonstrate the dance elements of PATHWAY and ENERGY.
- Identify and demonstrate the visual art elements of LINE and TEXTURE.
- Work cooperatively with others to create a Texture Suite.
- Respond to music cues.
- Reflect on their experiences.

Equipment: CD player; *Music for Creative Dance, Volumes II* and *III*; paper and crayons or colored pens; objects of different textures, such as sandpaper, sponges, toothpicks, twigs, pebbles, shells, fabrics, bubblewrap, etc.; whiteboard or chart paper on which to write conceptual vocabulary.

Warming-up

1. BrainDance: Students perform the BrainDance standing in self space for the first four patterns while focusing on texture and energy. For example, take smooth breaths, ragged breaths, "bumpy" breaths and relate the breathing to different textures such as silk, bark and bubble wrap. Students might name a texture and then try to describe the texture through breath. For the Tactile pattern, dancers can actually touch and rub various clothing and describe that texturally. Perform the last four patterns, traveling through general space in various Pathways and focusing on the lines being drawn through space. Students might visualize the line designs they are creating with feet and arms.

2. Introduce the Concept: Students "hear, see, say and do" the dance concepts of Pathway (straight, curved, zigzag) and Energy (smooth, sharp, shaky, swingy). Relate the visual art concepts of Line and Texture to Pathway and Energy.

Exploring the Concept

1. Designs: Dancers listen to music and draw line designs on paper, motivated by the various music selections. Then the music is repeated and they dance the line designs. Depending on the level of the students, they may hold the designs as they dance through space or place the designs, scattered through the space, dancing in straight pathways from design to design, curved pathways around the designs and zigzag pathways between designs.

Suggested Music: *Music for Creative Dance, Volume II, #7*

Reflection: "As you danced around the designs, did you notice many different line designs or were the designs similar? If you felt they were different, sit down. If you felt they were similar, stand up. Did you notice that you used different types of energy while moving in straight, curved and zigzag pathways? Discuss with a friend (or tell the class) what energy you associated with what pathway."

Developing Skills

1. Pathway Fences: Refer to the Exploring the Concept chapter for a detailed description of the basic Fence activity. After making a straight fence with straight shapes, dancers "build" one in a curved pathway out of curved shapes. They form a zigzag fence with zigzag shapes in a zigzag pathway. These fences are challenging and require teamwork, problem-solving and spatial intelligence. Remind dancers to closely follow the fence line (pathway) as they dance to the end of the fence. Incorporate the Energy and Texture concepts by calling out different textures as the dancers dance along the fence line. The dancers try to describe the texture through movement. For an added challenge, the dancers making shapes in the fence may move slightly.

Suggested Music: *Music for Creative Dance, Volume III,* #16 (This music has three sections that work well for three Pathways and changes in Energy.)

Creating

1. Texture Suites: Young students may create a dance together as a whole group under your guidance. More experienced dancers work in pairs, trios or small groups. Each group choreographs a three-part study, motivated by three textures. It is helpful to have a set of textured objects for each group to touch and manipulate. Dancers (or the teacher) choose three objects with different textures, such as sandpaper, silk and sponge. The dancers arrange the objects in an order (ABC), then compose a texture suite by focusing on different energies and pathways. Dancers create sounds for each section, motivated by the textures and energy. Encourage them to make the transitions between sections clear.

Cooling Down

2. Sharing and Reflecting: Groups perform the texture suites. Observers reflect on the clarity of Texture, Line, Energy and Pathway, the use of sound and other concepts included in the dances. Refer to the Cooling Down chapter for samples of reflection questions and evaluation tools.

Extended Visual Art Activity: Students create detailed line designs, texture collages or texture rubbings, motivated by the activities in the lesson.

(Endnote)

[1] Zull, 2002, Chapter 2

*Appendix H**
Resources – a Sampling

Organizations

The American Alliance for Health, Physical Education, Recreation and Dance (AAHPERD) is the largest organization of professionals assisting those involved in physical education, leisure, fitness, dance, health promotion and education and all specialties related to achieving a healthy lifestyle. AAHPERD is an alliance of five national and six district associations, including the National Dance Association. Members are welcome to visit the headquarters in Reston, VA, 25 miles west of Washington, DC. Programs, products and services, for both professionals and students, include publications, leadership/educational conferences, a national convention and other resources: www.aahperd.org

American Dance Guild (ADG) has reciprocal collegial benefit arrangements with the National Dance Association (NDA) and other dance organizations: www.americandanceguild.org

American Dance Therapy Association (ADTA) works to establish and maintain high standards of professional education and competence in the field of dance/movement therapy: www.adta.org

Black College Dance Exchange (BCDE) forms a coalition of dance departments from Historically Black Colleges and Universities (HBCU's): www.bcdexchange.org

Congress on Research in Dance (CORD) encourages scholars in dance to research, publish and discuss material from all areas of dance. CORD has an international membership of teachers, students, writers, performers, choreographers, researchers, archivists and librarians: www.cordance.org

dance and the Child international (daCi) is the international organization that is a fully constituted branch of the Conseil International de la Danse (CID), UNESCO, with the aim of promoting the growth and development of dance for children on an international basis (including conferences and resources): www.education.uregina.ca/daci

dance and the Child international USA (a chapter of daCi) promotes growth and development in dance for children and youth internationally, irrespective of race, color, sex, religion, and national or social origin (including national conferences and newsletters): www.daciusa.com

Dance Heritage Coalition (DHC) focuses on access to dance materials; the continuing documentation of dance employing both traditional methods and developing technologies; preservation of existing documentation and education regarding standards and practice: www.danceheritage.org

Dance Notation Bureau (DNB) advances the art of dance by creating dance scores using the symbol system called Labanotation: www.dancenotation.org

Dance/USA advances the art form of dance by addressing the needs, concerns and interests of the professional dance community: www.danceusa.org

*Please note that website addresses may change

Early Childhood Music and Movement Association (ECMMA) is an organization of professional educators dedicated to the ideal that all children should be given the advantage of music and movement instruction in their formative years from birth to age seven: www.ecmma.org

International Association of Blacks in Dance (IABD) provides initiates dialogue around issues that impact the Black Dance Community: www.howard.edu/collegefinearts/iabdassociation

International Council of Dance (CID) represents the interests of the world of dance by acting as a forum in close cooperation with UNESCO - bringing together international, national and regional organizations as well as any person working in the field of dance: www.unesco.org/ngo/cid

Laban/Bartenieff Institute of Movement Studies (LIMS) is an institution that provides the comprehensive study of movement as fundamental human experience, based on the work of Rudolf Laban and Irmgard Bartenieff: www.limsonline.org

National Dance Association (NDA), an association of AAHPERD, celebrates almost eighty years of advocating for dance as quality dance arts and physical education. NDA, the author of the *National Standards for Dance Education*, produces publications, conferences and other crucial resources to benefit its members and the arts community. Networking and creative, healthy lifestyles are two important objectives of NDA: nda@aahperd.org; www.aahperd.org/nda

National Dance Education Organization (NDEO) works in the field of dance education, encourages research and practical applications: www.ndeo.org

VSA arts is an international nonprofit organization founded by Ambassador Jean Kennedy Smith to create a society where all people with disabilities learn through, participate in and enjoy the arts: www.vsarts.org

Journals/Magazines

American Journal of Dance Therapy. Kluwer Academic/Plenum Publishers, New York, NY.www.kluweronline.com

Contact Quarterly: Biannual Journal of Dance and Improvisation. Contact Quarterly: Northampton, MA. www.contactquarterly.com

Dance Magazine. 333 Seventh Ave, 11th Floor, New York, NY 10001. www.dancemagazine.com

Dance Teacher. Lifestyle Ventures LLC. 250 W 57th St, Ste. 420, New York, NY 10107. www.dance-teacher.com

Early Childhood Connections: Journal of Music- and Movement-Based Learning. www.ecconnections.org

Journal of Dance Education (JODE). J. Michael Ryan Publishing, Inc., Official Publication of the National Dance Education Organization. 24 Crescent Drive North, Andover NJ 07821. www.ndeo.org

Journal of Dance Medicine and Science. J. Michael Ryan Publishing, Inc., 24 Crescent Drive North, Andover NJ 07821

Journal of Physical Education, Recreation, and Dance (JOPERD). American Alliance for Health, Physical Education, Recreation and Dance. www.aahperd.org

Research in Dance Education. www.tandf.co.uk/journals.

Research Quarterly for Exercise and Sport. American Alliance for Health, Physical Education, Recreation and Dance. www.aahperd.org

Spotlight on Dance. National Dance Association, 1900 Association Dr., Reston, VA 20191. www.aahperd.org/nda

The Orff Echo: Quarterly Journal of the American Orff-Schulwerk Association. www.aosa.org.

Young Children. National Association for the Education of Young Children (NAEYC), 1509 16th Street NW, Washington DC 20036. www.naeyc.org.

Web Sites

Arts

www.artslynx.org: international resources, publications.

www.arts4learning.org: resources, lesson plans, video clips of performances.

www.wwar.com: World Wide Arts Resources.

www.artsedge.kennedy-center.org: Artsedge – interactive lessons, quotes, resources.

www.dancemagazine.com: *Dance Magazine's Dance Annual Directory* – over 8,500 up-to-date dance resource listings.

www.aahperd.org/nda: The National Dance Association provides the latest in quality programs, products and services to strengthen dance education. Networking, advocacy and creative, healthy lifestyles are important objectives of this association.

Brain Research/Therapy/Education Resources

www.adta.org: American Dance Therapy Association.

www.amazingbabies.com: Beverly Stokes videos showing normal movement development of ages 0-3, books also – excellent resource for parents and teachers of young children.

www.ascd.org: Association for Supervision and Curriculum Development – resources for teachers.

www.BrainPlace.com: Brain SPECT information and many interesting resources.

www.bodymindcentering.com: School for Body-Mind Centering founded by Bonnie Bainbridge Cohen.

www.BrainConnection.com: BrainBuzz, books, resources, articles by Robert Sylwester and others.

www.dana.org: gateway to brain information and resources.

www.developmentalmovement.org: Developmental Movement and Education Center, Bette Lamont, Director, 206-525-8038, Seattle WA.

www.earlychildhood.com: resources for early childhood education.

www.jabadao.org: Jabadao is a British organization dedicated to movement and working towards an "embodied culture." Developmental movement resources, courses, research, etc.

www.loveandlogic.com: Love and Logic – resources for teachers and parents on class management and raising children.

www.learningbrain.com: brain research, training tips, future of learning.

www.aahperd.org/nda: The National Dance Association provides the latest in quality programs, products and services to strengthen dance education. Networking, advocacy and creative, healthy lifestyles are important objectives of this association. Publisher of *Dance Movement Therapy: A Healing Art* by Fran J. Levy and Anne Green Gilbert books.

www.talaris.org: brain development 0-3, monthly articles on key points in child development.

www.newhorizons.org: New Horizons for Learning – resources and information for teachers on brain research, best practices, cutting edge ideas.

www.nurturingpathways.com: resources for ages 0-3 created by dance educator Christine Roberts.

www.sparkplugdance.org: great articles and resources for early childhood dance, special populations and intergenerational dance. This site can be translated into several languages.

www.zerotothree.org: resources and information for parents and teachers of very young children.

Where to Order Dance Books, Music, and Videos

www.creativedance.org: Creative Dance Center – teacher training, workshops, events, books, music, videos, and more!

www.ravennaventures.com: Eric Chappelle's *Music for Creative Dance* CD includes idea booklets written by Anne Green Gilbert.

www.dancehorizons.com: Princeton Book Company Publishers/Dance Horizons – dance books and performance, historical and instructional dance videos.

www.erckids.com: Educational Record Company – CDs and videos.

www.folkstyle.com: folk dance CDs, instructional videos, and workshops by Sanna Longden.

www.johnsmusic.com: Johns Music – Shenanigans CDs, Rhythmically Moving CDs, world music, music for dance classes, videos, instruments, books, 800-473-5194.

www.kultur.com: instructional and performance dance videos.

www.lodc.org: Language of Dance Centre – LOD® resources, motif teacher aids, workshops.

www.aahperd.org/nda: National Dance Association – National Dance Standards, publications, research, conferences in dance arts education. Eric Chappelle and Anne Green Gilbert materials may be purchased from this site.

www.pbs.org: Public Broadcasting Service – great source for dance performance videos and teacher resources.

www.powells.com: Powells Books in Portland, Oregon has a good selection of dance books including some that are out of print.

www.stagestep.com: Stagestep for books, instructional and world dance videos, dance floors and barres, 800-523-0960.

www.treefrogpro.com: books, music, and workshops by Kerri Lynn Nichols, certified Orff-Schulwerk music and movement teacher.

www.westmusic.com: West Music – Shenanigans CDs, Rhythmically Moving CDs, world music, music for dance classes, videos, books, instruments.

Where to Order Dance Props

www.dancingcolors.com: Emily Day's dancing scarves and other dance products plus information about dance workshops and retreats.

www.displaycostume.com: Display and Costume Supply in Seattle, Washington sells dance scarf material, colorful plastic tablecloth for charts or dancing, costumes, fabric, art supplies, and more.

www.dyenamicmovement.com: Kimberly Dye's stretch band material products for dance, therapy, or exercise.

www.sportime.com: Sportime for balls, parachutes, cones, hoops, ribbon sticks, and more, 800-283-5700.

Music Recommendations

Instrumental Music for Creative Dance and Dance Technique Classes:

Eric Chappelle, *BrainDance Music*, BDM1, Ravenna Ventures, 2006, www.RavennaVentures.com. May order from the National Dance Association: 800-213-7193.

Eric Chappelle, *Music for Creative Dance, Volumes I-V*, Ravenna Ventures, 1993–2005, Includes idea booklets written by Anne Green Gilbert. www.RavennaVentures.com. May order from the National Dance Association: 800-213-7193.

Eric Chappelle, *Violin for Modern and Ballet*, Volume I, VMB1, Ravenna Ventures, 2006, www.RavennaVentures.com. May order from the National Dance Association: 800-213-7193.

Michael Cava, *Piano Solos*, www.johnsmusic.com

Peter Jones, *Gradual Motion*, 1989-1994, *Fifth Movement*, 1995, *Three Characters*, 1998, *Gradual Motion II*, 2004, www.joneschord.com or www.johnsmusic.com

American Gramaphone, *Sunday Morning Coffee*, www.amazon.com

Kerri Lynn Nichols, *Music for Dancers, I am the Song*, www.treefrogpro.com

Recordings by Cirque de Soleil, Brent Lewis, Jami Seiber, Bobby McFerrin, Yo Yo Ma, Baka Beyond, Ray Lynch, Windham Hill Samplers, Sweet Honey in the Rock, www.amazon.com

Activity Songs for Parent and Child Classes

Hap Palmer, *Homemade Band*, *Feel of Music*, *Walter the Waltzing Worm*, and others, www.johnsmusic.com

Greg and Steve Recordings, *Kids in Motion*, www.johnsmusic.com

Lullaby, A Collection (various artists), www.johnsmusic.com

Parachute Express, *Shakin It*, www.parachuteexpress.com

Paul Lippert and Sue Ribaudo, *In the Same Boat,* www.raspberryrecords.com

World and Folk Dance Music

Multicultural Folk Dance Treasure Chest Volumes I and II by Christy Lane: http://www.christylane.com: www.humankinetics.com

Putamayo World Music Recordings: www.putamayo.com; www.johnsmusic.com

Rhythmically Moving Series 1-9 (Traditional folk music selected especially for movement and dance) by Phyllis S. Weikart: www.highscope.org or www.johnsmusic.com

Sanna Longden Folk Dance Series: www.folkstyle.com

Shenanigans International Folk Dance: www.members.optusnet.com.au/shenanigan/band; www.johnsmusic.com

Bibliography

Brain Research, Learning, Behavior

Brandt, Ron. *Powerful Learning*. Alexandria, VA: ASCD, 1998.

Bresler, Liora, ed. *Knowing Bodies, Moving Minds*. Norwell, MA: Kluwer Academic Publishers, 2004.

Caine, Renate Nummela, and Geoffery Caine. *Making Connections: Teaching and the Human Brain.* Alexandria, VA: ASCD, 1991.

Caine, Geoffrey, and Renate Nummela Caine, Sam Crowell. *MindShifts: A Brain-Compatible Process for Professional Growth*. Chicago, IL: Zephyr, 1999.

Csikszentmihalyi, Mihaly. *Finding Flow: The Psychology of Engagement With Everyday Life.* New York, NY: Basic Books (a Division of HarperCollins Publishers, Inc.), 1997.

Damasio, Antonio. *Looking for Spinoza: Joy, Sorrow, and the Feeling Brain*. Orlando, FL: Harcourt, 2003.

Dennison, Paul E., and Gail E. Dennison. *Brain Gym*. Ventura, CA: Edu-Kinesthetics, Inc, 1992.

Dewey, John. *Art as Experience*. New York, NY: Berkley Publishers, 1959 (1st ed. 1934).

Diamond, Marian, and Janet L. Hopson. *Magic Trees of the Mind: How to Nurture Your Child's Intelligence, Creativity, and Healthy Emotions from Birth through Adolescence*. New York, NY: Penguin Putnam, Inc., 1999.

Dryden, Gordon, and Jeanette Vos. *The Learning Revolution*. Vista, CA: Accelerated Learning Systems Ltd, 1994.

Elin, Jane, and Boni Boswell. *Re-envisioning Dance*. (*Dance for all abilities*.) Reston, VA: AAALF/AAHPERD, 2004.

Eliot, Lise. *What's Going on in There? How the Brain and Mind Develop in the First Five Years of Life.* New York, NY: Bantam Books, 2000.

Gardner, Howard. *Intelligence Reframed: Multiple Intelligences for the 21st Century*. New York, NY: Basic Books, 2000.

___. *The Unschooled Mind: How Children Think and How Schools Should Teach*. New York, NY: Basic Books, 1993.

Fay, Jim, and Foster M. Cline, Bob Sornson. *Meeting the Challenge: Using Love and Logic to Help Children Develop Attention and Behavior Skills*. Golden, CO: Love and Logic Press, 2000.

Funk, David. *Love and Logic Solutions for Kids with Special Needs*. Golden, CO: Love and Logic Press, 2002.

Funk, David, and Jim Fay. *Teaching with Love and Logic: Taking Control of the Classroom*. Golden, CO: Love and Logic Press, 1998.

Gilbert, Anne Green. *BrainDance* (video/DVD, 85 minutes). Seattle, WA: AGG Productions, 2003. Available through www.aahperd.org/nda.

Glasser, William. *Schools Without Failure*. New York, NY: HarperCollins Books, 1975 (1st ed. 1969).

Goleman, Daniel. *Emotional Intelligence: Why It Can Matter More Than IQ*. New York, NY: Bantam Books, 1995.

Gopnik, Alison, Patricia K. Kuhl, and Andrew N Meltzoff. *The Scientist in the Crib: Minds Brains,and How Children Learn*. New York, NY: HarperCollins Publishers Inc., 2001.

Grubin, David (Producer). *The Secret Life of the Brain.* Series of five videos/DVDs about brain development from the baby's brain to the aging brain. Public Broadcasting Service, 2001.

Hanna, Judith Lynne. *Partnering Dance and Education: Intelligent Moves for Changing Times*. Champaign, IL: Human Kinetics, 1999.

Hannaford, Carla. *Smart Moves: Why Learning is Not All in Your Head.* Arlington, VA: Great Ocean Publishers, 1995.

Holt, John. *How Children Fail.* Jackson, TN: Perseus Books Group, 1995.

___. *How Children Learn*. Jackson, TN: Perseus Books Group, 1995.

Interview with Bonnie Bainbridge Cohen, "Sensing, feeling and action." *Contact Quarterly reprint No. 1,* 1981, p. 6.

Jensen, Eric. *Arts with the Brain in Mind.* Alexandria, VA: ASCD, 2001.

___. *Learning with the Body in Mind.* San Diego, CA: Brain Store Inc, 2000.

___. *Teaching with the Brain in Mind.* Alexandria, VA: ASCD, 1998.

Johnson, Katie. *Doing Words*. Boston, MA: Houghton Mifflin, 1987.

___. *More Than Words*. Chicago, IL: Zephyr Press, 1995.

___. *Reading Into Writing*. Chelsea, MI: Sheridan Books, 2000.

Lamont, Bette. "Learning and Movement." *Pathways: Creative Dance Center Newsletter.* Seattle, WA. Spring, 1996: 4-5.

Levy, Fran. *Dance Movement Therapy: A Healing Art.* Revised Ed. Reston, VA: National Dance Association/ AAHPERD, 2005.

Marzano, Robert J., and Jana S. Marzano, Debra J. Pickering. *Classroom Management that Works: Research-Based Strategies for Every Teacher.* Alexandria, VA: ASCD, 2003.

New England Journal of Medicine, 348:2508-2516. June 19, 2003.

Piaget, Jean. *Play, Dreams and Imitation in Childhood.* Trans. F. M. Hodgson and C. Gattegno. London, UK: Routledge, 2000 (1st ed. 1951).

Quinn, Thomas, and Cheryl Hanks. *Coming to Our Senses.* New York, NY: American Council for the Arts, 1988.

Ratey, John. *A User's Guide to the Brain: Perception, Attention, and the Four Theaters of the Brain.* New York, NY: Random House Inc., 2002.

Richmond, Virginia P., and James C. McCrosky. *Nonverbal Behavior in Interpersonal Relations.* 4th ed. Boston, MA: Pearson Education/Allyn and Bacon, 1999.

Randolph, Shirley, Margot Heiniger, and Kristin M. Tucker. *Kids Learn from the Inside Out: How to Enhance the Human Matrix.* 2nd ed. Boise, ID: Legendary Publishing Company, 1998.

Root-Bernstein, Robert S., and Michèlle M. Root-Bernstein. *Sparks of Genius: The Thirteen Thinking Tools of the World's Most Creative People.* New York, NY: Houghton Mifflin Company, 1999.

The Seattle Times, 5 April 2004, p. A13.

Sprenger, Marilee. *Becoming a "Wiz" at Brain-Based Teaching: How to Make Every Year Your Best Year.* Corwin Press, Inc., 2002.

___. *Learning and Memory: The Brain in Action.* Alexandria, VA: ASCD, 1999.

Stokes, Beverly. *Amazing Babies: Essential Movement for Your Baby in the First Year of Life.* Toronto, CAN: Move Alive Media, 2002.

Sylwester, Robert. *A Celebration of Neurons: An Educator's Guide to the Human Brain.* Alexandria, VA: ASCD, 1995.

___. Excerpts from "A Celebration of the Ordinary: The Key Role of the Arts in Educating a Brain." October 2002. www.BrainConnection.com

Thelen, Esther. "Grounded in the World: Developmental Origins of the Embodied Mind." *Infancy*, 1, 2000: Vol. 1 No. 1: 3-28.

Thelen, Esther, and Linda B. Smith. *A Dynamic Systems Approach to the Development of Cognition and Action.* Cambridge, MA: MIT Press (revised edition), 1996.

Verghese J., Lipton R. B., Katz M. J., Hall C. B., Derby C. A., Kuslansky G., Ambrose A. F., Sliwinski M., Buschke H. "Leisure Activities and the Risk of Dementia in the Elderly." *New England Journal of Medicine* (2003): 348:2508-2516.

Wagner, Wendi. "Movement and Cognition." Thes. Hollins University, 2004.

Wolfe, Patricia. *Brain Matters: Translating Research into Classroom Practice*. Alexandria, VA: ASCD, 2001.

Zull, James E. *The Art of Changing the Brain: Enriching the Practice of Teaching by Exploring the Biology of Learning*. Sterling, VA: Stylus Publishing, LLC, 2002.

Creative Dance

Baumgarten, S. and Langton, T. *Elementary Physical Education: Building a Solid Movement Foundation.* Champaign, IL: Stipes Publishing, 2005.

Benzwie, Teresa. *A Moving Experience: Dance for Lovers of Children and the Child Within.* Chicago, IL: Zephyr Press, 1987.

___. *More Moving Experiences: Connecting Arts, Feelings, and Imagination*. Chicago, IL: Zephyr Press, 1996.

Bissinger, Kristen, and Nancy Renfro. *Leap Into Learning! Teaching K-7 Curriculum Through Creative Dramatics and Dance*. Austin, TX: Nancy Renfro Studios, 1990.

Cone, Theresa Purcell, and Stephen Cone. *Teaching Children Dance.* 2nd ed. Champaign, IL: Human Kinetics, 2005.

Cornett, Claudia E. *The Arts as Meaning Makers: Integrating Literature and the Arts Throughout the Curriculum.* Upper Saddle River, NJ: Prentice-Hall, 1998.

Ellis, Becky. *Teaching Academics Through Movement.* Unpublished manuscript, 2nd edition. 1330 Apple Ave. Provo, Utah 84604. Email: movementacademic@aol.com, 1999.

Faber, Rima. *Primary Movers Move Russia.* (video, 30 minutes). Bethesda, MD: NDEO, 1997.

Gilbert, Anne Green. *Creative Dance for All Ages: A Conceptual Approach*. Reston, VA: National Dance Association/AAHPERD, 1992.

___. *Teaching Creative Dance* (video/DVD, 120 minutes). Seattle, WA: AGG Productions, 2002. Available through www.aahperd.org/nda.

___. *Teaching the Three R's Through Movement Experience: A Handbook for Teachers* Bethesda, MD: NDEO, 2002.

Gilbert, Debbie, and Joanne Petroff. *Dancing Science, Dancing Math, Dancing Cultures, Dancing Dance.* Seattle, WA: Whistlestop.

Gough, Marion. *Knowing Dance: A Guide to Creative Teaching.* Hightstown, NJ: Princeton Book Company, 1999.

Graham, George, and Shirley Ann Holt/Hale, Melissa Parker. *Children Moving: A Reflective Approach to Teaching Physical Education.* 6th ed. Ontario, CAN: McGraw-Hill Higher Education, 2004.

Griss, Susan. *Minds in Motion: A Kinesthetic Approach to Teaching Elementary School Curriculum.* Portsmouth, NH: Heinemann, 1998.

Herman, Gail, and Patricia Hollingworth: *Kinetic Kaleidoscope: Exploring Movement and Energy in the Visual Arts.* Tulsa, OK: University School, 2001.

Joyce, Mary. *First Steps in Teaching Creative Dance to Children.* 3rd ed. Mountain View, CA: Mayfield Publishing Co, 1993.

Landalf, Helen. *Moving is Relating: Developing Interpersonal Skills Through Movement.* Lyme, NH: Smith & Kraus, 1998.

___. *Moving the Earth: Teaching Earth Sciences Through Dance.* Lyme, NH: Smith & Kraus, 1997.

Landalf, Helen, and Pamela Gerke. *Movement Stories for Young Children: Ages 3-6.* Lyme, NH: Smith & Kraus, 1996.

Levete, Gina. *No Handicap to Dance: Creative Improvisation for People With and Without Disabilities.* London, UK: Souvenir Press, 1993.

Lloyd, Marcia L. *Adventures in Creative Movement Activities: a Guide for Teaching.* Dubuque, IA: Eddie Bowers Publishing, Inc, 1990.

Mettler, Barbara. *Materials of Dance as a Creative Art Activity.* Tucson, AZ: Mettler Studio, 1979.

Nichols, Kerri Lynn. *Music for Dancers.* Olympia, WA: Tree Frog Productions, 1999.

___. *Music Moments to Teach Academics.* Olympia, WA: Tree Frog Productions, 2001.

Overby, Lynnette Young, et. al. *Interdisciplinary Learning Through Dance: 101 MOVEntures.* Champaign, IL: Human Kinetics, 2005.

Reedy, Patricia. *Body, Mind, and Spirit in Action: A Teacher's Guide to Creative Dance.* Berkeley, CA: Luna Kids Dance, 2003.

Rowen, Betty. *Dance and Grow: Developmental Dance Activities for Three through Eight Years Old.* Hightstown, NJ: Dance Horizons/Princeton Book Company, 1994.

Stinson, Sue. *Dance for Young Children: Finding the Magic in Movement.* Reston, VA: National Dance Association/AAHPERD, 1988.

Willis, Cheryl M. *Dance Education Tips from the Trenches.* Champaign, IL: Human Kinetics, 2004.

Motif Notation

Brown, Ann Kipling, and Monica Parker. *Dance Notation for Beginners: Labanotation and Benesh Movement Notation.* London, UK: Dance Books Ltd., 1984.

Guest, Ann Hutchinson. *Dance Notation – The Process of Recording Movement on Paper.* Hightstown, NJ: Dance Horizons, 1984.

___. *Motif at a Glance.* London, UK: Language of Dance Centre, 2000.

___. *The Adventures of Klig and Gop* – A series of eight workbooks (introducing Motif symbols and movement for young children). Bethesda, MD: NDEO, 1999.

___. *Your Move: A New Approach to the Study of Movement and Dance.* 2nd ed. New York, NY: Routledge, 2005.

Modern Dance and Somatic Practices

Bartenieff, Irmgard. *Body Movement: Coping With the Environment.* New York, NY: Routledge, 1980.

Cohan, Robert. *The Dance Workshop: A Guide to the Fundamentals of Movement.* New York, NY: Simon and Schuster, 1986.

Cohen, Bonnie Bainbridge. *Sensing, Feeling, and Action: The Essential Anatomy of Body-Mind Centering.* Northampton, MA: Contact Editions, 1993.

Dowd, Irene. *Taking Root to Fly: Articles on Functional Anatomy.* New York, NY: Irene Dowd, 1995.

Erkert, Jan. *Harnessing the Wind: The Art of Teaching Modern Dance.* Champaign, IL: Human Kinetics, 2003.

Evans, Bill. *Bill Evans Creates and Teaches Modern "Dancing" Combinations* (to students at SUNY Brockport), video, 2005. www.billevansdance.org

___. *Bill Evans Teaches Barteneiff Fundamentals* (as they support the teaching of dance technique) video, 1999. www.billevansdance.org

___. *Bill Evans Teaches Modern Dance Technique* (to three members of his professional modern dance company), video, 1999. www.billevansdance.org

___. *Bill Evans Teaches Modern Dance Technique* (to two students at the University of New Mexico) video, 2002. www.billevansdance.org

___. *Reminiscences of a Dancing Man: A Photographic Journey of a Life in Dance.* Reston, VA: National Dance Association/AAHPERD, 2006.

Feldenkrais, Moshe. *Awareness through Movement: Easy-to-Do Health Exercises to Improve Your Posture, Vision, Imagination, and Personal Awareness* (Reprint ed). San Francisco, CA: HarperSanFrancisco, 1991.

Fitt, Sally S. *Dance Kinesiology*. 2nd ed. New York, NY: Wadsworth, 1996.

Franklin, Eric. *Dance Imagery For Technique and Performance*. Champaign, IL: Human Kinetics, 1996.

___. *Dynamic Alignment Through Imagery*. Champaign, IL: Human Kinetics, 1997.

___. *Conditioning for Dance*. Champaign, IL: Human Kinetics, 2004.

Hackney, Peggy. *Making Connections: Total Body Integration through Bartenieff Fundamentals*. New York, NY: Routledge, 1998.

Hay, Deborah. *My Body, the Buddhist*. Middletown, CT: Wesleyan University Press, 2000.

H'Doubler, Margaret. *Dance: A Creative Art Experience*. 2nd ed. Madison, WI: University of Wisconsin Press, 1989.

Joyce, Mary. *Dance Technique for Children*. Mountain View, CA: Mayfield Publishing Company, 1984.

Kimmerle, Marliese and Paulette Côté-Laurence. *Teaching Dance Skills.* Andover, NJ: J. Michael Ryan Publishing, Inc., 2003.

Knaster, Mirka. *Discovering the Body's Wisdom.* New York, NY: Bantam Dell Publishing Company, 1996.

Laban, Rudolph Von. *The Mastery of Movement*. Boston, MA: Plays, 1971.

___. *Modern Educational Dance*. 3rd ed. Philadelphia, PA: Trans-Atlantic Publications, 1988.

Metal-Corbin, Josie. *Reach For It: A Handbook of Health, Exercise and Dance Activities for Older Adults.* Peosta, IA: Eddie Bowers Publishing, 1997.

Minton, Sandra Cerny. *Dance, Mind and Body*. Champaign, IL: Human Kinetics, 2003.

Newlove, Jean, and John Dalby. *Laban for All.* New York, NY: Routledge, 2004.

Olsen, Andrea. *BodyStories: A Guide to Experiential Anatomy*. New York, NY: Barrytown Ltd, 1998.

Penrod, James, and Janice Gudde Plastino. *The Dancer Prepares: Modern Dance for Beginners*. Mountain View, CA: Mayfield Publishing Co, 1990.

Preston-Dunlop, Valerie. *Rudolf Laban, An Extraordinary Life.* London, UK: Dance Books, Ltd., 1998.

Scheff, Helene, Marty Sprague, and Susan McGreevy-Nichols. *Experiencing Dance: From Student to Dance Artist.* Champaign, IL: Human Kinetics, 2005.

Schrader, Constance A. *A Sense of Dance: Exploring Your Movement Potential*. 2nd ed. Champaign, IL: Human Kinetics, 2005.

Shapiro, Sheryl. *Dance, Power, and Difference: Critical and Feminist Perspectives on Dance Education.* Champaign, IL: Human Kinetics Publishers, 1998.

Sherbon, Elizabeth. *On the Count of One: Modern Dance Teaching Methods*. Mountain View, CA: Mayfield Publishing, 1975.

Sweigard, Lulu E. *Human Movement Potential: Its Ideokinetic Facilitation*. New York, NY: Dodd Mead, 1974.

Todd, Mabel. *The Thinking Body* (1937). (1st ed., 1937). Hightstown, NJ: Princeton Book Company, 1980.

Wetzig, Betsy, and Ginny Whitelaw. *Bodysmarts at Work.* In press.

Winton-Henry, Cynthia, and Phil Porter. *What the Body Wants: From the Creators of InterPlay.* Kelowna, CAN: Northstone Publishing, 2004.

Choreography

Blom, Linda Anne, L. Tarin Chaplin, and Alma M. Hawkins. *The Intimate Act of Choreography.* Pittsburgh, PA: University of Pittsburgh Press, 1982.

Ellfeldt, Lois. *A Primer for Choreographers*. Prospect Heights, IL: Waveland Press, 1988.

Hawkins, Alma M. *Creating Through Dance*. Hightstown, NJ: Princeton Book Company, 1988.

Hayes, Elizabeth. *Dance Composition and Production*. Hightstown, NJ: Princeton Book Company, 1993.

Humphrey, Doris. *The Art of Making Dances*. New York, NY: Grove Press, 1959.

Lavender, Larry. *Dancers Talking Dance: Critical Evaluation in the Choreography Class*. Champaign, IL: Human Kinetics, 1996.

McGreevy-Nichols, Susan, and Helene Scheff. *Building Dances: A Guide to Putting Movements Together*. Champaign, IL: Human Kinetics, 1995.

McGreevy-Nichols, Susan, Helene Scheff, and Marty Sprague. *Building More Dances: Blueprints for Putting Movements Together*. Champaign, IL: Human Kinetics, 2001.

Minton, Sandra. *Choreography: A Basic Approach Using Improvisation*. Champaign, IL: Human Kinetics, 1997.

Nagrin, Daniel. *Choreography and the Specific Image: Nineteen Essays and a Workbook*. Pittsburgh, PA: University of Pittsburgh Press, 2001.

Ririe, Shirley, and Joan Woodbury. *Teaching Beginning Dance Improvisation*. (Workbook and Video), Salt Lake City, UT: Ririe Woodbury Dance Company, 1989.

___. *Teaching Advanced Dance Improvisation*. (Workbook and Video), Salt Lake City, UT: Ririe Woodbury Dance Company, 1993.

Schneer, Georgette. *Movement Improvisation: In the Words of a Teacher and Her Students*. Champaign, IL: Human Kinetics, 1994.

Smith-Autard, Jacqueline M. *Dance Composition*. New York, NY: Routledge, 2000.

World Dance, Cultures, History

Anderson, Jack. *Ballet and Modern Dance: A Concise History*. Hightstown, NJ: Dance Horizons/ Princeton Book Company, 1992.

Arbeau, Thoinot. *Orchesography.* Mineola, NY: Dover Publications, 1995.

Caroso, Fabritio, and Julia Sutton, F. Marian Walker. *Courtly Dance of the Renaissance: A New Translation and Edition of the Nobilità Di Dame(1600).* Mineola, NY: Dover Publications, 1995.

Dils, Ann, and Ann Cooper Albright. *Moving History/Dancing Cultures: A Dance History Reader.* Middletown, CT: Wesleyan University Press, 2001.

Emery, Lynne Fauley. *Black Dance: From 1619 to Today.* Hightstown, NJ: Dance Horizons/Princeton Book Company, 1988.

Heth, Charlotte, Editor. *Native American Dance: Ceremonies and Social Traditions*. Washington, DC: Smithsonian Institution, 1992.

Laubin, Reginald. *Indian Dances of North America: Their Importance to Indian Life*. Norman, OK: University of Oklahoma Press, 1977.

Long, Richard A., and Joe Nash. *The Black Tradition in American Dance*. New York, NY: Smithmark, 1995.

Longden, Sanna, and Phyllis Weikart. *Cultures and Styling in Folk Dance.* Ypsilanti, MI: High/Scope Press, 1998.

Mazo, Joseph. *Prime Movers: The Makers of Modern Dance in America.* 2nd ed. Chicago, IL: Independent Publishers Group, 2000.

Pittman, Anne M., and Marlys S. Waller, Cathy L. Dark. *Dance A While: Handbook of Folk, Square, Contra, and Social Dance*. 9th ed. San Francisco, CA: Pearson Education, Inc., 2005.

Reynolds, Nancy, and Malcom, McCormick. *No Fixed Points: Dance in the Twentieth Century.* New Haven, CT: Yale University Press, 2003.

Spain, Louise, Ed. *Dance on Camera: A Guide to Dance Films and Videos.* Lanham, MD: Scarecrow Press, 1998.

Thorpe, Edward. *Black Dance*. New York, NY: The Overlook Press, 1990.

Weikart, Phyllis. *Teaching Folk Dance: Successful Steps*. Ypsilanti, MI: High/Scope Press, 1999.

World Dance Videos/DVDs

Black Dance America. Four-day gathering in 1983 of dancers and dance companies at the Brooklyn Academy of Music celebrating the evolution of black dance from the Cakewalk to the Alvin Ailey Company. Includes performances by Garth Fagan and Chuck Davis. www.dancehorizons.com

Dancing. Video series of eight tapes put out by PBS. Excellent resource for world and cultural dance and dance history. www.pbs.org or www.kultur.com

Holo Mai Pele, the Epic Hula Myth. www.pbs.org

Into the Circle, An Introduction to Native American Powwows. Full Circle Communications, 1131 South College Ave, Tulsa, OK 74104.

The JVC/Smithsonian Video Anthology of Music and Dance. This thirty videotape, nine-book collection contains over 500 performances and 1,200 pages of text from 100 countries. Volumes may be ordered separately or in Regional sets. www.multiculturalmedia.com

Moiseyev Dance Company. Russian Folk Dances. www.stagestep.com

Multicultural Folk Dance Treasure Chest. Produced by Christy Lane. Includes 2 Videos, 2 CDs and 2 Booklets. Eighteen dances from around the world demonstrated by people from the country in native costume. www.HumanKinetics.com

Road to the Stamping Ground. Australian Aboriginal Dance and Jiri Kylián. www.kultur.com

Russian Folk Song and Dance. www.kultur.com

Native American Indian Dances. www.erckids.com

Wongai 1 and 2. West African dance videos with Youssouf Koumbassa, www.westafricandance.com

Dance Standards, Assessments, Curriculum Guides

Contact your State Office of Education, State Arts Council or State Dance Association for information on State Dance Standards, Assessments and Curriculum Guides.

National Standards for Dance Education, What Every Young American Should Know and Be Able to Do in Dance. Reston, VA: National Dance Association/AAHPERD, 1994.

Opportunity-to-Learn Standards in Dance Education. Reston, VA: National Dance Association/ AAHPERD, 1995.

Standards for Dance in Early Childhood. Bethesda, MD: NDEO, 2005.

Brandt, R. (Ed.). *Assessing Student Learning: New Rules, New Realities*. Arlington, VA: Educational Research Service, 1998.

Hart, Diane. *Authentic Assessment: A Handbook for Educators*. White Plains, NY: Addison Wesley Publishing Co., 1992.

Herman, Joan, Pamela Aschbacher, and Lynn Winters. *A Practical Guide to Alternative Assessment.* Washington, DC: ASCD, 1992.

Koff, Susan, and Byron Richard. *Dance Teacher Licensure: State by State Requirements.* Bethesda, MD: NDEO, 1999.

Mirus, Judith, Elena White, Loren E. Bucek, and Pamela Paulson. *Dance Education Initiative Curriculum Guide.* Golden Valley, MN: Minnesota Center for Arts Education, 1993.

Wiggins, Grant P. *Assessing Student Performance: Exploring the Purpose and Limits of Testing*. San Francisco, CA: Jossey-Boss Publishers, 1999.

Wiggins, Grant, and Jay McTighe. *Understanding by Design.* Washington, DC: ASCD. 2nd edition, 2005. *Understanding by Design Handbook* is also available which includes assessment forms and samples.

Children's Books about Dance and Dancers

Ancona, George. *Let's Dance*. New York, NY: Morrow Junior Books, 1998.

Baylor, Byrd. *Sometimes I Dance Mountains*. New York, NY: Charles Scribner's Sons, 1973.

Brighton, Catherine. *Nijinsky*. New York, NY: Doubleday, 1989.

Cooper, Elisha. *dance*! Singapore: New York, NY: Greenwillow Books, 2001.

Evans, Richard Paul. *The Dance*. New York, NY: Simon and Schuster, 1999.

Hoffman, Mary and Caroline Binch. *Amazing Grace*. New York, NY: Dial, 1991.

Isadora, Rachel. *Isadora Dances*. New York, NY: Penguin Putnam, Inc., 1998.

___. *Max*. Aladdin, 1984.

Jonas, Ann. *Color Dance*. New York, NY: Greenwillow Books, 1989.

Jones, Bill T., and Susan Kulkin. *Dance*. New York, NY: Hyperion Books for Children, 1998.

Martin, Jr., Bill., and John Archambault. *Barn Dance*. New York, NY: Henry Holt and Co., 1988.

McMahan, Patricia. *Dancing Wheels*. New York, NY: Houghton Mifflin Company, 2000.

Moore, Libba. *My Mama Had a Dancing Heart.* New York, NY: Orchard Books, 1995.

Pinkney, Andrea Davis. *Alvin Ailey.* New York, NY: Hyperion Books for Children, 1993.

Price, Christine. *Dance on the Dusty Earth*. New York, NY: Simon and Schuster, 1979.

Sendak, Maurice. *Where the Wild Things Are*. New York, NY: HarperCollins Publishers, 1963.

Tadjo, Veronique. *Lord of the Dance*. New York, NY: J.B. Lippincott, 1988.

Note: The accuracy of all listings in Appendix H: Resources – a Sampling and the Bibliography is the sole responsibility of the author and not NDA/AAHPERD.

About the Author

Anne Green Gilbert is Director of the Creative Dance Center (CDC) and Kaleidoscope Dance Company, which she founded in Seattle, Washington in 1981. CDC is a unique private studio offering creative and modern dance for infants through adults. Kaleidoscope is a modern dance company of children ages 8-14 who perform throughout Washington State and tour internationally. Anne is recognized throughout the United States and abroad as one of the leading dance educators. When not teaching creative dance at CDC or choreographing for Kaleidoscope, Anne trains teachers through her Summer Dance Institute for Teachers and for Seattle Pacific University and Seattle University as an adjunct professor. Anne has conducted hundreds of workshops for children and adults in the United States, Japan, Australia, New Zealand, Canada, Finland, Russia, Denmark, France, Germany, Holland, Brazil and Portugal.

Anne is the author of the books *Teaching the Three Rs Through Movement*, *Creative Dance for All Ages, Brian-Compatible Dance Education* and videos *Teaching Creative Dance* and *BrainDance,* as well as numerous articles. She is also an active member of the National Dance Association, National Dance Education Organization and Dance and the Child International. Anne is founder and Past President of the Dance Educators Association of Washington, an organization promoting quality dance education in all Washington State schools K-12. As a member of the Arts Education Standards project, she helped write the Washington State Dance Standards and Learning Goals. Anne has received many awards including the WAHPERD Honor Award, NDA Outstanding Dance Educator Award (Northwest District), the NDA Scholar/Artist Award and the AAHPERD Honor Award.

Anne, the mother of three dancing children, currently lives in Seattle with her husband and two dogs.

About the Photographer

Bronwen Anne Gilbert started dancing at birth and received formal dance training at Creative Dance Center and was a member of Kaleidoscope Dance Company. Bronwen received her BA in Art History from Princeton University. She currently resides in New York where she works as a freelance photographer.

About the Graphic Designer

Alecia Rossano received formal dance training at Creative Dance Center and was a member of Kaleidoscope Dance Company. Alecia earned a BA in studio art from Scripps College and an MFA in sculpture from the New York Academy of Art. She is currently an Assistant Professor at the Digipen Institute of Technology in Redmond, Washington and resides in Seattle.

MISSION STATEMENT

The National Dance Association (NDA) leads in promoting and supporting creative, artistic and healthy lifestyles through quality services and programs in dance and dance education.

BRIEF HISTORY

The National Dance Association is an association of the American Alliance for Health, Physical Education, Recreation and Dance (AAHPERD), with a spirit and purpose that were advocated by the early leaders. AAHPERD was established in 1885 and today serves almost 30,000 members. AAHPERD is composed of six national, six district and fifty state organizations supporting the related fields. Modern dance icons like Margaret H. D'Houbler were instrumental in promoting dance education within AAHPERD and the nation. As early as 1905, the theme chosen for its national convention in New York City was multicultural dance. The dance section of AAHPERD was first established in 1932 and in 1974, NDA was welcomed as an association of AAHPERD.

PROGRAMS

For over 75 years, NDA continues to be the leader in dance education, as the founder of the national dance honor society Nu Delta Alpha, *Dance for Health!* Project and the author of *The National Standards for Dance Education*. NDA's highest honor, the Heritage Award, has been presented to such distinguished dance educators as D'Houbler, Louis Horst, Ted Shawn, Katherine Dunham, Hanya Holm, Donald McKayle and Gus Giordano. Other awards recognize both professionals and students for their achievements. NDA conducts workshops and conferences throughout the United States, publishes state-of-the-art materials and advocates for quality dance programs at all levels. The National Endowment for the Arts, Harkness Foundation for Dance, Capezio BalletMakers and the U.S. Departments of Education and Humanities have all supported NDA projects.